Books and Book People in 19th-Century America

Also by Madeleine B. Stern:

The Life of Margaret Fuller
Louisa May Alcott
Purple Passage: The Life of Mrs. Frank Leslie
Imprints on History: Book Publishers & American Frontiers
We the Women: Career Firsts of Nineteenth-Century America
So Much in a Lifetime: The Story of Dr. Isabel Barrows
Queen of Publishers' Row: Mrs. Frank Leslie
The Pantarch: A Biography of Stephen Pearl Andrews
Heads & Headlines: The Phrenological Fowlers
Old & Rare: Thirty Years in the Book Business [with Leona Rostenberg]
Between Boards: New Thoughts on Old Books [with Leona Rostenberg]

Books edited by Madeleine B. Stern:

Women on the Move (4 vols.)
The Victoria Woodhull Reader
Louisa's Wonder Book—An Unknown Alcott Juvenile
Behind a Mask: The Unknown Thrillers of Louisa May Alcott
Plots & Counterplots: More Unknown Thrillers of Louisa May Alcott

Books and Book People in 19th-Century America

by Madeleine B. Stern

R. R. Bowker Company
New York & London, 1978

Most of the chapters in this book have been previously
published and are being reprinted with the permission of the
publishers, as noted on the opening page of each chapter.
("Behind the Mask of Louisa May Alcott" and "Mind and
Body: The Fowler Family " were written especially for this
book.) The author also received permission to include a
number of illustrations in the book. An acknowledgment
appears below these illustrations.

Published by R. R. Bowker Company
1180 Avenue of the Americas, New York, N.Y. 10036
Copyright © 1978 by Madeleine B. Stern
All rights reserved.
Printed and bound in the United States of America

Library of Congress Cataloging in Publication Data

Stern, Madeleine Bettina (date)
  Books and book people in 19th-century America.

  Includes index.
  1. Publishers and publishing—United States—History—
19th century—Addresses, essays, lectures.   2. Book
industries and trade—United States—History—19th century—Addresses, essays, lectures.   I. Title.
Z473.S856   070.5′0973   78-12197
ISBN 0-8352-1109-6

Contents

Illustrations

Introduction

"BOOKS have always reflected the important questions of the day, and . . . the book trade may be regarded as a faithful barometer to world temperature. . . . [Its study] opens a new window upon the world and provides a fresh vantage point from which to look at history."[1] It is as an index to the history of 19th-century America that the articles in this book have been assembled. If they reveal something about trends in bookselling or publishing, they will hopefully reveal more about the time and place that form their backdrop—the American 19th-century, when there were frontiers to conquer and panaceas for every ill, when the individual was still a perfectible agent in an expanding country. Through the books that were published and sold, fresh insights may be yielded into that most exhilarating of times that began on the eastern seaboard at the opening of the 19th-century.

"In the year 1800, along the muddy roads of upstate New York, a portly, good-natured man on horseback might have been seen riding along, . . . his saddlebags filled with newspapers and a few books and pamphlets. . . . He was the post-rider," and he carried to the wilderness of upstate New York the news of all the world. The books and newspapers he purveyed "had been printed by a pioneer who had joined the agriculturist in [the] westward march, for the axe and plow had been followed by the schoolhouse and the printing press. The printer . . . had come . . . with 'as much type as a squaw could carry in her bag,' and . . . produced the books for the schools that were rising in the wilderness, books to spread the Gospel among the Indian tribes, . . . [to reach] to the farthest settlements of the State, forming public opinion at the same time as [they] mirrored forth the life of the people. So the pioneer printer lived history and made it, too." The "authentic annals of a group of pioneer bookseller-publishers of upstate New York" begin this story of geographical and intellectual expansion in which the chief characters are books and those who produced them.

One of those upstate pioneer printer-publishers was William Williams, who, armed with type and composing stick, did as much toward clearing the wilderness as those who felled the trees and turned the soil. By the time Williams died, in 1850, many other influences emanating from those who dealt in the printed word had been at work in the shaping of the country.

"No one individual can better mirror the events, the thought, and the writings of his time than the individual who deals in books, writing them, translating them, selling them, publishing them." One of those individuals happened to be Joseph Nancrede, a Franco-American bookseller-publisher who settled in Boston and flourished between the time of Crevècoeur and the time of de Tocqueville. As William Williams and his colleagues helped develop the villages of New York State, Joseph Nancrede helped introduce French thought to New England and increase the interchange of ideas between two countries. In so doing he played a part in creating a moment in history—that moment at which, according to de Tocqueville, "the literary genius of democratic nations has its confluence with that of aristocracies."

So many foreign influences helped shape the country, and how often they were introduced by those literary agents known as bookseller-publishers. The seeds of foreign thought were planted here not only by the transcendentalists—Emerson, Margaret Fuller, and their coterie—but by such publishers as that New York pair, Radde and Paulsen, who published the first German *Faust* in this country. They have been forgotten, but they too shaped a moment in American history. Nor should the early work of that bustling New England spinster and future kindergartner, Elizabeth Palmer Peabody, be overlooked, for it was at her Foreign Circulating Library on Boston's West Street that the literature of Europe was made available to American eyes.

While the eastern seaboard was absorbing and reacting to things and thoughts European, the push toward the West continued. Again, the tools used on the march to the Pacific included not only pans and shovels, hoes and spades, but books and news-sheets. And so, an Omaha surveyor named William Newton Byers arrived in the spring of 1859 at the place now called Denver. He brought with him "a few assistants, a Washington hand press, and a 'shirt tail full of type,' determined to publish the first newspaper in the diggings." His determination resulted in the *Rocky Mountain News*, which is almost as much a part of western history as the Gold Rush itself.

The Rocky Mountain Book Store established in Salt Lake City by a pair of Mormons, Charles R. Savage and George M. Ottinger, is far less celebrated but in its way equally interesting for it too gave an impetus to the development of the West. Here was "'a store, . . . three thousand miles west from New York, in the center of a vast Territory teeming with life'" that supplied "'the best literature of the Old World and the New'" along with the art and photography that helped awaken awareness of the beauties of western scenery.

Long before the Rocky Mountain Book Store opened, "a manifest destiny seemed at work not merely upon the lips of statesmen and historians, but upon the whole great continent itself." As settlers and farmers followed miners to the Pacific, bustling, roaring communities sprang up almost overnight and they needed books as much as they needed tools. "Books, in fact, were their tools, and in San Francisco as the 1850s rolled their swift, vivid course, the sharp need for men who could publish those books was answered. The Golden Fleece that was California had many Argonauts, not the least of whom was the Argonaut of Books." The "Argonaut of Books" in this publishing history is a bearded young man from Bavaria who migrated to America, crossed the plains to California in 1849, and joined the gold-seekers at Scott Bar. With 100 ounces of gold dust—his share of a claim on the Bar—Anton Roman invested in books, and "that little transaction opened an important page in the history of bookselling and publishing on the west coast." Indeed, by the mid-1860s, when Roman's publications were catering to the demands of an expanding state, another emigrant from Bavaria, the pioneer American Hebrew publisher Henry Frank, could establish a branch office in San Francisco. Through the forgotten stories of those who dealt in books, the westward move across the country can be traced. These men too were empire builders, their masonry the printed word.

Books and Book People in 19th-Century America has a background in time and ideology as well as in space, and the insights it offers are not always geographical. The isolated, seemingly disparate, and little-known facts about booksellers, publishers, and books that appear in these pages take on meaning to the bridge-builder. Those who perceive connections where none seem to exist will perhaps see them here and note from the stories that are told how the needs of a nation are reflected and answered.

That the first edition of Walt Whitman's *Leaves of Grass* was sold by a firm of publishers who were also practicing phrenologists, and that the equally significant second edition of that book was published—albeit anonymously—by that same firm, is surely an index to American trends and reactions. The evolution of *Leaves of Grass* is as American a story as it is possible to find, and the record of its first two editions reflects American gullibility and prudery, audacity and disenchantment.

That the first Beadle Dime Novel was written not by a "trailer in buckskin" or "a scout of the Great Plains," but by a New England woman "fair, fat and fifty," adds something to the history of American feminism. The fact that that orange-colored paperback has become "an American document," "'a landmark on the road of American literature,'" provides the historian of domestic mores with food for thought.

From behind her mask, Louisa May Alcott emerges in the early 1860s as a writer who delved in darkness, dipping her pen into "gory ink" and producing "tales of jealousy and revenge, murder and insanity, feminist anger, passion and punishment, drug addiction." The story of the detection of those gorgeous Gothics tells us much about the future author of *Little Women* and her publishers, but perhaps it tells us more about the country that devoured her page-turners.

Books and Book People in 19th-Century America carries us a long distance from the dime novel to the Bible, at least to the "first feminist Bible." Julia E. Smith, the learned maid of Glastonbury, Connecticut, was the first (and doubtless the last) woman to translate both Testaments into English in a solo performance. She did not publish the labor of her lifetime until the Centennial Year of 1876 when her Bible emerged from the press to prove to the world what one woman could accomplish. Here too is a tale that reveals as much about the country that required such proof as about the redoubtable translator, the maid of Glastonbury.

Consciously or unconsciously, the writers, publishers, and sellers of such books supplied demands whose nature mirrors the nation. Especially those publishers described here as "panacea publishers" aimed at filling the country's needs, and in filling them pin-pointed them. The Fowler family of phrenologist-publishers had its hand directly on the nation's pulse. Examining the national skull, it exhumed the national mind. It did more, for it presumed to improve that mind and ameliorate its functions. This it did not only in the dim recesses of an examining room, but through its presses. For a nation suffering from the ills of dyspepsia and alcoholism, wrong thinking and inadequate feeling, the Fowlers provided manuals that ranged from diatribes against tobacco to manuals on sex education, from handbooks on temperance and water cure to tomes on mental and physical health. "The publications of the Fowler firm . . . answered the purposes and reflected the tendencies of the nineteenth century. In its books designed to improve the physical and mental health of the nation, it . . . supplied a very real need. And so, thoroughly to understand that century, a knowledge of the work of the phrenologist-publishers becomes remarkably useful."

So too does a knowledge of the work of other publishers whose output embodies the spirit of their time. "Like a man, a nation must learn to laugh at itself." A publisher such as G. W. Carleton filled the need for humor in 19th-century America as assuredly as the humorists themselves. "Like the men whose works he published, Carleton was a humorist of sorts, and by placing their extravagant phrases, their vivid caricatures and atrocious spellings before the public, he helped a stumbling . . . nation to enjoy a laugh at its own expense. Setting his own unmistakable mark upon the humor that he published, he helped America become not only mature, but characteristically American."

The domesticity associated with 19th-century America was aided and abetted by such a publishing house as Dick and Fitzgerald, who provided for the family "those well-thumbed books of parlor tableaux and theatricals, social pastimes and songsters . . . needed for . . . winter evenings' entertainments. The books, indeed, are all that is left of this vanished age, and for a later time they recreate the picture, evoke the nostalgia, restore the yesterday." It was a yesterday to which Dick and Fitzgerald catered—"dealers in the printed word who . . . shaped history while they recorded it. . . . Across the years their books still reflect the warmth and glow of a hearthfire that has turned to ash." As we leaf through their dog-eared *Fireside Magicians* and *Sociables*, their *Kitchen Directories* and *Recitations and Readings*, we "brush the dust from yesterday's bandbox, revealing a way of life and a state of mind that have become historic."

Books and Book People in 19th-Century America strives not only to glimpse that way of life and that state of mind through the activities of a handful of booksellers and publishers, but to reveal something of the nature of bookselling and publishing as well. The 20th-century needs reminders of an age when the dividing line between printer, bookseller, and publisher was often thin or nonexistent, an age preoccupied by trade sales and seasonal trends, subscription sets and drummers, and the long struggle for international copyright.

"A Murder and a Meeting" affords us a cross-section of that book trade. In 1841, a publisher murdered his printer and the whole clan of printers, booksellers, and book manufacturers testified at the trial that followed. The roll of witnesses included Robert Hoe, who with his brother Richard, succeeded to the "great business of printing press manufacturers"; Cyrus W. Field, "just building up the paper firm of Cyrus W. Field & Company"; Robert Carter "who had opened his bookstore in 1834." "The trial in short was a free-for-all for the booktrade, whose members had the unprecedented opportunity of discussing at length their favorite subjects: printing and papermaking, publishing and bookselling."

Not many years later, in 1855, a "Fruit and Flower Festival" was held in New York's Crystal Palace, tendered by the publishers in honor of their authors. What a mass demonstration of goodwill in publisher-author relations this splendid occasion signaled! Under "lines of gaslights . . . arranged to represent the Temple of Wisdom," honor was paid to genius by the publishers of genius. Appleton acknowledged: "It is in our power, and therefore it becomes our imperative duty, to lend the most important aid in raising the intellectual and moral tone of the literature which is daily and hourly sent forth among the people of our native land." Putnam asserted: "The interests of writers, and publishers, and sellers of books, in this great and thriving country, . . . are, or should be, mutual and identical." And responding to a toast of the evening, William Cullen Bryant declared: "Authors and booksellers are each other's best allies. . . . When I hear of a rich bookseller, I know that there have been successful authors."

Even then, at the midcentury, a certain self-consciousness was emerging among members of the booktrade. Publishers who recognized their ethical responsibility gradually came to realize that they had another responsibility as well. By the nature of their product, publishers recorded and sometimes made their nation's history. Now the awareness grew that their own work needed dissecting, analyzing, recording. The trade, grown self-conscious, required its own examiners and historians.

One such examiner was a member of that firm of phrenologist-publishers who figure intermittently in this book. Nelson Sizer of Fowler and Wells applied his phrenological skills to describing the "organs" or faculties essential to booksellers and papermakers, bookbinders and printers, engravers and editors. Hopefully, all members or would-be members of the booktrade would know precisely what temperament and faculties were demanded for their specialties, and would hesitate to embark upon a bookish profession without a preliminary examination of the head!

If a phrenological chart could aid a novice printer, a catalogue of books could provide a more essential tool to a novice bookseller. This latter was supplied to the 19th-century American booktrade by a Polish refugee who called himself Francis G. Leon and who in 1885 compiled the first *Catalogue of First Editions of American Authors.* "The first catalogue to be devoted in its entirety to . . . American first editions as distinguished from Americana, . . . it was the first bibliography of American first editions. Its publication was an event, and the work still marks a milestone in the history of American bookselling and bibliography."

For a trade that has matured and grown self-conscious, a trade organ becomes essential, and 19th-century American publishers found this in *Publishers' Weekly.* "The nature of *Publishers' Weekly* makes it unique in trade journalism. . . . Publishers and booksellers, those indirect moulders and tracers of public opinion, demand . . . a trade journal that represents their spirit and guides their fortunes, that educates while it leads, and records the history in whose making it shares."

Some few aspects of that history have been trapped in these pages. Most collections of reprinted articles are preceded by an author's apologia, but this introduction was certainly not so designed. It is true that *Books and Book People in 19th-Century America* can make no claim to definitiveness. For that, the student must reach for John Tebbel's multivolume *History of Book Publishing in the United States.* Yet, if its chapters restore a partial portrait of some few booksellers, publishers, and books that illuminated the 19th-century in America, then this work needs no apology. Today, when what has been called "a best-seller mentality" based upon the pernicious "star system"[2] seems to characterize many members of the book trade; when the trade itself evolves more and more swiftly into "an electronic activity" that risks government regulation,"[3] it is enlightening to recall yesterday's individualistic, independent, and very human book trade. Surely it is salutary to remind the present of the past, and this *Books and Book People in 19th-Century America* seeks to do.

Notes

1. All quotations, unless otherwise indicated, are from *Books and Book People in 19th-Century America*.

2. Susan Braudy, "Paperback Auction: What Price A 'Hot' Book?" *The New York Times Magazine* (May 21, 1978), p. 109, quoting Peter Mayer on the paperback companies.

3. Ithiel de Sola Pool, "From Gutenberg to Electronics: Implications for the First Amendment," *The Key Reporter*, XLIII, no. 3 (Spring 1978), p. 8.

1
The Young Republic

Books in the Wilderness

Some 19th-Century Upstate Publishers

IN THE YEAR 1800, along the muddy roads of upstate New York, a portly, good-natured man on horseback might have been seen riding along, his neat pouch stuffed with parcels, his saddlebags filled with newspapers and a few books and pamphlets.[1] As he drew up before a store or tavern in a sparsely populated settlement, his arrival was announced by the sounding of a long tin horn, and the blasts attracted the villagers who came to learn the tidings of this "herald of a noisy world."

He was the post-rider, and the route he had taken passed near swampland and thick woods and wilderness, along wagon roads that had been broken through the forests over Indian trails. He had ridden over rough and muddy roads to settlements consisting of a saw and grist mill and a few rude log dwellings, to bring to the villagers the news of the world. It required a week to get intelligence from Albany, two weeks from New York, and two months from Europe; so the papers he carried in his saddlebags contained accounts of the timely visit of Bonaparte to the Directory and resolutions in honor of the memory of General Washington. They advertised European and India goods, Jamaica spirits, glass beads and dried codfish, muffs and caps and tippets, and Spanish hides. Perhaps, along with the papers, he took from his saddlebags a few books and pamphlets also, for the New Englanders, as they moved westward, had carried in one hand a Bible, in the other a spelling book.

Those books and newspapers had been printed by a pioneer who had joined the agriculturist in that westward march, for the axe and plow had been followed by the schoolhouse and the printing press. The printer, too, had come through a near-wilderness, with "as much type as a squaw could carry in her bag,"[2] and had printed those pamphlets and newspapers on an old Ramage press with a short screw and lever, after the pattern used in the days of

Reprinted from *New York History* XXXI, no. 3 (July 1950): 260–282; and XXXI, no. 4 (October 1950): 414–429.

Franklin. With four solid jerks he printed one page at each pull, while his apprentice made balls of wool covered with green sheepskin to ink the type, and the printer's wife folded the forms and stitched the pamphlets. So, with worn and indifferent type, the pioneer printer produced the books for the schools that were rising in the wilderness, books to spread the Gospel among the Indian tribes, and, paying his apprentice thirty or forty dollars a year to tread pelts, make the fires and cut the wood, he gradually developed an establishment where clean cotton and linen rags could be converted into Bibles and primers, grammars and spelling books. Only the nearest villagers could congregate at his bookstore, where he began to assemble imports from New York and where the neighbors could discuss the topics of the day. Most of his wares had to be distributed by colporteurs and post-riders, on wagons and pack-horses. By those means, the printed word reached to the farthest settlements of the State, forming public opinion at the same time as it mirrored forth the life of the people. So the pioneer printer lived history and made it, too.

By 1861, he had weathered many a panic, many a fire. The tangled forests of the wilderness had been converted into waving fields and cities. Log cabins had become mansions. Instead of the blind paths taken by the post-rider, railroads and steamboats carried the latest issues of the press to a region without a frontier. The newspapers and books they carried had been printed on a power press propelled by steam, and instead of honoring General Washington they reported the most recent developments in the secession movement, and advertised melodeons or sewing machines or Moffat's life pills.[3] The wilderness had flowered and borne fruit.

The printers had helped in that flowering. Who were they, who had published and sold the books that arose in the wilderness? As Cooper remarked, in his *Chronicles of Cooperstown*, "It is always desirable to possess authentic annals."[4] In the authentic annals of a group of pioneer bookseller-publishers of upstate New York, the legendary printer who set his type in the wilderness comes to life again.

The Phinneys of Cooperstown[5]

In 1795, a forty-year-old veteran of the Revolution penetrated a wilderness and broke a track through a deep snow with six teams of horses. Elihu Phinney, a native of Connecticut, had journeyed overland with his printing press and type, to establish, at the invitation of Judge William Cooper, the third newspaper west of Albany. Having managed a store and inn at New Canaan, where he had also printed the *Columbian Mercury*, he found Cooperstown dull by contrast—a village of some thirty-five families, "75 pr cent below Proof—no life—no society."[6] He believed, however, that "the progress of science as well as of agriculture was westward,"[6a] and the inhabitants were "civil, well-informed, and very sagacious."[7] Elihu Phinney proceeded to alleviate the dullness with his sallies of sparkling wit that were to make him a village favorite in short order, and to turn his bookstore into an attractive gathering place for Otsegans.

There, at the book and stationery store which he opened under his printing office and bindery, one door east of the courthouse, they could pick up their copies of the *Otsego Herald*, the little blue newspaper whose motto was "Historic truth our *Herald* shall proclaim,/The law our guide, the public good our aim."[8] There, too, they could watch the witty publisher alternate between literary composition and type-setting as he wrote a few lines and then put them in type. As the years passed, they could observe other activities going on at the Phinney store, where cotton or linen rags were bought for three pence a pound, and peddlers were supplied with chapbooks, pamphlets, and almanacs on commission. There, writing and wrapping paper, bonnet and clothier's press papers were for sale, along with ledgers and quills, wafers and sealing wax, India rubber and slates, playing cards, conversation and wool cards. The Cooperstown ladies could find a full supply of fashionable paper for their rooms, window curtains, cornices and fire boards, while their spouses could pick up an assortment of watch seals, keys and trinkets.

The books displayed at Phinney's store were offered on as low terms, wholesale or retail, as at any of the capitals of the Union, and attracted the Otsegans, who chatted with the proprietor about the Court of Common Pleas, of which he was Judge, as they considered the literary and historical works on his shelves. At his printing office and bindery, they could see blank books ruled and bound to any size or pattern, sheepskins exchanged for books and stationery, fonts of new type used in the printing of cards and handbills. There, too, they might observe young Fenimore Cooper learning to set type for fun, or his father, Judge Cooper, lending a hand in Phinney's editorial labors. If the *Otsego Herald* did not satisfy their reading interests, they could purchase a copy of *Phinney's Calendar*, first issued in 1797, and thumb its pages until they came upon such moral advice as, "When you are married, study Addition, practice Multiplication, and avoid Division," or such astute meteorological information as, "Expect a change of weather."[9] Indeed, by a typographical error, snow, predicted one year for July 4th, actually fell on that day, increasing the general reverence for Phinney's almanac.

By 1813, when Elihu Phinney died, the villagers had developed a reverence for the founder of the printing establishment also, and doubtless watched with extreme interest as his two sons, Elihu and Henry, proceeded to expand the business until it became one of the most important manufactories in the interior. Though they discontinued the *Otsego Herald* in 1821, the brothers persisted in publishing *Phinney's Calendar* until it boasted a yearly circulation of 100,000. They had learned to print in their father's office, and had watched the publications that emerged from his press, the sermons and addresses that had been delivered in the village. These were merely a beginning, for in every phase the business was to be enormously expanded by the industry of Elihu Phinney's sons.

For the distribution of their books, they ordered the construction of large wagons with movable tops and counters, and these locomotive bookstores were stocked with hundreds of varieties of books and driven to distant villages by colporteurs or traveling agents. After the completion of the Erie Canal, the Phinneys developed a floating, canal boat bookstore which anchored in winter at large towns on the Canal and spread their wares throughout the interior. The money collected from this expanded circuit was spent by the enterprising brothers at their Cooperstown manufactory, which developed into one of the most important businesses of the village. By 1820, they had a stereotype foundry which cast quarto Family Bible plates. By 1838, the plant was the largest in the village, employing forty hands and consuming three thousand reams of paper a year. Five presses were in constant use, and with Todd, the Phinneys owned the first paper mill in the neighborhood.

It was doubtless the type of book published by the brothers that developed their father's bookstore into so huge a business enterprise. The works that issued from their busy presses circulated through the State and indicated the tides of taste at the same time that they helped create those tides of taste. The Phinneys manufactured, first and foremost, over 150,000 copies of the quarto Family Bible, and could boast that no other quarto Bible in the United States was so extensively circulated. The proofs were read with the greatest care, the text was compared with other editions, and a premium was offered to the men in the establishment for the discovery of errors. In addition, they published books for the schools: Starkweather's *Arithmetic*, Smith's *Geography*, Salem Town's *Spelling and Defining Book*, Crandall's *Columbian Spelling-Book*. For the amusement of the children, they turned out chapbooks such as *The Farm-Yard Journal* and *The History of Goody Two Shoes, The Popular Story of Blue Beard*, or *The Pride of Peter Prim*. These miniature juveniles, embellished with neat engravings, appealed to all, and with volumes by Jacob Abbott became household favorites for a generation afterward. In their publications the Phinneys kept local interests in mind also, issuing Barber's *Pictorial History of the State of New York*, or addresses delivered before the Otsego County Agricultural and Education Societies. They could boast, too, of one local author on their lists—James Fenimore Cooper, whose *Chronicles of Cooperstown, American Democrat, Battle of Lake Erie*, and *Naval History* appeared under the local imprint of H. & E. Phinney.

With their almanacs, their school and toy books, their Bibles, they stocked and maintained bookstores in Utica, Buffalo, and Detroit, and in the Cooperstown offices developed a policy that was to continue undisturbed until 1849. Arrangements were made to receive frequent and large supplies of new works from New York, Boston, and Philadelphia, as fast as they were published. Any books found unsatisfactory might be exchanged within four weeks. Professional men, students, teachers, parents, representatives of school districts, academies, and library associations were invited to examine the huge stock of spellers and primers, toy books and Bibles, historical, theological and classical books, and Sunday School periodicals which the Phinneys assembled and offered at advantageous terms. The bookstore that their father had opened one door east of the courthouse had expanded into a four-story building on West Street that housed machinery and stock, with a second building for paper and other material. In 1839, Henry Frederick Phinney, the founder's grandson, became a partner, giving yet another fresh impulse to an establishment whose wares reached to the farthest corners of the interior.

Ten years later, in 1849, the Phinneys introduced new power presses into their concern, at the same time discharging a number of workmen. It was this move that led to a succession of anonymous threats and finally to the burning of their manufactory. The plant was ruined by the fire and moved to Buffalo, where Phinney & Company became one of the largest book establishments in the State, though a smaller local business was continued in Cooperstown. In 1854, the younger Phinney moved to New York, joining Henry Ivison as educational publishers, and bringing into the concern a number of important books, among which were some by James Fenimore Cooper, his late father-in-law. By that time, not only Cooper had changed from the boy who had learned to set type for fun into an author remembered as one of America's most distinguished writers; the village, too, had flourished, developing into a town with six churches, an academy, and a Collegiate Institute, as well as a bookstore that boasted a long and colorful history. In the growth of the village, as well as in the circulation of books throughout the State, the Phinney family had played a significant part, since that momentous day in 1795, when a veteran of the Revolution had plowed through the snows armed with printing press and type.

William Williams of Utica

Henry Ivison, the man who became Phinney's partner and the head of one of the largest schoolbook publishing houses in the world, had been apprenticed as a boy to William Williams of Utica. It was Williams' public spirited enterprise which, when Utica was merely a thrifty little village of a few thousand inhabitants, made of it one of the most productive and important book distributing centers of upstate New York. Williams was, first and foremost, a man who recognized and paid his debt to society, and published the books that his generation needed. This is the explanation for the enormous spate of books that flowed from his presses when Utica was little more than a rude and straggling village, lately risen from an Indian crossroads. Nearly every book that bore the Williams imprint was related, in one way or another, with his own intense interest in the development of his section of the country, and so those books reveal to us the history that he helped to make. . . .

No one better illustrates the combining of a career of public service with private enterprise than William Williams, who published the books that would advance the causes in which he believed. [For a detailed account of William Williams see pages 30–43.]

Ebenezer Mack of Ithaca [12]

While William Williams was serving at the front, in 1813, a young man twenty-two years old, with large, penetrating eyes and tousled hair was delivering an oration before the New York Typographical Society, declaring to his audience that "the Art of Printing arose as a sun, which should dispel the clouds of Ignorance and Superstition, . . .

". . . the first blow which is aimed at the Freedom of the American Press, would be the step by which a tyrant would attempt an ascent to power." [13]

Throughout his life, Ebenezer Mack was to use the art of printing to dispel ignorance and enlighten the public mind. At the time he delivered his speech, he was serving as journeyman foreman in the *Columbian* printing office of Charles Holt of New York. He had been born in 1791, at Kinderhook Landing, and when his father, Stephen Mack, migrated to Owego and published the *American Farmer*, young Ebenezer acquired from him his knowledge of the craft of printing. The boy had carried the newspaper and the mails on horseback, through Ithaca to Auburn and Geneva, learning the trails and highways, and planning one day to establish a newspaper in Ithaca.

Only a year and a half after he had made his declamation before the Typographical Society, his employer, Holt, provided the young man with a letter of recommendation, stating that "The bearer, Mr. Ebenezer Mack, is a young man of genius, intelligence, sobriety and integrity, a good writer (in verse and prose) and correct republican, and a capable and quick workman as a printer." [14] Ebenezer's father had died, and after a short partnership with Stephen Leonard in the publication of the *Owego Gazette*, Mack was ready to fulfill the ambition of his youth.

With his brothers he arrived in Ithaca, finding it a village of some fifty houses, and finding also that a printing press, on which Jonathan Ingersoll issued the *Seneca Republican*, had been established there. Ebenezer soon purchased the press, and, in a small wooden building, published, with his partner, Erastus Shepard, the *American Journal*, later dubbed the *Ithaca Journal*—a sheet destined to survive until the present day. It appeared at first on job sheets, dodgers and handbills, printed on a Washington hand press, one sheet at a time, from type set by hand, one letter at a time. Mack stood at the type case, setting up his editorials as he thought them out, editorials that would dispel the clouds of ignorance and superstition, and fulfill the promises made in his prospectus:

> Some may be disposed to think, that now the states and empires of the world are so generally at peace, . . . there can be little of interest to fill the columns of a paper. . . . Indeed, good friend!—and is there no subject left to concern the mind? . . . When was there a time more favorable to the propagation of useful knowledge? for the impressing upon the character of a people that stamp of intelligence and virtue which may ensure to them the . . . preservation . . . of the natural and dignified rights of man? [15]

There were other ways, too, by which a printer could preserve the rights of man and propagate useful knowledge. Mack's purpose from the beginning had been to develop the village by building mills on its streams and manufacturing paper from which he could make stationery, publish books, and establish a retail and wholesale business, using the newspaper to advertise his goods and work up a large trade. He was well aware that his own advancement would march hand in hand with the progress of his village. Attached to his newspaper, therefore, was a large and fashionable job printing office, where the raw material amounted to $700 a year, which, after being wrought up, was valued at $2,800. There, books, pamphlets, cards and handbills were executed with neatness, accuracy, and dispatch. When, in 1826, he offered his half interest in the establishment for sale, he could describe it as an office where

> a more than ordinary share of Job and Book printing is done . . . the sale of books is considerable and increasing, and the location for publishing extensively, is scarcely surpassed; there are some copyright, and other valuable privileges, with a share in a Paper-Mill. [16]

By that time, and continuing later on, his business, conducted with various partners, had indeed expanded from a limited book and stationery trade connected with his newspaper to one of the largest establishments of its kind in western New York. It included a bindery, where ledgers and day books, county books and justices' dockets were bound to order and ruled to any pattern. It included a bookstore, where, along with musical instruments, stationery, lottery tickets, globes, snuff boxes, macassar hair oil, cologne water, portable shaving apparatus, and paper hangings, books of all kinds were offered for sale or barter: books religious and moral, historical and biographical, juvenile and classical, scientific and medical. There, one might find *A Sketch of the Internal Condition of the U.S. By a Russian* or Miss Porter's *Tales round a Winter Hearth*. There, a literary farmer might exchange a supply of wheat or salt for the *Memoirs of Major General Andrew Jackson*, and there, too, it was that Ezra Cornell made his first purchase in Ithaca—a copy of Pope's *Essay on Man*. As early as 1825, Mack could announce that he had appropriated a number of volumes from the shelves of his bookstore "as a *foundation* for a Circulating Library," [17] which was to serve the public for several years, and by 1842, his firm, Mack, Andrus, and Woodruff, could issue a sixty-page catalogue of the books sold at wholesale or retail. Its interest is such that one is glad to find that at least two Ithacans heeded the booksellers' advice to preserve "this Catalogue for future usefulness, as it will not only prove a valuable auxiliary in selecting books for a Library, but also serve to show the different works that have been published." [18]

To facilitate him in the publication of those works, Mack was also a manufacturer of paper. Besides operating the Phenix flour mills and doing custom grinding, he was one of the proprietors of a paper mill at the foot of the Tunnel Stream on Fall Creek, where, by 1835, thirty hands were employed, and the paper manufactured annually amounted to $20,000 and the rags used annually consisted of one hundred forty tons. The Fall Creek Paper Mill manufactured and kept constantly on hand cap and letter paper, printing and wrapping paper, tea and tobacco paper, and its products were put to good use in Mack's own printing establishment.

That establishment was a publishing concern also, turning out a *Farmer's Calendar* and *Almanac*, such schoolbooks as Cobb's *Spelling Book* and Day's *District School Grammar*, and such literary works as Johnson's *Rasselas* and Pope's *Essay on Man*. In addition, the firm lent its imprint to a fine group of American biographies, including Humphrey's *Memoirs . . . of Israel Putnam*, Ramsay's *Life of George Washington*, and Linn's *Life of Thomas Jefferson*. Perhaps their most interesting publications were those that were concerned with Ithaca itself, ranging from *Facts relative to the Trade, . . . of the County of Tompkins* to reports on the Ithaca and Owego Railroad and the catalogues of the Ithaca Female Seminary and Tompkins Teachers' Institute. Of all these local works, the most attractive today is doubtless Horace King's *Early History of Ithaca*, a lecture delivered at the village hall in 1847. That pamphlet was published at the expense of the author, a promising young Ithaca lawyer, and forms the first and one of the most trustworthy accounts of the settlement of the village. Only a small edition was printed, and since nearly all the copies remaining unsold were destroyed by a fire in the printing office, that work is now extremely rare as well as significant in the early history of Ithaca. The firm could serve as publishers to still another local author—Ebenezer Mack himself, whose *Life of . . . Lafayette* appeared under their imprint, an attempt "to elevate the taste . . . of the American people, and increase in them the desire of investigating the history and biography of their own country." [19]

Mack did not content himself with investigating the country's past. Like William Williams, he served its present enterprises also, acting as school and village trustee, assemblyman and senator, one of the first directors of the Ithaca Bank, and the first secretary of the Ithaca and Owego Railroad, offices which went hand in hand with his desire to preserve the rights of man.

This printer-publisher-bookseller-binder-paper manufacturer-and-public servant evinced throughout his life not only his industry but his astuteness. He was particularly wise in the selection of his partners, especially William Andrus, who, as traveling auctioneer for his brother, the well-known Hartford publisher, Silas Andrus, had visited Ithaca to sell books and was in 1824 induced to join Mack as partner. The combined imprint of Mack and Andrus appeared upon many of the books published to "dispel the clouds of Ignorance and Superstition," and William Andrus helped in no small way to develop the firm's reputation for commercial and financial soundness.

By 1849, when Mack died of consumption in his fifty-ninth year, he, too, had developed no less enviable a reputation for his personal contributions to the growth of his State. His obituary could, without exaggeration, declare him "a man of rare endowments; . . .

". . . a man of the most sterling integrity, . . . none more ready to engage in any work of public importance and utility, and push it to a successful issue." [20]

He pushed all his enterprises to a successful issue. His printing office was continued until 1942,[21] and his newspaper survives to this day. What is more, he helped mold the character of the place of his adoption, propagating, as he had promised years before, useful knowledge, and using the art of the printer to insure to his community "the natural and dignified rights of man."

James C. Derby of Auburn[22]

In 1840, the year when Ebenezer Mack's firm published Ramsay's *Life of George Washington*, a new bookstore was opened in a town north of Ithaca by a man destined to play an important part in American publishing history. The village of Auburn offered several attractive opportunities for the sale and publication of books. Its Theological Seminary was frequented by students and professors who were active book patrons and the institution itself could use the services of a local printer. Moreover, the presence in Auburn of William Henry Seward, who was to become Lincoln's secretary of state, would give a capable publisher the chance of issuing his numerous addresses.

James Cephas Derby was well aware of these possibilities. The oldest of four brothers, all destined for publishing careers, he had been born in 1818 at Little Falls, and at the age of fifteen had been apprenticed to none other than Henry Ivison, the man who was later to become Phinney's partner, and who at that time was running a bookstore in Auburn. For a village of some five thousand inhabitants, the Ivison establishment was well appointed with a fair stock of miscellaneous books and stationery and a bindery in the rear. There, for fifty dollars a year, young Derby worked from seven in the morning until nine at night, learning the trade, observing the rapid sale of works by Cooper,

Irving, and Scott, and developing the quick perceptions and attractive social qualities that were to bring him success. After four years, he entered the rival bookstore of Ulysses F. Doubleday, but later returned to Ivison as managing clerk. In that capacity he was sent east to buy new stocks, journeying for three days by stage coach to New York City, where, having learned to sell books, he studied the no less essential art of how to buy them.

In 1840, when, with Doubleday's retirement, an opportunity for another Auburn bookstore presented itself, Derby was—as he would always be—quick to seize the opportunity, and with capital contributed by Ivison as special partner, the twenty-two-year-old bookseller set up his own business in the village. On August 6th he proudly wrote to his mother:

> I have at last succeeded in getting into business under the name and firm of J. C. Derby & Co., at the old stand of U. F. Doubleday, and have opened with an entire new stock purchased in New York in July.[23]

For the next thirteen years, his firm, both as J. C. Derby & Company, and as Derby, Miller & Company was to remain an important factor in the prosperity of Auburn, giving employment to many, including Derby's brother George, who later headed a Buffalo concern, consuming the products of the paper mill, and selling books profitably and on a large scale.

Four years after he had opened his store, Derby branched out as a publisher of books, and in that year his mother wrote him a letter regarding the purchasing of books which might equally well apply to their publication:

> You now stand upon the pivot of general improvement in almost everything, and it is your special province to go forward in this particular branch of progression.[24]

In the publishing "branch of progression" Derby soon manifested his keen awareness of Auburn's literary needs. His very first publication, an edition of *Conference Hymns* prepared by Henry Ivison and the local pastor, was doubtless designed for the use of the Auburn Theological Seminary, and Derby continued to supply the demands of that institution by publishing *The Christian's Instructer*, *The Missionary Offering*, Winfield's *Antidote to the Errors of Universalism*, and *Rational Psychology* by a professor at the Seminary.

In 1840, when log cabins were being constructed for William Henry Seward by ardent Whigs, a committee, headed by J. C. Derby, had greeted the local celebrity with one on his arrival at Auburn just before election. Later on, as publisher, Derby eagerly grasped the opportunity of lending his imprint to Seward's *Argument . . . in defence of William Freeman, on his trial for murder* or the statesman's *Oration on the Death of Daniel O'Connell*. When an Auburn lawyer prepared an edition of New York Statutes, or John Jenkins compiled a *New Clerk's Assistant*, Derby was on hand to issue the legal requisites of his town.

In most of his other publications, however, James C. Derby evinced an interest more general and comprehensive than the supplying of local needs, and proceeded to publish books that were timely or popular. All America could be eager purchasers of the first *Memoirs of the Mother and Wife of Washington*. The whole country could be attracted to a *Life of . . . Andrew Jackson*, or a timely *History of the Mexican War*, or Headley's fascinating *Life of the Empress Josephine*. Solomon Northrup's *Twelve Years a Slave*, dedicated to Harriet Beecher Stowe and published in 1853 when interest in slavery was at a height, caused a sensation. Goodrich's *History of All Nations*, erroneously described by Derby as the first subscription book published west of New York City, was actually his firm's first subscription book and, with its fine illustrations, sold in the tens of thousands despite its high price. *Facts In Mesmerism*, its yellow paper covers adorned with a picture of Miss Helen, Who Remained Three Weeks in the Mesmeric Sleep, and who therefore "is not dead, but sleepeth,"[25] doubtless provided food for thought to the sceptics as well as the followers of the much debated animal magnetism. Derby reaped the rewards of appealing to popular interest and timing his publications astutely. A *Life of . . . Zachary Taylor*, written by the editor of the *Auburn Journal* in time for the General's nomination to the Presidency, sold 40,000 copies, as did Seward's *Life . . . of John Quincy Adams*, published soon after Adams' death. *Fern Leaves from Fanny's Portfolio* ran to the even more exalted figure of 80,000 copies in its first year.

There were several reasons for the remarkably large sale of books published in the little town of Auburn. Derby was, first and foremost, quick to seize the moment of intense public interest in a subject, publishing appropriate books at the time of the death of national heroes or during the period of presidential elections. The books he issued were not only timely, but popular, as his imprints on works concerning such debated topics as slavery and mesmerism reveal. Finally, he had the opportunity for a wide distribution of his publications, for after his brothers had set up businesses in Buffalo, Cincinnati, and Sandusky, the Auburn firm could publish in connection with them, their numerous double or triple imprints testifying to the efficacy of the family's enterprises.

Through 1853, Derby's firm published over one hundred books, and his biographies and standard histories, his school and law publications were designed to attract not only local patrons, but general readers throughout the country. Brought out in attractive styles, they met with very large sales, and indicated that an alert upstate publisher could vie with the magnates of large cities, and by issuing books of popular appeal could branch out into big business.

Derby himself branched still farther afield in December, 1853, when he joined the magnates of New York City, disposing of his interest in the Auburn concern and establishing himself as a publisher at 8 Park Place, where he engaged as readers George Ripley and later Thomas Bailey Aldrich. Derby was to have a varied and colorful career after his departure from Auburn, joining with Edwin Jackson, who hailed from Cooperstown, in the firm of Derby & Jackson, and later associating himself with Appleton. Meanwhile, the Auburn firm he had founded continued under various reorganizations, and in the 60's, Derby and his former partner, Norman C. Miller, were again united for a time in the publication of books. As late as 1891, the two old colleagues organized one last time to bring out an appropriate reminder of their early career—the *Autobiography* of William Henry Seward.

James C. Derby died the next year, but not before he had written his *Fifty Years among Authors, Books and Publishers*, an autobiography that is itself a history of many phases of 19th-century publishing, not before he had given an impetus to the publication of general books of wide appeal in a small upstate town, and proved that a village printer with his finger on the pulse of the nation could produce books for all the people everywhere.

James Bogert of Geneva[26]

In 1806, before James Derby had been born, when Ebenezer Mack was carrying his father's newspaper on horseback through the trails and highways near Ithaca, and William Williams was serving his apprenticeship in Utica, when Elihu Phinney was supplying Cooperstown with general "intelligence" in his little blue newspaper, a printer arrived in yet another village to establish a newspaper and publish books that would extend the development of New York State still farther west. In that year, Geneva was a post town of three hundred twenty-five people and seventy-five houses, on the margin of Seneca Lake, and James Bogert was a twenty-year-old member of the craft of printing.

Born in 1786, he had served his apprenticeship with the firm of Thomas and James Swords of New York, where, for forty dollars a year, and board that included rancid butter, mouldy bread, and spoiled meat, he had learned the art of printing. When young James was forced to shake the snow from his bed on arising and retiring, it soon became apparent that many hogs were better fed and housed, and his articles were cancelled. After a short period as journeyman for Daniel Longworth of New York, Bogert arrived in Geneva, where he doubtless hoped for better food if not for the spirit at least for the body. There, in November, 1806, he established the weekly *Expositor*, the second newspaper of the village, which, with its name changed to *The Geneva Gazette*, was to continue under his control for twenty-seven years and was to prove that the proprietor was in all respects a worthy member of the craft.

Like most early 19th-century upstate printers, Bogert, as the years passed, branched out into allied phases of his trade. At his establishment opposite the hotel on Main Street, Genevans found a lively store, where they could select from an extensive assortment of ciphering books and quills, marbled paper and inkpowder, elegant albums and ever-pointed pencil cases, printing ink and justices' blanks. There, too, were displayed a variety of flutes and fifes, violins and clarinets, strings and reeds for the amateur musicians of the village, while those with a taste for gambling could buy their tickets for the Literature Lottery at the Geneva Bookstore, and those suffering from poor vision could choose from a supply of plain and colored spectacles. There, bookbinders could purchase a quantity of sheep and lambskins, and candidates for Mr. Lindsley's course of lessons in penmanship could leave their names at Bogert's bookstore.

With so many diverse attractions to patrons, there were few who would have left the Main Street emporium without a glance at Mr. Bogert's books. There were volumes to whet a variety of tastes, from novels and romances to psalms and hymns, from books on travels and voyages to books on medicine and science. For the village pastor, a copy of *Arguments for the Immortality of the Soul* waited on Bogert's shelves, and for the village doctor there was Burns' *Obstetrical Works* or North on the *Spotted Fever*. For the teacher, Ostrander's *Arithmetic* and Kirkham's *Grammar* offered their charms, while the merchant could pick up a copy of the *American Magazine and Review* as his wife reached for *Charlotte Temple* and his daughter for *Scottish Chiefs*. All of Bogert's books—chapbooks and primers, pamphlets and toybooks—were offered "at prices that cannot fail of being satisfactory," and when his fall and winter stock was received, the villagers must have congregated at the Geneva Bookstore with considerable alacrity.

One young villager was so enthralled by Bogert's bookstore that he made it his "daily resort, in all leisure hours."[26a] As a boy, George Washington Doane, who later became Bishop of New Jersey, lived with his family in the dwelling part of the building in which Bogert's business was conducted, and found "a welcome place, in that storehouse of information." Frequently, Bogert would leave young George in charge, and if his presence were required at home, he was usually "sought and found in the store." Doane never forgot the riches of the Geneva Bookstore or the kindness of its proprietor, and in recalling them, wrote, "These were the days of few, but those good books: and never shall I forget, never *can* I repay, the debt I owe to James Bogert, then . . . the chief bookseller in the West, for the kindness with which he gave me access to his more than treasures."[26b]

As at Mack's establishment in Ithaca, printing and bookbinding were pursued by Bogert, in their various branches, and cash was paid for clean cotton and linen rags. Like all his colleagues in upstate New York, the Geneva printer issued his *Western Almanac*, where, as in his newspaper, he could advertise the wares that he offered to his customers, and he, too, proceeded to supplement those publications with books and pamphlets of keen interest in the development of his part of the State. As Derby was to publish books that would appeal to members of the Auburn Theological Seminary, Bogert directed a few of his publications to the needs of Geneva College, now Hobart College, but, whereas Derby was to try to attract general readers throughout the country, Bogert, for the most part, confined his imprints to works that would serve the local citizenry and improve their welfare.

The Geneva Light Infantry naturally turned to him for the publication of its *Constitution* in 1812, for Bogert was not only a printer, but a captain and later a colonel. For the Geneva College, the Genesee Missionary Society, or the Domestic Horticultural Society of Western New York, he was a likely publisher, but of all his imprints the most significant were those that pertained to the Erie Canal. Bogert was, throughout his life, aware of the advantages of Geneva's location on Seneca Lake. As early as 1821, he pressed those advantages by publishing *A Vindication of the Claim of Elkanah Watson, . . . to the merit of projecting the Lake Canal Policy*, and he continued to advocate the great scheme by issuing the *Report of a Committee appointed for the purpose of ascertaining the most eligible route for a canal from the Seneca Lake to the Erie Canal*. He was indeed the most appropriate printer for the broadside of 1825 that announced the *Grand Celebration* on the completion of the Canal. Throughout his life, Bogert demonstrated his awareness of the needs of a community that happened to be situated on Seneca Lake, and proceeded to publish books in accordance with those needs. After he had served the local public through his imprints, he continued to serve it as collector of canal tolls at Geneva.

Bogert's deep interest in Geneva's past and future is indicated also by a collection of newspapers, broadsides, books, and manuscripts now deposited in the New York State Library and known as the Bogert Journalistic Collection. Assembled by the publisher during his long career, this material contains, in addition to many unique western New York political posters and carriers' addresses, the manuscript of Elkanah Watson's *Observations respecting the practicability of opening a western navigation as far as the Seneca Lake*. The geographical position of Geneva influenced Bogert's collecting and publishing interests, and when, by the time of his death in 1862, Geneva was a flourishing town at the foot of Seneca Lake, the seat of a Water Cure and Hygienic Institute, as well as of Hobart Free College, no little credit for its expansion was due to Colonel James Bogert, who had kept his weather eye on the Lake that bordered its shores while he wielded the composing stick in his hand.

Everard Peck of Rochester [27]

There was one upstate celebrity who could have written an authoritative account of the printing activities that were pursued in western New York during the early 19th century. Thurlow Weed worked for William Williams of Utica and went to the front with him during the War of 1812. He served in the office of the Phinneys at Cooperstown, and doubtless was well acquainted with the craftsmanship of Ebenezer Mack and James Bogert. There was still another upstate printer whose biography Thurlow Weed could have sketched from first-hand knowledge.

In 1822, when Rochester was a bustling little village where the woodman's axe was hewing down the forest to make room for streets, this tall, well-built young man, in search of employment, stopped before the printing establishment of Everard Peck and asked for a position as journeyman. Since the interview proved to be a turning point in his career, Weed left a record of it.

> Mr. Peck replied, that though a bookseller, and prepared to print books as well as his newspaper, he had nothing then in press, and no work, consequently, for a journeyman. . . .
>
> On the following morning Mr. Peck informed me that he had concluded to put a small work to press, which would, he said, give me employment for a couple of months. On expressing the gratification I felt, I added that as I had been accustomed . . . to select copy and prepare matter for a weekly newspaper, I would, after my day's work was over, if he would permit it, very cheerfully take that labor off his hands. We then conversed for some time in relation to the tone, spirit, and general character of a newspaper adapted to the condition of the village and county, and the tastes of the people.[28]

For $400 a year, Thurlow Weed was engaged to work as journeyman in the office and to assist in editing the *Rochester Telegraph*—a position that was to start him on his extraordinary career.

The man with whom Thurlow Weed conversed on that memorable day was Everard Peck, a thirty-one-year-old printer who well remembered his own struggles to embark upon his career in the frontier village of Rochester six years before. A native of Berlin, Connecticut, he had, after learning the book-binding trade at Hartford under Silas Andrus, the brother of Ebenezer Mack's partner, worked as journeyman in Albany, but in 1816 he had moved to Rochester before the village had been incorporated, when it was little more than a place at Genesee Falls, favorable for mills but surrounded by wilderness and numbering only a few hundred inhabitants. With the implements of his trade and a small stock of books on commission, Everard Peck had seen "through the discomforts and rudeness of the settlement, indications which promised a prosperous future,"[29] and, opening his slender stock of books and tools, had set up the double business of bookselling and binding.

The business so founded was to grow by leaps and bounds until it comprehended a newspaper and printing establishment, a paper mill, and a publishing concern that kept pace with the extraordinary expansion of Rochester itself. Only two years after his arrival in the place at Genesee Falls, Everard Peck could advertise that he had for sale hundreds of books—books moral and religious, medical and juvenile, schoolbooks and poetry—books to match the tastes of the enterprising millers and merchants who were already beginning to convert the settlement into one of the great cities of the State. Those books, from the *Communicant's Companion* to the *Seraphic Shepherd*, from *Rob Roy* to the *Fudge Family in Paris*, from the *Dyer's Assistant* to a *Dream Dictionary*, were offered at large discounts to merchants and library companies. In addition, through his arrangements with booksellers in Albany and New York, Peck could supply any requests for books not on hand, in a few weeks, and at his bookstore on Carroll Street orders could be left for works published by subscription.

There, too, this Connecticut Yankee put in a supply of garden seed and elegant paper hangings, along with writing and wrapping paper, wafers and quills, gold leaf and mathematical instruments. On Carroll Street, the merchants and farmers and mechanics who were flocking to the village would find pocket match lights and pounce boxes, spy glasses and Chinese puzzles, "a Philosophical amusement" for their leisure moments. For them also, at the printing office over the Carroll Street bookstore, the type was inked by deer-skin balls and at the press was "expeditiously executed" printing of every description.

On July 7, 1818, Everard Peck could advertise his wares in his *Rochester Telegraph*, the first number of which appeared on that day with the announcement:

"It shall be our fixed aim to conciliate and harmonize. . . .
. . . no pains shall be spared in the mechanical execution of the paper."[30]
It was that weekly for which one hardy subscriber was to pay in advance by chopping wood for the proprietor, and it was in its office that Thurlow Weed was to stagger "into the shop under bales of paper, pulling with bare, ink-spattered arms at the hand press set on a rickety table, the press from which ran the scanty sheets of the weekly *Rochester Telegraph*."[31]

From its press room were issued other publications, too—works that include such bibliographical rarities as the first book printed in Rochester and the first directory of the village. The first publication that bears the name of E. Peck & Company displays also in its imprint the name of Silas Andrus of Hartford, but this *Circumstantial Narrative of the Campaign in Russia*, dated 1816, was not published in Rochester. Neither was *A Journal, . . . of the Loss of the Brig Commerce* of 1818, though it was the first book bearing only a Rochester imprint. The first book actually printed in Rochester did not appear until 1819, when *The Whole Duty of Woman . . . To Which Is Added, Edwin And Angelina A Tale* was published in type faces that are the same fonts as those used in the *Telegraph*. Until its discovery, another work, published the next year by Peck, was considered Rochester's first book, but though that distinction can no longer be claimed for it, *The Life and Adventures of James R. Durand* doubtless thrilled the villagers with the tale of a man impressed on board the British fleet and held in detestable bondage for more than seven years.

There was pleasure for the Geneseeans, too, in a series of almanacs started by Peck with astronomical calculations by Oliver Loud, a tavern keeper on the road not far from Rochester. Today those almanacs are treasured because of their unique woodcuts depicting the characteristic rural life of each month on the farm. But when they were originally circulated, readers probably enjoyed more the "Advice to all Ladies" to "be like an echo, to speak when spoken to; but . . . not be like an echo, always to have the last word."[32] In the *Western Almanac* that Peck had founded, they could later on chuckle over a candid announcement that doubtless held as well for the period when Peck was its publisher:

> Some persons are so foolish that they consult the Almanack to learn what is to be the state of the weather. They do not know that all the information which Almanacks contain on this subject, is inserted at random, and as often as otherwise by the printer's boy, who makes it hot or cold, wet or dry, whenever and wherever best suits his fancy.[33]

The interest of these almanacs with their unusual woodcuts, and of the first book printed in Rochester, is equaled only by the village's first directory of 1827. A gazetteer and local history too, it was printed by Peck and published by Elisha Ely after the remarkable progress in the village in a period of ten years had caused such inquiries at home and abroad as to create a demand for the undertaking. A copy, sent to De Witt Clinton, brought the enthusiastic reply:

> When I saw your place in 1810, without a house, who would have thought that in 1826 it would be the source of such a work? This is the most striking illustration that can be furnished of the extraordinary progress of your region in the career of prosperity.[34]

Indeed, so rapidly did the population grow and shift about that Peck's *Rochester in 1827* appeared without a directory of residents.

Other books flowed from Peck's press as the years passed—Rochester sermons, the *By-laws of Fire Company, No. 1,* an *Address to the . . . Rochester Athenaeum,* the *Minutes of the Genesee Baptist Association,* along with books of wider appeal, such as *The Fashionable Letter Writer* and Charles Yale's *Outlines of General History,*—but none are of greater interest today than those early publications that testify to a printer's pioneer work in a frontier village.

In addition to his publishing and bookselling activities, Everard Peck, like Ebenezer Mack, operated a prosperous paper mill on the east side of the river, between the aqueduct and market bridge. It supplied the wants of the rapidly growing village until, in December, 1827, a fire that probably started in the bleaching room consumed it. At that time its size was such that there were about six hundred reams of paper and a large quantity of rags in the building, and the estimated loss was about five or six thousand dollars, of which one half was covered by insurance.

Ironically enough, Peck had journeyed that same year to New York and Philadelphia in search of the best model fire engine for his village. This was only one of the numerous public services he rendered to Rochester, for, like William Williams, he spared "no exertions to promote the welfare and happiness of the community."[35] Everard Peck was one of the first village trustees, and a member of the stock company organized to construct a railroad connecting the head of ship navigation on the Genesee with the Erie Canal in Rochester. At his fine home on the corner of Spring and Fitzhugh Streets, the Rochester Female Charitable Society was formed, and there, too, conferences were held regarding the founding of the University of Rochester.

In 1825, Weed had assumed full control of the *Telegraph*, and until 1831, Peck gave his exclusive attention to the book business as well as to the public institutions of Rochester. After a period of ill health, he then proceeded to embark upon a new and successful career in banking, and when he died, in 1854, one of his former clerks could write of him: "He was literally one of the 'City Fathers,' . . .

. . . One among ten thousand."[36] Another, named Thurlow Weed, wrote of him, too, recalling the "early benefactor"[37] who had more than thirty years before given him employment, and at the close of his first year added $100 to the salary agreed upon. Everard Peck, quiet in manner, equable in temperament, had left his mark not only upon Thurlow Weed, but upon a city whose busy, thronging population and well-paved streets bore evidence not merely of the passing of time, but of the life work of yet another upstate printer.

The Salisburys of Buffalo[38]

The memorable scene that took place between Thurlow Weed and Everard Peck was preceded by an interview that closely paralleled it, though it occurred in a village still farther to the west. Shortly before Peck had moved to Rochester, a man with two shillings in his pocket might have been seen walking along the Main Street of Buffalo, a settlement in the westernmost reaches of the State on the shores of Lake Erie. He stopped before a signboard that read "Printing Office," and after placing a cigar in his mouth, boldly walked in. Like Thurlow Weed, Eber D. Howe had come to seek employment, and he, too, was engaged by the proprietors.

That signboard marked not only a printing office, but a small bookstore on the ground floor. At the time it had been established, in 1811, it was the only bookstore in the State west of Canandaigua, for its proprietors, Hezekiah A. and Smith H. Salisbury, had brought their printing equipment and small stock of books and stationery to Buffalo when other pioneers were bringing their axes and rifles to the rising young hamlet of five hundred.

The Salisbury brothers had pushed westward from Canandaigua,[39] where they had learned the craft of practical printing under James D. Bemis, the great entrepreneur who set them up in business as proprietors of the *Buffalo Gazette*, the first paper in Erie County. Though the early numbers of the paper were largely indebted to their stationery business for advertising patronage, the *Gazette* weathered the storms of the day, and it was the amusing articles in that rough little sheet printed on coarse paper that clipped the final superfluous "e" from the spelling of Buffalo. It was not long before the newspaper, which required two days to be printed on the hand press the young craftsmen had brought with them, achieved a circulation of one thousand copies. With the War of 1812, the brothers, anticipating an attack by the British, had to move their *Gazette* establishment to Harris' Tavern, at Harris Hill, near Williamsville, where a friend, Stephen K. Grosvenor, was wont to throw off his broadcloth coat and help mail the papers on publication days in order to secure the company of a Salisbury for the evening whist party. There, while the British were applying the torch to the little settlement of Buffalo, the *Gazette* safely surveyed and reported the scene from the heights of Harris Hill. It continued to report the scene after 1815, when the brothers returned to Buffalo, advertising also the legal, medical, religious, historical, and philosophical books offered for sale at the Salisbury bookstore.

On its press—one made after the old pattern used in the days of Franklin—were struck off the handbills and blanks, cards and labels required by the community. But, like Everard Peck's press in Rochester, the Salisbury press made its claim to fame not by its ephemeral job printing, but by the rare Buffalo items that issued from it. The names of the brothers appear on the first recorded Buffalo imprint, a work entitled *The French Convert; being a true relation of the happy conversion of a Noble French Lady, From the Errors . . . of Popery*. Another work, however, also dated 1812, vies with *The French Convert* in bibliographical importance and far outranks it in historical significance. In July, 1812, Erastus Granger, the Indian Agent, and Red Jacket, Chief of the Seneca Nation, spoke at the village of Buffalo concerning the part the Six Nations would take in the war with Britain. Their *Public Speeches* were long considered to constitute Buffalo's first book, and still are of notable bibliographical rarity, a work "printed and sold by S. H. and H. A. Salisbury," and, interestingly enough, "sold also at the Canandaigua and Geneva Bookstores."

Between 1812 and 1818, few imprints rolled from the Salisbury press, for the destruction and then the rebuilding of Buffalo took precedence over literature. In 1818, however, Hezekiah Salisbury again produced an interesting item, *Hymns, in the Seneca Language*, and in 1825, having printed Buffalo's first almanac, an *Astronomical Calendar* published by Oliver Spofford, he topped these rarities by printing S. Ball's *Buffalo in 1825*, the first history of the village. Later on, the imprint of Salisbury and Clapp appeared on a *Pictorial Guide to the Falls of Niagara* which is of great regional interest, though it was issued eight years later than the first guide to Niagara Falls. The distinction of publishing Ingraham's *Manual* of 1834, a book whose paper was manufactured at the Falls so that "the waters of the Niagara . . . are intimately blended with its every fibre,"[40] goes not to a Salisbury but to Charles Faxon of Buffalo.

In 1825, when Hezekiah Salisbury was printing Buffalo's first history, his brother Smith, the more talented but also the more unsteady of the two, purchased the *Black Rock Gazette*, in whose office his son Guy took up the composing stick and learned to be a practical printer. By 1830, Smith H. Salisbury had moved to Rochester, where he died, poorly circumstanced, two years later. His son Guy later became editor of the Buffalo *Daily Commercial Advertiser*, of which Hezekiah was a proprietor. Hezekiah, who never pretended to brilliance, persevered and prospered, a frugal, honest, upright man, printer to the city and commissioner of deeds, ending his days in Buffalo in 1856. By that time, Buffalo was the second commercial city of the State and the largest and most important on the Great Lakes. He could remember when he had pushed westward to the little hamlet on Lake Erie; he could remember its destruction and rebuilding, and the days when two brothers had broken ground in establishing a press in Erie County, days whose history Guy H. Salisbury was later to record. He could take pride, too, in the part he had played in printing the books that declared to the world that Buffalo was taking her place among the cities of the land.

In 1847, a Printers' Festival was held at Rochester to celebrate the one hundred forty-first aniversary of the birth of Franklin. At the Blossom House, printers from all parts of the State gathered, and when they entered they saw, near the head of the center table, a model of the old Ramage Press, for the equipment they had once used had become historic in the annals of printing. They met to exchange reminiscences of the days when a few rude dwellings had formed scattered oases in the wilderness of western New York, and they gave voice to their amazement at the complete change that had come over the face of the country, converting wilderness into cities. "This," they concluded, "is the result of civilization, coupled with industry, intelligence, and indomitable perseverance."[41]

It was the result of a civilization that came bearing in its arms books as well as axes, printing presses as well as rifles. Westward across the State they came, those pioneers who smelled of printer's ink, bringing with them the first rude tools for producing more books, and in their wake came the cylinder press and the stereotype press and the power press, came the people to read their books and buy their wares. Across the State they came, William Williams, Derby and Peck, Ebenezer Mack and James Bogert, the Phinneys and the Salisburys, publishing the newspapers and almanacs, the books and pamphlets that guided the taste of the people at the same time that they recorded it, that bade the settlers pause and ponder the history they were living.

They, too, made history, through the books that bore their imprints as well as through their work as village trustees and committeemen. They built the schools and laid the railroad tracks and planned the canal, though their tool was neither brick, nor steel, nor stone, but the composing stick. There were others, too, who came, some preceding, some following, building on the foundations until the wilderness had literally "blossomed like the rose." In the story of the development of upstate New York, the printer takes his proud place with the woodsman and the planter, for he, too, cleared ground and planted seed, and, what is more, he published to the world the history he had helped to make.

Notes

1. For details regarding post-riders, newspapers, and printing methods of this period, see *The Albany Register* (January 3, 1800); *The Centennial History of Chautauqua County* (Jamestown, N. Y., 1904), II, 96; [Franklin Ellis], *History of Columbia County, New York* (Philadelphia, 1878), 117; Frederick Follett, *History of the Press of Western New-York* (Rochester, 1847), 67; William H. Hill, *A Brief History of the Printing Press in Washington, Saratoga and Warren Counties* (Fort Edward, N. Y., 1930), 95; Eber D. Howe, *Autobiography and Recollections of a Pioneer Printer* (Painesville, Ohio, 1878), 20; John W. Moore, *Moore's Historical, Biographical, and Miscellaneous Gatherings, . . . relative to Printers* (Concord, N. H., 1886), 23, 143; Joel Munsell, *Chronology of the Origin And Progress of Paper And Paper-Making* (Albany, 1876), 64; J. Munsell, *The Typographical Miscellany* (Albany, 1850), 146; Elliot G. Storke, "History of the Press of Cayuga County," *Cayuga County Historical Society Collections* No. 7 (Auburn, 1889), 53 & 55; Harriet A. Weed, ed., *Autobiography of Thurlow Weed* (Boston, 1883) I, 22.

2. See Barrows Mussey's sketch of Charles R. & George Webster in Rollo Silver's notes on publishers at the Grolier Club. The author wishes to thank Barrows Mussey & Rollo Silver for help in the preparation of this article.

3. See, for example, *Newburgh Highland Chieftain* (February 16, 1861).

4. [James Fenimore Cooper], *The Chronicles of Cooperstown* (Cooperstown, 1838), 3.

5. Sources for the lives and careers of the Phinneys include Edward P. Alexander, "A View of a New York State Community," *New York History* XX: 3 (July, 1939), 249; *Almanacs Now in the Possession of The Rochester Museum of Arts and Sciences* (Rochester, September, 1935), 10 ff; Levi Beardsley, *Reminiscences; . . . Early Settlement of Otsego County* (New York, 1852), 65–66; Ralph Birdsall, *The Story of Cooperstown* (Cooperstown, 1917), 129 ff; Alexander V. Blake, *The American Bookseller's complete Reference Trade List* (Claremont, N.H., 1847), 142–143; John L. Blake, *A Biograhical Dictionary* (Philadelphia, 1856), 990–991; "The Book Trade," *Norton's Literary Gazette* N. S. I:8 (April 15, 1854), 191–192; Clarence S. Brigham, *History and Bibliography of American Newspapers 1690–1820* (Worcester, 1947), I, 568. The author wishes to thank Dr. Brigham for his help in the preparation of this paper; Advertisement at end of *The Constitutions of the United States, and of the State of New-York* (Cooperstown: H. & E. Phinney, 1815); [Cooper], *op. cit.*, 42, 62, 68, 96; James Fenimore Cooper, *Reminiscences of Mid-Victorian Cooperstown* (Cooperstown, N. Y., 1936), 19; Cooperstown Imprints in Imprint Catalogue at New York Public

Library; "Death of Henry Phinney, Esq.," *Otsego Democrat* (September 21, 1850, Courtesy James Taylor Dunn, Librarian, New York State Historical Association); Adolf Growoll, *American Book Trade History* (Scrapbooks at *Publishers' Weekly* office), VII, 133 ff; Milton W. Hamilton, *The Country Printer New York State* (New York, 1936), 54, 74, 291; Milton W. Hamilton, "The Spread of the Newspaper Press In New York Before 1830," Reprinted from *New York History* (April, 1933), unpaged; *A History of Cooperstown* (N. p., 1929), 33, 48, 51–52; *History of Otsego County, New York* (Philadelphia, 1878), 32; Rev. S. T. Livermore, *A Condensed History of Cooperstown* (Albany, 1862), 41, 58, 62, 104–105, 158 ff; Barrows Mussey's sketch of H. & E. Phinney in Rollo Silver's notes at Grolier Club; E. Phinney's advertisements in *Otsego Herald* 1796–1811, passim (Courtesy James Taylor Dunn, Librarian, New York State Historical Association); "Obituary," *Otsego Herald* (July 17, 1813, Courtesy James Taylor Dunn); "Obituary," *Otsego Republican* (February 5, 1863, Courtesy James Taylor Dunn): "Obituary. Henry F. Phinney," *Publishers' Weekly* VIII:21 (November 20, 1875), 772; E. B. O'Callaghan, *A List of Editions of the Holy Scriptures . . . Printed in America Previous to 1860* (Albany, 1861), passim; *The Otsego Herald* (July 3, 1795, May 19, June 9, & June 23, 1796); *Phinney's Calendar, . . . For . . . 1806–1849* (scattered numbers); Frank H. Severance, "The Story of Phinney's Western Almanack," *Publications of the Buffalo Historical Society* XXIV (1920), 343 ff; S. M. Shaw, ed., *A Centennial Offering* (Cooperstown, 1886), 31; "Sketches of the Publishers," *The Round Table* III:24 (February 17, 1866), 106; Robert E. Spiller & Philip C. Blackburn, *A Descriptive Bibliography of the Writings of James Fenimore Cooper* (New York, 1934), passim; Carl J. Weber, *A Bibliography of Jacob Abbott* (Waterville, Me., 1948), passim; Harry B. Weiss, *A Catalogue of the Chapbooks in the New York Public Library* (New York, 1936), passim; Rev. John Wright, *Early Bibles of America* (New York, 1894), 364.

6. James Fenimore Cooper, *The Legends and Traditions of a Northern County* (New York & London, 1921), 162.

6a. Elihu Phinney, *Reminiscences of the Village of Cooperstown* (Cooperstown, 1891), 13 (Courtesy James Taylor Dunn, Librarian, New York State Historical Association).

7. William Cooper, *A Guide in the Wilderness* (Cooperstown, 1936), 49.

8. Livermore, *op. cit.*, 104.

9. Severance, *op. cit.*, 349, & *Phinney's Calendar, . . . For . . . 1806.*

12. For Ebenezer Mack's life and the various aspects of his career, see Henry Edward Abt, *Ithaca* (Ithaca, 1926), 55, 58, 61, 74; *American Journal* (August 20, 1817, Courtesy Mrs. J. B. Smelzer, Curator, DeWitt Historical Society of Tompkins County). The author is grateful to Mrs. Smelzer for her help in the preparation of this article; Blake, *American Bookseller's . . . Trade List*, 141 & 157; Brigham, *op. cit.*, I, 589–590 & 715–716; Information from Dr. Clarence S. Brigham, American Antiquarian Society; Beman Brockway, *Fifty Years in Journalism* (Watertown, N. Y., 1891), 420; Thomas W. Burns, *Initial Ithacans* (Ithaca, 1904), 69; Information from Edwin F. Church, Jr.; W. Freeman Galpin, *Central New York* (New York, 1941), I, 238 & II, 337; H. C. Goodwin, *Ithaca As It Was, and Ithaca As It Is* (Ithaca, 1853), 9; Hamilton, *Country Printer*, 18, 41, 46, 74, 126, 256, 284; Information from Thelma L. Harrington, Cornell University Library; Mack's advertisements in *Ithaca*

Journal (October 25, 1826); *The Ithaca Journal. Centennial Number* (August 28, 1915, Courtesy Mrs. J. B. Smelzer); *The Ithaca Journal* (October 28, 1939). passim (Courtesy Dr. Clarence S. Brigham & Mrs. J. B. Smelzer); Horace King, *Early History of Ithaca* (Ithaca: Mack, Andrus & Co., 1847), MS note at end of copy in New York Public Library; Information from Frances W. Lauman, Cornell University Library; William Andrew Leonard, *Stephen Banks Leonard of Owego* (N. p., 1909), 127 ff; Douglas C. McMurtrie, *A Bibliography of Books and Pamphlets Printed at Ithaca, N. Y., 1820–1850* (Buffalo, 1937), passim; [H. B. Peirce & D. Hamilton Hurd], *History of Tioga, Chemung, Tompkins, and Schuyler Counties, New York* (Philadelphia, 1879), II, 382, 403, 434; John H. Selkreg, *Landmarks of Tompkins County New York* (Syracuse, 1894), 23, 39, 42–43, 120, 147, 161; Rev. Thomas C. Strong, *In Memoriam. Memorial Discourse of William Andrus* (Ithaca, 1870), passim (Courtesy Mrs. J. B. Smelzer); Ebenezer Mack Treman & Murray E. Poole, *The History of the Treman . . . Family in America* (Ithaca, 1901), I, 394 ff; *Views of Ithaca and Its Environs. By An Impartial Observer* (Ithaca, 1835), 36–37.

13. Ebenezer Mack, *An Oration, delivered before the New-York Typographical Society, on the Fifth of July, 1813* (New York, 1813), 10 & 14.

14. Treman & Poole, *op. cit.*, I, 395.

15. *The Telegraph* [Newtown Village] (September 9, 1817), 2.

16. Auburn *Free Press* (October 18, 1826, Courtesy Edna L. Jacobsen, New York State Library).

17. *Ithaca Journal* (June 15, 1825, Courtesy Frances W. Lauman, Cornell University Library).

18. *Catalogue of Religious, Scientifick, Historical, Classical, School, and Miscellaneous Books; . . . For Sale, . . . at the Bookstore of Mack, Andrus, & Woodruff* (Ithaca: Mack, Andrus, & Woodruff, 1842), 2 (Courtesy Mrs. J. B. Smelzer).

19. Ebenezer Mack, *The Life of Gilbert Motier De Lafayette* (Ithaca: Mack, Andrus, & Woodruff, 1841), ii.

20. Treman & Poole, *op. cit.*, I, 395.

21. Mack's printing office was continued till 1942, operated during its last period by Mrs. Hugh D. Reed, daughter of William Andrus Church (Information from Mrs. Hugh D. Reed).

22. Sources for J. C. Derby's life and career include information from Henry M. Allen, Auburn, N. Y.; Alexander V. Blake, *The American Bookseller's . . . Trade List*, 140 & 155; John L. Blake, *A Biographical Dictionary*, 360; "The Book Trade," *Norton's Literary Gazette* I:8 (April 15, 1854), 191; J. C. Derby, *Fifty Years among Authors, Books and Publishers* (New York, 1884), 21 ff, 63, 117, 210, 213; "James C. Derby—Obit.," *Publishers' Weekly* XLII:14 (October 1, 1892), 559–560; Growoll, *American Book Trade History* (Scrapbooks at *Publishers' Weekly* office), V, 31; Douglas C. McMurtrie, *A Bibliography of Books, Pamphlets and Broadsides Printed at Auburn, N. Y. 1810–1850* (Buffalo, 1938), passim; Joel H. Monroe, *Historical Records of a Hundred and Twenty Years Auburn, N. Y.* (N. p., 1913), 125; Barrows Mussey's sketch of Derby, Miller & Co., in Rollo Silver's notes at Grolier Club; *Norton's Literary Gazette* I:1 (January 1, 1854), 20; William H. Seward, *An Autobiography* (New York: Derby & Miller, 1891), I, 503, II, 109, 294, & III, 505; Elliot G. Storke, *1789. History of Cayuga County, New York* (Syracuse, 1879), 54; Elliot G.

Storke, "History of the Press of Cayuga County," *Cayuga County Historical Society Collections* No. 7 (Auburn, 1889), 77 ff; Walter Sutton, "The Derby Brothers: 19th Century Bookmen," *The University of Rochester Library Bulletin* III:2 (Winter, 1948), 21–24 (Courtesy Margaret Butterfield, University of Rochester Library & Walter Sutton, Syracuse University. The author wishes to thank Miss Butterfield for her help in the preparation of this article); Information from Lester Grosvenor Wells, Seymour Library, Auburn.

23. Derby, *op. cit.*, 25.

24. *Ibid.*, 26.

25. Prof. W. H. Rodgers, *Facts In Mesmerism, Three Weeks In The Mesmeric Sleep, Advice to Californians, Etc. Also, Davis' Cure For Cholera* (Auburn: Derby, Miller & Co., 1849), cover.

26. Sources for the life and career of James Bogert include Lewis Cass Aldrich, *History of Ontario County New York* (Syracuse, 1893), 312; "The Bogert Journalistic Collection," *New York State Library 125th Annual Report 1942*, 34–35 (Courtesy Edna L. Jacobsen, New York State Library); Brigham, *op. cit.*, I, 572–573; Follett, *op. cit.*, 45; *Geneva Courier* (January 29, 1862, Courtesy Elizabeth Thalman, Librarian, Hobart and William Smith Colleges); Bogert's advertisements in *The Geneva Gazette* (November 18, 1812, October 19, 1825, December 21, 1825, January 14, 1829); Hamilton, *Country Printer*, 36, 103, 259–260; Information from Milton W. Hamilton, Albright College, Reading, Pennsylvania; George M. B. Hawley, Unpublished notes on James Bogert (Courtesy Elizabeth Thalman, Hobart and William Smith Colleges, Geneva); Ulysses P. Hedrick, "Early Geneva," *New York History* XXIII:2 (April, 1942), 155; [W. H. McIntosh], *1788. History of Ontario Co., New York* (Philadelphia, 1876), 26 & 66–67; Douglas C. McMurtrie, *Additional Geneva Imprints 1815–1849* (Buffalo, 1936), passim; Douglas C. McMurtrie, *A Bibliography of Books and Pamphlets Printed at Geneva, N. Y. 1800–1850* (Buffalo, 1935), passim; Charles F. Milliken, *A History of Ontario County, New York and Its People* (New York, 1911), I, 354–355; Joel H. Monroe, *A Century and a Quarter of History Geneva* (Geneva, N. Y., 1912), 33; Information from Elizabeth Thalman; O. Turner, *History of the Pioneer Settlement of Phelps and Gorham's Purchase* (Rochester 1851), 459; *The Western Almanac, for 1832* (Geneva: J. Bogert, 1832), advertisement at end.

26a. William Croswell Doane, *A Memoir of the Life of George Washington Doane* (New York & London, 1860), 16–17. See also Mrs. S. H. Bradford, "History of Geneva," *Brigham's Geneva, Seneca Falls and Waterloo Directory . . . For 1862 and 1863 . . . Compiled . . . by A. DeLancey Brigham* (Geneva, N. Y., 1862), 23–24, (Courtesy Ridgway McNallie. Grosvenor Library, and Margaret Butterfield, University of Rochester Library).

26b. "More babble about books," *The Churchman* X: 51 (February 27, 1841), 202 (Courtesy Niels H. Sonne, General Theological Seminary, Barney Cheswick, Library Company of Philadelphia, & George W. Adams, Trinity College, Hartford).

27. Sources for Everard Peck's life and career include *Album* (December 25, 1827, Courtesy of Dr. Blake McKelvey); James M. Angle, "Early Rochester Records," *The Rochester Historical Society Publication Fund Series* VI (Rochester,

1927), 257 & 259; Raymond H. Arnot, "Rochester; Backgrounds of Its History," *Rochester Historical Society Publication Fund Series 1* (Rochester, 1922), 99; Beardsley, *op. cit.*, 153; George C. Bragdon, ed., *Notable Men of Rochester* (Rochester, 1902), xvi, xxv, 61; Brigham, *op. cit.*, I, 728; Information from Margaret Butterfield, University of Rochester Library; "Death of Everard Peck," *Albany Evening Journal* (February 21, 1854); "Death of Everard Peck," *New Haven Daily Palladium* (February 10, 1854); [John Devoy], *Rochester and the Post Express* (Rochester, 1895), 26; *Early History of Rochester, 1810 to 1827* (Rochester, 1860), 6, 9 ff; "Evidences of Culture in Early Rochester," *Rochester History* VII:3 (July, 1945), 4 (Courtesy Dr. Blake McKelvey); Follett, *op. cit.*, 9, 46, 49; Edward R. Foreman, *Centennial History of Rochester, New York,* (Rochester, 1931–1934), II, 21 n. 3 & 107; Edward R. Foreman, *Proposed Bibliography of Rochester Publications*, reprinted from *The Rochester Historical Society Publication Fund Series V* (1926), passim; Donald B. Gilchrist, "The First Book Printed in Rochester," *Rochester Historical Society Publication Fund Series* IX (Rochester, 1930), 275 ff; Hamilton, *Country Printer*, 290; Amy Hanmer–Croughton, "The Rochester Female Charitable Society," *The Rochester Historical Society Publication Fund Series* IX (Rochester, 1930), 65–66; *Landmarks of Monroe County, New York* (Boston, 1895), 111–112, 143, 167, 169; *The Life And Adventures of James R. Durand* (Rochester: E. Peck & Co., 1820), advertisement on back cover; Blake McKelvey, "Early Almanacs of Rochester," *Rochester History* III:1 (January, 1941), passim (Courtesy Dr. Blake McKelvey); Blake McKelvey, *Rochester the Water-Power City 1812–1854* (Cambridge, Mass., 1945), 59, 101–102, 116, 126, 138, 149 ff, 295; Douglas C. McMurtrie, *Rochester Imprints 1819–1850, in libraries outside of Rochester* (Chicago, 1935), passim; Munsell, *Chronology of the Origin And Progress of . . . Paper-Making*, 61; John Clyde Oswald, *Printing in the Americas* (New York, 1937), 230; William F. Peck, *History of Rochester and Monroe County New York* (New York & Chicago, 1908), I, 54 ff, 158, 204, 208, 446 ff; William F. Peck, *Semi-Centennial History of the City of Rochester* (Syracuse, 1884), 108 ff, 345–346, 664–665; Peck's advertisements in *Rochester Telegraph* (July 7, July 14, August 25, September 1, September 8, October 6, October 20, 1818, November 23 and November 30, 1819); Henry B. Stanton, *Random Recollections* (New York, 1886), 18; Turner, *op. cit.*, 618, 622; "Two Interesting Letters," *The Rochester Historical Society Publication Fund Series* VI (Rochester, 1927), 293; Glyndon G. Van Deusen, "Thurlow Weed in Rochester," *Rochester History* II:2 (April, 1940), 1 ff; Glyndon G. Van Deusen, *Thurlow Weed Wizard of the Lobby* (Boston, 1947), 20, 35; Glyndon G. Van Deusen, "A Young American, Frontier Style: The Early Years of a Famous Citizen of Rochester," *Rochester History* VI:1 (January, 1944), 16–17; Weed, *op. cit.*, I, 95 ff, 207, II, 23, 195.

28. Weed, *op. cit.*, I, 95–97.

29. W. F. Peck, *History of Rochester and Monroe County* I, 446.

30. *Rochester Telegraph* (July 7, 1818).

31. Van Deusen, "Thurlow Weed in Rochester," *Rochester History* (April, 1940), 3.

32. McKelvey, "Early Almanacs of Rochester," *Rochester History* (January, 1941), 4.

33. *Ibid.*, 19–20.

34. Henry O'Reilly, *Settlement in the West. Sketches of Rochester* (Rochester, 1838), 416.

35. Angle, "Early Rochester Records," *Rochester Historical Society Publication Fund Series* VI, 259.

36. "Death of Everard Peck," *New Haven Daily Palladium* (February 10, 1854).

37. "Death of Everard Peck," *Albany Evening Journal* (February 21, 1854).

38. Sources for the lives and careers of the Salisburys include Robert W. Bingham, "The Cradle of the Queen City," *Publications of the Buffalo Historical Society* XXXI (1931), 233; Brigham, *op. cit.*, I, 557–558; *Buffalo Directory* 1835, advertisement of H. A. Salisbury; *Buffalo Times* (March 10, 1929), 13 C (Courtesy Edith B. Krebs, Buffalo Public Library); "Carrier's Addresses," *Publications of the Buffalo Historical Society* XXV (1921), 89, 101; "Contributions Towards A Bibliography of The Niagara Region. Pamphlets and Books Printed in Buffalo Prior to 1850," *Publications of the Buffalo Historical Society* VI (1903), Appendix, passim; "Death of a Veteran of the Press," *Buffalo Morning Express* (March 17, 1856, Courtesy Buffalo Historical Society); [John Devoy], *A History of the City of Buffalo* (Buffalo, 1896), 120; "Editorial Notes," *Publications of the Buffalo Historical Society* XIX (1915), 341; "Millard Fillmore Papers," *Publications of the Buffalo Historical Society* X (1907), 71 n; Follett, *op. cit.*, 52–53, 57; David Gray, "The Charles Lamb of Buffalo Memoir of Guy H. Salisbury," *Publications of the Buffalo Historical Society* IX (1906), 407 ff; Hamilton, *Country Printer*, 81, 83–84, 295–296; Henry W. Hill, ed., *Municipality of Buffalo, New York* (New York & Chicago, 1923), I, 460 & II, 894–895; Eber D. Howe, *Autobiography and Recollections of a Pioneer Printer* (Painesville, Ohio, 1878), 19–20; Crisfield Johnson, *Centennial History of Erie County, New York* (Buffalo, 1876), 194–195; William Ketchum, *An Authentic and Comprehensive History of Buffalo* (Buffalo, 1865), II, 258–259; J. N. Larned, *A History of Buffalo* (New York, 1911), I, 22 & II, 191 ff; "Literature of Buffalo," *Americana* XVII (January, 1923), 1; Douglas C. McMurtrie, *Additional Buffalo Imprints. 1812–1849* (Buffalo, 1936), passim; Douglas C. McMurtrie, *Pamphlets and Books Printed in Buffalo Prior to 1850* (Buffalo, 1934), passim; Oswald, *op. cit.*, 227–228; *Rochester Daily Advertiser* (January 25, 1832, Courtesy Dr. Blake McKelvey); Guy H. Salisbury, "Buffalo In 1836 And 1862," *Thomas' Buffalo City Directory for 1863* (Buffalo, 1863), 18; Guy H. Salisbury, "Early History of the Press of Erie County," *Publications of the Buffalo Historical Society* II (1880), 200 ff; Hezekiah A. Salisbury, "A Guardsman of Buffalo," *Publications of the Buffalo Historical Society* IX (1906), passim; Frank H. Severance, "The Periodical Press of Buffalo 1811–1915," *Publications of the Buffalo Historical Society* XIX (1915), 180 ff & facsimile opp. 230; Frank H. Severance, "Random Notes on the Authors Of Buffalo," *Publications of the Buffalo Historical Society* IV (1896), 340 ff; Severance, "The Story of Phinney's Western Almanack," *Publications of the Buffalo Historical Society* XXIV (1920), 355; "Some Pioneer Printers and Representative Editors and Publishers of the Earlier Buffalo," *Publications of the Buffalo Historical Society* XIX (1915), 282; Truman C. White, *Our County and Its People . . . Erie County New York* (Boston, 1898), I, 183, 296, 813 ff.

39. Smith H. Salisbury appears to have gone to Buffalo a little in advance of his brother. See Brigham, *op. cit.*, I, 557 & Follett, *op. cit.*, 57.

40. "Contributions Towards A Bibliography of The Niagara Region," *Publications of the Buffalo Historical Society* VI (1903), Appendix, 572. [Horatio Adams Parsons], *A Guide to Travelers Visiting the Falls of Niagara* (Buffalo: Charles Faxon, [1834]) disputes priority with Ingraham's *Manual.* See Douglas C. McMurtrie, *The First Guides to Niagara Falls* (Chicago, 1934), 6.

41. Follett, *History of the Press of Western New-York; . . . Together with the Proceedings of the Printers' Festival, Held . . . in . . . Rochester, on . . . Jan. 18, 1847* (Rochester, 1847), 43.

William Williams

Pioneer Printer of Utica, New York, 1787–1850

In 1800, when the boy William Williams migrated to Utica to serve as printer's apprentice, he found himself in a straggling village situated in a frontier region.[1] Indeed, Utica had been incorporated as a village only two years before, and not long since had been little more than an Indian crossroads. When the young apprentice arrived, he walked along unpaved streets with boarded sidewalks. Actually there were but three roads, of which Genesee Street, where Williams was to settle, was a newly made causeway of bare logs with swamp and forest on both sides. The woods were celebrated as a hunting ground for squirrels, owls, and pigeons, but in the village itself there were less than two thousand inhabitants and ninety houses. Yet that small hamlet was shortly to become a printing center that could vie in production with the publishers' row of any great city.

Despite enormous difficulties, both in the manufacture and the distribution of books, this vigorous and vital printing acitivity was to manifest itself. The Canal would not be completed until 1825. Hence, to distribute newspapers, books, and pamphlets, colporteurs had to be sent out, and wagons and pack-horses hired.[2] The mails—and often the books, too— were carried in the pouch of the postrider, who announced his arrival by the sounding of a long tin horn. The books themselves were printed on an old Ramage press with a short screw and lever, two pulls to the form. While the printer's wife folded the sheets and stitched the pamphlets, his apprentice trampled pelts, cut wood, and made the fire in the printing office. Yet, for all these difficulties, there was an avid public for the books that rolled at length from the press with its worn and indifferent type; for the New England

Paper read before the Oneida Historical Society of Utica, New York, February 12, 1951. Reproduced for distribution to members of the Bibliographical Society of the University of Virginia, Charlottesville, Va., 1951.

ancestors, as they moved west, had carried in one hand a Bible and in the other a spelling book. As the years passed, they would be eager for more and more books, and the hearty response to their demands, in Utica, would be owing in large measure to the activities of one great printer.

William Williams had been born in Framingham, Massachusetts, on October 12, 1787, the son of Susanna Dana and Thomas Williams of Roxbury.[3] His father had been one of the Roxbury minute men and had joined the Boston tea party, a man "distinguished for his suavity of manners, amiability of temper and exemplary piety."[4] With his father's family, young William had migrated to New Hartford, whence he removed to Utica. First as apprentice to William McClean, and later to his brother-in-law, Asahel Seward, who had in turn been apprenticed to Isaiah Thomas, the boy was to develop not only his "stiff handwriting at the printing office,"[5] but his versatile accomplishments in the trade. As a master printer he eventually set type, ran the hand press, worked as a practical bookbinder, manufactured paper, wrote editorials, and engraved notes and woodcuts to illustrate his letterpress.

By 1807, when Williams was twenty years old, his capabilities were rewarded when he was taken into partnership with Asahel Seward.[6] At the office, one door east of the Coffee House on Genesee Street, Williams soon became the master of other apprentices and journeymen also, among them Henry Ivison,[7] destined to be the head of one of the largest schoolbook publishing houses in the world, and Thurlow Weed, who was to recall how Williams

> put a composing stick in my hand, placed some copy before me, and in an encouraging way remarked that he would see what I could do. When he returned two or three hours afterwards, he read over the matter that I had been "setting up," and remarked kindly that I could go with the other boys to supper. I was therefore at work in the office and domiciled in the house of a gentleman . . . who became and ever remained my warm friend, and for whose memory I cherish a grateful remembrance.[8]

The partnership between Seward and Williams terminated in 1824, with Seward's withdrawal,[9] but both before and after that date, Williams exhibited such a many-faceted skill in book production that Utica could boast itself one of the liveliest publishing centers in the state.

Williams' career, both in partnership under the firm name of Seward and Williams, and alone, ran along four different lines, all of them fused and integrated. He was a publisher of books; he was a newspaper proprietor; he was a bookseller; and finally, he was an active and productive citizen. The thread that unified these varied activities was, indeed, Williams' social consciousness as a citizen. Captain of a company of volunteers in the War of 1812, he was to become brigade major and then colonel on the staff of General Oliver Collins in 1813 during the Sacketts Harbor incident.[10] With

Thurlow Weed, he left for the "front" in a sleigh and remained there most of the time until July 1814. Eighteen years later, when the village was stricken with an epidemic of cholera, Williams was still on hand to attend the sick "with such entire disregard of comfort and safety, that he narrowly escaped with his life having himself suffered an attack." [11]

Between those two events, during years that called for less heroic but no less creative efforts, Williams served his community well. For its religious needs, he acted as elder of the First Presbyterian Church, instructor in the Bible Class, and superintendent of the Sunday School. To advance the educational demands of a growing frontier settlement, Williams served as president of the Western Education Society and director of the Utica Library. To give an impetus to other local community requirements, he became village trustee, a stirring member of the fire department, and delegate to political conventions at which he evinced his Federalist–Clintonian inclinations or his championship of anti-masonry. Incidentally, Williams was naturally on the reception committee that welcomed Lafayette to Utica, and "the unbuilt miry road which had recently been laid in front of the Williams house received the name of the distinguished French visitor." [12]

This vital and active public career was reflected in the books that bore the imprint of Seward and Williams and later of William Williams alone. [13] The printer's church interests naturally led him to undertake the publication of numerous religious works that could be used by local pastors and Sunday Schools. It was said that "when a stray clergyman turns up in Utica with a manuscript, he instinctively goes to William Williams." [14] The first edition of the Devereux Testament, so-called because Nicholas Devereux of Utica owned the stereotype plates from which the volume was printed, appeared under his imprint, along with several other Bibles and New Testaments. For the sermons delivered by the pastor of the First Church of Clinton or of Onondaga, or by the first president of Hamilton College, Williams was the most likely publisher, as well as for that pathetic *Farewell sermon, to the First Presbyterian Church on the occasion of the dismission of their pastor, who had for some months, by the weakness of his voice, been unable to discharge the duties of his office.* And to his list of Bibles and sermons, he added an assortment of plums for the benefit of clergy, from *Discourses on the Temptations of Christ* to a *Defense of the Trinitarian System*, from a *Young Christians' Guide* to a *Brief History of the First Presbyterian Church . . . in Utica*, of which Williams was elder.

Just as he combined his church activities with his trade as publisher, Williams reflected his educational interests in the books that rolled from his press. From Noah Webster his firm purchased the right to publish the *Elementary Spelling Book* in the Western District of New York, and for many years that work not only afforded them an annual income of $2,000,[15] but at the same time supplied the schoolbook needs of a frontier settlement. Other books bearing the Williams imprint helped develop the community's educational enterprises also: Murray's *English Reader*, Hull's *Spelling Book*, the *New England Primer*, Thayer's *Geography*, a school Bible—the last in press because the "increasing demand, in this section of the country, and west of it, for the Testament as a School Book, has induced the proprietor to procure standing forms, of new letter, from the Cambridge stereotype edition." [16] Since he could not stereotype in Utica, Williams was not averse to spending months in Ohio to produce stereotype editions of his publications. [17] All these educational books, including the Hamilton College catalogues and, characteristically, the catalogue of the Utica School District Library, were "calculated to improve the minds and refine the taste of youth" at a period when schoolhouse and printing press had followed in the wake of farmer and pioneer.

Williams' publication of an Iroquois speller and a Hawaiian grammar bears direct evidence of how the printer combined his religious and educational interests. The spread of the Gospel among the Indian tribes led to the demand for books printed in Mohawk and Choctaw, and Williams served also as an accredited agent of the American Board of Commissioners for Foreign Missions. In this capacity he undertook the interesting task of printing the *Missionary Herald* in an edition for upstate New York. The December 1822 number contains a revealing statement regarding this Utica edition:

> On account of difficulties and delays, which have been experienced in transporting our work to subscribers in the western part of New-York, and the adjacent regions, an agreement has been made with Mr. William Williams, of Utica, N. Y. to reprint, from sheets forwarded to him from Boston, so many copies, as shall be necessary to supply the counties, and other sections . . . the work will generally come into the hands of our western subscribers sooner than it does at present, and, in most cases, with less expense of postage. [18]

Farther afield, the Hawaiian Mission Press profited from Williams' labors. It was in the office of Seward and Williams that Elisha Loomis, the missionary printer, met his wife, who folded in the bindery. When, in 1827, Loomis returned from the Sandwich Islands to get certain tracts printed more expertly than was possible in Honolulu, he wrote to Levi Chamberlain of the Hawaiian Mission about the arrangements he had made, adding, "I engaged Wm. Williams of Utica to print 20,000 copies of each [of two tracts]. The cost of paper, printing, and folding of these was $200, but Mr. Williams had made *a donation of the whole*, to the Board." [19] Loomis' great-granddaughter visited Honolulu in 1936 and, mentioning the firm of Seward and Williams to the librarian of the Hawaiian Mission Children's Society, heard the response, "Oh, that must have been the Mr. Williams who did so much for the Mission by printing free of charge a large number of its pamphlets!"

Once the basic needs of school and church had been supplied, Williams could branch out into the publication of more general instructional works that would be useful in a pioneer region. For the tradesman, he undertook a *Domestic manufacturer's assistant, and family directory in the arts of weaving and dyeing*, or an *Artist and tradesman's guide.* For the legal requirements of the community, he published a report of a case in chancery or a judge's opinion on a local trial. Nor did Williams neglect the lighter side of his trade. For the children, he produced juveniles, such as Mrs. Sherwood's *History of little Henry*; for the musical, his imprint appeared upon a variety of *Gamuts, Preceptors* for fife and violin, and *Flute Melodies*, as well as the *Musica Sacra* of Thomas Hastings, who had come to Utica in 1797 to lead the church music and had written the hymn, "Rock of Ages," there. For the literary, Williams undertook such intriguing titles as *Escalala: an American Tale; Purraul of Lum Sing; or, the missionary & the mountain chiefs; by an officer of the Madras army;* and the *Memoirs of Mrs. Harriet Newell* in an edition which would "have the preference to preceding editions, it being printed from a copy lately received from India, with corrections and additions by the Rev. Samuel Newell." [20]

None of the works bearing the Williams imprint indicates so clearly his interest in the local citizenry as the books he published for various county societies. He was the perfect candidate for issuing addresses delivered before the Oneida Agricultural Society and the Utica Temperance Society, or the tracts of the Tract Society of the Oneida Association. To him, the Oneida Medical Society, the Maternal Association of Utica, the Oneida Bible Society, the Oneida Institute of Science and Industry, and the Western Education Society naturally turned when they wished a publisher for their reports and discourses.

Still other works of purely local interest rolled from the Williams press. When Alexander B. Johnson, the Utica banker, delivered an Independence Day oration in the village, or when John Sherman wrote a description of Trenton Falls in Oneida County, Williams, as a matter of course, published their effusions. To Maynard's *Speech on the bill for the construction of the Chenango canal* and Beach's *Considerations* on the great Canal, this prolific and versatile publisher added his own *Tourist's Map of the State of New York* as well as his *Stage, Canal, and Steamboat Register.* Of all these local works, the most interesting both from the historical and the antiquarian points of view, is the *Utica Directory* of 1817, the first directory of the village as well as the first book bearing the name of Williams alone as printer. Included in the *Directory*, with its street addresses and Utica census, is an almanac. By 1817, Williams had had copious experience in the publication of almanacs, for the imprint of Seward and Williams had appeared on the *Farmers' Calendar; or, Utica Almanack* for many years, and later on, Williams was to issue *Williams' Calendar; or, the Utica Almanack.* Like most of the almanacs published by upstate New York printers, Williams' offered "a great variety of useful and entertaining pieces," including instructions for whitewashing fruit trees, anecdotes on rustic shrewdness, and versified warnings to the drunkard to "spurn the treacherous bowl," advice from which the thrifty citizenry doubtless profited.

They profited also from Williams' political views, which might be reflected in such a work as Bernard's *Light on Masonry*, appearing at a time when popular indignation rose high after the abduction of William Morgan.[21] A far more satisfactory medium, for the dissemination of news as well as of political opinion, was, however, the newspaper, and of this William Williams was well aware. In his *Farmers' Calendar* he had announced that the word NEWS was derived from the four cardinal points of the compass marked with the letters N.E.W.S.,[22] and in his experience as newspaper proprietor he had and would continue to have ample opportunity to apply the great powers of a free press. In all his activities, Williams worked with a large hand. By far the most prolific publisher outside the largest cities, he could boast an annual output of from six to twenty titles, in four years issuing fifty-one books and pamphlets, and after 1821 publishing one hundred thirty works, ranging from a Welsh hymn book to tracts in Choctaw. This same generous "wholesale" spirit Williams evinced in his proprietorship of newspapers.[23] Between 1814 and 1834, his name was connected with seven periodicals, from the *Utica Club* to *The Elucidator*, in all of which he could write editorials on canals or railroads or slavery, on the colonization of free blacks in Haiti or the People's Party *vs.* the Regency. Perhaps the most interesting of the newspapers with which he was associated was *The Patrol*, which later became the Clintonian *Patriot, & Patrol*. The first issue of January 5, 1815, contains a statement of purpose and policy:

> Various considerations have induced the Publishers to undertake the publication of a newspaper.
>
> Among the most prominent of these considerations, are the growing wealth of the village and its vicinity, the increased importance of its local situation, arising from the peculiar state of political affairs, and the advantages which will necessarily arise to the community from a more frequent communication of the occurrences of public transactions than the present sources of information afford.[24]

Important news was promised, along with biographical sketches of distinguished characters; the proprietors would not be unmindful of agricultural and manufacturing interests, nor would they "neglect the muses." Party politics would be excluded. "We choose rather to extinguish than fan the coals of political contention."

Yet political affairs themselves were not excluded. In the *Patriot, & Patrol*, distributed by one Mr. Parkhurst and other postriders, subscribers could find, for example, a strikingly prophetic article on the Power of

Russia, along with news of the death of the Princess Charlotte of Wales, and the "Latest" from France, carried via a New York communication nearly three weeks old.[25]

When the *Patriot, & Patrol* was abandoned, the *Utica Sentinel* took its place, and there, too, "the interesting crisis of our public affairs"[26] could be reflected, as well as in the anti-masonic *Elucidator*, which Williams undertook in 1830. Indeed, when the latter was transferred to Williams, the *Oneida Observer* announced that the "Messrs. Northway & Porter, finding that the Sentinel and Elucidator, like the Kilkenny cats, were in a fair way to destroy each other, if both were longer kept in their possession, have transferred their half of the latter establishment to Mr. Wm. Williams."[27]

In all these newspapers, William Williams found the opportunity not only for grinding his political axe and advancing the public welfare according to his lights, but also for the more practical advertising of his own wares. Williams was not only the public-spirited citizen who plied a trade as printer-publisher and newspaper proprietor, but he was also bookseller of 60 Genesee Street. By 1820, his bookselling establishment was the largest in the state west of Albany. As the years passed, Genesee Street,[28] with its mantuamaker's establishment, its Utica Fashionable Clothing Emporium, its Looking-Glass Factory, its Yellow Store, and Peale's Utica Museum, became notable for the stand at No. 60. The bookstore[29] on the ground floor was topped by a bindery, where ladies stitched and thousands of sheepskins or bark-tanned skins were piled high, along with tons of sizing. On the third story the printing office flourished, and there apprentices might be seen pushing the hand roller over the forms on the press, washing the rollers, or carrying wood and water. The activity on the second and third stories was matched by that on the ground floor, where the bookstore offered its varied attractions. There, Williams, the proprietor, a figure of noble presence and winning manners, his clear dark eye beaming upon his patrons,[30] might be seen extending the hospitality of his establishment to those who came in search of books.

The needs of almost every profession could be met at No. 60 Genesee Street.[31] If Montgomery Bartlett wandered there in quest of suitable reading matter for his Young Ladies School on Bleecker Street, or if the Rev. William Weeks wished to find texts for the Clinton Grammar School of which he was in charge, the search was sure to be rewarded at No. 60. For the Utica Academy or the Clinton Liberal Institute or Hamilton College, William Williams offered a variety of schoolbooks and instructional works, and had on hand such quantities of each that none need go without. His bookstore housed 10,000 copies of a School Testament, 8,000 of Murray's *English Grammar*, 2,000 of Thayer's *Geography*, 2,000 *American Preceptors*, as well as hundreds of copies of Starkweather's *Arithmetic*. There were, in addition, Greek *Lexicons*, or Crabb's *English Synonymes*, *The Cabinet History of England, Scotland, and Ireland*, or *Familiar Lectures on Botany* by Mrs.

Almira H. Lincoln, Vice-President of the Troy Female Seminary. From *Peter Parley's Geography* to Gillie's *History of Ancient Greece*, books were available for all who would teach and all who would learn, at prices ranging from a few cents up to $24 for a nine-volume *Universal History*.

Williams catered to the legal profession as well, and there is little doubt that such Utica lawyers as William Maynard, Ezekiel Bacon, or Samuel Beardsley were on hand when a case of new law books arrived at No. 60. There they could browse to their hearts' content, thumbing the leaves of Starkie on *Evidence*, or Jeremy's *Equity*, of Hoffman's *Legal Outlines* or a set of the *Revised Laws of New York*.

For the physicians of Utica—Alexander Coventry or William Watson—indeed for the entire Medical Society of Oneida, the proprietor offered an assortment of works on *Remittent* or *Intermittent Diseases*, on *Practical Obstetrics*, or *Diseases of the Skin*, not to omit one important item entitled *Bell on the Teeth*, with plates.

The Utica pastors—whether they served the First Presbyterian Church, like Samuel C. Aikin, or the Universalist Society, like John Samuel Thompson; whether they represented the Oneida Bible Society or the Tabernacle Baptist Church—found on the shelves of 60 Genesee Street enough Bibles and Testaments to answer the needs of their flocks, and surely one of them picked up a copy of the *Antidote to the Miseries of Human Life* which sold at the nominal price of thirty-one cents.

For so small a village, Utica could boast a comparatively large number of musicians, and for them, too, the bookstore of William Williams had many attractions. William Whitely, who made musical instruments, and George Dutton, who ran a music store in Utica, doubtless enjoyed browsing among the *Musical Readers* and *Instrumental Preceptors* on hand, while Ebenezer Leach, who taught flute playing, could examine the hundreds of *Flute and Fife Preceptors* on the shelves. The Oneida Musical Society need wander no farther afield for its supplies, for Williams could offer 3,000 *Gamuts* for singing schools, along with hundreds of copies of the *Musica Sacra*.

Nor were the ladies and children reglected. For the latter, No. 60 Genesee Street had assembled 10,000 assorted toy and picture books, as well as 5,000 chapbooks, while the ladies could enjoy such varied works as *Rob Roy*, *Manners, a Novel*, Godwin's *Mandeville*, or *Tales of Wonder, of Humour and of Sentiment*, by Anne and Annabella Plumptre. The titles alone were enticing: *Rosabella, or a Mother's Marriage*; *Sea Serpent*; the *Bower of Spring*; the *Balance of Comfort, or Old Maid and Married Woman*. And, of course, no shelves would have been complete without being graced with Lord Byron's *Siege of Corinth*, Moore's *Lalla Rookh*, and Cooper's *Novels*.

For all his varied customers, William Williams offered astute techniques of salesmanship. He was, as he advertised, "constantly receiving new supplies of Books, Stationary [*sic*], &c. which would enable him to supply orders for Books and articles in his line, in general use, with facility and on good terms." [32] The terms were good indeed. Library companies, merchants and town libraries were offered special inducements. Bible Societies were furnished with Bibles at sixty-four cents a copy, and the initials of the Society were marked on the same, gratis. When books were received from New York or Baltimore, they were offered for sale "on as reasonable terms as they could be had elsewhere in the state." [33] Books in quantities were of course sold wholesale, and besides advertising his wares in the newspapers of which he was proprietor, Williams also issued catalogues in pamphlet form "for gratuitous distribution." [34] He purchased books with the same acumen he used in selling them, a fact to which one of his letters to the Philadelphia firm of McCarty and Davis [35] bears witness:

> Far be it from me to blame you for doing as well as you can with your own books, but at the same time, if you do not furnish them to me on as good terms as your neighbors, it will be for my interest to trade with them, and thereby you might fail in disposing of some of your books . . . I shall never wish you to take an article of me that is not *good*, that is that will not *sell*, for the goodness of a book with book sellers depends upon its sale, and what may be *good* at Utica is not of course *good* at Philadelphia.

Another letter to the same concern [36] indicates the unusual difficulties Williams occasionally faced in shipping his books from the comparatively remote location of Utica:

> Your letter of inquiry respecting the Box of Books was duly received. Business having called me to this City [Albany] I have enquired of my Agent here, and find the vessel containing two boxes from me for yourselves and Grigg ran aground near Hudson and was there frozen in. The weather is now so mild that there is reason to hope they will get afloat soon. The accident has no doubt produced a serious disappointment to you, and is much regretted on my part, as these delays, from whatever cause, are calculated to prejudice you against dealing with a person at so remote a distance.
>
> I trust you will make all due allowance for an accident entirely beyond my control.

In addition to handling books and shipping them to remote distances, Williams was the agent for a variety of periodical works, from the *Edinburgh* and *Quarterly Reviews* to *Niles' Weekly Register*, from the *North American Review* to the *Library of Useful Knowledge*, soliciting in their behalf the "patronage of an enlightened and liberal public." [37] There were few aspects of his trade as bookseller that Williams had not mastered.

Besides the many thousands of books that flowed in and out of No. 60 Genesee Street, there were numerous other attractions for the public. [38] Williams kept on hand a supply of 12,000 Holland Quills, selling at from twelve shillings to $40 a thousand, along with hundreds of reams of foolscap writing paper priced at from $3.25 to $6 a ream. He offered a variety of fine and common wafers, as well as fancy and billet papers. There was, indeed, little that No. 60 did not keep on hand, from tinted paper albums, "elegantly bound," to clean linen rags from Rome and Hamburg. To complete his services, Williams also acted as agent for the New York type and stereotype founders, William Hagar & Company, and for the patent printing presses of Robert Hoe & Company. He kept constantly on sale, at reduced prices, news and book ink, and, besides the kegs of printing ink, his extensive stock included a general assortment of small fancy and job type, cuts and ornaments, brass rules, composing sticks, and chases.

Not content with being merely a printer-publisher-newspaper proprietor-and-bookseller, William Williams was also an engraver, and had associated himself with the firm of Balch and Stiles, who issued maps and bank notes for Utica and some western banks. Under the firm name of Balch, Stiles & Company, they advertised that they would "receive and execute orders for Bank Bill and other kinds of engraving, on the shortest notice,"[39] together with copper plate printing of every description. In 1831, orders for all but the bank bill engraving were executed at No. 60 Genesee Street. Just the year before, Williams had also opened a commission paper warehouse in Utica, where he offered to "receive on sale, and make liberal advances on consignments of merchantable Printing, Writing, and Wrapping Paper . . . Bonnet Board, and Press Papers."[40]

It may have been that William Williams had too many irons in the literary fire, although in those days before specialization and division of labor, it was more or less customary for a printer in a small community to publish books, sell them, and own a newspaper in which he could advertise them. It may have been that the Panic of 1837 was already casting its shadows before, or it may have been a combination of Williams' many-faceted career and the fore-warning of national economic depression. At any rate, by 1833, Williams was suffering financial reverses which could be attributed to a few more specific causes.[41] He had been endorsing notes for others;[42] his anti-masonic *Elucidator* detracted from his revenues; and an edition of the *Edinburgh Encyclopedia*, begun years before in connection with J. and E. Parker of Philadelphia, brought a heavy loss to its publishers. In 1834, there were two sheriff's sales of Williams' stock, after which his creditors ran the business under his name, retaining him as manager, until 1836.

In that year, Williams removed to Tonawanda to take charge of some lumber interests for his friends, but anxiety about his Utica book business continued to pursue him, as a privately owned letter, dated Tonawanda, May 9, 1837, indicates:

> I would close the store [in Utica] at once, were it not that my binder and clerk would have to seek other employ, and the establishment could not readily be resusitated [*sic*]. If the Tracys would have paid me one half of the real value of Musica Sacra copyright I should have sold my lease and given up the idea of

again going into the Bookselling business. As it is, I cannot but hope a way may be opened by which I can consistently resume it. Unless this can be done as early as next fall it will be economy to shut up at once, for . . . the broken assortment now on hand will not defray expenses.[43]

In 1840, all his Utica affairs were closed out by his creditors; the famous bookstore and printing house of No. 60 Genesee Street were disposed of; and the stirring activities of the celebrated Utica printer-publisher-bookseller had become annals for the historian.

The next year, Williams was thrown from the top of a stage coach when it overturned,[44] and as a result of the injuries he sustained, he suffered from a mental disorder. Early in that year he had written pathetically, "I now pay $2 a week for my board . . . have no money worth naming."[45] After that accident he failed constantly and was completely separated from society. On June 10, 1850, in his sixty-third year, he died in Utica, where he had returned.

By that year, the population of the village had increased to over 17,000. The Utica and Schenectady Railroad Company had long since been incorporated, and the Chenango Canal completed. There is no doubt that the community owed a great part of its development, not only to those who had come with axe and plow, but to the printer whose tool had been the composing stick. It was the printer, who, with books and newsprint, had advanced the communication of ideas, without which no other form of communication was possible. And it was one printer, in particular, one whose social consciousness had motivated his every undertaking, who had cleared the ground and planted the seed for the expansion of a small community. Thurlow Weed wrote, after the death of William Williams, that "as a citizen, he was public spirited beyond his means; his counsel, his exertions, and his purse were ever at the service of any enterprise calculated to benefit the place."[46] The place—and the nation, too—were benefited by William Williams, the master printer, who, armed with type and composing stick, had paid a larger debt than he owed not only to his trade, but to his country.

Notes

1. For Utica during this period, see *A Bibliography of the History and Life of Utica* (Utica, 1932), 5, 139, 229 (Courtesy Alice C. Dodge, Utica Public Library); W. Freeman Galpin, *Central New York* (New York, [1941]), II, 327; Glyndon G. Van Deusen, *Thurlow Weed, Wizard of the Lobby* (Boston, 1947), 8; [Thurlow Weed], "Death of Col. William Williams," *Albany Evening Journal*, June 12, 1850; "William Williams," *DAB*.

2. For early methods of printing and book distribution, see *A Bibliography . . . of Utica, op. cit.*, 139; *The Centennial History of Chautauqua County* (Jamestown, N. Y., 1904), II, 96; Harriet A. Weed, ed., *Autobiography of Thurlow Weed* (Boston, 1883),

I, 22; John Camp Williams, *An Oneida County Printer, William Williams* (New York, 1906), xxii–xxiii.

3. For Williams' early life and apprenticeship as a printer, see M. M. Bagg, ed., *Memorial History of Utica, N.Y.* (Syracuse, 1892), 76; Milton W. Hamilton, *The Country Printer New York State, 1785–1830* (New York, 1936), 308; Hon. Ellis H. Roberts, "Chief of Our Early Printers," *Utica Daily Press*, January 12, 1907 (Courtesy Alice C. Dodge, Utica Public Library); [Thurlow Weed], "Death of Col. William Williams," *op. cit.*; George Huntington Williams, "The Genealogy of Thomas Williams of New Hartford, Oneida County, N. Y.," *The New-England Historical and Genealogical Register* (Boston, 1880), XXXIV, 72; John Camp Williams, *op. cit.*, 13–14; "William Williams," *DAB*.

4. *Utica Patriot, & Patrol*, August 5, 1817, p. 3.

5. Hamilton, *op. cit.*, 34.

6. For the Seward–Williams partnership, see Henry J. Cookinham, *History of Oneida County New York* (Chicago, 1912), I, 283; Roberts, *op. cit.*; [Thurlow Weed], "Death of Col. William Williams," *op. cit.*; John Camp Williams, *op. cit.*, 25.

7. Bagg, ed., *Memorial History of Utica, op. cit.*, 164–165; James C. Derby, *Fifty Years among Authors, Books and Publishers* (New York, 1884), 50–51. Williams found an Auburn opening for Ivison and purchased his first stock for him.

8. Harriet A. Weed, ed., *Autobiography of Thurlow Weed, op. cit.*, I, 25–26.

9. Bagg, *op. cit.*, 76.

10. For Williams' activities in the War of 1812, the cholera epidemic, and his general services to the community, see Bagg, *op. cit.*, 77; M. M. Bagg, *The Pioneers of Utica* (Utica, 1877), 165–166; *A Bibliography . . . of Utica, op. cit.*, 75; Franklin B. Hough, *American Biographical Notes* (Albany, 1875), 429; Roberts, *op. cit.*; Daniel E. Wager, *Our County and Its People a Descriptive Work on Oneida County New York* (Boston, 1896), 301; Harriet A. Weed, ed., *Autobiography of Thurlow Weed, op. cit.*, I, 26; [Thurlow Weed], "Death of Col. William Williams," *op. cit.*; George Huntington Williams, "The Genealogy of Thomas Williams of New Hartford," *op. cit.*, 72; John Camp Williams, *op. cit.*, xxiv–xxv; "William Williams," *DAB*.

11. [Thurlow Weed], "Death of Col. William Williams," *op. cit.*

12. Elizabeth Dunbar, *Talcott Williams* (n.p., c. 1936), 19.

13. For the books published by Seward and Williams, and William Williams, in various fields, see, besides the works themselves, Advertisements of Williams' publications in *Utica Patriot, & Patrol*, January 21, 1818, p. 3, and September 2, 1817, p. 3; Bagg, *The Pioneers of Utica, op. cit.*, 165; *A Bibliography . . . of Utica, op. cit.*, 204 ff; Cookinham, *op. cit.*, I, 283; Joseph Gavit's additions to Utica imprints (Courtesy Laura A. Greene, New York State Library); E. B. O'Callaghan, *A List of Editions of the Holy Scriptures . . . Printed in America Previous to 1860* (Albany, 1861), *passim*; Roberts, *op. cit.*; Alexander J. Wall, *A List of New York Almanacs 1694–1850* (New York, 1921), *passim* (Copy at New York Historical Society contains Joseph Gavit's additions); J. C. Williams, *op. cit.*, xviii–xix and *passim*; Rev. John Wright, *Early Bibles of America* (New York, 1894), 364.

14. Dunbar, *op. cit.*, 19.

15. Bagg, *Memorial History of Utica, op. cit.*, 76; Hamilton, *op. cit.*, 78.

16. *Utica Patriot, & Patrol*, September 2, 1817, p. 3.

17. Dunbar, *op. cit.*, 20.

18. *The Missionary Herald* XVIII:12 (December 1822), 400. See also Dunbar, *op. cit.*, 19. For this phase of Williams' activities, the writer is indebted to information from Mary A. Walker, Librarian, American Board of Commissioners for Foreign Missions.

19. Information from Albertine Loomis, Detroit, Michigan, great-granddaughter of Elisha Loomis. For this phase of Williams' activities, the writer is also indebted to Robert E. Moody of Rushville, N. Y. See also Howard M. Ballou and George R. Carter, "The History of the Hawaiian Mission Press," *Papers of the Hawaiian Historical Society* (Honolulu, 1908), No. 14, p. 26. Williams bequeathed this interest to his son, the Rev. S. Wells Williams, who went to China as a missionary printer.

20. *Utica Patriot, & Patrol*, February 10, 1818, p. 3.

21. Williams was, in fact, accused by his opponents of "reaping a rich reward from the *printing* and *selling* of Anti-masonic books." See *Oneida Observer*, February 23, 1830.

22. In *The Farmers' Calendar*, or *Utica Almanack, For . . . 1825.*

23. For the newspapers and periodicals published by Williams, see, besides the papers themselves, Bagg, *Memorial History of Utica, op. cit.*, 477 ff; *Bibliography . . . of Utica, op. cit.*, 38, 41; Clarence S. Brigham, *History and Bibliography of American Newspapers 1690–1820* (Worcester, 1947), I, 748–750, 752; [S. W. Durant], *History of Oneida County, New York* (Philadelphia, 1878), 302; Hamilton, *op. cit.*, 149, 308; Wager, *op. cit.*, 353; J. C. Williams, *op. cit.*, 97.

24. *The Patrol*, January 5, 1815, p. 2.

25. See *Utica Patriot, & Patrol*, January 13, 1818, pp. 2–3.

26. *The Patrol*, December 25, 1815, p. 1.

27. *Oneida Observer*, February 23, 1830.

28. For the establishments on Genesee Street, see *Utica Directory* for 1828.

29. J. C. Williams, *op. cit.*, 153–154. The copy of a statement of real estate owned by William Williams, dated February 27, 1834 (Courtesy of Mr. and Mrs. E. Frank Evans of Rome, N. Y.), indicates that by that date Williams also owned a bindery on Main and First Street. In the statement the inventory of his bindery is given as $10,772; of his printing office as $7,422; of his store as $22,982.

30. Williams is described in Bagg, *The Pioneers of Utica, op. cit.*, 166–167.

31. For the books sold at 60 Genesee Street, see Williams' advertisements in *Utica Patriot, & Patrol*, September 2, 1817, p. 3; January 6, 1818, p. 3; January 21, 1818, p. 3; February 10, 1818, p. 3; April 7, 1818, p. 3; April 14, 1818, p. 3; April 20, 1819, p. 1; and in *The Elucidator*, February 16, 1830, p. 3; July 20, 1830, p. 4; September 7, 1830, p. 4; September 11, 1830, p. 3.

32. *The Elucidator*, July 20, 1830, p. 4. For Williams' selling techniques, inducements to buyers, and his agencies, see also *Utica Patriot, & Patrol*, January 6, 1818, p. 3; April 14, 1818, p. 3; October 27, 1818, p. 2; *Utica Sentinel*, December 28, 1824, p. 1.

33. *Utica Patriot, & Patrol*, January 6, 1818, p. 3.

34. *Ibid.*, October 27, 1818, p. 2.

35. William Williams to McCarty & Davis, Philadelphia, June 26, 1818. In McCarty–Davis Collection, IV, 572, American Antiquarian Society. For this letter, as well as for numerous other aids in the preparation of this paper, the writer is indebted to the late Dr. Clarence S. Brigham.

36. William Williams to McCarty & Davis, Albany, January 26, 1825. In McCarty–Davis Collection, IX, 470, American Antiquarian Society (Courtesy Dr. Clarence S. Brigham).

37. *The Elucidator*, February 16, 1830, p. 3.

38. For Williams' trade in paper, type, and ink, see *Utica Patriot, & Patrol*, January 6, 1818, p. 3; *The Elucidator*, February 16, 1830, p. 3; April 20, 1830, p. 4; July 20, 1830, p. 4; August 23, 1831, p. 4.

39. *The Elucidator*, April 12, 1831, p. 4.

40. *Ibid.*, February 16, 1830, p. 3.

41. For Williams' financial reverses, decline, and death, see Bagg, *The Pioneers of Utica, op. cit.*, 165; Cookinham, *op. cit.*, I, 283; Roberts, *op. cit.*; [Thurlow Weed], "Death of Col. William Williams," *op. cit.*; George Huntington Williams, *op. cit.*, 72; John Camp Williams, *op. cit.*, 156, 159; "William Williams,"*DAB*.

42. For example, Pell & Brother, and Collins & Hannay. See William Williams to Henry Huntington, Utica, March 6, 1834, letter owned by Mr. and Mrs. E. Frank Evans of Rome, N. Y.

43. William Williams to Henry Huntington, Tonawanda, May 9, 1837, letter owned by Mr. and Mrs. E. Frank Evans of Rome, N. Y.

44. A letter from William Williams to Henry Huntington, Buffalo, April 14, 1841 (Courtesy Mr. and Mrs. E. Frank Evans) describes the accident in detail: ". . . we went over with great force. I was thrown through the window . . . I was so much stunded [sic] as not to be able to know where I was. . . ."

45. Roberts, *op. cit.*

46. [Thurlow Weed], "Death of Col. William Williams," *op. cit.*

2
Foreign Influences

Joseph Nancrede

Franco-American Bookseller-Publisher, 1761–1841

Books have been written to illuminate the course of Franco-American relations—relations that played so vital a part in the germinal years of this country and the years of revolution in France. Historians have investigated the reciprocal events that helped shape both nations between the time of the French Revolution and the Orleans monarchy. Scholars have dissected the interplay of concepts between the French *philosophes* and the founding fathers and their sons. Students of comparative literature have traced the sources of certain American books to France and of some French books to an exotic America.

Yet history, philosophy, literature are all molded and reflected by individuals. No one individual can better mirror the events, the thought, and the writings of his time than the individual who deals in books, writing them, translating them, selling them, publishing them. And who can trace more clearly the graph of Franco-American relations than a Franco-American who happens also to be a bookseller-publisher? The introduction of French thought into America and the interchange of ideas between the two countries, especially during the years of the French Revolution, the Directory, and the Consulate are provocative themes. The French newspaper press in this country, the French books that were published here, and the French books that were translated and distributed here all elucidate those themes. Much of France that is still woven into the fabric of this country was made part of the American pattern by the Franco-American publisher.

Reprinted from *The Papers of the Bibliographical Society of America* LXX (First Quarter, 1976): 1–88.

PLATE 1. The Franco-American publisher Joseph Nancrede. Courtesy of Professor Allen J. Barthold, Nazareth, Pa.

Joseph Nancrede flourished between the time of Crèvecoeur and the
time of Tocqueville. (See Plate 1.) He was part of what Crèvecoeur called
"this promiscuous breed" from which "the race now called Americans have
arisen." And although he was what Crèvecoeur described as an American—
"a new man, who acts upon new principles"—he was also ineluctably
French and by nature highly political. He lived a long span of over eighty
years, beyond the time that Tocqueville, questioning whether American
liberties could survive "their new penchant for equality and democracy,"
analyzed the tyranny of the majority in this country. In the course of that
long life which he lived partly in America and partly across the seas, he
remained a hyphenated American whose loyalties were less to America and
less to France than to a harmonious Franco-America. In the interests of that
united if nonexistent utopia he wrote, he translated, he published, and he
sold books that in his view helped tie his two countries together. His eyes
were brown, his nose long, his manner Gallic, and although he survived
many changes of costume from knee-breeches to pantaloons he carried
always in one hand an American flag and in the other a French tricolor.
Though much has been written about his times, little has been written about
him. Yet as a Franco-American publisher active in this country especially
during the eventful decade of 1794 to 1804 he illuminated those times and in
a minor fashion helped shape their thoughts and their events.

Like his divided loyalties, his name was an acquisition, not a birthright.

He was born at Héricy, near Fontainebleau, on 16 March 1761, [during] the reign of Louis XV, and was baptized not Joseph Nancrede but Paul Joseph Guérard, "legitimate son of Jean Joseph [Guérard] and Jeanne Françoise Gauthier; godfather Sr. Paul François Cecile, master of surgery, and godmother Jeanne Le Moine Pallate." Though the six brothers and sisters who had preceded him had departed this life by the time Paul Joseph made his appearance, he seems to have been born with all the trappings of fortune, descendant of a line of Marie Marguerites and Marie Josephes, with legitimate parents, godparents, and the blessings of the parish of Héricy, diocese of the "Sens Election de Melun, généralité de Paris."[1]

To those who read between the cold lines of his genealogy, however, a different, less auspicious tale is disclosed. In 1768, after the birth of her tenth child, Paul Joseph's mother died. Two weeks later his father followed her to the grave. Paul Joseph Guérard, a seven-year-old orphan and the only surviving child of a fecund union, appears to have been raised by his maternal grandfather Louis Gauthier.

Though the next decade of his life cannot be documented with any extant letters or certificates, it may reasonably be assumed that Paul Joseph Guérard was educated in the rudiments of his language and his national history and attained young manhood in the pleasant environs of Fontainebleau without any further untoward tragic events. On 19 August 1779 he entered military service, and with this traditional act required of most eighteen-year-old French boys Paul Joseph Guérard altered the course of his life, broke with the past and marched—in full regalia—toward an unlikely future.

The company he joined was the Regiment of the Soissonnais, and the Regiment of the Soissonnais happened to be part of the Army of Rochambeau. Young Paul Joseph Guérard was a member of the French expeditionary force destined to serve in the American Revolution. After the Americans' success at Saratoga, Benjamin Franklin had in 1778 been able to effect an alliance between France and the colonies that provided for French support until American independence was attained. The destiny of Paul Joseph Guérard of Héricy near Fontainebleau, age eighteen, was in a sense an outcome of that alliance.

His military history was the history of his regiment and so can be reconstructed by inference. On 6 April 1780 two battalions (including Private Paul Joseph) embarked at Brest with the Count de Rochambeau. Three months later they landed at Newport, Rhode Island, with the Bourbonnais and together both regiments defended the forts of Rhode Island and "participated in all the principal operations of the Army of Rochambeau."

The final operation of that Army was the Siege of Yorktown. On 21 July 1781 the Soissonnais took part in the expedition of the Chevalier de

Chastellux at Kingsbridge. In mid-August, after the Army had forced English withdrawal, the Soissonnais arrived in Philadelphia "to render honors to Congress" and was there "loudly acclaimed." On 28 September, Paul Joseph and his companions were at Yorktown. In October they fought with the Bourbonnais, Guérard's "captain commandant" Jean-Baptiste de Marin was seriously wounded, and on the nineteenth Cornwallis surrendered.[2]

At Yorktown nearly half of Washington's troops were French. While he remained in winter quarters at Hampton with the Soissonnais, Paul Joseph Guérard had time to contemplate the stirring fact that the French had indeed helped make the American Revolution a success. He himself had therefore helped unite the two countries. Years later he would indulge in more elaborate personal fantasies about his military service, claiming he had been not a private but a captain in Rochambeau's Army and that he had lost a twin brother "killed by his side" at Yorktown. As "an officer in the army of Count Rochambeau, it was his fortune to contribute with Washington & Lafayette, to the capture of Yorktown, at which he had the command of a Bastion, deemed of great importance by the British. In the course of the contest, they succeeded in entering it, & even spirited some of our cannon, but every individual of the enemy's party, finally remained dead in our recovered Bastion."[3]

Washington and Lafayette, Rochambeau and—Paul Joseph Guérard! Understandably, the quartet of names struck the young soldier's fancy. It is entirely possible that it was at this point in his life that he found the inspiration for the new name he would one day assume, that of Joseph Nancrede or Joseph de Nancrede. One of his companions in arms, a member of the Bourbonnais and a sublieutenant in the Soissonnais, was named De Dreux de Nancre, a name so similar to Guérard's later choice of Nancrede that it may well have been its source and its suggestion.

After three years of military service, Paul Joseph embarked with his regiment in March 1783 and returned to France.[4] He did not remain there long. The following February his grandfather Louis Gauthier died at the age of eighty-four. Whatever other ties the young soldier may have had in Héricy or Fontainebleau were apparently not strong enough to keep him there. He had played a part in an American Revolution that had resulted in American independence and had observed enough of what was coming to be called an American character to attract him to that new country.

On 13 October 1785 a passport was issued at Fontainebleau giving "free passage" to a man with a new name: Paul Joseph Guérard de Nancrede. On the twenty-first he embarked at Le Havre aboard "La Diligence de Cadix," Captain De la Roque, bound for Philadelphia and "l'Amérique Septentrionale."[5] His compatriot, "An American Farmer," had already posed the question "What Is An American" and answered it: "The American is a new man, who acts upon new principles; he must therefore entertain new ideas, and form new opinions." The young man who had fought at Yorktown had a new name and, having cast off for the time his old life in France, was on the way to becoming a new man in a new country.

Between his 1785 passport and a Harvard College Record of 1787, the name of Nancrede appears on no extant document that reflects his earliest activities in or his reactions to independent America. He disembarked from "La Diligence de Cadix" in Philadelphia in 1785 and cannot again be pinpointed until August of 1787 when it was voted at Harvard College "that the President, Mr. Storer and Mr. Lowell be a Committee to agree with Mr. Nancrede upon the terms on which he shall instruct the students of the University in the French language."[6]

There was much to appeal to the twenty-six-year-old Frenchman in "a place called Cambridge." Brissot de Warville, future leader of the Girondist party during the French Revolution and strong advocate of Franco-American accord, a man whom Nancrede deeply admired, described that "place" during a visit in 1788. It was "surrounded by delightful country houses used by Boston merchants for vacations, and here the students can find pleasant company and agreeable conversation. . . . The air is infinitely pure; the environs are charming. . . . The university consists of several buildings very well laid out." And he proudly added, "The heart of a Frenchman beats faster to find Racine, Montesquieu, and the Encyclopedia in a place where a century and a half ago the Indians smoked their calumets."[7]

It was in some small measure because of Nancrede's presence that Brissot de Warville found Racine, Montesquieu, and the Encyclopedia in that "place." Nancrede was not—despite some allegations to that effect—the first teacher of French at Harvard. As early as 1735 permission had been given for the teaching of French and occasional instructors had been brought in from Boston one day a week for that purpose. Between 1782 and 1783, when private Guérard was in winter quarters at Hampton, Albert Gallatin, Jefferson's future financier, had taught French at Harvard.[8] Now in 1787, thanks perhaps to the intercession of some anonymous benefactor, Nancrede and Harvard had been brought together.

Mutual benefits would result from this relationship. "The course of study," Brissot would comment, "is almost the same as at Oxford University. It is impossible that the recent revolution will not bring about a great reform. Free men must quickly cast off their prejudices and realize that they must be, above all else, men and citizens, and that the study of dead languages and of tedious philosophies . . . should occupy few hours of their lives." Nancrede's teaching of French would introduce to his students both the language and the philosophy of his compatriots. In turn, Nancrede's work as an instructor in French would awaken in him a growing awareness of the literary needs of his pupils and their families and so lead him eventually to fulfill those needs with books compiled, imported, or published for the purpose.

Joseph Nancrede, coupling his teaching with other literary, political, and publishing activities, would be associated with Harvard College for a decade—the decade that was marked by the French Revolution. Lovers of France who believed that "the French had made our revolution a success, and we in turn precipitated theirs" sang in the streets and "mounted the tri-colored cockade." Later, however, as event followed event, as a king was executed and news of French excesses aroused protest in Boston, regard for the precisions of the French language fell, and French dancing masters and teachers of French lost stature.[9]

Nancrede's path at Harvard was far from smooth and from year to year the College Records amusingly disclose his difficulties. In 1794 at a College Faculty Meeting "it appeared that Shattuck insulted Mr Nancrede while he was in the College Hall instructing the Class . . . in the French language, by throwing water-melon peele into one of the windows." A later student with heavier ammunition and more violent tendencies threw "stones . . . at the door of his Lecture-Room" and upon several occasions pupils were admonished or reprimanded for "disorderly and insulting behavior" to their French instructor.[10] One pupil who bore the name of Washington Allston exercised his artistic faculties by "representing his French class seated around a table, except one boy reciting, the French master holding a pig in his hands and directing the boy to pronounce 'oui' just like the noise made by the little brute."[11]

Despite his trials Nancrede persisted and to a great extent succeeded. Through his influence, the French consul at Boston, Mozard, presented the University with the gift of "a very curious, valuable and scarce" French scientific work.[12] One of Nancrede's star pupils, John Pickering, became a creditable linguist, and it was to him that the Boston minister John Clarke wrote *Letters to a Student in the University of Cambridge, Massachusetts* that contain oblique but laudatory recognition of the French instructor's influence. French, Clarke wrote, is "a qualification for an elegant intercourse with the world. . . . To read the French language with ease; to speak it with propriety; and to write it correctly, are enviable attainments. . . . I hope, soon to hear that you have made considerable progress in Telemachus, . . . The Studies of St. Pierre will afford you much entertainment. If his philosophy is sometimes lame, his language is good; . . . France has produced numberless writers, who do honour to human genius. To mention the most eminent, I must extend this letter to an unreasonable length. I therefore, refer you to the French instructer, . . . who will put into your hands such works as will aid his own labours; and make you a proficient in his language."[13]

Desirous as he was to place in his pupils' hands the works of Rousseau and Saint-Pierre, Racine and Montesquieu, Joseph Nancrede found it extremely difficult to do so. Often the books had neither been imported from abroad nor published in American editions. In November 1791 therefore he determined to provide for his scholars a compilation of his own which would eventually be published under the title *L'Abeille Françoise* and rank as the first such French textbook in this country. Nancrede's letter about this project to the Gentlemen of the Corporation of Harvard College reflects both the state of French studies there and his own intentions. In it he is already thinking like a Franco-American publisher. The letter is significant enough to be cited almost in its entirety:

> It is now upwards of four years, since you were pleased to appoint me to the instruction of French, in the University of Cambridge. You have since thought proper to establish that Language a branch of study, by successively enjoyning it on the students, and assimilating it, in some measure, to the other studies of the College. . . .
>
> I beg leave to submit to you a disadvantage under which every one of my pupils, at college, has laboured, ever since the establishment of French. . . .
>
> There never was, at College, any French classical book. The students have ever been obliged to read and construe, each in a different book. The inconveniencies and discouragements consequent upon such a deficiency must have been obvious to you; for one only can read and construe, at the same time; the rest do not improve by it; whereas, if they had all the same author, every one might join; . . . I would reckon for nothing the additional trouble it gives me, if it could turn to the advantage of my scholars; but here it is felt by them as well as by me. A considerable loss of time for the diligent and a pretence for the idle is always the consequence. The scholar, who can find no such pretence, in any other study, when he has no lesson, in french, never fails to say he has no book. . . .
>
> With a view to supply this deficiency, I have been engaged, for upwards of a twelve months, in collecting pieces, in several different styles, from our best authors. I requested the leave and approbation of Mr. President, to publish it for the use of the University. A little sum of money, and some Subscriptions, I thought would have enabled me to print it, without troubling this board; but my domestic circumstances, which put it out of my power, at present, do not diminish my zeal or my attachment to the interest of the university. I see what should be done; but cannot do it; yet think it incumbent on me, to expose the difficulty to you.
>
> The expences of printing . . . would amount to about 188 dollars for 500 copies: those for the paper, would be 100 more. The Subscriptions would defray part of these expences. If the Corporation would make up the rest, by taking as many copies, as would amount to the sum advanced; the number of scholars who should want it, would repay it, in a couple of years. In other respects, the board would lose nothing, for an advance might be laid on the price of every copy, so as to pay for the interest. The scholars would be properly supplied with a cheap book, which uniting different styles, would equally suit the beginners, and those more advanced. They would study with

pleasure, and find, in those fugitive pieces, a relish for the different authors, from whom they are taken. The negligent would have no pretence left.

The correction, and the whole care of the press, I would most cheerfully take upon myself. . . .[14]

L'Abeille Françoise, ou Nouveau Recueil, De morceaux brillans, des auteurs François les plus celebres. . . . A l'usage de l'Université de Cambridge. par P.J.G. de Nancrede, Maître de langue Françoise, en cette Université would be published at Boston by Belknap and Young in 1792. As an outcome of Nancrede's tutorial work it requires immediate mention, but as a pioneer text of enormous significance in the introduction of French thought to America it deserves more extensive study and so *L'Abeille Françoise* will be dissected and analyzed in due course.

One of the subscribers to that volume would be Caleb Bingham, pioneer textbook writer and French scholar who helped reorganize Boston's public schools in 1789 before setting up as bookseller-publisher on Cornhill. Four evenings a week Joseph Nancrede used Mr. Bingham's schoolroom to teach French privately. Between 1789 and 1794 the zealous Frenchman combined his Harvard teaching with his private classes. In the *Massachusetts Centinel*, 14 November 1789, he advertised that "A Small number of young Ladies, by assembling every day might be instructed in that [French] language on very reasonable terms," and announced to "such parents as wish to procure their children the knowledge of this useful tongue, that a French School for young Gentlemen might be opened in this town— punctual attendance given, and upon the same terms as those of other schools, if a sufficient number (from 20 to 30) of Scholars should offer."

In the *Massachusetts Centinel* of 19 August 1789, Nancrede made a long and eloquent plea "To The Publick" on behalf of his language and its service to America: "The French Language," he began, "is obviously of much importance to the Youth of this town, and is becoming more so every day. . . .

"The Subscriber, whose ambition shall ever be to justify the favours of the citizens of this town, by projects of *real utility*, begs leave to represent . . . that the French Language could and should be taught, in this town, upon the same terms with every other branch of education. . . . For the two most powerful springs, pleasure and profit, which are wanting in the study of dead languages, and which are strongly excited in that of French, . . . would be in a continual motion in a publick school. . . . "

From the language of Montesquieu and Rousseau, Voltaire and Raynal, and from the profundities of Helvetius, pleasure could be derived. But Joseph Nancrede, ever alive to the importance of trade relations, made the profit motive part of the concept of French for Americans. As he lucidly explained: "To open a source of knowledge, whence commerce, navigation, philosophy, the necessary arts, &c. may derive useful information, must be beneficial to the citizens of the United States, but especially to those of

Boston, whose affability to strangers, . . . has created a predilection in their favour. . . .

"It is rendering an immediate service to such individuals, as are in any wise interested in the trade or politicks of Europe; while the republican may discover in the abuse of power . . . the means of guarding his countrymen. . . . it is expected that the rising commercial intercourse with France, will receive additional encouragement. The new government being put in operation, will open the ports of America to the multitude of foreigners . . . every observer sees that the commerce of America must, in a few years, become as universal as that of any nation; therefore a sign of communication, as universal, if possible, as that trade itself, must be agreed upon, and what other can it be than the French language? . . . This language seems to be necessary to America." [15]

To provide that essential language, that "sign of communication," to the citizens of Boston, Joseph Nancrede, instructor of French at Harvard, private teacher, future compiler of the first French textbook, sported still another cap as the editor of an early and influential French newspaper in this country.

The preceding summer—in July of 1788—the French journalist-politician who had aroused Nancrede's admiration, Brissot de Warville, had arrived in Boston. "With what pleasure," he wrote, "did I look upon this city, the first one to shake off the English yoke, . . . What a delight it was to wander along that long street whose simple wooden houses face Boston's magnificent harbor, and to stroll past the shops which displayed for sale all the products of the Continent I had just left!" [16] Nancrede was well aware of Brissot's interest in close commercial ties between France and the new nation. Indeed he had already attempted a translation of a work by Brissot and Clavière on that subject—one of several translations by Nancrede which will be analyzed. Now, Brissot had come to America for a variety of related purposes one of which keenly influenced Nancrede.

To assemble information on the commerce of the United States and to further reciprocal trade relations with France, the Gallo-American Society had been formed in Paris under Brissot's aegis. As Brissot himself put it, "If a like society be formed in free America, as there is reason to hope for such a measure, it will be employed in publishing in America, every useful discovery which French genius can make." The Society's motto reflected its aim: *The utility of the two worlds.* [17] Joseph Nancrede was quick to become a member of the Boston chapter and equally quick to respond to the proposal that he found a French newspaper in America. [18]

The paper Nancrede eventually established was not, in spite of statements to that effect, the first French paper in this country. Nor did it have a long life. It lasted only six months, from 23 April to 15 October 1789, but what six months they were!—months that witnessed the first session of the American Congress, the inauguration of George Washington, the Fall of the Bastille.

Armed with his inspiration and his purposes—to bring France and America into closer commercial relations, to dispel erroneous views about the new nation, and, still Harvard's French instructor, to stimulate the study of French language and literature in this country—Joseph Nancrede embarked upon the preliminary operations for his scheme.

On 3 January 1789 the *Massachusetts Centinel* carried his lengthy address "To the Publick" concerning a French newspaper entitled the *Courier de Boston:*

> The advantages which must accrue to the United States from a periodical publication, calculated to inform foreigners, and above all, merchants, in their own language, of the natural, moral, and political resources of this country, are obviously of so much importance, and must prove so beneficial to the Commerce of America, that I shall ever view the attempt alone (should it fail of success) as one of the most happy, and most favourable circumstances that could recommend me to the citizens of the UNITED STATES.
>
> To be the Interpreter, the Organ of every citizen . . . to convey adequate ideas of the MAJESTY OF CONGRESS to nations who scarcely know that there is one existing: . . . to convince them, . . . that "WHERE LIBERTY DWELLS, GREAT MEN ARE NOT WANTING";—to afford a vehicle to merchants (that numerous and wealthy part of the community, whose individual interest is so immediately connected with that of the people); to be instrumental in removing commercial obstacles; to contribute to its extension; . . . are objects, to which, I confess, I have the rashness to extend my ambition. Such are the principles upon which the COURIER DE BOSTON is offered to the patronage of the Americans; . . . .
>
> What American . . . has not been shocked at the descriptions given of America in foreign parts, by the most learned men— . . . what could rectify these errors better than a WEEKLY PUBLICATION. . . ?
>
> The other local recommendations to this establishment, such as the *stimulus* to learning French, . . . are too trivial, when compared to those GREAT OBJECTS, to be enlarged upon here.
>
> I am well aware, that the undertaking of a paper, in a language, which is not yet prevalent in America, is arduous, and will be attended with difficulties, to which I have little . . . to oppose, than perseverance; but as I have reason to think that the number of foreign subscribers from Canada, the West-Indies, and Europe, will by far exceed those of America, . . . I am determined to begin the publication as soon as the number of subscribers will appear sufficient to defray the most necessary expenses.

Subscriptions would be received by the *Centinel*'s printer Benjamin Russell, at whose office copies of the prospectus were also available.

The day after his announcement had been printed Joseph Nancrede sent a copy of his prospectus to John Adams with a flattering letter soliciting the influence of one whose "thorough knowledge of Europeans, and their Ideas of America, . . . has no doubt, long since, convinced you of the necessity of a periodical paper that might, propagate in france, through every class of people, just and adequate Ideas of the United States." [19]

By the following month Nancrede had stirred up enough interest not only among the sizable French population in Boston but among the Americans themselves to elicit a letter from "A Boston Merchant" to the publisher of the *Centinel* announcing "I am extremely well pleased with Mr. de Nancrede's project of publishing a *French periodical paper* in this town. It is a project that merits the encouragement and patronage of the citizens of America. . . . France and America, although politically allied, are yet *strangers to each other*. . . . we now have an opportunity of seeing a work published weekly in this town, in which the Editor drawing this stream of knowledge immediately from the *source* of French politicks, will present us with the *truth* . . . and dam out the usual torrent of English *lies*. . . . The *rage* for *belittleing* every thing American among the French philosophers, though neatly *allayed* by Mr. Jefferson, will be totally extinguished by a *present tense* journal of the kind now proposed." [20]

On 23 April 1789 the first number of that *"present tense* journal" the *Courier de Boston*[21] was published. Consisting of eight pages, crown quarto, with double columns, and priced at five pence, it sported as its running motto that of the Gallo-American Society, *"L'Utilite des deux Mondes"* but nowhere stated the name of its editor. Instead, the imprint, at the foot of the last page, read: "A Boston, de l'Imprimerie de Samuel Hall, Libraire, dans le *Cornhill*, No. 53." Samuel Hall, "a correct printer, and judicious editor; industrious, faithful to his engagements, a respectable citizen, and a firm friend to his country,"[22] had opened a printing house, book and stationery store in Cornhill in November 1785, just after Nancrede had returned to America. Now, less than four years later, the two were united in a significant enterprise attended, as Nancrede perceived, with "an arduous task—which very few printers can undertake, unless armed with a stock of industry, patience and attention" (*Massachusetts Centinel*, 11 February 1789). Subscriptions for the *Courier de Boston* could be arranged for "chez les principaux Imprimeurs des Etats-Unis," among them Greenleaf and Fenno in New York and Mathew Carey in Philadelphia.

Despite the availability of agents there were never enough subscribers to warrant the *Courier* a long life. Yet during its six months it did indeed fulfill its editor's aims to provide a useful and instructive sheet that would do justice to America and help tighten commercial ties with France. Moreover, the weekly reflected political affairs both in France and in America during one of the most eventful half years in history. News from France, doubtless obtained through Nancrede's connection with the Gallo-American Society, was both copious and accurately reported. It traced a period of upheaval with accounts concerning Necker and Mirabeau, Calonne and—of course— Brissot de Warville. It commented upon the "millions" of brochures and pamphlets emanating from France and it described the pomp attending the opening of the States–General. It reported revolt and confusion as well as tranquillity. It offered details on Lafayette and the Declaration of Rights; it quoted Rousseau; it announced the Fall of the Bastille and the onset of the Revolution.

The *Courier de Boston* was equally responsible in its recital of domestic events. The sessions and debates of Congress were reported as well as news of Washington's arrival in New York against a background of ringing bells and crowded streets. Washington's speech to Congress, the annual meeting of the Society of Cincinnatus, the presence of French ships in Boston Harbor, the state of the Creek Indians, and sessions of the American Academy of Arts and Sciences, even an account of Cambridge and its University found their way to the columns of the *Courier de Boston* and to the eyes of such subscribers as remained faithful.

Nancrede's weekly was enriched with several feature articles: essays on commerce, free trade and speculation, on the science of government, and one of particular interest gave "Advice to Emigrants to America." Possibly written by Brissot de Warville, this noted the presence of a middle class in America, the unimportance of birth, and the emphasis upon toil, not "*cocagne*," in "a country of work."

The *Courier de Boston* could be sustained only by subscriptions. Since Massachusetts levied a heavy tax upon advertisements in gazettes, the editor did not solicit them. Despite the fact that the weekly clearly reflected the activities of a new American government and the approaching upheaval of an old French government, it did not succeed. Nancrede was pursued with difficulties and problems. He sustained two thefts. A French refugee from St. Domingo stole 800 piastres from him, and a black woman whom he "had taken to board, to oblige her owner, pending a proposed sale" relieved him of another 120. Basically, however, it was a faulty subscription list that ended his newspaper. That list, burdened by many delinquents and apparently lacking those foreign subscribers the editor had anticipated, was never large enough to defray expenses. On 15 October 1789, the last number was issued and Joseph Nancrede was forced to seek other ways to improve Franco-American relations and advance the utility of two worlds.

He was forced, too, to seek other ways of earning a livelihood both for himself and his family. On 11 November 1788, before the *Courier* had been issued but after he had been appointed French instructor at Harvard, Joseph Nancrede had married and begun to experience those "domestic circumstances" he had mentioned in his letter to the Harvard Corporation. The *Massachusetts Centinel*, which would carry Nancrede's *Courier* address, now carried the following announcement (12 November 1788): "Married— By the Rev. Mr. Parker, Mr. P. J. G. de Nancrede, to Miss Hannah Dixcey [*sic*]."

Irony accompanies the biographer's pursuit of Miss Dixey, for considerably more may be unearthed about the Rev. Samuel Parker who performed the service than about Nancrede's bride. Dr. Parker, then rector of Trinity Church, Boston, would become Bishop of the Protestant Episcopal Church in the State of Massachusetts before his death in 1804.[23] Little over a week before the wedding, the first Catholic mass had been celebrated in Boston by Claude Florent Bouchard de la Poterie. Yet Nancrede, a Catholic, was married not by him but by Dr. Parker. The assumption is that Miss Dixey was Episcopalian. As for her appearance, no assumptions are necessary. She was described by the Canadian Pierre de Sales La Terrière, who studied at Harvard Medical School at the time, as "a very pretty woman." La Terrière rounds out the picture of the Nancredes:

> I was already intimate with several Frenchmen who lived in Boston, particularly with M. Joseph de Nancred, professor of French at the college, whom I frequently invited to dine with me at my boarding house; he reciprocated every Thursday in Boston. I came to have a close friendship with him, as he was a most estimable person. He rendered me great services. . . . He was married to a very pretty woman.[24]

Hannah Dixey Nancrede was also a fecund woman. Between 1789 and 1803, nine children were born of the union, all but one—Anacharsis, named after the ill-fated humanitarian Anacharsis Clootz—surviving well beyond childhood.[25] Two would become noted physicians; one would work for the illustrious Philadelphia printer Mathew Carey. All required some degree of education and a letter from Nancrede written to his son Joseph in 1803 indicates that they received it: "Louisa is still at Miss Burges' academy"; brother Nicholas adds a legible and literate message; and a good report of the recipient's scholastic progress in Montreal had been received.[26] Besides the rudiments, the children must be fed and clothed, and the necessary quantity of smallclothes and vests, hose and stocks, not to mention cocked hats, provided for the growing family. Despite the size of that family, Nancrede's marriage was not destined for success. After 1804 he and his wife would live apart and there would be but infrequent references to her during the remainder of his long life.

Meanwhile Nancrede was definitely a family man. Through his teaching privately and at Harvard, and his collateral activities, he was able in time to acquire some substance. In 1789 the Boston Directory places him at "William's-court, Cornhill" and characterizes him as an "instructor of the French language." Some years later he was proprietor of a brick house at the corner of Middle and Cross Streets, a wooden house in Cross Street, and the two-story brick house at 49 Marlborough Street where he would live and conduct his publishing business.[27]

The long-nosed Frenchman with dark hair and round chin, a man short in stature being only five feet seven inches tall,[28] could not have made a particularly imposing appearance at Harvard, at Samuel Hall's printing office, or in his wanderings about Boston. Yet, through his varied activities, either directly or indirectly he would make himself felt.

Joseph Nancrede had become a habitué of Boston, that "fine maritime town, the population of which . . . amounted to about twenty-two thousand souls." With his friend La Terrière he doubtless agreed that the "harbor, with its long wharf, is very commodious; . . . The promenades on the side of Beacon Hill are very pretty. But the most remarkable thing is the North Bridge, ornamented with lamps. The fair sex here surpasses in beauty any that I have seen in America. A very pure English is spoken. All the roads that approach the town are excellent. . . . The meadows and the fields between Boston and Cambridge are all bordered with hedges of barberry." [29]

Of those "twenty-two thousand souls," some of course were French and they must have been known to Nancrede: the rich Lothario from Martinique, "a fop to his fingertips"; the instructors in grammar, gavotte, and the eighteenth-century art of pleasing; Consul Letombe who brought his cook to Boston and remained faithful to the White Cockade until Louis' imprisonment; the Abbé de la Poterie who turned the brick building used as a stable by General Gage's troops into a Roman Catholic Chapel.

Nancrede's character developed along with his familiarity with Boston. His political interests were shaped by the earthshaking events of the time. His attachment to Rousseau and the *philosophes*, his fervent desire to explain, defend, and advance his native country in the country of his adoption, mingled with a hatred of fanaticism as the aims of the French Revolution became corrupted. "The real *fanatics*," he was to write, "are that dreadful tribe of *revolutionary men, assassins, oppressors, calumniators.*" [30] In this point of view he reflected the changing attitude of those Americans to whom he taught French and for some of whom he edited his *Courier de Boston*. Those who had danced in the streets at the start of the French Revolution tolled church bells and wore black roses when news of the execution of Louis XVI reached the United States. By the time of the arrival of Genêt, the new French ambassador, the people's pro-French enthusiasm had been restored, for news of England's joining the "coalition of kings" had preceded him. Nancrede watched the swing of the pendulum in a land that was both independent and supposedly neutral.

He did more, however, than watch. On 19 February 1799 Joseph Nancrede, "formerly of the City of Paris, in the Republic of France, now of Boston in the County of Suffolk" came personally into the Supreme Judicial Court of the Commonwealth of Massachusetts and swore that he had resided in the United States for more than five years, that he would "support the Constitution of the United States of America" and "renounce and abjure all allegiance and fidelity to any foreign Prince, Potentate, State or Sovereignty . . . particularly to the Republic of France," and that he had "never borne any hereditary title or been of any of the orders of nobility in the State from whence he came. Whereupon the Court upon due enquiry made that during the term aforesaid Joseph Nancrede, has behaved as a man of good moral character, attached to the Constitution and Administration of the United States" decreed that "the said Joseph Nancrede" was "agreeably to his petition admitted to become a Citizen of the United States."[31]

By that time, as the century was drawing to a close, Joseph Nancrede had served or attempted to serve both France and America in many ways: through his writings and translations, through his political machinations, and finally through his selling and publishing of books. He had begun first with the most obvious means of explaining one country to another—the art of translation.

On 25 June 1788 Nancrede offered "Translation from the English into the French language, and from French into English," which would be "done with fidelity and expedition."[32] He ran similar advertisements in the public prints from time to time and by 1793 he was translating not only for Cézar Dubuc, a French gentleman in Boston, but for Governor John Hancock.[33] Three years later it was thought "necessary to name a French interpreter for the service of the French in this Department and for authentic translations often necessary to be made for acts of justice." Because of "the zeal for the Republic and the devotion to the cause of liberty and the study which Citizen Joseph Nancrede has made in the English language during his long sojourn on this continent," he was named and commissioned "sworn translator of the English language for the service of the French." In July 1796, Citizen Nancrede received his Interpreter's Commission.[34] In the course of time he developed his own theories of translation, favoring adherence to the spirit rather than the letter of the original and advocating simplicity, purity, and moderation in style.

Nancrede's earliest major translation was, predictably, a work on Franco-American trade relations which had been written by Brissot de Warville in collaboration with the refugee banker Etienne Clavière. *De la France et des Etats–Unis; ou l'Importance de la Révolution de l'Amérique pour le Bonheur de la France* had appeared in 1787, a study dilating upon the commercial advantages opened to France by the American Revolution. Anti-mercantilist and pro-Adam Smith in its economic philosophy, it stressed the commercial interdependence of a France on the verge of revolution and an America emerging from revolution. The theme was after Nancrede's heart. Although his translation, "On France and the United States," was never published in book form, excerpts from it appeared in the newspaper press. Moreover, in his attempts to publish the translation, Nancrede learned much of printing-publishing methods which he would one day put to use.

As early as 22 May 1788, the *Independent Chronicle* carried his "Proposals for printing by Subscription, A System Of French *and* American

Trade, under the title of '*On* France *and the* United States.'"[35] Priced at three shillings, sixpence, the work would be "committed to the press as soon as 300 copies" were subscribed for. Surely this was not beyond the realm of possibility since "several gentlemen in this town, after a perusal of the original, have expressed the strongest marks of their approbation; nor have the English (who should always be believed when they bestow praises on the French, and their productions) hesitated to pronounce it a very useful and judicious work."

The *Massachusetts Centinel* (2 April and 2 August) and the *Independent Chronicle* (17 July) both proceeded to carry excerpts from Nancrede's translation. By July, when Brissot de Warville arrived in this country aboard the *Cato*, his translator had collected some 150 advance subscriptions and interested not only the French-speaking population of Boston in the enterprise but Governor Hancock and Hancock's predecessor James Bowdoin. Nevertheless, 150 subscriptions were inadequate to meet projected expenses, and Nancrede, in order to lower costs, contemplated deletions in the text. To this Brissot objected; indeed, he threatened to make the publication still more costly by furnishing Nancrede with additional sections to be incorporated in the work.

At this stage the frustrated translator tried to enlist the aid of Isaiah Thomas of Worcester, the great printer whom Brissot de Warville called "the Didot of the United States."[36] Nancrede's letter of 5 August 1788 to Thomas reflects both his enthusiasm for the text and his powers of persuasion:

> Of all the publications in which the Americans are concerned, none can arrest their attention so immediately as a system on trade; and if any publication can receive encouragement it must certainly be this; for among that class of men who can afford to buy books there are certainly more Merchants than any other. Besides every American whether Merchant farmer, or Navigator is too immediately interested in *commerce* not to read with avidity so useful a performance. . . .
>
> From these considerations together with—your patriotism and circumstances those gentlemen who have the encouragement of the work at heart among whom may be reckoned Mr Baudouin [Bowdoin] the pres. Gov. the comptroller general and many others equally learned and well-wishers to their country seem to be of opinion that you should undertake to print it and agree with me for the manuscript. There is a prospect of a large profit in printing 1000 copies. *Baltimore Virginia* and *Charlestown* seem to offer a large sale for it. . . .
>
> I wish to know what would be your lowest terms (in case we should not agree this way) for printing a 1000 copies upon good paper with good types . . . and the notes . . . of a smaller type in a large 8° and—likewise what would be the lowest price for half that number, that is 500[.] The work is ready for the press you may begin it when you please. . . .[37]

Isaiah Thomas never began the printing of Brissot in English. As it happened, Nancrede's efforts had already been anticipated, for another English translation, *Considerations on The Relative Situation of France, and the United States of America*, was published in London at the Logographic Press in 1788. It would take another six years for still a third English translation to be published. *The Commerce of America with Europe* appeared in London in 1794 and was republished the following year in New York.[38] Despite a strain in Franco-American relations, there was still sufficient interest in trade between the two countries to spur a demand for Brissot's work. But it was not Nancrede's translation that supplied that demand. This time the translator was none other than Joel Barlow, the Hartford wit who resided abroad, the poet-statesman and liberal thinker whose path would once again, years later, cross that of Joseph Nancrede.

Meanwhile Nancrede had been more successful with another Brissot translation. On 10 July 1791 the great revolutionary delivered before the Society of the Friends of the Constitution his *Discours sur la Question, Si le Roi Peut être Jugé* which Nancrede subsequently translated into English. This time his translation was published by Belknap and Young of Boston and the name of "P.J.G. de Nancrede, Preceptor of the French Language, in the University of Cambridge" appeared as translator on the title page of "The First American Edition."

In a two-page Advertisement Nancrede explained his purposes in translating a *Discourse* which would never cease to remind the world that *"The American Revolution brought forth the French Revolution."* [39]

> Ever unable to suppress those National feelings, excited by the reading of the energetic and masterly pieces which our Revolution has produced, though a citizen of this country and happy under its government, I still remember that I am a Frenchman, and indulge those enthusiastic feelings, always consequent upon the perusal of a spirited and beautiful piece of composition, especially when it comes from that quarter. To communicate these feelings to the Public was my intention in the undertaking of the present translation; . . .
>
> The subject upon which the following Discourse was delivered, is one of the newest and most interesting in the world. It is of the utmost importance to the French Nation: It cannot be indifferent to the Americans. . . .

Nor was the English version indifferent to Brissot, for he wrote to Nancrede from Paris, "I owe you thanks for the pains you have taken with this translation." [40]

Between 1791, when Louis was imprisoned, and 1793, when the monarch was guillotined, Joseph Nancrede published one of his most important compilations, *L'Abeille Françoise*, whose purposes he had outlined to the Harvard Corporation and in which he included some of his own translations. Like the *Discourse upon the Question, Whether the King Shall be Tried*, this bears the imprint of Belknap and Young, and the arrangement for publishing it is revealed in a receipt of 15 December 1791 that is also a contract: "Rec^d of Joseph de Nancrede of Boston fifteen pounds LM, it being a part of £48.15. LM for which sum we have this day agreed to print him a book, in french 12mo the book to contain 360 pages, the pages to be of the same width & length as that we are now printing of the Life of Baron Trenck, the Number of Copies to be 1000, the balance to be paid as soon as 100 copies can be bound after they are printed. *& the book to be printed at the rate of one sheet per week as soon as the paper is had.*" [41]

Under such terms *L'Abeille Françoise* made its bow in 1792—the first French textbook of its kind published in this country, a tangible tie between France and the United States. Its title page carried a quotation from the admired Brissot de Warville: "*L'Amérique doit être l'asyle de tous les hommes: les Américains doivent être en rapport avec tous les habitants de la terre; ils doivent chercher à se faire entendre de tous, et sur-tout de ceux avec les quels ils ont plus de communication, tels que les François.*" In its more than 350 pages Nancrede advanced that understanding by presenting the thoughts of Fénelon and Rousseau, Voltaire and Montesquieu, Helvetius and Brissot de Warville, Marmontel and Bernardin de Saint-Pierre. His anthology was not only a textbook for his Harvard students but a manual for all who believed in the interdependence of France and America. A three-page "Liste des Souscripteurs" included some illustrious names: John Q. Adams, Esq., His Excellency John Hancock, Esq., Josiah Quincy, along with those who had been associated in one way or another with Nancrede such as Caleb Bingham and the printers Benjamin Russell and Isaiah Thomas.

In a lengthy bilingual introduction, the compiler not only expounded his purpose but indicated his awareness of its significance:

> The attention with which the French language has lately been honored at the University of Cambridge, is a necessary consequence of its utility and of its importance. This is a happy presage of the empire it is about to acquire in this new world. Several causes have united to give this language so universal a utility. The political Constitution of France; its situation; the nature of its climate; the genius of its writers; the character of its inhabitants; and the opinion, which she has known how to give of herself to the rest of the world, have made her language attain to that universality which it possesses, and which, by its own genius, it will probably maintain.

From the time of the seventeenth century, Nancrede insisted, "France has continued to give a stage, dress, taste, manners, a language, a new mode of living, to the greatest part of the states, which surround her." The French language was "enriched by the revocation of the edict of Nantz [*sic*], by every thing which the state lost. The refugees carried into the north their hatred for the prince, and their sorrows for their country; and this sorrow, and this hatred, was vented in French." From Fontenelle and Buffon, from the "*philosopher of Geneva*" and Raynal came ideas and words that expanded the concepts and polished the language of France—a language which "must be indispensably necessary to the Americans, who, by their commercial connexions, are called to deal and correspond with" European travelers in their country. Finally, Nancrede summed up: "The persons who study the French language, and especially the students at Cambridge, had for a long time felt the want of a book which might serve them to read and construe. We have endeavoured to render this collection the best possible, by uniting in the choice of different kinds of styles, the most brilliant pieces of our literature; that, by this variety, we might indemnify the students, for the dryness which always accompanies the beginning of the study of languages."[42]

Even after Joseph Nancrede had established himself in the business of bookselling and publishing he continued the work of translating and compiling. It was under his own imprint in 1795 that his translation of the *Projet de Constitution pour la République Française* was published with French and English text on facing pages. Two years later Nancrede issued a new edition—the first American edition—of Fénelon's *Les Aventures de Télémaque Fils d'Ulysse* which he himself had revised and corrected. This ambitious bilingual project was dedicated "To the American Youth of Both Sexes," for, as Harvard's French instructor put it, "The young persons of no country have shewn a greater love of literature, or a more ardent thirst of knowledge, than in America; and among the books which daily fall into your hands, . . . none have a higher claim to your regard than Telemachus. . . . The fatal effects of indulging the passions are exemplified, . . . and the happiness attending innocence and virtue, printed in the liveliest colours. Whatever can incite to virtue and deter from vice; whatever can enlighten the understanding, charm the imagination and improve the heart, is to be found in this interesting work."

As late as 1804, when his career as Boston publisher was drawing to a close and he was about to revisit France, Joseph Nancrede published another "interesting work" which he himself had compiled, an anthology in English entitled *The Forum Orator; or the American Public Speaker*. Designed for those "whose business it is to teach, to learn, or to practise the art of being persuasive and commanding in public speaking," it offered within a single volume orations from the British Parliament and the American Congress, pleadings of distinguished advocates in both countries, commentaries by Burke and Fox, Pitt and Sheridan.

The Forum Orator, like many of the works translated or compiled by Joseph Nancrede, nowhere bears his name. It was not always modesty that induced him to seek anonymity. Upon some occasions it was that discretion which is the better part of valor. While he was still teaching French at Harvard and translating letters for Governor Hancock, and before he hung out his shingle as bookseller-publisher, Joseph Nancrede wrote an intriguing and virulent pamphlet. The anonymous *Les Citoyens Francois* reflects not only his style in the French language but his fascinating role in the complicated affair of Citizen Genêt. Joseph Nancrede, teacher and translator of French, compiler and editor, was also a dabbler in politics.

On 8 April 1793 the handsome, arrogant, hotheaded Edmond Charles Genêt, minister plenipotentiary to the United States, arrived in Charleston, South Carolina. He arrived on the heels of news that France and Great Britain were at war; he was received enthusiastically by a pro-French public; and he precipitated such violent party conflict that he was repudiated. Much of the agitation aroused by the impulsive diplomat centered around the interpretation of a treaty. By terms of the Franco-American Treaty of Alliance and Commerce signed in 1778, America was pledged to support France in any defensive war. The France of 1778, however, was not the France of 1793. Although the United States recognized the French Republic, it was divided in its interpretation of the treaty. The pro-French Jefferson insisted it was still binding; the pro-British Hamilton insisted it was not. On 23 April 1793 Washington issued his Proclamation of Neutrality.

Edmond Charles Genêt, ever a law unto himself, had brought with him 250 letters of marque to commission privateers in American ports. He disregarded American neutrality, commissioned four privateers, ordered the French consul in Boston to set up a French prize court on American soil, and finally threatened to appeal for his mandate directly to the people over the head of President Washington.

Against this background the Harvard French instructor and translator Joseph Nancrede, armed with cloak, dagger, and pen, played a clandestine role agitating if not actually provoking a little consular war. His war was directed not against Minister Genêt, whom he attempted to aid, but against the consular system in general, for he insisted that the French Republic was appointing as consuls salaried "serpents" whose abuses were destroying Franco-American commerce. His war was directed against the Boston consuls in particular—Duplaine, "a violent and indiscreet *sans culotte*";[43] his predecessor Dannery, a man who spoke no English, an "ancien mignon du Tiran" whose "anti-republican conduct" especially in connection with the privateer "La Marseilloise" in Boston Harbor conflicted with Nancrede's views. It is quite possible that Nancrede's patriotic aversion to consular corruption was mingled with his own mercenary desire to have a share in a prize agency.

At all events, by the time of Dannery's arrival in Boston, in September 1793, Citizen Nancrede was employing his tireless pen in an extraordinary correspondence with Citizen Genêt.[44] Those lengthy letters, written in French from Boston in September and October 1793, reveal the writer as both plaintiff and informer if not spy. In them Nancrede reports the arrivals of ships and the state of French prizes, the intricate campaigns in his consular war and the political agitation of a people in ferment who will surely "se declarent pour la France." In them too he complains of the unpaid hardships he has endured: he has been cheated out of an agency for prizes; Genêt's packet to him was opened by Duplaine. "Depuis le commencement de la Revolution j'ai sacrifié la moitié de mon tem[p]s à en soutenir la cause, dans ce pays." And again: "Je travaille nuit et jour, à soutenir l'état dans les gazettes." There are allusions to persecutions, interceptions, threatened lawsuits, until, on October 23, Genêt rapped Nancrede's knuckles soundly. In a letter from New York the imperious diplomat reprimanded his informant for his negative attitude about French consuls and agents, charging that he regarded everything with rancor and bitterness instead of indulgence. He should no longer impede the work of the Republic's authorities or use his talents in bringing to popular attention struggles that scandalize without interesting the public.

The rebuke was apparently not taken to heart. Probably toward the end of the year Nancrede published a vitriolic seventeen-page pamphlet that is unsigned and undated. It bears merely a caption title: *Les Citoyens Francois, habitans des Etats-unis de L'Amérique Septentrionale, à leur patrie, à ses Réprésentans.*[45] Addressed to the "Peres des francois," it speaks eloquently for the French residents in America. The French fathers have regenerated everything in France and have freed the blacks in the colonies, but the native Frenchmen in America have been forgotten and disdained. They are served by those salaried "serpents" called consuls and are victims of their cruelty and a tyranny unequaled in "Constantinople." The "Marseilloise" was detained in the port of Boston while English ships were allowed to pass. As a result of all this the royalists and Anglomaniacs have triumphed and Franco-American commerce has been destroyed. The consuls, in league with émigré aristocrats, are partisans of the "treason of Toulon."

The author of *Les Citoyens Francois* has been identified because a copy of that extremely rare pamphlet was enclosed in a packet of "Correspondance Consulaire Boston" and deposited in the Diplomatic Archives of the Ministry of Foreign Affairs on the Quai d'Orsay. It was sent there by Consul Dannery whose invective against Nancrede outdoes Nancrede's invective against him. The Boston consul describes Citizen Nancrede as an associate of Brissot de Warville (who had been guillotined on the last day of October), a man who "played the patriot" with Citizen Genêt (who had recommended Nancrede as translator to Dannery), the member of a kind of Jacobin Club, and a wicked husband who daily beat his wife even when she was pregnant. In short, Nancrede was a torment to the consulate—a man who had publicly insulted Dannery and narrowly escaped imprisonment. To crown his misdemeanors he was the author of a vicious libel, a copy of which was presented by the French consul to Boston to the Commission of Foreign Affairs.

Joseph Nancrede of Héricy near Fontainebleau had already lived several lives in America. As Revolutionary soldier, as Harvard's French instructor, as newspaper editor, as translator and compiler and as pamphleteer and would-be politician, he had come to know the pulse of his new country, especially the needs of Boston's *Citoyens Francois*. In 1795, having, temporarily at least, doffed his cloak and dagger, he embarked upon still another life, one that would be more productive than any he had as yet attempted, one that would directly advance the cause of Franco-American understanding. During the next decade Joseph Nancrede would help supply the literary needs of Boston's French residents and elucidate to the citizens of his adopted country the thought and language of France. On 25 July 1795 the *Columbian Centinel* printed under its New Advertisements the announcement that launched the thirty-four-year-old Nancrede upon the most fruitful of his many enterprises, the métier that was most truly his:

> A FRENCH *and* ENGLISH BOOK-STORE. Tho's Hall & Joseph Nancrede, *Inform the public in general, and the friends of literature in particular, that they have opened, on the north side of the State-house,* . . . A French and English Book-Store.
>
> The principal object of this establishment, is to keep a constant, and extensive assortment of *Foreign books*, such as *French, Latin, Italian, and Spanish*. A regular and well established correspondence, with . . . Booksellers in almost every capital in France, a personal acquaintance with some men of science and literature; and other local advantages, flatter them with the prospect of gratifying the ingenious and inquisitive of all classes. . . .
>
> They expect to receive soon a large supply of Foreign books, principally French; and have now for sale a general assortment of English books and Stationary [*sic*]—English and American publications. . . .
>
> *They have also for sale*, Account Books . . . Music paper . . . gentlemen's Morocco Pocket-Books . . .
>
> Writing-Paper of all sizes . . . Inkstands . . . Playing Cards.

With the additional promise of printing in foreign languages—a project requiring "Two Journeymen and two Apprentices," but never realized—and with a quotation in Italian from Beccaria, the new firm of Hall and Nancrede made its bow to the Boston public.

Thomas Hall, who had been active in 1794 as a bookseller and printer in Boston, was doubtless to provide business acumen in both those specialties while Nancrede brought to the partnership his own wide knowledge of French language, thought, and literature. Actually the partnership, while it gave Nancrede his introduction to the trade, did not last long. By March of 1796 advertisements that had been styled "Hall & Nancrede, Imprimeurs-Libraires," became "Joseph Nancrede, Imprimeur-Libraire" and by the end of that month Joseph Nancrede had set up shop independently at his own building, 49 Marlborough Street—that two-story brick edifice where the translator and French instructor was metamorphosed into bookseller.

Printing, despite the style of his advertisement, figured little if at all in Nancrede's business. Between 1796 and 1803, the Boston Directory lists him as "bookseller and stationer" at "No. 49 Marlborough street," a street leading from Summer to School Street. There, as the proprietor, self-styled *"young in the trade,"* [46] grew more expert, his shop became a bustling center of literary activity. Prospectuses of other editors and publishers were hung up; browsers came to indulge in book talk, "flying opinions of the flying lounging Gentlemen, who often innundate [*sic*] Bookstores," "Chitchat of my lounging customers." [47]

One of those loungers was an "illustrious wanderer" who would one day wear the crown of France but who at the moment needed money sorely. Louis Philippe d'Orléans, eldest son of the late Egalité, arrived with his brothers and Prince Talleyrand in Boston in October 1797. He had come to dispose of "some valuable books" to Benjamin Russell, but he surely dropped in at his compatriot's shop on Marlborough Street; for many years later Nancrede would recall the visit that honored him in Boston. [48] Indeed Nancrede won the praise of Orléans' companion Count Gustave de Montjoie, who described the bookseller as a man of letters who had given a strong impetus to bookselling in New England and at the same time served as a benefactor to his own country. [49]

It was largely through the books he made available that Nancrede achieved that reputation. Thanks to his catalogues and his advertisements, his business methods can be reconstructed and the stock that once graced the shelves of 49 Marlborough Street can be restored. It was primarily a stock of imports—imports from "London, Dublin, Paris, and other Capitals of Europe"—books imported not on those French privateers that had figured in Nancrede's consular war but on such ships as the *Victory,* the *Gallen* and the *Minerva.* "In order to extend his business, J. N. intends keeping a general assortment of old Books, scarce Tracts, and new Publications: and, from the Correspondence he has established in Europe as well as in the Continent, he expects he shall be able to give general satisfaction." [50] "Orders from the country, though never so trifling," were "executed by the first conveyances." [51] Exchanges were offered to those who had duplicates to sell; wholesale customers, country booksellers and purchasers for "Social Libraries" were offered discounts and, along with the books, paper, inkstands and mathematical instruments, spectacles, "Gaugles" and reading glasses, wafers, sealing wax and "India Ink, by the box or stick," "Segar Cases," paint boxes, and writing desks were offered. [52]

At times Nancrede's stock was large indeed and his inventory, which included the usual assortment of miscellanies and English sermons, anatomical textbooks, and dramas, was remarkable for its emphasis upon French authors and French authors in translation. Voltaire and Rousseau, Brissot de Warville and Condorcet, Condillac and Raynal, Molière and Mirabeau, Montesquieu and Scarron were all available on Marlborough

Street. Books in the French language were present in great quantities, from *L'Abeille Françoise* to *Zélie au Bain*, while among the pamphlet collections could be found a *Constitution of the French Republic* or a *Defence of Louis XVI*. Students from Harvard, lounging gentlemen, vendors of duplicates, Frenchmen in pantaloons and liberty caps who called each other Citoyen could dip into the *Code Noir* or the *Order of Cincinnatus*, savor the *Esprit* of Voltaire or the *Histoire Secrete* of Mirabeau and, in the late 1790s, indulge in the delights of an *An 2440* on Marlborough Street.

Despite his abiding interest in providing French reading matter for his customers Nancrede did not neglect the field of English books. Indeed in June 1798 he boasted that his recent "Importation, added to the stock of Books already on hand, forms a collection of nearly twenty thousand volumes, principally English, in the various branches of Science, and ancient and modern Literature:—As great pains and much time were bestowed on the choice, it is hoped it will be found as judicious and as interesting as any in the United States:—In THEOLOGY, LAW, POLITICS, AGRICULTURE, HISTORY and VOYAGES, particular attention has been paid to selecting all that is rare and valuable in the English Language; all new works and scarce tracts, many of which were never seen before in America, are comprised in this assortment. . . . Gentlemen of Science and of taste in general:—Young gentlemen intended for the superior departments of commercial life, or the learned professions, have now an opportunity of completing or of forming their libraries, from the latest and best editions of the best works, and on the most reasonable terms." [53]

It is not only to gentlemen forming libraries in Boston that Joseph Nancrede sold his books but to gentlemen abroad also, especially in Canada where he would form connections that would play an important part in his later life. Meanwhile he was also forming connections with his colleagues.

One of Nancrede's most interesting business relationships was the one he shared with Médéric-Louis-Elie Moreau de Saint-Méry, bookseller-stationer-publisher of Philadelphia. Before the end of 1794, when Moreau de Saint-Méry set up his shop in that city, he had played a colorful role in the French Revolution. Born in Martinique, he had gone to Paris to arrange for the publication of his books and at the Fall of the Bastille it was he who had received the keys of that prison. For the next three days he governed the city as King of Paris. Subsequently, hounded by Robespierre, he had escaped the guillotine by fleeing to America. His shop on Philadelphia's First Street with its "beautiful signboard" became the meeting place of the French émigrés who congregated there daily "to chat . . . discuss the fate of the world and drink madeira." As early as April 1795, before the formal opening of his French and English Bookstore, Nancrede had visited Moreau de Saint-Méry. The former King of Paris made an entry in his journal: "I had M. Nancrède, a Frenchman, to dinner. He is a bookseller in Boston, and my correspondent there. He already showed a strong and habitual satisfaction with his own ideas. . . ."[54]

It was to provide news of Boston events for the *Courrier de la France et des Colonies* which Moreau was printing that Nancrede became his correspondent. Subscriptions for the *Courrier* could be obtained at Nancrede's office and the two booksellers formed a business relationship revealed in a series of four letters written—or scrawled—by Moreau de Saint-Méry to Nancrede between 1795 and 1797. Primarily the French Philadelphian and the French Bostonian exchanged information and books, discussing editions of dictionaries, importations from abroad, deliveries of consignments, payments, translations, commissions, and that particular brand of gossip transmitted by the bookseller's special grapevine. "Mathew Carey," Moreau reported slyly to Nancrede, "says you offered him 2 dozen copies of your Abeilles for 2 American Museum."[55]

Still another bookseller in Philadelphia—William Cobbett, translator of Moreau de Saint-Méry's works on St. Domingo and pamphleteer with whom Nancrede would have closer dealings later on—received from 49 Marlborough Street a consignment that included "10 English pamphlets" at 10 percent discount.[56]

Joseph Dennie, editor of the *Farmer's Museum* in Walpole, New Hampshire, and future editor of the Philadelphia *Port Folio*, was another of Nancrede's correspondents with whom he established business relations. Nancrede's letters to Dennie intimately reveal the bookseller's problems, successes, and methods as well as the affairs of 49 Marlborough Street. Nancrede wrote in November 1796:

"I did express to Mr Carlisle [David Carlisle, Boston publisher], that I should wish for a few copies of the *Lay-preacher*; I could have put off since, a good number, say about 40 or 50 had I had them. A subsequent letter . . . by the same G[n] . . . intimated a disposition on yr part of sending me some, when bound. It is a disadvantage, which probably you are not acquainted with, not to have those publications when they first come out. I will take, to dispose of, on your acc[t] 2 dozens of the Lay-preacher if it be agreeable to you. . . . I have just given to the bearer of your letter one of my last catalogues. . . . my European Magazines that are left me are in N[os] for 1795 and one vol. only from July 95 to December id. The Boston & other libraries have taken what I had. . . . I expect for the future, a *regular, complete*, & *plentiful* supply of periodical publications, all of which shall be at your service. I would exchange some, many European publications for some & many home productions, and I would with Mr Dennie extend the common rules of exchange adapted by exchanging Booksellers; . . ."[57]

By February of 1797, Nancrede imparted to Dennie his hopes for the enlargement of his stock: "I expect in the next season a most complete assortment of *books of taste:* Books, for Gentlemen *to buy*, as well as for

Booksellers *to sell*; add to that, a regular and constant supply of the *critical* &
monthly reviews, & European Magazine— . . . the first publications of the
kind in England. . . ."[58] Subscriptions for Dennie's paper were taken at
Nancrede's office and its prospectus was hung up there. Those "flying
opinions of the flying lounging Gentlemen, who often innundate Bookstores" were reported as they related to the *Farmer's Museum* and Nancrede's
letters make it clear that he had a rapport with his colleagues in and on the
fringe of the trade.[59]

With one colleague, Edmund March Blunt, hydrographer and bookseller
of Newburyport, Massachusetts, Nancrede's relations left something to be
desired. Although he was doubtless aware that the Newburyport Book
Store was headquarters for American nautical publications, Nancrede
imported fifty copies of Bowditch's *New American Navigator* in English
edition. Blunt proceeded promptly to start a suit against him for infringement
of copyright.[60]

By and large, however, Nancrede's business relations with his colleagues
were amicable and productive. Between 1796 and 1800, his name appears on
the imprint of some fourteen different works as one of the sellers of books
published by others. Speeches and sermons, almanacs and astronomical
diaries printed by his former partner Thomas Hall or by Isaiah Thomas or by
the Russells of Quaker Lane were sold by a variety of local dealers as well as
"at Nancrede's Bookstore, Marlborough-street." These joint imprints,
including Oulton's *The Wonderful Story-Teller*, a *Pilgrim's Progress* published
at Boston in 1800, Surr's "New Novel" *George Barnwell* and L'Estrange's
version of Seneca's *Morals*, are all interesting indications of Nancrede's
membership in the bookselling fraternity.

Far more interesting, however, are those imprints that bear his name
alone, for Joseph Nancrede was not only a bookseller but a publisher. At 49
Marlborough Street, where his children played and his colleagues conferred,
where loungers gossiped and periodicals were sold, where books were
exchanged and prospectuses hung from the walls, where readers browsed and
French and English were spoken with equal facility—the trade of publishing
was also carried on. It was primarily through his publications issued between
1795 and 1800 that Joseph Nancrede helped to introduce French thought
into America and reflected if he did not shape the taste of his day.

Nancrede's imprints relating to France mirror not only his own intense
interest in his native country but the rise and fall of American partisanship in
French affairs. His entry into the book trade had coincided with the defeat of
the terrorists and the beginning of the Directory. In 1795, the Year IV of the
French Republic, Americans were still sufficiently involved in the fate of
France to provide an eager market for French books. Their own
Constitution, whose fabric had in part been woven from the concepts of
Rousseau and the *philosophes*, had of course been translated into French to be

in turn interwoven into the French Constitution. One of the earliest of Nancrede's imprints, undertaken while he was still in partnership with Hall, was the bilingual edition of the *Projet de Constitution pour La République Française* (Evans No. 28695) which he himself had translated. The same year, Hall and Nancrede issued from their establishment on the "n. side Town-House, State-St.," *Treaties with France, Great Britain, and the United States* (Evans 29757) containing Alexander Dallas' study of Jay's Treaty and Noah Webster's "Vindication of that instrument." Jay's Treaty—the answer in a sense to the demand of pro-French factions for war with England—aroused considerable indignation among friends of France and mobs who burned John Jay in effigy, but provided required reading matter for merchants, shipowners, and all who were caught up in the intricate affairs of the time.

One of the first if not the first publication undertaken independently by Nancrede was a reprint in French of the French Constitution proposed to the people of France by the National Convention. Its imprint is a reminder that the publisher was also interpreter and "sworn translator . . . for the service of the French": "Réimprimée à Boston, d'après le voeu des citoyens françois, assemblés au consulat de la République Françoise: par Joseph Nancrede, libraire; et se vend à son magazin de livres, no. 49 Marlborough street." Under a second title of *Procès-verbal de l'assemblée, . . . pour prendre connoissance de la constitution* (Evans No. 30439) the imprint points still more directly to Nancrede's double service to the French in Boston for it reads: "Imprimé conformément à la souscription formée par les citoyens françois, actuellement à Boston."

It was not only for the "citoyens françois, actuellement à Boston" that Joseph Nancrede though "*young in the trade*" embarked upon and brought to fruition his most ambitious and perhaps most influential publishing project. His scheme, grandiose enough for an established publisher, was conceived to inform and enlighten a wide public among French- and English-speaking readers in America. Between 1796 and 1797 Nancrede introduced to his new country the major works of Bernardin de Saint-Pierre both in French and in English translation—an undertaking involving multivolume sets, engraved illustrations, elaborate prefaces, and one exalted dedication.[61]

Paul et Virginie, Histoire Indienne, the masterpiece of the botanist-philosopher-physiocrat-moralist-poet-artist Bernardin de Saint-Pierre, was set in an exotic land that offered a haven from the struggles of civilization and so appealed to a world caught up in change and revolution. Its contrast between natural good and the ills of civilization reaffirmed the doctrine of Rousseau. In it the French romantic school found a new vocabulary. The initial appearance of *Paul et Virginie* had been followed by some fifty counterfeit editions, and Joseph Nancrede, French instructor at Harvard, had included lengthy extracts from Saint-Pierre in his anthology, *L'Abeille Françoise*.

Now, as independent publisher, he would do far more to spread the philosophy and language of a writer who did "honour to human genius." Joseph Nancrede would actually issue the first American editions of Saint-Pierre in French and in English. On 30 September 1796, he announced as *"This Day Published" Paul and Virginia* "in a pocket-size vol. with *two neat Plates*. . . . An interesting Story founded on Fact. . . . The denoument," he quoted from the *Mercure de France*, "rends the heart of the reader, who is deprived of the very consolation of believing that it is a romance." In addition to the pocket-size English edition he issued "The same Work . . . in French: also in French and English, in 2 volumes, with plates."[62] For all those editions—the French, the English, and the two-volume bilingual—Nancrede entered into a temporary partnership with the Catholic publisher William Spotswood.[63]

The following year, in spite of Spotswood's withdrawal, Nancrede published still another major work of Saint-Pierre in several versions: *Studies of Nature* in three volumes, illustrated; *A Vindication of Divine Providence* in two volumes, "compiled from those parts of the 'Studies of Nature' which relate to religion"; and *Botanical Harmony Delineated*, a translation of the eleventh of Saint-Pierre's *Studies of Nature* (Evans Nos. 32795–97). In all cases the English translation used was that of the British divine, Henry Hunter, translator of Lavater and Euler. And in all cases the imprint read not "Spotswood and Nancrede," but "Worcester for J. Nancrede. 1797." The volumes had been printed for publisher Nancrede by the distinguished firm of Isaiah Thomas: Thomas, Son and Thomas.

In a letter of 14 March 1797 to Joseph Dennie, editor of the *Farmer's Museum*, Nancrede confided a few of the difficulties he was encountering in his ambitious publishing project:

> altho' I have three hundred subscribers, yet it is a very heavy undertaking: . . . the fraternity of Booksellers had pronounced my ruin, for pursuing a publication, on which *they had given their last judgment*, and in which I was *cruelly* disappointed by having the whole burden thrown on my shoulders. . . . there is perhaps a degree of merit, resulting from the unfavorable situation of the publication I struggled against the current to bring forward, and from an intimate satisfaction that the work was excellent and would meet with the flattering approbation it has already received.

The details of this "very heavy undertaking" are disclosed in a series of six remarkable letters written between November 1796 and February 1797 by Nancrede to his printer Isaiah Thomas.[64] The stages in the publication of Saint-Pierre's *Studies of Nature*, the selection of paper and type, the engravings and binding, the rate of production and the number of copies in an edition, the preparation of preface and dedication, the typographical errors and the sale of the work, not to mention the publisher's petulant impatience—all emerge from this correspondence. In it Nancrede dilates upon the quantity of "wove" and "philadelphia" paper needed for one thousand copies; mentions Thomas' rate of production as "*five sheets a week*" and refers to "the sorting & harmonizing of the type" which he leaves "to Mr Thomas's taste & judgment." Despite Nancrede's confidence in the printer's "consummate experience & ingenuity" he cautions: "Beware of other folks correcting the press, some bad faults have been detected."

A touch of humor alleviates his worries when Nancrede, discussing Saint-Pierre's *Vindication of Divine Providence*, advises: "After striking off 450 of the first vol. [that is, the one-volume edition] it will be well . . . to put '*the end*' at the end of it, . . . I have been induced to make this arrangement from the advice of a Gentleman who, having read the work attentively, observed to me that *it goes on vindicating further than the* end I have assigned."

Sending a box of paper and "various articles," Nancrede frets, "I request you or those you may employ in the opening of this box, may exercise the greatest care & caution—I have taken a great deal of pains in packing it up." And again: "I have fear respecting Tufts who carried the paper as he was tolerably drunk, last Saturday night . . . is the paper arrived safe?" Finally, on 2 February 1797, he confides to Thomas another of his anxieties: "The dedication to the president of the U.S. which must come in the Ist vol. is another difficulty of which I did not think, when you were last in town. I have it ready but rather choose to wait till you come to town, which as you inform me, will be tomorrow."

The dedication of *Studies of Nature* to the President of the United States involved the tyro publisher in another interesting though brief correspondence. To obtain permission to dedicate the first American edition of Saint-Pierre's work to George Washington, Joseph Nancrede bethought himself of the highly placed father of two of his Harvard students, John and William Pickering, and did a bit of politicking. On 13 May 1796, in a clever maneuver, he had approached John's father, Secretary of State Timothy Pickering, with his proposal:

> In submitting to your patronage, the inclosed work we flatter ourselves, that our particular application or its mode will not be deemed presumptuous or intrusive, when you consider that, although it be acknowledged by those who have read it, one of the most ingenious and moral works of the age, yet there are few copies of it in America; and as it is the particular province of men of talents, whose abilities have acquired them public confidence, to disco[u]ntenance the propagation of immoral works, . . . so it is the peculiar satisfaction of talents and fortune to patronize those calculated to promote virtue, science and submission to the laws.

> We propose to inscribe this first American edition to the President of the United States; and it is conceived here, by men of discernment, that *no American publication was ever more worthy the acceptance of that great and good man.*

> To sollicit your particular intercession with the president to grant us our request, as also your influence in favour of the work, I have no particular

claims, unless you would consider as one my having instructed, for four years past, and since, your two sons, in the french Language, at the University of Cambridge. I will however confess that this is a weak recommendation, for the satisfaction I have derived from it (especially with John) has amply repaid me for the extra trouble I might take with him.[65]

In reply Pickering not only conveyed to the publisher "the President's ideas relative to the proposed dedication" but enclosed Washington's subscription for one set of *Studies of Nature*.[66] It was indeed a prestigious subscription list Nancrede was assembling for the first American edition of Saint-Pierre. The names of the three Pickerings, Timothy and his sons, along with those of such dignitaries as James Bowdoin, Thomas Paine, Harrison Gray Otis, Timothy Dwight, and Josiah Quincy followed the most illustrious name of all, General Washington, President of the United States. The 326 subscribers could read not only the concepts of Saint-Pierre but the dedication written by Joseph Nancrede to George Washington, a dedication which doubtless incorporated such of "the President's ideas" as had been conveyed to the publisher by Timothy Pickering. Here publisher addressed eminent dedicatee and here in a sense one who had fought at Yorktown addressed his commander in chief:

> The Editor of the *Studies of Nature*, indulges the idea that in dedicating to you the AMERICAN EDITION of a work, so much esteemed, he does not take a disrespectful or unwelcome license. As a member of the human family, he finds a superior gratification, in testifying his respect for a character, equally known and revered among mankind. As an AMERICAN CITIZEN, he feels a sweet satisfaction in paying the tribute of gratitude and veneration, . . . to the MAN, whom his country delights to honour and to bless, as having eminently contributed to establish her independence, by his military command; to insure her peace and prosperity, by his civil administration; . . . The belief that the general intention and execution, if not all the peculiar sentiments of the STUDIES OF NATURE will coincide with your views, encourages him to offer them to your attention. Such a belief is the natural consequence of his opinion that the work is calculated to interest the Philosopher, by presenting ingenious and useful speculation . . . the Philanthropist, by exciting "A WARMER INTEREST IN FAVOUR OF SUFFERING HUMANITY" . . . the Friend of Religion and Morals, by illustrating the being and providence of DEITY . . . and the Lover of Nature, by displaying the harmony and proportion, the beauty and utility that mark her productions.[67]

With this dedication, in which he sought to relate the President of the United States to an eighteenth-century French philosopher, and with engravings by Samuel Hill of Boston and William Rollinson of New York, the three-volume *Studies of Nature*, priced at $8, $7 in boards, $9.50 in gilt calf, was ready for distribution. Advertising that "no pains nor expense" had been "spared in procuring suitable paper and able artists,"[68] Nancrede sent several copies to Moreau de Saint-Méry in Philadelphia,[69] made a selling trip to Salem,[70] and solicited sales and notices from Joseph Dennie of Walpole.[71]

The *"This Day Published"* advertisement, dated 24 July 1797, described *Studies of Nature* for the Boston press as a "very ingenious, interesting and instructive work" in which "St. Pierre has enabled us to contemplate this universe with other eyes; has furnished new arguments to *combat atheism*, has established beyond the power of contradiction, the doctrine of a Universal Providence; has excited a warmer interest in favour of suffering humanity, & has discovered sources unknown before of moral and intellectual enjoyment."[72] Nancrede's "heavy undertaking" had also, although he did not say so, introduced to this country the philosophic romanticism of a distinguished French writer and so had quickened American understanding of French thought.

Despite the warnings pronounced by "the fraternity of Booksellers," Joseph Nancrede was encouraged to yet another major undertaking, the publication of Fénelon's *Telemachus* (Evans Nos. 32123–24), edited and corrected by the publisher himself, in French, in English, and in a two-volume bilingual edition. In 1798 he chose an oblique way to remind the American public of the nature of revolution by publishing an English translation of Claude Rulhière's *History, or Anecdotes of the Revolution in Russia in the Year 1762* (Evans No. 34492). Printed on "fine paper, with an elegant Portrait of the last Empress of Russia, neatly bound and lettered"[73] and priced at 75 cents, the work of Rulhière joined the small library of books by French authors that were serving to explain one country to another.

By the last year of the century, however, despite Nancrede's efforts, France and the United States were facing estrangement. During the period following the demand for the recall of Citizen Genêt, the two countries had moved apart. In 1796 France threatened to seize American ships. The three commissioners sent by the United States to Paris to solve the problem were found "subject to solicitation for bribes" and the infamous XYZ affair not only ruptured diplomatic relations between the countries but opened naval hostilities.[74] Joseph Nancrede's three publications of French interest in 1799 reflect the collapse of pro-French feeling in America.

In February of that year he issued in a broadside his PROPOSALS *For Publishing, By Subscription, The History of the Destruction of the Helvetic Union and Liberty.*[75] *By J. Mallet Du Pan.* That work, purportedly about Switzerland, related primarily to France, the scourging nation. Thus it expressed the current views of many Americans and of some disillusioned Franco-Americans:

> That the people of the United States may profit by the errors and calamities of Switzerland, is the object of the present undertaking. Here, the same means are employed, the same engines set at work, which, in their destructive progress, annihilated the Helvetic Union and Liberty. Those who have a Union and a

Liberty to preserve, will do well to attend to the pages of *Mallet Du Pan*, and from his interesting details, . . . learn the salutary lessons drawn from the downfal [*sic*] of his own country.

If there be yet one nation that flatters itself that its existence is reconcileable with that of the *French Republic*, let it study this dreadful monument of their *friendship*. Here every man may see how much weight treaties, alliances, benefactions, rights of neutrality, and even submission itself, retain in the scales of the Directory, who hunt justice from the earth, and whose sanguinary rapacity seeks plunder, and spreads ruin alike . . . in Republican Congresses as well as in the hearts of Monarchies.

This denunciation of the French Republic especially in its relations to the Helvetic Union[76] was issued from 49 Marlborough Street in March 1799 and among the subscribers was that John Jay who had negotiated Jay's Treaty and who now wrote to Nancrede from Albany: "I have been fav^d with your's of the 10th Instant, enclosing a subscription paper for 'a Republication of the History of the Destruction of Helvetic Union and Liberty, by M. Mallet du Pan'—I have subscribed that paper for six copies; and shall immediately send it to Messrs Websters printers in this city, with a Request that they will give it a place in their store, and patronize it." [77]

With a similar end in view, to expose French oppression, Nancrede proposed publication—"should a decent subscription appear"—of La Harpe's *Du Fanatisme dans la Langue Révolutionnaire.* "It treats largely," he wrote, "of the word *Fanaticism*, as applied by revolutionary men, in the revolutionary language" and shows "that the real *fanatics* are that dreadful tribe of *revolutionary men, assassins, oppressors, calumniators*." [78]

With the publication, the same year of 1799, of Vittorio Barzoni's *The Romans in Greece*, in English translation, Nancrede broadcast the reactionary author's message "that the French were like the ancient Romans"—crude conquerors who subjected the Greeks to "wanton extortion and plunder, ruthlessly imposing themselves while forever talking of 'liberty.'" [79]

In a few short years the publisher had come almost full circle. Nancrede, who through his imprints had served as an importer of French civilization, now used the same means to denounce French barbarity. His publications catered to the tides of American reaction to France. During the early years of the nineteenth century, French influence would be on the wane in this country. Yet Nancrede, who might castigate his country's government, would never lose his love of France nor his desire to interpret its culture to America. Throughout his life he would remain what he had long been, a Franco-American.

Even in his general publications for an English-speaking American market there are occasional French overtones. The publication of *Joan of Arc* (Evans No. 34583), Southey's epic poem, surely appealed to students of French history as much as to students of English literature. In a preface or advertisement to other publications too Nancrede would find opportunity to exalt the wisdom of French writers.

Meanwhile, one of his first non-French imprints had been a folio broadside executed in Latin for Harvard University (Evans No. 28809). This list of theses in the various faculties of the University of Cambridge bore the Hall and Nancrede imprint and the date 15 July 1795—ten days before the *Centinel's* announcement of the partnership. Thanks to his connections, Nancrede was also enabled to publish two years later Joseph Perkins' *Oration upon Genius, Pronounced at the Anniversary Commencement of Harvard University, in Cambridge* (Evans No. 32671), a commencement doubtless attended by the French publisher-teacher whose short figure and long nose had become familiar on the college grounds.

Nancrede's own publishing list served to some extent the various faculties that had been listed on his Harvard broadside. Several of his imprints were designed for the student of literature. The first American edition of Southey's *Poems* (Evans No. 36345) in 12mo boards, priced at 62 cents, followed *Joan of Arc*. In a joint undertaking with two Philadelphia publishers, Nancrede issued *Pursuits of Literature*,[80] a satirical poem in four dialogues by Thomas James Mathias, "copied from the 8th London edition." For better or worse the scholar in rhetoric could peruse Lindley Murray's *English Grammar*[81] in Nancrede's First American Edition of 1800, a work that "set the pattern followed by generations of children . . . learning to speak and spell . . . in a way that would later have to be undone." In 1803, toward the end of his career as publisher, Nancrede issued, perhaps as a kind of literary farewell to the city that had been "first . . . to shake off the English yoke," a poem entitled *Boston* by Winthrop Sargent (Shaw and Shoemaker No. 3871).

For the theologian, the office at 49 Marlborough Street provided Thomas Cogan's *Letters to William Wilberforce . . . on the doctrine of Hereditary Depravity* (Evans No. 35318), a volume heralded by an interesting Advertisement regarding current ethical concepts: "It might have been expected in the present day, that the general prevalence of good sense, and more accurate ideas of the nature of justice in general, and of the divine benignity in particular, would have committed such a doctrine as that of *hereditary guilt*, to the oblivion it deserves. But as it has met with an eloquent defender in . . . Mr. Wilberforce, the error may acquire new strength to the injury of genuine Christianity."

It was also to advance "genuine Christianity" that Nancrede published *The Pulpit Orator*, an anthology comparable to his own *Forum Orator* except that it was directed to a clerical readership. This "new Selection of Eloquent Pulpit Discourses, accompanied with Observations on the Composition and Delivery of Sermons" contained the work not only of Knox and Jerningham but of Bossuet and Massillon. As the chauvinistic preface put it,

"Many have learnt the fame, who are precluded from the works of Bossuet, Massillon, and other French preachers and . . . orators. They must be pleased to get portions of them in an English dress sufficient to give some idea of the kind of merit they possess." The translation, it was conceded, was more "an abridgement . . . than a translation," for the "many local and incidental passages arising from the peculiar habits, the popular opinions, and religious persuasions of France, so well understood and felt by the audience before which these Discourses were delivered, would pall upon the English reader." [82]

It was in the course of his temporary partnership with Spotswood that Nancrede published a work aimed at "the Merchants and other Gentlemen connected with Naval Affairs in the United States of America." The Rev. John Malham's *The Naval Gazetteer; or, Seaman's Complete Guide*[83] was an important and ambitious project. Containing "a Full and Accurate Account . . . of the several coasts of all the Countries and Islands in the Known World," the two-volume geography was illustrated with "a Correct Set of Charts" and the binder was "desired to beat the Books before he places the Charts." For this first American edition, "the American Ports, Harbours, &c. have been corrected by a gentleman of great abilities, and extensive information on the subject," and the editors took pains to point out that the "dangers of Navigation, so intimately connected with the Mercantile Profession, are well known, . . . Whether public or private emolument be considered; the aggrandizement of the country, or of individuals—in every point of view, the following sheets deserve attention and encouragement." Nancrede was well aware of the close relationship between navigation and commerce and at all times worked for a market among those "merchants . . . whose spirited and patriotic exertions have given no less stability to our Government than increase to our Commerce."

The machinations and deliberations of politicians fascinated Nancrede. One of his earliest publications in the "Hall and Nancrede" period had been "*A Little Plain English*" *addressed to the people of the United States on the Treaty and on the Conduct of the President; in answer to the Letters of Franklin; by Peter Porcupine* (Evans No. 28438). "Peter Porcupine" was of course William Cobbett, who bought pamphlets from bookseller Nancrede and with whom years later the publisher would be rather closely involved.

It was "to rescue from the common fate of newspaper publications," where it had first appeared, a "deserved tribute to . . . a distinguished Patriot" and so to aid "the cause of real liberty" and perform "an acceptable service to the American public" that Nancrede included on his list in 1796 John Gardner's *Brief Consideration of the Important Services and Distinguished Virtues and Talents, which Recommend Mr. Adams for the Presidency of the United States* (Evans No. 30472). It is an interesting concatenation of events that the following year John Adams became President of the United States and in 1798, when a son was born to Joseph Nancrede, he was named for the author of that work, John (or Jean) Gardner Nancrede.

The year 1800 was remarkable for many reasons in publishing history, not the least of which was the great number of Washington eulogies issued by patriotic publishers in pamphlets bordered with black or adorned with the title vignette of an urn. Nancrede added three to the extensive list: one by Josiah Dunham, a Captain in the Sixteenth United States Regiment; one by Major-General Henry Lee, Member of Congress from Virginia; and one by John Miller Russell whose oration carried on its title page the vignette not only of an urn but of a cypress and a setting sun.[84]

Nancrede's publications in English were varied, offering something for almost every taste—the literary, the theological, the political. For American farmers he provided the first American edition of Charles Marshall's *Introduction to the Knowledge and Practice of Gardening* along with *An Essay on Quick-Lime, as a Cement and as a Manure* by James Anderson (Evans No. 35770). For all who had a thought to their health and their stomachs, he issued one of his most interesting publications, the two-volume *Lectures on Diet and Regimen* by A. F. M. Willich.[85] In his advertisement to the first Boston edition Nancrede explained his purposes and once again slyly interjected his praise of France. "Books are not wanting," he averred, "which profess to teach us how to become our own physicians, when we are sick." But, he insisted, "Before the present, no author had expressly undertaken to instruct mankind in the faculty of shunning disease by means so simple as the regulation of Diet." It was entirely possible, he considered, that epidemics were caused by "the *vicious diet* and *incautious regimen* peculiar to the Americans. Such are . . . the grounds of a very judicious treatise, written in French, and sent to the President of the United States, that he might render it public. The author, who has resided several years in America, paints . . . the abuses of *American diet* [and] . . . attributes . . . their yellow fever, to that cause." In conclusion, Nancrede wisely commented, thinking perhaps of that cook whom Consul Letombe had brought with him to Boston, "we find all foreigners, who visit this country, . . . exclaiming against *our copious* and *everlasting* dinners." Willich's work on the relation of diet to disease and to health was thus given by Nancrede a strong American slant when he issued it for a large American public—a public that included "mothers and guardians of families" as well as "friends of society . . . who are solicitous to preserve their health, and to adopt the parental hints of nature, rather than submit to the palliative relief of art." Was there perhaps a touch of Rousseauean doctrine in Nancrede's devotion to nature?

Although he was active as bookseller and as publisher between 1795 and 1804, Nancrede was never active as printer. Therefore, to publish the works on his list, whether they were designed for French, American, or

Franco-American readers, whether they related to politics or literature, theology or health, he required the services of his colleagues in the printing trade. He especially required the services of early French-language printers. The great firm of Isaiah Thomas—exalted as the "Didot" or the "Baskerville" of America—had declined to print Nancrede's translation of Brissot de Warville on Franco-American commerce, but had undertaken with consummate skill his more ambitious Saint-Pierre project. Indeed it had been Brissot himself who, after a visit to Worcester, commented: "This town is elegant and well-peopled; the printer, Isaiah Thomas, has rendered it famous throughout the Continent of America. He has printed a large part of the works which appear; and it is acknowledged that his editions are correct and well edited. Thomas is the Didot of the United States." [86]

The director of Isaiah Thomas' firm of Thomas and Andrews was at one time William Manning. In partnership with James Loring, Manning set up a printing office on Boston's Quaker Lane and Spring Lane, and the firm of Manning and Loring served as printers for many of Nancrede's publications. Among the papers kept by the bookseller-publisher long after he left Boston was an invoice of 11 April 1799, recording the price charged by Manning and Loring for the bookmaking involved in Mallet Du Pan's *History of the Destruction of the Helvetic Union:*

> Mr. Joseph Nancrede, to Manning & Loring,—D^r
>
> To printing "The History of the Destruction of the Helvetic Union and Liberty," $9.83 ⅓ cts. pr. Sheet, eleven sheets, ——————————————— $108.16 ⅔
>
> To the case-work of four half sheets, composed the second time, ——————————————— 10.66 ⅔
>
> To five quires of printing paper, used on the above, 1.0
>
> Manning & Loring $119.83 ⅓ [87]

Although "case-work . . . composed the second time" indicates perhaps a certain dissatisfaction on the part of the publisher with the case work that had been composed the first time, Manning and Loring accounted for a goodly proportion of Nancrede's publications.

Some years later, in 1805, Samuel Hall would sell out to that firm. In 1789, when Hall had been located at 55 Cornhill as printer-bookseller, he had printed Nancrede's own newspaper, the *Courier de Boston*, "the first publication in the language of any importance in Boston." [88] Nancrede relied upon other printers too for his presswork, among them Belknap and Hall, a firm consisting of Joseph Belknap, who in partnership with Alexander Young had printed Nancrede's pioneer textbook, *L'Abeille Françoise*, and his own early partner Thomas Hall. Occasionally using the firms of Samuel Etheridge, John Russell, or David Carlisle, Joseph Nancrede apparently found in Boston a sufficient number of printing houses capable of producing the presswork he desired.

Once his books had been manufactured, the publisher confronted the perennial problem of sales and distribution. Though there was a sizable French population in proportion to the non-French population in Boston, there was never a sufficient number of French readers to guarantee anything like a wide market for his books. As a Franco-American publisher in Boston, therefore, Nancrede faced serious problems. He advertised his books in his own publications of course; and between 1796 and 1803 he issued four major catalogues in which he took occasion to publicize not only his stock of books for sale but those that bore his own imprint. Joseph Nancrede's forty-six page *Catalogue of Books in the Various Branches of Literature; Lately Imported from London, Dublin, Paris, and other Capitals of Europe* announced, besides his general inventory in English and French, Malham's *Naval Gazetteer, Paul and Virginia,* and *Télémaque.* Two years later, in 1798, Nancrede published a list of over eighty pages entitled *Joseph Nancrede's Catalogue of Books Just Imported from London* which devoted considerable space to Rulhière's *History . . . of the Revolution in Russia,* Saint-Pierre's *Studies of Nature,* and Malham's *Naval Gazetteer.* Toward the end of his publishing career Nancrede issued two *Fixed-Price Catalogues,* one of his importation aboard the *Gallen* and *Minerva* from London and another of a "large collection of books, which has, for several years past, been accumulating every production of merit, in the English language." In both those catalogues the bookseller-publisher took occasion to advertise his own imprints.

Printing his Proposals in the newspaper press or in broadside form, dispatching them to prospective subscribers, enlisting the aid of fellow booksellers, traveling to Salem or Philadelphia, Joseph Nancrede, bookseller-publisher, was also his own extremely active salesman. Toward the end of the eighteenth century, Philadelphia especially was becoming a cosmopolitan city and its bookstores were "richly stocked with French books."[89] After the Philadelphia bookseller-publisher Moreau de Saint-Méry, the erstwhile King of Paris, dismissed from his employ an assistant named Decombaz, Nancrede availed himself of that knowledgeable gentleman's services. Moreau had dismissed Decombaz, as he confessed, "regretfully, because of his knowledge of the details of my business, which long experience had given him to a superior degree. But his plans were too ambitious and I couldn't tolerate them."[90] Nancrede apparently could, for, among the methods he used to sell his wares was an arrangement with "G. Decombaz, No. 48, North Third Street, Philadelphia" to sell "Books Published by J. Nancrede, Boston."[91] Indeed, one edition of *The Adventures of Telemachus* "Revised and Corrected By Joseph Nancrede" was actually published by G. Decombaz of Philadelphia in 1797, and the work contained at the end an advertisement of Nancrede's Boston publications. By such means Nancrede exported or attempted to export, sold or attempted to sell, his merchandise.

His efforts were not always successful and upon several occasions his publishing plans were frustrated. It was that very Moreau de Saint-Méry for whom Decombaz had clerked who thwarted one of Nancrede's well advertised projects. In a four-page list of the kind that might be distributed separately or tipped in at the end of a volume, Nancrede had announced "A New Standard of French Pronunciation, wherein the sounds of French are faithfully indicated by typographical signs, in so distinct a manner, as to render the attainment of French pronunciation equally easy and accurate."[92] Such a French phonetic dictionary was never published by Nancrede. A letter from Moreau (4 March 1795) expresses regret that his own comparable project had caused the Boston publisher to abandon his scheme. Such disappointments were to be expected in the publishing trade in the 1790s when interest in French events and the French language was still strong.

In negotiations with authors too a degree of frustration could be anticipated by a publisher especially when he was bargaining with a well-known writer. Nancrede had apparently hoped to publish a book of Moral Tales written for American youth by the respected Vermont lawyer and author of *The Contrast* and *The Algerine Captive*, Royall Tyler. However Nancrede insisted upon his own terms while Tyler not only insisted upon his but entertained several reservations about the entire project. Although Nancrede claimed the manuscript had gone to press, it never appeared in book form. Both the bargaining and the frustration are revealed in a fascinating correspondence recently published, a correspondence that indirectly discloses Nancrede's publishing policies. On 10 February 1800, he writes concerning Tyler's manuscript: "How will it answer *my* purpose or *your* purpose?" The book was too short. "Books for youth must not have empty pages; and it would hardly bear binding. It must be highly puffed, and repeatedly advertised; and it cannot sell for so much as it would if it were as large as we expected." Despite these objections, Nancrede made his offer: "as the price of the absolute copy-right, 200 copies of the book . . . neatly bound, free of all expense to you. If this arrangement suits you, be so obliging as to send me the Contract of the copy-right; I shall copy it, and send you the double, signed. It shall then be put to press immediately. If I have an answer in time, I will annex a small engraving as a frontispiece." Although Nancrede sweetened the offer with the gift of "a paper of ink powder, and a bunch of quills," Tyler declined. He had expected cash, not books in payment, specifically $200, not 200 books. Moreover he was quick to call the publisher's bluff. "If . . . it will require much expensive advertisement, and artful puffing to be succeeded by a slow sale, it cannot certainly be your interest to publish it; and if the copy-right is worth merely your proffer, it cannot be mine to usher it to the public with my name at length." Although he was "willing" he was not "anxious—to write again for the press." "If writing for the public is attended with no more profit, I had rather file legal process in my attorney's office, and endeavor to explain unintelligible law to Green Mountain jurors." The elegantly couched complaints, the more or less subtle negotiations continued, Nancrede observing, "You have a very exalted idea of the price of a manuscript, and a very diminutive one of the money of the Bookseller. . . . I will not make any comment on your very 'explicit and absolute answer' of an advance of 200 dollars for 100 small pages of a work for youth, which the author says have cost him 'eight days' amusement;' but request you will furnish me with an instance of an author—the gigantic Johnson, Pope, Swift, Voltaire, Rousseau (I will not compare you to meaner writers) or any other, selling the amusements, or even the hard labors, of eight days for '200 dollars cash,' in an old and rich country, populated by 20 millions of readers." Between Nancrede's protestations and Tyler's real or assumed indifference, the possibility of agreement evaporated. The correspondence was discontinued and Royall Tyler's Moral Tales joined A New Standard of French Pronunciation as one of Nancrede's ghosts.[93]

A third Nancrede ghost proved a far more serious disappointment, for this unrealized scheme had been a major enterprise involving elaborate labors and expenditures. The project concerned an ambitious multivolume "complete System of Universal Geography." A preliminary circular and two pamphlets were printed to publicize the work; scholars and libraries were tapped for information; Nancrede actually went abroad to obtain maps for it; but in the end the venture was abandoned.[94]

With a temporary partner—Barnard B. Macanulty, Irish-born bookseller of Salem—Nancrede on 1 September 1801 launched the venture with a preliminary circular indicating the shortcomings of preceding works in the field of geography and adumbrating the planned compilation. Its author, James Tytler, was described as "a man of learning and talents, author of several Geographical works of reputation, who has resided several years in America."[95] The description was accurate enough though it omitted much of interest regarding James Tytler. Born in Scotland, that "intelligent and candid stranger" had had a checkered career before he came to America, having been not only a literary hack but a pioneer astronaut known as Balloon Tytler. Because of advanced views that did not sit well with the Scottish establishment, Balloon Tytler had been threatened with arrest, a predicament he avoided by a sudden departure for the new world. He was indeed "a man of learning" but he was also a man who drank heavily. It was this impecunious eccentric of Salem who had been engaged by Macanulty and Nancrede to compile a "complete System of Universal Geography" and to be paid for his labors at the rate of 12½ cents an hour.

The labors were Herculean not only for Tytler but for Nancrede. Nancrede used his Harvard connection to obtain the privilege of borrowing books, "three volumes at any one time . . . Mr. Nancrede to be accountable for the books, and to return them uninjured."[96] In September 1801 the publisher solicited the assistance and influence of William Duane, editor of the Philadelphia *Aurora*, who replied, "What aid I could lend I would most cheerfully do it, but I think the most serviceable aid I could give would be to point out the *fallacies* and *mistakes* of former Systems."[97] Dr. William Bentley of Salem was contacted and although he looked down his ministerial nose at the publishers, he grudgingly offered to help with their project.[98] While James Tytler was perusing the books supplied by his publisher, Nancrede in November 1801 had his naturalization papers copied and by 15 December had reached London. There he remained for several months, settling in St. Michael's Alley, Cornhill. In his search for books and maps he contacted a wide range of people including his old associates William Cobbett,[99] the pamphleteer, who had recently opened a bookshop in Pall Mall and begun *Cobbett's Weekly Political Register*, and Louis Philippe d'Orléans, who promised lively interest and the purchase of a Geography.[100] In the course of his field trip Nancrede also journeyed to Paris. By mid-1802 he was back in Boston with the spoils of his journey.

The project being thus far advanced, a fifteen-page pamphlet was issued at Salem in June 1802 to acquaint the public with complete details of the enterprise, to obtain subscribers and insure a wide circulation for the Universal Geography. "Our resources," the *Proposals* boasted, "are numerous and authentic; and we have the encouragement and countenance of many men, eminent for literature and learning. As no expense will be spared, we trust that we shall strictly fulfil the expectations of the public in the extent of our design." The work would consist of "three close and large octavo volumes, with a *folio Atlas*" and would be priced at $9.[101]

Those promises were never realized. Between June 1802, when the *Proposals* were circulated, and December 1802, when a third pamphlet relating to the Geography was issued, an event occurred that threatened its success. A rival work—John Pinkerton's two-volume *Modern Geography*—was published in London and imported to the United States. Obviously the urgent need for another "complete System of Universal Geography" had diminished. Despite the Pinkerton publication, Nancrede and Macanulty persisted, issuing a fourteen-page review of Pinkerton's *Geography* castigating that work.[102] Unfortunately, the threat imposed by Pinkerton was followed by another event that gave to Nancrede's ambitious plan its death blow. On a freezing January night in 1804, Balloon Tytler "in a fit of intoxication . . . deceived by the lights . . . slipt into the wash, the tide being up and perished."[103] So too did his work. Tytler's Universal Geography never saw the light of day. One of Nancrede's most ambitious enterprises had failed. A major undertaking, it proved a major disappointment.

This failure may indeed have played no small a part in the publisher's decision to abandon both his trade and, for a period of time, his adopted country. It takes more than one or two failures to end a productive career, however, and there were doubtless other forces that motivated Nancrede. Some of those forces may be deduced from his subsequent actions; some of them must remain speculative. Facts, however, are not speculative, and these may be put together in an attempt to recreate the mosaic of his life at this time.

After Nancrede had returned from his business trip abroad in connection with Tytler's Geography, a notice appeared in the 15 June 1803 issue of the *Columbian Centinel* announcing that the firm of Dyer and Eddy "have taken the store, and greater part of the stock lately owned by Mr. *Joseph Nancrede, No. 49 Marlboro'-Street, Boston*, where they offer for sale, a large assortment of *Books and Stationery*, as usual, and hope . . . to be in future honoured with the commands of those, who have been in the habit of purchasing of Mr. *Nancrede.*" After 49 Marlborough Street had been taken over by Dyer and Eddy, who sold watches, fancy goods, and jewelry along with books, Nancrede moved to 24 State Street. According to the *Centinel* of 20 August 1803: "JOSEPH NANCREDE has moved his BOOKS to No. 24, *State-Street*, corner of *Kirby-Street, over Sam'l Bradford*'s Auction store—*Where he has for sale, at reduced prices*, a much larger, and more varied . . . collection of *English, French, Latin, Spanish* and *Italian* BOOKS than he ever before was able to offer the public." A twenty-eight-page *Fixed-Price Catalogue* was issued from his new address but Nancrede's emphasis upon the size and variety of his stock does not remove the suspicion that he was a man terminating, not expanding a business—a man tying up loose ends.

In January 1804 that suspicion was corroborated. Some two weeks after James Tytler's death a notice appeared in the Boston papers: "BOOKS. On THURSDAY, 8th February next, And the following days, will be sold, at *Public Auction*, by SAMUEL BRADFORD, at his Office, No. 5, *Kirby-Street*, The whole STOCK OF BOOKS, of Joseph Nancrede; consisting of upwards of 7000 Volumes, and being a Collection which has for several years past been accumulating every production of merit, in the English language; and is now grown into as valuable and rare a variety in the useful, ornamental and classical branches of science and literature, as was ever offered for sale in *America*. . . . Catalogues of the above Stock having largely been liberally distributed through the Country . . . Gentlemen are requested to preserve these, as no new ones will be printed."[104]

Nancrede's last *Fixed-Price Catalogue* was, in other words, to serve as an auction catalogue for the remainder of his stock. The sale, postponed to 14 February "and the following days" when the "Law, Classical, Latin and French with other Foreign BOOKS" were auctioned,[105] was apparently successful, for Dr. Bentley of Salem, whose aid had been enlisted for the Tytler Geography, recorded in his journal (III, 77) under the date of 2 March 1804: "Nancrede's Sale of Books . . . sold for their highest value this week, so that the demand must necessarily be great."

In January, Bentley, referring to the announced auction of Nancrede's stock, had remarked, "It is not often that valuable or general collections are sold. The importers commonly receive upon a limited Catalogue & have seldom an opportunity to enlarge it in America. Such as go to England, generally bring the best selection. Nancrede has been lately. But his domestic affairs & his general manners have not contributed to the public confidence."

There is little doubt that Nancrede's "domestic affairs" played as large if not a larger part than the Tytler failure in his decision to end his American business career. Despite the fecundity of his union, his relations with his wife had apparently never been happy. Nonetheless he had eight children to support and to educate—six sons and two daughters ranging from one-year-old Charles to fifteen-year-old Louisa, the others having appeared in steps every year or two. Despite his allegiance to the United States, despite the fact that he had become a naturalized citizen, despite such success as he had had in this country, Joseph Nancrede, faced with the necessity of educating his eight children, determined to perform that task not in America but in France. Moreover, he determined to do it on his own and without his wife.

Other factors too may have played a role in Nancrede's decision to return to his native country. He had visited Paris briefly in 1802 during his map-searching journey, and that year had been a splendid one in the history of France. Peace had been restored after conquests had been achieved; order had returned and trade had been revived. Perhaps an opportunity for some kind of preferment, political or literary or economic, had presented itself. Paris fashions again delighted the eye. *Citoyens* were once more *Monsieurs*. Revolutionary zeal had given way to the art of pleasing and the fame of Bonaparte was an effulgence upon the land. The man who in 1802 had been made Consul for life was two years later crowned Emperor of the French. On the surface at least there seemed much to attract a native Frenchman back to his own country.

Yet for twenty years Nancrede had lived a rich life in his adopted land. The former soldier of Yorktown had exerted a decided influence as French instructor at Harvard; in his *Courier de Boston* he had produced a pioneer French newspaper and in his *L'Abeille Françoise* he had compiled the first French textbook for use in this country; he had helped spread in the United States the doctrine of Brissot de Warville, of Rousseau, of Saint-Pierre. In the course of his little consular war and the affair of Citizen Genêt he had stirred up considerable political agitation. As bookseller and as publisher he had reflected and illuminated the changing tides of American feeling toward France. When in January 1804 what has been called the first American book-trade catalogue was issued by the Boston booksellers as a *Catalogue of all the Books printed in the United States*, the imprints of Joseph Nancrede found a place.[106]

Now, owing in some measure to a few trade disappointments, to an unhappy marriage, to the need to educate eight children, to the memory of the splendors of France during a recent visit, and possibly to a promise of some office or assignment, Joseph Nancrede pulled up his American roots.

Nancrede's "Permis de Séjour"—his pass to reside in France, dated 1804—requested free passage to Mr. Nancrede, "Négocian, Amé* ricain" as well as to his eight children, his baggage, and one domestic.[107] The forty-three-year-old Franco-American "merchant" in books had lived half of his life in America. In the course of the many years that remained he would return to his adopted country but he would never again set out a shingle as bookseller-publisher. Instead he would live quite successfully on the fringe of the book world and on the fringe of the political-economic world. His life as a professional bookseller-publisher was over. His life as dabbler, as negotiator behind scenes was about to begin.

Nancrede's papers—his *permis de séjour*, his passport—record his appearance, the black hair and brown eyes, the large mouth and long nose, and so restore the portrait of a Franco-American who in 1804 returned to his native country. Another extant paper, a short letter written by the French astronomer Lalande thanking Nancrede for sending Nathaniel Bowditch's notes on Lalande's *Astronomie*, reanimates another aspect of his life abroad. Lalande's letter is addressed: "A Monsieur Joseph Nancrede chez M. Recamier rue du Montblanc . . . a Paris."[108]

The house on the Rue du Montblanc was one of the most elegant mansions in Paris, a masterpiece of the Directory style where "returned exiles . . . rubbed shoulders . . . with . . . army suppliers" and political survivors of the Revolution consorted with the "young officers of a new regime." It had been purchased by the great banker Jacques-Rose Récamier who had married the fifteen-year-old Juliette, destined to become a queen of Thermidorian society. Her salon on the Rue du Montblanc attracted so many statesmen that Napoleon inquired "if the counsel of ministers took place there." Presumably Joseph Nancrede, late bookseller-publisher of Boston, enjoyed their company for a time, watching the social triumphs of Madame Récamier as she entertained in her flowing Grecian robes, discussing the vacillations of the French franc, observing from a corner while political plots were hatched and political gossip was exchanged.[109]

There was much to discuss in Paris in 1804. Napoleon had become Emperor of the French in May, and in December the famous coronation took place, Pius VII journeying to the city for the occasion. In between there had been a treaty—the Franco-Dutch—and a war—Spain's against Britain—and in the year that followed Trafalgar and Austerlitz would punctuate the long Napoleonic saga of triumph and defeat.

The events in Nancrede's life are far more difficult to reconstruct than the events of the France in which he lived. He remained abroad from 1804 to 1812 and during those eight years he doubtless succeeded in educating his eight children and in establishing himself as a man of some means if no great wealth and a man of some small influence if no great name. Among the shadows of his life at this time a few lights penetrate, most of them in the form of correspondence still extant. In 1805, Philippe-Jean-Louis Desjardins, a French theologian who had remained in Canada for some time, presented his compliments to Monsieur Nancrede along with a list of the paintings in his possession and the prices they had fetched.[110] Had Nancrede become a collector of paintings or an art dealer? Or simply a consultant in Scriptural portraiture?

Austerlitz had been followed by Friedland and Wagram before the next extant letters offer a glimpse of Nancrede's activities. In 1810 his correspondent is no theologian but a general and the subject of the letters is more closely related to Nancrede's bookish than his artistic interests. In them General Baron Henri Jomini, aide-de-camp to Marshal Ney, discusses at some length the second and a possible third edition of his *Traité des grandes opérations de la Guerre*: the revisions he has incorporated into it, the additional material now available, and his reaction to a possible English translation.[111] The inference is that Nancrede had been invited to participate in some way, as editorial adviser if not as publisher, in a revised edition of a French military treatise.

It is at least clear that Nancrede during his long Paris sojourn had been dabbling in both art and letters. That he dabbled also in real estate is suggested by still another correspondent, the Prince de Neuchatel, who, writing in April 1811, acknowledges Monsieur's offer to sell a house and land near "grosbois."[112]

The outcome of Nancrede's different ventures during this period remains shadowy. At least once he met his former associate Moreau de Saint-Méry, who recalled that Nancrede had not ceased to show the "strong and habitual satisfaction with his own ideas" that he had evinced years before in Philadelphia.[113] Moreau de Saint-Méry did not trouble to record those ideas; they doubtless concerned not only the books but the politics of the period both in France and in America. It is tempting to believe that the Nancrede who had once striven to explain France to America would now make a similar effort to explain America to France. Especially during those climactic months before the War of 1812 when America vacillated as to which country was more offensive to her interests, France or Britain, a resident of France who was also a naturalized American citizen must have pondered long upon the political fabric of his time.

Shortly before he returned to his adopted country, Nancrede emerged as a dabbler not only in art, literature, and real estate, but in politics too. The man who had listened to political musings "chez M. Recamier" and exchanged political ideas with Moreau de Saint-Méry, actually entered the political arena himself in 1812. Yet even then he entered stealthily as it were and behind the scenes.

Having announced an impending declaration of war, the *Salem Gazette* of 9 June 1812 carried the following provocative paragraph: "A letter from Paris mentions, as the confidential advisers of our minister there, *Daniel Parker, Mark Leavenworth, Big Lee, and Nancrede* (formerly a bookseller in Boston) and that, 'Parker, Leavenworth, Nancrede and the Minister are all French citizens de facto as well as de jure.'"

It is interesting to be able to trace the former Boston bookseller to a diplomatic sphere of action in Paris. Nancrede's "confidential" role becomes still more interesting when it is recalled that "our minister there" was none other than the Hartford wit who had translated the work of Nancrede's admired Brissot de Warville, Joel Barlow. Prior to that August day in 1811 when he sailed to France as Madison's Minister, Barlow had had a hand in so many Franco-American activities that he was almost as much a hyphenated American as Nancrede. He had been associated with the Ohio Company that sold western land to the French; he had been an agent of the Scioto Company. As a reward for his *Letter to the National Convention . . . on the Defects in the Constitution of 1791* he had been made a citizen of France. When his *Advice to the Privileged Orders* was suppressed by Britain and he himself proscribed, the author had sought refuge in Paris. He had translated Brissot de Warville's *New Travels in the United States*, been active in French politics, and written to George Washington to prevent an Anglo-French war. Finally, Madison had appointed the author of the *Hasty Pudding* and *The Columbiad* Minister to France.

The prime purpose of Barlow's ministry was to intercede with the Emperor for improved commercial relations with America, the removal of restraints upon American merchants, the reduction of customs duties on American goods. This was a subject after Nancrede's heart. Had he not translated Brissot and Clavière on Franco-American commerce, and urged the advantages of trade relations between the two countries in his *Courier de Boston*? Now, as "confidential adviser" to a minister plenipotentiary with whom he had so much in common, Nancrede could at last attempt to put his beliefs into practice and make of "l'utilité des deux mondes" something more substantial than a motto.

He was joined in his efforts by the American merchant William Lee— the "*Big Lee*" mentioned by the *Salem Gazette*—who had sailed with Barlow aboard the *Constitution* for France. As Secretary of the Legation, however, Lee had no need to hide behind the scenes. When Joel Barlow, dressed in his "plain bottle green coat," went to St. Cloud for a private audience with Napoleon, William Lee, arrayed in full regalia, accompanied the Minister as far as the "*salon des ambassadeurs*." [114] If Nancrede was in the company his presence remained unrecorded. Yet there is no doubt that he was involved in some commercial activity and that his path crossed Joel Barlow's at this time. To the paragraph in the *Salem Gazette* may be added as evidence a letter found among Nancrede's papers, written by Joel Barlow to Peter Stephen Du Ponceau, Steuben's aide-de-camp in the Revolution, who had become a specialist in international law. Written from Paris in February 1812, the letter recommends Nancrede to Du Ponceau's "good offices" and discusses a commercial transaction involving Du Ponceau, General Duportail, and Nancrede.[115]

Still another letter that would be treasured by Nancrede and found among his effects links him with the negotiations going on in Paris in 1812. That letter was written to Secretary of State James Monroe by "America's Cultural Ambassador in France," David Bailie Warden, author of a work on the *Origin, Nature, . . . and Influence of Consular Establishments*. Besides being a diplomat, Warden was a book collector, and Nancrede, who kept a copy of "Warden's precious confessions" all his life, must surely have discussed with him not only the disappointments of diplomatic ambition but the books of the hour.[116]

Meanwhile Barlow's mission proceeded, or failed to proceed. While he did accomplish the release of unjustly seized American vessels, he found French officials extremely evasive and the Emperor himself reluctant to sign a treaty. It was not until October 1812 that Napoleon, facing the disasters of his invasion of Russia, agreed to meet Barlow in Poland to discuss the treaty. The Minister set out for Wilno but his hopes of meeting the Emperor were never realized. Napoleon, defeated at the Berezina, returned to Paris in December. The same month Barlow, who had been taken ill in Poland, died near Cracow.

By that time both Nancrede's situation and the politics of Europe had undergone considerable change. On 18 June the War of 1812 had been declared. The next month, without waiting for the outcome of Barlow's diplomacy, his "confidential adviser" sailed aboard the *Mary Anne* for America. Napoleonic defeats and French economic decline doubtless governed his decision to depart. Yet, despite current unemployment and scarcities in Paris, Nancrede appears to have garnered some tangible substance from his years abroad, from his dabblings in art and literature, property and trade. If his confidential advice to Barlow had come to nought, at least his children had been educated. If his activities on the political fringe had failed of any solid achievement, at least he had circulated among diplomats. He had been involved in the intricacies of Franco-American trade relations and surely he had discussed Franco-American books with the poet Joel Barlow and the collector David Warden.

As mementoes of his service as "confidential adviser" to "our minister" in Paris, Nancrede carried with him aboard ship several papers. One was the letter in which Joel Barlow had recommended Nancrede to the "good offices" of Du Ponceau in Philadelphia. Another was a note from William Lee stating: "The bearer . . . M Nancrede goes to Dunkerque with his family to embark in the Mary Ann. He agreed for the passage of himself and family at five thousand francs one half to be paid in France and one half in the UStates."[117]

After eight years abroad, Joseph Nancrede, now fifty-one, was ready to take up again a life in America. This time he would live it not in Boston but in another center of French culture, Philadelphia. Still on the fringe of the world of books and the world of politics, he would continue his career of Franco-American against the background of the City of Brotherly Love.

Stephen Du Ponceau, to whom Nancrede carried Barlow's letter, was not only a member of the Philadelphia Bar but the "orator" or mouthpiece of the city's French colony. Emigrés and exiles from the Revolution had settled around Second, Third and Fourth Streets near the waterfront and made of Philadelphia a "French Noah's Ark" where men in pantaloons and liberty caps had greeted each other as "citizen." At the University of Pennsylvania, where Nancrede's son Joseph was enrolled in the medical school, French had been taught before Harvard's French instructor had been born. With the teaching of French came the demand for French books, and "in Philadelphia the most popular single book over a long period of time was Telemachus," Nancrede's beloved *Télémaque* which he had edited and published in his Boston days. Moreau de Saint-Méry, whom Nancrede had visited in Philadelphia, had for a short time been part of the French colony there, and there were still in 1812 enough survivors of that colony to give to the city a Gallic flavor. Frenchmen who had "passed through the imperial court of Napoleon" without losing their republicanism would join exiles from the Revolution in a place that continued to be, if not a French Noah's Ark, at least a Cosmopolis.[118]

There were obviously enough attractions to prompt a Franco-American to settle in Philadelphia. Another inducement for Nancrede was doubtless the absence of his wife who apparently remained in Boston and who seems by this time to have unofficially stepped out of his life. In 1813 young Joseph Guerard was graduated from medical school; after a few years in Louisville, Kentucky, he was back in Philadelphia by 1816 when he opened his office on South Tenth Street, an address he shared with his father.[119] Nearby, son Nicholas also set up his shingle as a physician, and Philadelphia's French community was in competent medical hands.

Another of Nancrede's sons seemed ready to follow more closely in his father's footsteps, for Henry Walstane Nancrede was employed by the distinguished Philadelphia printer-publisher Mathew Carey. Years before Nancrede had had some dealings with Carey, having purchased a Hebrew Bible from him in 1796,[120] and indeed he had much in common with the Irish Catholic printer who had settled in Philadelphia. As Nancrede had deplored French fanaticism, Carey had attacked English oppression of Irish Catholics. While Nancrede was soldiering in the Army of Rochambeau, Carey, sent to Paris, worked at Franklin's printing office in Passy and through Franklin met Lafayette. In 1784 he set sail for America, landing at Philadelphia, a twenty-four-year-old Irish immigrant whose capital consisted of twelve guineas and an ambition to be a printer. With the aid of Lafayette he fulfilled his ambition in a city that soon attracted refugees from the French Revolution. By 1796, when Nancrede purchased a Bible from his colleague, Carey was prospering as bookseller-printer-publisher. In 1817 the Carey firm published Dr. Joseph G. Nancrede's translation of Orfila's work on toxicology. Nancrede père and Mathew Carey shared not only professional but economic interests, both being consistently involved in problems of commerce and trade.

In 1817 the young son of the Franco-American who had been a publisher in Boston began work for the Irish-American who was still a publisher in Philadelphia. Receipts in the Mathew Carey Collection indicate that Henry Nancrede received $200 a year in quarterly payments for his services.[121] By 1819 he was acting as a firm agent, soliciting subscriptions in New York and Albany, in Troy and "along the North River" for an edition of the Carey atlas—an enterprise that must have evoked in Nancrede père some half-bitter recollections of the Tytler failure. Later on Henry was sent to Georgetown to solicit the nation's Congressmen and notables for the Carey publication.[122] At the end of 1820 a certificate testifies that Henry W. Nancrede "attended our store for above three years; and that his conduct during that period has merited & recd. our warmest approbation. We have found him honest, attentive, faithful, and industrious—& possessing a spirit that wd. revolt at any mean or improper action." [123]

Meanwhile, Henry's father not only rejoiced in his son's good conduct but enjoyed his own friendship with the Philadelphia publisher. Although Nancrede was not officially in business, he still dabbled in books and his business relations with the Carey firm preceded his son's employment there. A document of 30 August 1813 signed by Nancrede's son Joseph acknowledges the receipt of "fifty-nine 4/100 dollars in full for nine second hand Charts, belonging to Malham's Naval Gazetteer," and other receipts indicate that Nancrede was selling off what was probably the remainder of his Boston stock to Mathew Carey.[124]

To the few official records of the business relationship between Nancrede and Carey may be added one or two letters that help reconstruct their friendship, letters that refer to a call from the French consul and an exchange of claret bottles.[125] One letter in particular, bearing the date 5 July 1819,[126] elucidates the Nancrede-Carey connection:

> As I was saying, before Henry, that I wished you had 2 papers, *Ephemeris* which Mr. Duane had just given me, Henry cried out—"oh Papa, let me carry them to Mr Carey's—Our store is shut up—I have nothing to do, to day."—I conclude that if there be any impertinence or intrusion in that it is due to Mrs Carey, or the Young Ladies goodness in making too much of him—so, they must bear the penalty—of their goodness—
>
> I read yesterday with very great pleasure a piece in Niles Register—I pray you to read it. It expresses my answer to "let trade regulate itself" better than I could

have expressed it myself.—I spent the last evening with friend Ronaldson now agrees perfectly to have a new series—but have a good many things to say to you, which, if, as a *rank tory*, you had not absented yourself from the city, on such a day as this, I would have told you. Notwithstanding all which I am Your friend & hble servant

Jos. Nancrede

In 1819, when the Bourbon Louis XVIII was occupying the French throne after the Napoleonic years had passed and James Monroe was occupying the American presidency during a time of economic depression, the regulation of trade preoccupied both Mathew Carey and Mathew Carey's humble servant. Indeed Carey had been moved to establish a society to improve the country's trade, recording in his *Autobiography*: "At the crisis of the affairs of the country . . . there was a small society formed in Philadelphia entitled the 'Philadelphia Society for the promotion of National Industry.'— There were only ten members—. . . The object of the society was to advocate the protection of national industry generally, but more particularly of manufactures, as perishing for want of protection."[127]

One of the ten members of that society was Joseph Nancrede. Another was James Ronaldson, mentioned in the letter to Carey, the typefounder whose tools had originally been brought from France by Franklin. At the Society's meetings, Nancrede listened to addresses on the cotton trade or the encouragement of national manufactures or aired his own views on commerce and the wealth of nations. Years later he would recall that Ronaldson had "been the first man who . . . proposed him [Andrew Jackson] in Philadelphia as candidate for the presidency, and to our society, when . . . your proposition was hooted, by every member but myself."[128] In addition, Nancrede supplied the French consul in Philadelphia, the Comte de Lesseps, with books and pamphlets, receiving in exchange a lengthy discourse on economics designed for Nancrede's "respectable société."[129]

During his Philadelphia years, the city directory described Nancrede as a "gentleman," and indeed his pursuits, revealed by his correspondence, were those of a gentleman. Speculations on politics and trade vied for his attention with books and letters. He acted as self-appointed entrepreneur for many French visitors to Philadelphia, and with acquaintances in France he continued his connections. In 1815 a Paris correspondent regrets that "my purse will not permit me to execute your small commission for Books. The *fourteenth* volume of the Dictionaire des Sciences medicales was published a month or two ago, which brings down the work only to the middle of the letter F. Hence you may judge what a voluminous production this will be.

"You do not mention whether you received the two numbers of M. Magendie's Experiments I sent you . . . I am sorry you did not send me a letter of thanks for that gentleman. I would then have had an opportunity of asking him for a continuation of his Experiments for your sons' perusal."[130]

To Dupont de Nemours, Nancrede wrote in 1816, asking him to visit South 10th Street should he pass through Philadelphia on his way to New York and France.[131] One of the most interesting letters retained by Nancrede was sent in 1819 by the French dramatist Victor-Joseph Etienne Jouy, whose tragedy *Belisaire* had been denied presentation. After referring to various periodicals—Duane's *Aurora* and his own *Minerve français*—Jouy adds an intriguing postscript: "You will receive with this letter 17 Copies of my tragedy of *Belisaire*."[132] Was gentleman Nancrede an unofficial distributor of books or an informal press agent for French writers?

Throughout the years, from the Hundred Days to Waterloo, from the return of Louis XVIII to the death of Napoleon, Nancrede had not and would not discard his self-made role of interpreter of France to America. He transmitted his Franco-Americanism to his son and namesake Dr. Joseph G. Nancrede, and it was surely with gratification that he heard young Joseph's *Address* before the New England Society of Philadelphia in 1820. The speaker not only quoted Rousseau at length but exalted the role of the emigré to America: "To their emigration, provoked by religious fanaticism, we owe the liberty of conscience we enjoy—to intolerance, our toleration; to despotism our liberty; to tyranny the security of our lives, reputation and property; and to persecution in the parent country, we are indebted for the country which secures us all these blessings, and is at once, our happiness, and our pride."[133]

One especially exalted emigré was numbered among Dr. Nancrede's patients and gentleman Nancrede's acquaintances. In July 1815, at the time of the "White Terror" in France, Napoleon's older brother Joseph sailed for America, using the pseudonym of the Comte de Survilliers. Settling near Philadelphia, as did other Napoleonic exiles, the former King of Spain later purchased a country seat near Bordentown—Point Breeze—where his hospitality was extended to all French emigrés and where he remained for sixteen years. In the course of them, Dr. Joseph Nancrede ministered to his physical well-being, and the doctor's father upon at least one occasion ministered to his spiritual well-being. In 1825, having left America for the last time, Nancrede presented to Joseph Bonaparte a copy of a book that attempted to avenge the memory of his late brother: *Napoléon et la Grande Armée en Russie*. Nancrede's intention to present the book was conveyed to the royal master of Point Breeze by his secretary, the French historian Méneval, who added, "I have taken a lively pleasure in hearing M. Nancrède, who is so sincerely devoted to you, speak to me of you."[134]

Nancrede's devotion was extended not only to Joseph Bonaparte but to some of the erstwhile monarch's pet schemes. Many of the French exiles, including Joseph Bonaparte and former members of the Imperial Guard, projected a variety of plans to obtain land grants—from the Champ d'Asile in Texas to Demopolis in Alabama. Long before his final departure for France, while he was still very much the gentleman of Philadelphia,

Nancrede involved himself in one such scheme known as the Renaut Claim, and so the former dealer in books was transformed temporarily into a dealer in land and in dreams.

Nancrede had been in Philadelphia when some hundred and fifty French exiles set sail from the port for Champ d'Asile, Texas. In that "futile attempt . . . to found a Napoleonic state in the Southwestern wilderness" Joseph Bonaparte, who saw it possibly as the path to a kingdom in Mexico, had had a stake, approving the plan and contributing money to it.[135] Nancrede's own stake was not in Champ d'Asile but in the Renaut Claim, whose history was as long as it was involved.[136] As with most of Nancrede's fringe activities, his role in the scheme was puzzling and mysterious.

In 1719, Philip François Renault, an American colonist born in France, and principal agent for the Company of St. Philip, sailed for Illinois. His company, a branch of John Law's famous Mississippi scheme, obtained large land grants before Renault returned to France. A century later Renault's heirs petitioned for confirmation of his grant in the Territory of Illinois. In 1816, when French refugees who had flocked to America needed land to clear, a group of interested persons apparently banded together to purchase the Renaut Claim. Negotiations were complicated, involving not only the Committee on Private Land Claims, but a variety of agents and attorneys, capitalists and sleeping partners, official and unofficial advisers. Among them were Albert Gallatin, Minister to Paris; Henry Baldwin, Pennsylvania lawyer; Joel Barlow's nephew Thomas, a relative of Baldwin; and the Philadelphia gentleman Joseph Nancrede.

Once again it is a dossier of letters kept by Nancrede that throws a flickering light upon his role in purchasing an asylum for French refugees in the Illinois Territory. As Henry Baldwin indicates, Nancrede served as unofficial adviser. Apparently because of his familiarity with the complications involved in the land grant, Nancrede was to give "advice and instructions" to Barlow, who in turn was to go to France and ascertain whether or not the deed was genuine.[137] "If any thing is ever done by us to purchase the Renaut Claim," wrote another correspondent to Nancrede, "it must be done *quickly* but how is it to be done?"[138] An essential preliminary was authentication of the claim, a task assigned to Thomas Barlow with Nancrede's help. Prior to sailing for France, Barlow wrote to Nancrede: "I should be glad to receive from you . . . any advice or instructions you may think will be of service to me in this business in France. . . . I have seen all the papers relating to this business & have the Deed with me. . . . I shall do every thing in my power to endeavour to trace this business & I should be glad to receive any information or direction you can give me. . . . I sail in the ship Rubicon, Capt. Holdrige for Havre de Grace."[139]

Despite the crossing of the *Rubicon* the purchase of the Renaut Claim joined the Tytler Geography as another of Nancrede's ghosts. Henry Baldwin had complained to Nancrede: "This business has been from the

beginning involved in . . . mystery and difficulties have . . . thickened."[140]
The mystery obfuscated and the difficulties complicated the project and the
Renaut Land Claim was still being considered by the Congress of the
United States in 1834. By that time Nancrede had gone on to other interests
and other mysteries. His unofficial role in the Renaut Claim is merely
another indication of his continuing identification with the affairs of the
French community in America, this time as it sought to reach out and
establish itself in western lands.

Meantime Joseph Nancrede had neither forgotten nor abandoned his
interest in the press through which he had also served the Franco-American
community. One of his earliest publications, issued in 1795 during the
partnership of Hall and Nancrede, had been William Cobbett's *"A Little
Plain English"* addressed to the people of the United States on the Treaty and on
the Conduct of the President (Evans No. 28438). Subsequently, at the turn of
the century, when "Peter Porcupine" was a Philadelphia bookseller, he had
purchased from Nancrede English pamphlets as well as Nancrede's
publication on *Helvetic Union and Liberty*. Shortly after, when the
vituperative pamphleteer had set up a bookshop in London's Pall Mall,
Nancrede, seeking maps for the ill-fated Universal Geography of Balloon
Tytler, had contacted him. Now, years later, the journalist William Cobbett,
who had once taught English to French refugees and translated such books
as Martens' *Law of Nations*, was back in America. Between 1817 when he
arrived in New York, and 1819 when, with the bones of Thomas Paine in
his baggage, he returned to England, William Cobbett's path once again
crossed that of Joseph Nancrede. This time the path bore the signpost:
Liberty of the Press.

During his days as a Philadelphia bookseller, the English-born Cobbett
had violently attacked Dr. Benjamin Rush for treating, or mistreating,
yellow fever victims with violent purges and excessive bleedings. Rush sued
for libel; the case came to trial in 1799, and Cobbett, relieved of $5,000,
returned to England. Now that he was back in America, he determined to
obtain reimbursement from the Pennsylvania legislature and at the same
time take a firm stand on the freedom of the press. It was in this endeavor
that he involved his former colleague Joseph Nancrede.[141]

Cobbett's first petition having been rejected as "highly indecorous and
grossly libellous," he tried again, explaining to Nancrede: "It is my earnest
wish, that the assembly should do me justice, not only for my own interests'
sake, but for the sake, too, of the character of free institutions of
government. But, be consequences what they may, I *will* have justice, either
in money or in exposure. I should be the meannest of all mankind, were I to
hold my tongue upon this subject, while I am daily calling upon my
countrymen to *resist* acts of oppression less cruel, and far less base."[142]

Why Nancrede should have been selected as Cobbett's abettor and
been given power of attorney in this case is puzzling until it is recalled that

the two men had much in common, especially that common ground upon which bookseller-publishers in general stand—the liberty of the press. Eight letters from Cobbett to Nancrede and the draft of a letter from Nancrede to Cobbett survive to reanimate not only one of the many litigious episodes of the journalist's life, but the stand taken by Nancrede on such abstract subjects as tyranny and justice.[143] On 16 November 1818, he wrote to Cobbett:

> I will with pleasure receive the power of attorney, as well as do any thing else, within the narrow compass of my abilities to serve you.
>
> I have made many enquiries, and talked with many people, I love justice for the sake of justice; I love it, when it is reparatory of the abuse of power, of tyranny. . . . The general apology for not doing what is evidently right in your case, is that *you were too stiff.*—what has the man to do with the honor of the state of Pennsylvania? was my reply. Does its legislature do justice to none, but to such as are base and cringing, or, are none right but such as are base and cringing? is not right independent of the man who demands it.—It is favours are thus granted, not justice. You denied justice to Mr. Cobbett, because he did you the honor not to sollicit you to do your duty. . . . I wish therefor, that the publick mind may be prepared, by some previous anonymous instruction, by which the people may all know all about the whole transaction. The legislature are not corrupt but they are narrow, uninformed, cowardly of publick reproof, which they think they always expose themselves to, when they vote away any money however justly.

Nancrede added that he had "done something in the case of Napoleon" which he wished Cobbett to examine, "alter it, correct it, both in style & shape, . . . I would be much obliged to you—or if you should think of publishing it." This allusion to his own writing at the time had been prompted by a postscript from Cobbett: "I shall, I think, take up the subject of Napoleon's treatment. It is certainly one of the most atrocious acts of the most atrocious of all tyrants" (11 November 1818). But in a subsequent letter (20 December 1818) Cobbett chided Nancrede: "*One thing at a time*, if we would do things *well*. I will write to you very soon on the subject of *Napoleon*; but, *now* I must confine myself wholly to that of *the Petition*."

Yet Nancrede's two preoccupations at this time did have something in common over and beyond Cobbett's interest in them. Presenting Cobbett's petition to the Pennsylvania Congress advanced in a small way "justice for the sake of justice," as writing of Napoleon castigated "the abuse of power, of tyranny." By the fall of 1819, Cobbett was off to England and "in the rush of affairs after his return . . . this matter [of the petition] probably faded to insignificance."[144] Yet throughout his life Nancrede retained among his papers a six-page document in French entitled "De la liberté de la presse, et de M. William Cobbett."[145] Doubtless composed by Nancrede himself, the essay, with apt quotations from Chateaubriand, is a panegyric of Cobbett and of the freedom of the press. The "something in the case of

Napoleon" that Nancrede produced was apparently not kept by its author. Yet there can be little doubt as to its tenor. The French Revolution that had begun with such high hopes had ended in terror and the fanaticism that repulsed Nancrede. Napoleon, who had come to power as the savior of France, had ended his career as one of "the most atrocious of all tyrants." The only constant through all the years of change had been France itself— and Nancrede's love of France.

Joseph Nancrede remained in Philadelphia until 1825. There were many pursuits and diversions to fill the years of an aging gentleman with a taste for politics and letters. Visits to Mathew Carey, discussions about Joseph Bonaparte, the Renaut Claim or the Cobbett petition certainly occupied him. So too did his correspondence and his correspondents. Among the latter was James Swan, former financier and agent of the French Republic, who remained in debtors' prison twenty-two years because he refused to have what he regarded as an unjust debt paid by his wife. In 1816 Swan wrote to Nancrede from Paris informing him that the "government decidedly put their face against all persons known to have been attached to the Buonaparts or democratic party." [146] Nancrede retained not only his own voluminous correspondence but letters addressed to others. His Collection—for such it was becoming—included a lengthy letter written in November 1818 by Thomas Jefferson to Mathew Carey about a reprint of Hume's *History of England*, a letter perhaps forwarded to Nancrede by Carey or given by Carey to young Henry Nancrede. [147]

Nancrede's children naturally played a part in his Philadelphia life, especially Dr. Joseph G. Nancrede with whom he lived. In 1822 Nancrede solicited the city's vaccine agency for his son in a letter that reveals as much about Nancrede père as about Nancrede fils: "His claims, as a physician, and as one, well versed by a long and assiduous study of the subject of vaccination, in having been for the last five years, and being now the sole vaccinator for this city, will be exhibited by physicians and other gentlemen of Philadelphia:—as a favor, if his qualifications are balanced, he has only to depend on his father's services in Rochambeau's Army, in the U.S. as 2.' Capt. in *Soissonnois* reg^t in which he lost a twin brother, killed by his side, at York-town, on the 12th of Oct 1781, while moving to the 2^d parallel line of the siege; and in his father's attachment and respect as well as his own, for the present chief magistrate of the United States." [148]

While Joseph Nancrede was weaving a legend about the past, the chief magistrate of the United States, James Monroe, was weaving a doctrine for the future. Surely the concept of noncolonization and nonintervention by Europe in the Western Hemisphere must have deeply affected the Franco-American Nancrede, threatening as it did to stop the sometimes easy and sometimes uneasy intercourse that had prevailed in the past between his two countries. In 1824 Lafayette's visit to the United States merely emphasized the lack of harmony between France and America. The same year a personal tragedy occurred that may have played a part in Nancrede's determination to live abroad. On 20 September his young son Henry, who had worked for Mathew Carey, died at Alvarado, Mexico.[149]

Much had happened since the young French soldier had fought at Yorktown. As Boston publisher and more recently as Philadelphia gentleman he had played diverse roles and had a hand in many varied enterprises. Although his passport application described his hair as chestnut and his complexion as fair, Joseph Nancrede was now in his early sixties and according to such a demographic authority as Déparcieux his life expectancy could not be long. Perhaps it was with the thought of eventually dying in his native land that Nancrede sailed for France. Yet he would live another sixteen years, years divided between literary accomplishments and political aspirations. This time he was accompanied not by eight children but by one daughter, Miss Louisa Nancrede. This time the throne of France was occupied not by Emperor Napoleon I but by the Bourbon monarch Charles X. And this time Nancrede carried with him the mementoes of what had been a rich life in the City of Brotherly Love. Although many things had changed, he himself was still seeking to understand and to serve the two countries between which his life had been divided.

Nancrede settled for a time at No. 7 on the Rue des Moineaux—the Street of Sparrows—in Paris.[150] Since at his death in 1841 he would leave to his heirs not only his books and furnishings but an interest in Belgian loans and several canals as well as an abundance of silver money and sound investments, it must be assumed that the gentleman of Philadelphia was fast becoming a Parisian man of property. It is apparent that Joseph Nancrede had not only the inclination but the wherewithal to devote his leisure to the dual preoccupations that had always intrigued him—books and politics. Often those two interests were interrelated.

It was in 1825 that the Baron de Méneval, secretary to Joseph Bonaparte, charged Nancrede with dispatching to the former King of Spain a copy of *Napoléon et la Grande Armée en Russie*. As Méneval wrote to the erstwhile monarch: "M. Nancrède veut bien se charger de vous transmettre un livre où le général Gourgaud et moi avons cherché à venger la mémoire d'un grand homme."[151] Though Napoleon's reputation had undergone a metamorphosis, Nancrede never doubted that he had been a "great man" and it must have interested him to learn that Joseph Bonaparte's reply to Méneval was carried by none other than Lafayette, who had been entertained at Bordentown.[152] Subsequently, Nancrede and Joseph Bonaparte had some lively correspondence about revolution and exile, literature and politics.[153]

Meanwhile Joseph Nancrede was assiduously transforming his own political opinions into literature. In America he had compiled several books—*L'Abeille Françoise, The Forum Orator*—and translated others, the work of Brissot de Warville, the *Projet de Constitution*. He had edited the *Courier de Boston* and revised Fénelon's *Télémaque*. Upon at least one occasion he had produced an original work, the vituperative pamphlet *Les Citoyens Francois*.

Now in Paris in 1825, another original work by Joseph Nancrede was published by J. G. Dentu. Though it was less vituperative and more informative than *Les Citoyens Francois*, this too was a pamphlet, 62 pages long, and this too was anonymous. It concerned France less than it concerned England, but its message was one that the former bookseller-publisher had never ceased to stress—the importance of trade relations between nations and the economic basis of war.

Nancrede's pamphlet made up in the length of its title for the absence of any author's name: *De La Politique de L'Angleterre, de Ses Rapports avec les autres puissances, et des causes qui l'empêchent d'adhérer aux principes de la Sainte-Alliance: Avec Quelques Réflexions Sur les effets que cette politique a dû produire et doit continuer de produire sur les nations commerçantes du monde entier.*[154] According to the preliminary pages, it had been written some eighteen months before in order to clarify the designs of Britain. In it Nancrede expatiated on his fear of England's disavowal of the Holy Alliance, her attitude toward America, and the growth of her naval power. As a commercial market for England, he insisted, the United States was indispensable. Trade and freedom were inextricably interrelated. The old soldier of Yorktown reminded his readers: "The American Revolution taught England that the commerce of a free and independent nation can be ten times more precious than that of the same nation bent under the weight of slavery and colonial monopoly. . . . An independent people offers more advantages to a commercial nation than . . . a colony." As for the French Revolution, England had opposed that only because of her fear that France would become an economic rival.

Nancrede, addressing himself to England, had not forgotten Brissot de Warville. Despite the Monroe Doctrine, the author was writing as a citizen of the world who, for all his distrust of perfidious Albion, was mindful that internationalism must play a role in the politics of 1825.

Between 1825, when *De La Politique de L'Angleterre* was published, and 1841, when Nancrede died, he witnessed many changes in the France that was now his home. The Revolution of 1830 called his former visitor, the Duke of Orléans, to power as Louis Philippe, and the Bourbons gave way to the Orléans monarchy. Paris in the thirties was a vibrant city filled with a million people and as one observer put it, "the industry for the arts of taste and luxury" had developed prodigiously and "the love of equality is stronger here than in America."[155] As for Nancrede, he was living in Batignolles Monceaux, 12 Boulevard Monceau, 17 Rue de l'Ecluse.[156] He could stroll, if he wished, through the Parc Monceau. To visit an increasing number of acquaintances he could take the White Barrier omnibus that stopped periodically at Batignolles. He could also wander along the quais among the bookstalls.

Upon at least one occasion the former bookseller of Boston picked up a volume about the Jesuits to send to Count Roederer, the French politician-economist who had been Joseph Bonaparte's minister of finance at Naples.[157] Much of Nancrede's time was spent now upon literary pursuits. When he was not writing "a long letter" to the *Courier Français*[158] he was translating from English into French an article on the law of primogeniture.[159] Research on the "droit d'aubaine"—the feudal right by which French kings could claim the property of aliens who died in their dominions—took much of his time, for that right involved him personally and prompted him to examine not only questions of Franco-American citizenship but the interpretation of a Franco-American treaty and its limitations.[160]

Researcher and antiquarian, scholar and collector, bibliophile and critic, Joseph Nancrede was indeed becoming a Parisian litterateur. In publications of Americans he took a deep interest, reading and approving a narrative about William Duane's "defensive course"[161] or recommending as "très-brillante et très-vraie" a work by Gallatin on the northeastern boundary.[162] Among Nancrede's papers when he died would be found a document entitled "Autographes de quelques hommes distingués des Etats Unis."[163] At least one letter written in 1838 by a friend to the British politician John Arthur Roebuck suggests that Nancrede might still have had a hand in publishing, for it advises Roebuck: "To have your eloquent pleas printed in Paris you could interview him [Nancrede]."[164] Though there is no evidence that he ever actually resumed his profession of publishing, he developed so many literary connections during his years abroad that he could boast to a friend: "Je vous procurerais toutes les ressources litteraires, et autres. J'en puis commender de puissante et de plus d'un genre."[165]

The "other" connections to which Nancrede alluded were surely political, for when the bibliophile of Paris was not involved in books and pamphlets he was involved in the machinations of government. He was regarded by his son Dr. Joseph G. Nancrede as "puissant, dans un certain quartier,"[166] certainly an allusion to his political interests. But, despite his son's description, Nancrede, once the fomenter of a little consular war in Boston, was not sufficiently "puissant" to become American consul in Paris. A letter of 29 July 1829 to his Philadelphia friend, the typefounder James Ronaldson,[167] reanimates his political hopes and their disappointment and, for all its protestations of reluctance, discloses the ambition and the drive of the Franco-American resident in Paris:

> Since my arrival in this country I have frequently been advised and pressed, by American residents and others travelling in France, . . . to apply for the office of Consul in this city, . . . I have uniformly rejected the proposition. But since the election of General Jackson, they have been more pressing, and have got from me a promise that I would write to some friend to make the application. I

have thought of the subject for some time and concluded to sollicit your advice; and if you approved of the application, to assist me with your support.

I feel the conscience of possessing the qualifications necessary to discharge the duties of an office, . . . the main requisite for which, next to integrity, is a general acquaintance with the institutions, laws, spirit and purpose of our countrymen, and above all, principles, by a constant adherence to which, our country can arrive at the degree of prosperity and power, which its information, industry and courage have assigned it.

My early services in the revolution . . . might have furnished some claims to the notice of former administrations, from whose favors, on account of my political obduracy, I have ever been excluded—and, on the other hand my personal respect for General Jackson, and support of his election in 1823 & 4 . . . may be produced, to shew that I was his friend, before he was president.

. . . If I may obtain the office, by fair and honorable means, I will endeavor to discharge its duties, as becomes a man who is attached to the honor and respectability of his country, and support of its administration, that is to say, with correctness and integrity. . . .

As a result of this importuning, James Ronaldson wrote as follows to Andrew Jackson, President of the United States:

A perusal of the enclosed will give a clearer view of my friend Nancredes application, then [*sic*] might be done by any explanation of mine in the absence of his letter. I knew Mr Nancrede and that he is governed by the strictest principles of integrity, and most ardent feelings in favor of every thing that contributes to the independence of the United States and the happiness of her citizens. My good opinion of Mr Nancrede is founded on an intimate acquaintance of twenty years. He is one of the officers [*sic*] of Rochambeau's army, that after the Revolutionary war returned to the U States and adopted it for his country and except Genl Lafayette, I believe little notice has been taken of the French officers who served in the Revolution.

I think it reasonable to presume the appointment of Mr Nancrede would be gratifying to the liberal thinkers in France, while at the same time it would be kindly felt by the Bourbons as a compliment to them.

Mr Nancrede besides being a man of business, is a classical schollar intimate with the literary men of France; and would be most usefull in correcting the misrepresentation, illiberal writers may put forth against us.

But what is of most essential importance to us is his intelligence, and extensive knowledge of the world, combined with his strong American attachment; he would keep the Government fully & correctly advised of all that was goeing on; that it was the interest of the Government to know or was interested in. . . . I do not apply for his appointment as a favor to me, . . . but as the friend of the administration I recommend the appointment on account of my belief that should the office be vacant there are very few men to be found who would fill it with so much advantage to the nation's honor and interest. . . . [168]

In further support of the appointment Nancrede's son Dr. Joseph addressed a letter to the Chief Magistrate in which he declared that his father was "perfectly conversant with the nature of our political Institutions, as well as our commercial interests, and to an enlightened & liberal mind, adds a thorough & familiar acquaintance with the French & English languages. Besides . . . a residence of some years in Paris, has made him acquainted with the nature of the duties of the consulship."[169]

Despite such strong endorsements, Isaac Coxe Barnet of New Jersey continued as Agent for Claims and for Seamen, and Consul in Paris. Although he never became American consul in Paris, Nancrede did not lose his taste for the stew of politics and the garnish of diplomacy. The matter of claims of soldiers in the American Revolution, especially of those no longer resident in the United States, engaged his attention. In connection with their requests for pensions and land grants he corresponded with Lafayette whose reply was duly kept among Nancrede's papers.[170]

Franco-American relations naturally affected him deeply: the vacillations of Louis Philippe's government over the so-called Spoliation Claims; Jackson's suggestion of reprisals by the United States on French property in America. It was not until 1836, when Nancrede was seventy-five, that the matter was finally settled. By that time Egalité's eldest son was securely ensconced on the Orléans throne. Nancrede later took occasion to write a letter to Louis Philippe recalling the time, forty years before, when he had honored the bookseller with a visit in Boston.[171]

Like most aging men Joseph Nancrede must have thought much of the past but this did not prevent his keeping time with the present. Although his relations with his family were obviously not close—after his death his son would recall that his father "lived some years in a state of irritation against his family"[172]—nonetheless he must have rejoiced at his son Joseph's Memorial to Congress in behalf of vaccination against smallpox,[173] and he must have been deeply grieved by the death of his son John Gardner in 1831 and the death of Charles William five years later.[174] He could leave Boulevard Monceau No. 12, near the Clichy Barrier, to visit his friends, enjoying a little music and more conversation. He could invite the Roman Catholic Bishop John Joseph Hughes to dinner. He could pursue his connections and the connections of his connections. He could attend the annual celebration of America's Independence Day at dinner on the Rue de Richelieu, and he could visit the Museum of Natural History in Paris to which his old friend Ronaldson sent grains from America.[175]

For several months in the early 1830s Nancrede was in England, where his daughter—probably a natural daughter—was married.[176] Some years' later, in 1838, he crossed the Channel again, this time to use his political connections in the service of a friend.[177]

The friend was Louis-Joseph Papineau, former speaker of the legislative assembly of Lower Canada, a man regarded by some as the head of the French Canadian party, by others as a radical agitator. Papineau had denounced the British government, attended the celebrated meeting at St.

Charles at which armed rebellion was decided upon, and after a warrant had been issued for his arrest for high treason had fled to the United States. There he had been for a time the guest of Dr. Joseph G. Nancrede in Philadelphia. The interest of the Nancrede family in French-Canadian affairs in general and in the Papineaus and their cause in particular had been of long standing. Now, in 1839, the French-Canadian Papineau, age 53, sought refuge in Paris where he found a warm welcome from the 78-year-old French-American Nancrede.

In June 1838 Nancrede had written to Papineau assuring him that the "triumph of your cause has been merely delayed" and promising him "secure asylum. . . . I offer you the consolations of a man whose life has been filled with troubles with disasters and with catastrophes of more than one kind." Nancrede offered still more: the intercession of "S.M. le roi des Francais!!— Cette intercession Monsieur, j'ose vous assurer que vous pourriez l'obtenir." [178] Moreover, a "Canadian would find himself more at home in France than anywhere else" and "on peut toujours consulter l'histoire contemporaine avec profit." [179]

By the following March, Papineau's "doating, dozing but sincere friend" Joseph Nancrede welcomed the exile to Paris, inviting him to share his home—an invitation which Papineau declined—and assembling a little reunion to greet the newcomer. [180] Along with the welcome Nancrede provided advice, lined up his various connections, planned visits to Cass and Hume, and reveled in his role of political seer and manipulator. [181] He reveled too in a Paris in ferment with parliamentary agitation and hatred of Britain, where journals were constantly read and as constantly discussed and where the songs of Béranger were sung.

In 1840, Napoleon's remains were returned to the city and transferred with pomp to the Hotel des Invalides. Nancrede, hearing of or perhaps seeing the ceremony, must have thought of the long history he himself had lived. He could look back to the American Revolution in which he had served and to the French Revolution he had at first supported, to the Terror and fanaticism he had abhorred, to the empire and defeat of the man whose body was now interred in the Invalides.

It was an extremely cold winter, that winter of 1840 in Paris, especially for a man nearly eighty. Taking the omnibus at the White Barrier that left St. Sulpice every ten minutes, Papineau visited his old friend at Batignolles, finding him as the new year advanced, "toujours malade," "un peu mieux," "languissant". [182] On 4 December 1841 Nancrede wrote a short note: "Je prie M Pappineau [*sic*] de vouloir bien passer chez moi le plutot qu'il pourra." [183] It was doubtless his last. By 15 December Nancrede was dead. Two days later his obsequies took place. After a dignified service in the Batignolles church, the American consul and some fifteen or sixteen other gentlemen accompanied the body to the cemetery near Clichy. [184]

The day before he was buried, Nancrede's will[185] was read—the will in which he disposed of his earthly possessions, his money, his investments, and his property, leaving to his surviving children and grandchildren the accumulation of a long lifetime. For the recorder of that life one bequest transcends all others in interest, that by which Joseph Nancrede left to his French-Canadian friend Louis-Joseph Papineau his books and papers. For these were the testimonials to his intellectual life and to his lasting achievements.

Papineau proved a faithful legatee. Although he may have complied with the request of Nancrede's son Joseph to "destroy as much as possible the traces of his unhappy family relations,"[186] the French-Canadian guarded his legacy well. In 1844 he wrote to his wife: "J'ai acheté des livres et fait relier un nombre considérable des brochures que ma laissées Mr. Nancrède. Je paie des copistes pour m'aider à hâter le beau le consolateur travail que je fais aux archives."[187] And when his own exile was ended, Papineau carried back to Canada the bulk of Nancrede's correspondence, a correspondence that eventually found its way to the Public Archives of Canada where it provided the materials to illuminate a life.

That life had been as long as it had been unusual. Nancrede's son may have been astute when he wrote that his father had had "at his disposition all the elements of happiness" but had "thrown them far from him without wishing to enjoy them."[188] But if accomplishment is cause for happiness, then Joseph Nancrede must have found gratification in the most significant aspects of his life. He had observed America between a Crèvecoeur and a de Tocqueville. From the American Revolution to the Monroe Doctrine he had watched and participated in the development of a new society. And later he had been, as his acquaintance Duane put it, "a calm observer in a foreign land of all that passes in your adopted country."[189] His son, writing in 1840, had unwittingly written his epitaph when he remarked of his father: "He has lived long enough to know the injustices, not only of despotic governments, but . . . even in the so-called free government of my country."[190] Yorktown and Harvard, Citizen Genêt and Joseph Bonaparte, Napoleon and Louis Philippe, Isaiah Thomas and Mathew Carey—all had played a part in his varied career.

Nancrede's death certificate describes him as a "rentier,"[191] but surely he had been less of a "rentier" than a man of books, and the most sparkling facet of his many-faceted life had been his career in books. All his life had been bookish, for Joseph Nancrede had ever turned to his pen for self-expression and to his books for self-education. Yet it is especially for that Boston decade when he had published and sold books that he must be remembered. His early Franco-American newspaper, the *Courier de Boston*; the French textbook he compiled, the *Abeille Françoise* were signal achievements. But it was as bookseller-publisher during ten years of crisis in

Franco-American affairs that he most effectively interpreted the one country to the other. De Tocqueville had written: "There is . . . a moment at which the literary genius of democratic nations has its confluence with that of aristocracies, and both seek to establish their joint sway over the human mind. Such epochs are transient, but very brilliant: they are fertile without exuberance, and animated without confusion." In that moment of literary history Joseph Nancrede came most alive. Indeed, as a Franco-American publisher-bookseller he helped create that moment. The confluence of the two countries was brief but exhilarating. It owed much to that citizen of two worlds, Joseph Nancrede.

Notes

1. Extrait des registres de baptemes, mariages, et sépultures de la paroisse d'Héricy, du diocese du Sens Election de Melun, généralité de Paris, pour . . . 1761; Paul Joseph Guérard, Acte de Naissance, Archives Départementales de Seine-et-Marne; Guérard Genealogy, Katharine de Nancrede Pond Papers (Collection of Prof. Allen J. Barthold, Stroudsburg, Pa.)

2. *Les Combattants Français de la Guerre Américaine 1778–1783 Listes établies d'après les documents . . . aux Archives Nationales et aux Archives du Ministère de la Guerre. 58th Congress, 2d Session, Senate Document No. 77* (Washington, 1905), pp. 270, 278; Howard C. Rice, Jr., to Madeleine B. Stern, Brattleboro, Vt., 19 Jan., 23 March 1973.

3. Joseph Nancrede to Sir, Philadelphia, 28 March 1822; Nancrede to James Ronaldson, Paris, 29 July 1829; Joseph G. Nancrede to Andrew Jackson, Philadelphia, 22 Sept. 1829 (National Archives).

4. Allen J. Barthold, "A Propos du Rédacteur du 'Courier de Boston' Paul-Joseph Guérard de Nancrède," *Le Messager de New-York*, 4 (15 June 1932), 10.

5. Paul Joseph Guérard de Nancrede, Passport, 13 Oct. 1785 (Prof. Allen J. Barthold Collection).

6. College Records, 3 (5 May 1778–31 Aug. 1795), p. 299 (Harvard University Library, Archives).

7. J. P. Brissot de Warville, *New Travels in the United States of America 1788* (Cambridge, Mass., 1964), pp. 94–95.

8. Charles Hart Handschin, *The Teaching of Modern Languages in the United States* (Washington, 1913), p. 21.

9. Francis Baylies, *Eulogy on the Hon. Benjamin Russell* (Boston, 1845), p. 49; Donald C. McKay, *The United States and France* (Cambridge, Mass., 1951), pp. 79, 82.

10. Records of the College Faculty, 6 (1788–1797), p. 244; 7 (1797–1806), pp. 46, 64 (Harvard University Library, Archives).

11. Jared B. Flagg, *The Life and Letters of Washington Allston* (New York, 1892), p. 34.

12. College Records, 4 (23 Sept. 1795–1 Oct. 1810), p. 490 (Harvard University Library, Archives).

13. John Clarke, *Letters to a Student in the University of Cambridge, Massachusetts* (Boston, 1796), pp. 74–79.

14. Joseph de Nancrede to the Gentlemen of the Corporation of Harvard College in the University of Cambridge, Cambridge, Nov. 1791, Harvard College Papers 3 (1785–1796), p. 61.

15. *Massachusetts Centinel*, 17 Sept. 1788.

16. Brissot de Warville, *New Travels in the United States*, p. 84.

17. J. P. Brissot de Warville and Etienne Clavière, *Considerations on the Relative Situation of France, and the United States of America* (London, 1788), pp. 322–323.

18. Allen J. Barthold, "French Journalists in the United States 1780–1800," *The Franco–American Review*, 1 (1937), p. 219; *Massachusetts Centinel*, 11 Feb. 1789.

19. J. Nancrede to John Adams, Boston, 4 Jan. 1789, Adams Papers, Microfilm (Columbia University Library).

20. *Massachusetts Centinel*, 4 Feb. 1789; George Parker Winship, "Two or Three Boston Papers," *PBSA*, 14 (1920), 60–61.

21. *Courier de Boston*, 1–26 (23 April–15 Oct. 1789). For studies of the weekly see Allen J. Barthold, *History of the French Newspaper Press in America 1780–1790* (Ph.D. Dissertation Yale University, 1931); Samuel J. Marino, *The French-Refugee Newspapers and Periodicals in the United States, 1789–1825* (Diss. University of Michigan, 1962).

22. Isaiah Thomas, *The History of Printing in America* (Barre, Mass., 1970), p. 178.

23. John Sylvester J. Gardiner, *A Sermon preached . . . on the death of the Right Reverend Samual Parker, D.D.* (Boston, 1804).

24. [Pierre de Sales La Terrière], "The Harvard Medical School in 1788–89," *Boston Medical and Surgical Journal*, 162 (1910), 520.

25. Nancrede Genealogical Papers, Katharine de Nancrede Pond Papers (Prof. Allen J. Barthold Collection, Stroudsburg, Pa.).

26. Joseph Nancrede and family to Joseph G. Nancrede, Boston, 30 Aug.–3 Sept. 1803, Monk Family Papers (Public Archives of Canada).

27. Fernard Baldensperger, "Le premier 'instructeur' de français à Harvard College: Joseph Nancrède," *Harvard Advocate*, 5 Dec. 1913, p. 77.

28. For Nancrede's appearance see copy of his passport certified Paris, 15 June 1810, Katharine de Nancrede Pond Papers (Prof. Allen J. Barthold Collection).

29. [P. de Sales La Terrière], "The Harvard Medical School in 1788–89," *Boston Medical and Surgical Journal*, 162 (1910), 520–521.

30. [Thomas Cogan], *Letters to William Wilberforce, Esq. M.P. on the doctrine of Hereditary Depravity* (Boston, 1799), Nancrede's advertisement, pp. 126–127.

31. Joseph Nancrede, Copy of Naturalization Paper, Boston, 19 Feb. 1799, Katharine de Nancrede Pond Papers (Prof. Allen J. Barthold Collection); William E. Lind, National Archives and Records Service, to Madeleine B. Stern, Washington, 30 March 1973.

32. *Massachusetts Centinel,* 25 June 1788.

33. Citizen F. Lequoy to Edmond Charles Genêt, Boston, 17 Nov. 1793; Joseph Nancrede to E. C. Genêt, Boston, 19 Sept. 1793, Genêt Papers (Library of Congress).

34. Theodore Charles Mozard, Interpreter's Commission to Nancrede, July 1796, L. J. Papineau Papers (Public Archives of Canada).

35. Repeated in the 19 June 1788 issue.

36. Clifford K. Shipton, *Isaiah Thomas Printer, Patriot and Philanthropist 1749– 1831* (Rochester, [1948]), p. 51.

37. Letter in American Antiquarian Society. See also Madeleine B. Stern, "Brissot de Warville and the Franco-American Press," *SB* 29 (1975).

38. Jacob Blanck, *Bibliography of American Literature* (New Haven, 1955), I, Nos. 882 and 887; Robert F. Durden, "Joel Barlow in the French Revolution," *The William and Mary Quarterly,* 8 (1951), 327–354.

39. J. P. Brissot de Warville, *A Discourse upon the Question, Whether the King shall be tried?* (Boston, 1791), p. 28. The advertisement of the translator appears on pp. iii–iv.

40. J. P. Brissot de Warville to Nancrede, Paris, 23 July [?] 1792, L. J. Papineau Papers (Public Archives of Canada). This and all subsequent translations are by Madeleine B. Stern.

41. In Massachusetts Historical Society. See also Sinclair H. Hitchings, "Joseph Belknap's Printing in Boston," *Printing & Graphic Arts,* 6 (1958), 100.

42. P. J. G. de Nancrede, *L'Abeille Françoise, ou Nouveau Recueil, De morceaux brillans, des auteurs François les plus celebres* (Boston, 1792), pp. [3], 5–7, 10–11.

43. Meade Minnigerode, *Jefferson Friend of France 1793—The Career of Edmond Charles Genêt* (New York and London, 1928), p. 238.

44. Nancrede to Citizen Genêt, Boston, 19, 20, 30 Sept., 3, 9 Oct. 1793; Genêt to Nancrede, New York, 9, 23 Oct. 1793; Citizen F. Lequoy to Genêt, Boston, 17 Nov. 1793, Genêt Papers (Library of Congress).

45. One copy is in the New York Public Library; another is enclosed in Correspondance Consulaire, Boston, 3 (1793–1795), Archives Diplomatiques (Ministère des Affaires Etrangères, Paris) where Dannery's correspondence is also deposited.

46. Nancrede to Isaiah Thomas, Boston, 2 Feb. 1797 (American Antiquarian Society).

47. Nancrede to Joseph Dennie, Boston, 6 July 1797, Joseph Dennie Papers (Houghton Library, Harvard University).

48. Nancrede to Louis Philippe, [Paris], 25 June 1838, L. J. Papineau Papers (Public Archives of Canada). See also Francis Baylies, *Eulogy on the Hon. Benjamin Russell . . . March 10, 1845* (Boston, 1845), pp. 15–16; Jane Marsh Parker, "Louis Philippe in the United States," *The Century Magazine,* 62 (1901), 756.

49. Gustave de Montjoie to MM d'Orléans, Boston, 20 Oct. 1797, L. J. Papineau Papers (Public Archives of Canada).

50. *Joseph Nancrede's Catalogue of Books in the Various Branches of Literature; Lately Imported from London, Dublin, Paris, and other Capitals of Europe* [Boston, 1796].

51. Robert Southey, *Poems* (Boston, 1799), advertisement at end.

52. James Henry Bernardin de Saint-Pierre, *Studies of Nature* (Worcester, 1797), advertisement at end of Vol. I.

53. Joseph Nancrede, *Catalogue of Books Just Imported from London* (Boston, 1798), pp. 65–66.

54. Kenneth Roberts and Anna M. Roberts, *Moreau de St. Mery's American Journey* [*1793–1798*] (Garden City, N. Y., 1947), p. 181. See also Bernard Faÿ, *L'Esprit Révolutionnaire en France et aux Etats-Unis a la Fin du XVIIIe Siècle* (Paris, 1925), pp. 269–270.

55. Moreau de Saint-Méry to Joseph Nancrede, Philadelphia, 11 March 1795; see also 23 Jan., 4 March 1795, 21 April 1797, L. J. Papineau Papers (Public Archives of Canada).

56. William Cobbett, Philadelphia, Booksellers Ledger, 1796–1800, p. 84 (American Antiquarian Society).

57. Nancrede to Dennie, Boston, 8 Nov. 1796, Joseph Dennie Papers (Houghton Library, Harvard University).

58. Ibid., 8 Feb. 1797.

59. Ibid., 14 March, 6 July 1797.

60. *Salem Gazette*, 5 Oct. 1802. Three years later Blunt threw a skillet at his engraver James Akin who retaliated by publishing a caricature of that act entitled "Infuriated Despondency" which was reproduced upon English crockery, "pitchers, wash bowls and chamber vessels." See John J. Currier, *History of Newburyport, Mass. 1764–1909* (Newburyport, 1909), II, 372.

61. Madeleine B. Stern, "Saint-Pierre in America: Joseph Nancrede and Isaiah Thomas," *PBSA*, 68 (1974), 312–325.

62. *Joseph Nancrede's Catalogue of Books in the Various Branches of Literature; Lately Imported from London, Dublin, Paris, and other Capitals of Europe* [Boston, 1796], p. 33.

63. John Tebbel, *A History of Book Publishing in the United States* (New York and London, 1972), I, 188.

64. 29 Nov., 1, 22 Dec. 1796, 27, 30 Jan., 2 Feb. 1797.

65. Nancrede to Timothy Pickering, Boston, 13 May 1796, Timothy Pickering Papers (Massachusetts Historical Society).

66. Pickering to Nancrede, Philadelphia, 7 June 1796, L. J. Papineau Papers (Public Archives of Canada).

67. James Henry Bernardin de Saint-Pierre, *Studies of Nature* (Worcester, 1797), I, i–iii.

68. Joseph Nancrede, *Catalogue of Books Just Imported from London* (Boston, 1798), pp. 68–69.

69. Moreau de Saint-Méry to Joseph Nancrede, Philadelphia, 21 April 1797, L. J. Papineau Papers (Public Archives of Canada).

70. *The Diary of William Bentley, D.D. Pastor of the East Church Salem, Massachusetts* (Salem, 1907), II, 235.

71. Nancrede to Dennie, Boston, 8 Feb., 6 July 1797.

72. *Independent Chronicle*, 17, 31 Aug. 1797.

73. Joseph Nancrede, *Catalogue of Books Just Imported from London* (Boston, 1798), p. [2].

74. Donald C. McKay, *The United States and France* (Cambridge, Mass., 1951), p. 83.

75. In the American Antiquarian Society.

76. Jacques Mallet Du Pan, *The History of the Destruction of the Helvetic Union and Liberty* (Boston, 1799); Evans Nos. 35765–66.

77. John Jay to Nancrede, Albany, 22 Nov. 1799, L. J. Papineau Papers (Public Archives of Canada).

78. [Thomas Cogan], *Letters to William Wilberforce, Esq. M.P. on the doctrine of Hereditary Depravity* (Boston, 1799), advertisement at end, pp. 126–127.

79. Evans No. 35160; R. R. Palmer, *The Age of the Democratic Revolution: A Political History of Europe and America* (Princeton, N. J., 1964), pp. 318, 541.

80. Evans No. 37940; [Thomas Cogan], *Letters to William Wilberforce, Esq. M.P. on the doctrine of Hereditary Depravity* (Boston, 1799), advertisement at end.

81. Evans No. 38013; John Tebbel, *A History of Book Publishing in the United States* (New York and London, 1972), I, 198.

82. *The Pulpit Orator; Being a new Selection of Eloquent Pulpit Discourses, accompanied with Observations on the Composition and Delivery of Sermons* (Boston, 1804), pp. iv, [132].

83. Evans No. 32415; Joseph Nancrede, *Catalogue of Books Just Imported from London* (Boston, 1798), p. 70.

84. Evans Nos. 37334, 37804, 38435.

85. Evans No. 39111; Joseph Nancrede, *Fixed-Price-Catalogue Of a large collection of Books* (Boston, [1803?]), p. 21.

86. Clifford K. Shipton, *Isaiah Thomas Printer, Patriot and Philanthropist 1749–1831* (Rochester, [1948]), p. 51.

87. Manning & Loring, Invoice to Joseph Nancrede, 11 April 1799, L. J. Papineau Papers (Public Archives of Canada).

88. Tebbel, I, 165.

89. Howard Mumford Jones, "The Importation of French Books in Philadelphia, 1750–1800," *Modern Philology*, 32 (1934), 176–177.

90. *Moreau de St. Méry's American Journey*, p. 203.

91. François de Salignac de La Motte Fénelon, *The Adventures of Telemachus* (Philadelphia, 1797), I, advertisement at end.

92. *Books Published by Joseph Nancrede* [Boston, 1797?] (Rare Book Division, Library of Congress).

93. G. Thomas Tanselle, "Author and Publisher in 1800: Letters of Royall Tyler and Joseph Nancrede," *Harvard Library Bulletin*, 15 (1967), 129–139.

94. Madeleine B. Stern, "A Salem Author and a Boston Publisher: James Tytler and Joseph Nancrede," *The New England Quarterly*, 47 (1974), 290–301.

95. Nancrede and Barnard B. Macanulty to Sir, Boston, 1 Sept. 1801, printed circular (American Antiquarian Society). For Tytler see also Sir James Fergusson, *Balloon Tytler* (London, [1972]), pp. 142–145.

96. Harvard College Records, 4 (1802), p. 638 (Harvard University Library, Archives).

97. Duane to Nancrede, Philadelphia, 30 Sept. 1801, in *Proceedings of the Massachusetts Historical Society*, Second Series, 20 (1906), 268–270.

98. *The Diary of William Bentley, D.D. Pastor of the East Church Salem, Massachusetts* (Salem, 1907), II, 410.

99. Cobbett to Nancrede, Pall Mall, 22 March 1802, L. J. Papineau Papers (Public Archives of Canada).

100. Louis Philippe d'Orléans to Nancrede, Twickenham, 29 July 1802, L. J. Papineau Papers (Public Archives of Canada).

101. Joseph Nancrede and Barnard B. Macanulty, *Proposals for Publishing, by Subscription, A New System of Geography, Ancient and Modern. By J. Tytler* (Salem, June 1802).

102. Joseph Nancrede and B. B. Macanulty, *Review of Pinkerton's Modern Geography* (Boston, 1 Dec. 1802) (Boston Athenæum).

103. *Diary of William Bentley*, III, 69.

104. *Columbian Centinel*, 21 Jan. 1804; *Independent Chronicle*, 23 Jan. 1804.

105. *Columbian Centinel*, 8, 15, 18 Feb. 1804.

106. A. Growoll, *Book-Trade Bibliography in the United States in the XIXth Century . . . to which is added A Catalogue of all the Books printed in the United States . . . January 1804* (New York, 1939).

107. Joseph Nancrede, Permis de Séjour, 1804, Katharine de Nancrede Pond Papers (Prof. Allen J. Barthold Collection).

108. Joseph Jérôme de Français de Lalande to Nancrede, Paris, 15 June [1804] (Boston Public Library).

109. Hoefer, *Nouvelle Biographie Générale*, XLI, 811; Maurice Levaillant, *The Passionate Exiles: Madame de Stael and Madame Récamier* (New York, 1958), pp. 15–17, 70–71.

110. Desjardins to Nancrede, Paris, 7 March 1805, L. J. Papineau Papers (Public Archives of Canada).

111. Jomini to Nancrede, 18 June 1810 and n.d., L. J. Papineau Papers (Public Archives of Canada).

112. Louis-Alexandre Berthier, Prince of Neuchatel to Monsieur [Joseph Nancrede], Paris, 26 April 1811, L. J. Papineau Papers (Public Archives of Canada).

113. *Moreau de St. Méry's American Journey*, p. 181. The year of the meeting is given incorrectly as 1813.

114. "Joel Barlow," *D.A.B.*; James Woodress, *A Yankee's Odyssey: The Life of Joel Barlow* (Philadelphia and New York, [1958]), pp. 286–290.

115. Barlow to Du Ponceau, Paris, 23 Feb. 1812, L. J. Papineau Papers (Public Archives of Canada).

116. Francis C. Haber, "David Bailie Warden, A Bibliographical Sketch of America's Cultural Ambassador in France, 1804–1845," *Bulletin de L'Institut Français de Washington*, N.S. 3 (Dec. 1953), pp. 75–118; David Bailie Warden to

James Monroe ["Warden's precious confessions"], Paris, 8 July 1812, L. J. Papineau Papers (Public Archives of Canada).

117. Lee to Sir, Paris, 4 July 1812, L. J. Papineau Papers (Public Archives of Canada).

118. Russell E. Durning, *Margaret Fuller, Citizen of the World An Intermediary between European and American Literatures* (Heidelberg, 1969), p. 53; John L. Earl III, "Talleyrand in Philadelphia, 1794–1796," *The Pennsylvania Magazine of History and Biography*, 91 (1967), 84, 291; A. Levasseur, *Lafayette in America in 1824 and 1825* (Philadelphia, 1829), I, 146.

119. Philadelphia Directory entries for J. G. Nancrede, M.D., Nicholas C. Nancrede, and Joseph Nancrede (1816–1824), courtesy Ellen S. DeMarinis, Reference Librarian, University of Pennsylvania Library.

120. Mathew Carey to J. Nancrede Book Store, Receipted Invoice, Boston, Aug. 1796, Mathew Carey Collection, Receipts 8 No. 2911 (American Antiquarian Society).

121. Messrs. M. Carey & Son to J. Nancrede, Receipt, Philadelphia, 8 Nov. 1817, 21 Jan., 10 July 1818, Mathew Carey Collection, Receipts 30 No. 4927, 31 No. 5428 (American Antiquarian Society).

122. Peter J. Parker, Chief of Manuscripts, The Historical Society of Pennsylvania, to Madeleine B. Stern, Philadelphia, 11 May 1973.

123. M. Carey & Son, Certificate, Philadelphia, 4 Dec. 1820, L. J. Papineau Papers (Public Archives of Canada).

124. Receipts 27 No. 3321, 29 No. 4534, Mathew Carey Collection (American Antiquarian Society).

125. Nancrede to Carey, Wednesday afternoon; Philadelphia, 6 Sept. 1820 (Historical Society of Pennsylvania).

126. Nancrede to Carey, 5 July 1819 (Historical Society of Pennsylvania).

127. Mathew Carey, *Autobiography [1835–37]*, p. 101. See also *Addresses of The Philadelphia Society for the Promotion of National Industry* (Philadelphia, 1820), pp. 99–155; [Mathew Carey], *Auto Biographical Sketches* (Philadelphia, [1829]), I, 46–47; Kenneth Wyer Rowe, *Mathew Carey A Study in American Economic Development* (Baltimore, 1933), p. 74.

128. Nancrede to James Ronaldson, Paris, 29 July 1829 (National Archives).

129. Matthieu-Maximilien-Prosper de Lesseps to Monsieur [Nancrede], Philadelphia, 24 Jan. 1820, L. J. Papineau Papers (Public Archives of Canada).

130. D. C. Swan to Nancrede, Paris, 20 Dec. 1815, L. J. Papineau Papers (Public Archives of Canada).

131. Nancrede to Pierre Samuel Dupont de Nemours, Philadelphia, 20 June 1816 (Eleutherian Mills Historical Library).

132. Jouy to Monsieur [Nancrede], 10 April 1819, L. J. Papineau Papers (Public Archives of Canada).

133. Joseph G. Nancrede, *An Address delivered before The New England Society of Philadelphia, at their Semi-Annual Meeting, May 1, 1820* (Philadelphia, 1820), p. 15.

134. Joseph Bonaparte, *Lettres D'Exil Inédites . . . Publiées par Hector Fleischmann* (Paris, 1912), pp. 73–75.

135. *The Story of Champ d'Asile as told by two of the Colonists* (Dallas, [1937]), p. 7; [Just Jean Etienne Roy], *The Adventures of a French Captain* (New York, [1876]), pp. 43–45, 53, 59.

136. *American State Papers. Documents, Legislative and Executive, of the Congress of the United States, From the First Session of the Fourteenth to the First Session of the Eighteenth Congress, Inclusive: commencing December 4, 1815, and ending May 27, 1824* (Washington, 1834), 30, Public Lands, p. 281 No. 255; B. P. Poore, *A descriptive catalogue of the government publications of the United States, September 5, 1774–March 4, 1881* (Washington, 1885), pp. 119, 198; Sabin No. 69604.

137. Baldwin to Nancrede, Pittsburgh, 6 July 1816, L. J. Papineau Papers (Public Archives of Canada).

138. Seth Hunt to Nancrede, New York, 25 Feb. 1816, L. J. Papineau Papers (Public Archives of Canada).

139. Barlow to Nancrede, New York, 20 July 1816, L. J. Papineau Papers (Public Archives of Canada).

140. Baldwin to Nancrede, Pittsburgh, 6 July 1816, L. J. Papineau Papers (Public Archives of Canada).

141. Mary Elizabeth Clark, *Peter Porcupine in America: The Career of William Cobbett, 1792–1800* (Philadelphia, 1939), pp. 120–123.

142. Cobbett to Nancrede, Hyde Park, 11 Nov. 1818, Charles Roberts Autograph Letters Collection (Haverford College Library).

143. All the letters are in the Charles Roberts Autograph Collection, Haverford College Library.

144. *Peter Porcupine in America*, pp. 122–123.

145. In L. J. Papineau Papers (Public Archives of Canada).

146. Swan to Nancrede, Paris, 23 Feb. 1816, L. J. Papineau Papers (Public Archives of Canada).

147. Thomas Jefferson to Carey, Monticello, 22 Nov. 1818, holograph, L. J. Papineau Papers (Public Archives of Canada); Julian P. Boyd to Madeleine B. Stern, 24 April, 3 May 1973.

148. Nancrede to Sir, Philadelphia, 28 March 1822 (National Archives).

149. Nancrede Genealogical Documents, Katharine de Nancrede Pond Papers (Prof. Allen J. Barthold Collection).

150. *L'Intermédiaire des Chercheurs et Curieux* 11 (1878), cols. 202–203.

151. *Mémoires et Corrrespondance Politique et Militaire du Roi Joseph* 10 (1854), p. 283.

152. Joseph Bonaparte, *Lettres D'Exil Inédites* (Paris, 1912), p. 76.

153. Bonaparte to Nancrede, Point Breeze, 29 Feb. 1826, 17 June 1831; Nancrede to Bonaparte (draft), Paris, 25 March 1831, L. J. Papineau Papers (Public Archives of Canada).

154. Copy in Bibliothèque Nationale, Paris.

155. L. J. Papineau to Mrs. Papineau, Paris, 15 March 1839, L. J. Papineau Papers (Public Archives of Canada).

156. Mme. Nicole Felkay, Conservateur d'Archives de Paris, to Madeleine B.

Stern, Paris, 31 Jan. [1973]; Joseph G. Nancrede to Louis-Joseph Papineau, Philadelphia, 10 Aug. 1838 (Archives Nationales, Quebec).

157. Nancrede to Pierre Louis, Count Roederer (draft), 31 March 1826, L. J. Papineau Papers (Public Archives of Canada).

158. Ibid.

159. Louis Stanislas Cécile Xavier de Girardin to Joseph Nancrede, Paris, 18 March 1826, L. J. Papineau Papers (Public Archives of Canada).

160. Maurice Duval to Nancrede, 15 May 1830, L. J. Papineau Papers (Public Archives of Canada).

161. William J. Duane to Nancrede, Philadelphia, 12 June 1840, L. J. Papineau Papers (Public Archives of Canada).

162. Lactance Papineau, Journal, Archives Provinciales du Québec (Courtesy Ruth White, Vancouver, Canada).

163. In L. J. Papineau Papers (Public Archives of Canada).

164. Louis-Joseph Papineau to Roebuck, 28 and 30 Sept. 1838, John Arthur Roebuck Papers (Public Archives of Canada).

165. Nancrede to Papineau, [Paris], 29 June 1838, L. J. Papineau Papers (Public Archives of Canada).

166. Joseph G. Nancrede to Papineau, Philadelphia, 10 Aug. 1838 (Archives Nationales, Quebec).

167. In National Archives.

168. Ronaldson to Jackson, Philadelphia, 20 Sept. 1829 (National Archives).

169. Joseph G. Nancrede to Jackson, Philadelphia, 22 Sept. 1829 (National Archives).

170. Lafayette to Nancrede, Paris, 12 March 1829, L. J. Papineau Papers (Public Archives of Canada).

171. Nancrede to Louis Philippe, [Paris], 25 June 1838, L. J. Papineau Papers (Public Archives of Canada).

172. Joseph G. Nancrede to Papineau, Philadelphia, I Feb. 1842 (Archives Nationales, Quebec).

173. Joseph G. Nancrede, *Memorial* (Washington, 1828) 20th Congress, 1st Session, HR Doc. No. 66.

174. Nancrede Genealogical Documents, Katharine de Nancrede Pond Papers (Prof. Allen J. Barthold Collection).

175. For these activities see Invitation to Joseph Nancrede to attend 4th of July Dinner, Paris, 29 June 1829, L. J. Papineau Papers (Public Archives of Canada); Muséum d'Histoire Naturelle to James Ronaldson, Paris, 6 Aug. 1840, L. J. Papineau Papers (Public Archives of Canada); Julie Bruneau Papineau to Amédée Papineau, Paris, Nov. 1839 (Archives de Québec) in *Rapport de l'Archiviste de la Province de Québec pour 1957–1958 et 1958–1959*.

176. Nancrede to Bonaparte (draft), Paris, 25 March 1831, L. J. Papineau Papers (Public Archives of Canada).

177. Louis-Joseph Papineau to Roebuck, 28 and 30 Sept. 1838, John Arthur Roebuck Papers (Public Archives of Canada).

178. Nancrede to Papineau, Paris, 19 June 1838 (Archives Nationales, Québec).

179. Nancrede to Papineau, [Paris], 29 June 1838, L. J. Papineau Papers (Public Archives of Canada).

180. Papineau to Julie Bruneau Papineau, Paris, 29 April 1839, in Fernand Ouellet, ed., "Lettres de L.-J. Papineau à sa femme," *Rapport de l'Archiviste de la Province de Québec pour 1953–1954 et 1954–1955*, p. 419; Papineau to Julie Bruneau Papineau, Paris, 15 March 1839, L. J. Papineau Papers (Public Archives of Canada).

181. Nancrede to Papineau, Paris, n.d., 2 letters (Archives Nationales, Quebec).

182. Lactance Papineau, Journal, Archives Provinciales du Québec (Courtesy Ruth White, Vancouver, Canada).

183. In Archives Nationales, Quebec.

184. Lactance Papineau, Journal (Archives Provinciales du Québec).

185. Déclarations des Mutations par Décès, 15 June 1842, Nos. 282–283 (Archives de Paris); Mme. Nicole Felkay, Conservateur d'Archives de Paris, to Madeleine B. Stern, 31 Jan. [1973]; Lactance Papineau, Journal (Archives Provinciales du Québec).

186. Joseph G. Nancrede to Papineau, Philadelphia, 1 Feb. 1842 (Archives Nationales, Quebec).

187. Papineau to Julie Bruneau Papineau, Paris, 27 April 1844 in Fernand Ouellet, ed., "Lettres de L.-J. Papineau à sa femme," *Rapport de l'Archiviste de la Province de Québec pour 1955–1956 et 1956–1957*, p. 263.

188. Joseph G. Nancrede to Papineau, Philadelphia, 1 Feb. 1842 (Archives Nationales, Quebec).

189. William J. Duane to Nancrede, Philadelphia, 12 June 1840, L. J. Papineau Papers (Public Archives of Canada).

190. Joseph G. Nancrede to Papineau, Philadelphia, 15 March 1840 (Archives Nationales, Quebec).

191. Joseph Nancrede, Acte de Décès, Batignolles Arrondissement de Paris, 1841 (Archives de Paris).

The First German Faust
Published in America

THE IMPORTANCE OF GOETHE in the cultural life of 19th-century America has been so well documented that any further evidence may seem superfluous and all but impossible. Yet a footnote, in the form of a previously underestimated "first," may now be added to the towering superstructure of the bibliography on the subject.

From the time of Edward Everett's return from abroad in 1819, the fame of German literature and philosophy began to spread in this country. The foreign seeds were sowed here by Margaret Fuller, Emerson and others. Carlyle's influence was effective and in time copies of Goethe's writings appeared upon American shelves and articles on Goethe enriched American periodicals. James Freeman Clarke wrote in the *Western Messenger* (August 1836): "Five years ago the name of Goethe was hardly known in England and America. . . . But now a revolution has taken place. Hardly a review or a magazine appears that has not something in it about Goethe." Margaret Fuller planned a biography of the great German poet. At Harvard, at Longfellow's Bowdoin and elsewhere, German lessons and German readings prepared the ground for an understanding of that "restorer of faith and love" whose universality and whose affirmations began to infiltrate American transcendental thought.

Goethe's *Werke*, published in forty volumes between 1827 and 1830 at Stuttgart and Tübingen, were followed between 1832 and 1834 by fifteen volumes of the *Nachgelassene Werke*. These fifty-five volumes found their way to Emerson's shelves and when Elizabeth Peabody opened her Foreign Library at 13 West Street, Boston, Items 15–70 consisted of Goethe's *Sammtliche Werke* in *55 Banden*.

Of all Goethe's works, his *Faust*—that "national poem of the German people"—seemed most meaningful to the American mind. As Margaret Fuller put it in *The Dial* (July 1841): "Faust contains the great idea of his

Reprinted from *American Notes & Queries* X, no. 8 (April 1972): 115–116.

life, as indeed there is but one great poetic idea possible to man, the progress of a soul through the various forms of existence. All his other works . . . are mere chapters to this poem." *Faust* was known to this country both as part of the *Werke* and in translation. A copy of Lord Francis Leveson-Gower's verse translation of Part I (London: J. Murray, 1823) was in Thomas Dowse's library in Cambridge; Emerson read the Gower translation. Abraham Hayward's prose version, published in London by Edward Moxon in 1833, was the first translation to be published in this country, bearing the 1840 imprint of Lowell: Daniel Bixby; New York: D. Appleton and Company. A copy of that edition "in which Emerson wrote his name, is still in his house, at Concord." The Hayward translation of *Faust* was also in Elizabeth Peabody's circulating foreign library despite the feeling expressed in *The Dial* (July 1841) that "All translations of Faust can give no better idea of that wonderful work than a Silhouette of one of Titian's beauties."

Although it appears to have escaped general notice, *Faust* in the original German was made available in this country three years before the American edition of the Hayward translation. The Curator of the William A. Speck Collection of Goetheana at Yale cities as the "earliest *Faust* in German with an American imprint" the 1864 edition published by S. R. Urbino of Boston and F. W. Christern and others of New York. Yet a generation earlier—in 1837—a German *Faust* was published in this country. Its title-page reads simply: Faust./Eine Tragödie/von/Goethe./New-York:/Zu haben in der Verlags-Handlung,/471 Pearl-Strasse./1837. An octavo of 432 pages, it contains both parts of *Faust* in continuous pagination with a second title-page, no more informative than the first, preceding the "Zweiter Theil." [It turns out that Yale's William A. Speck Collection of Goetheana does include the New York 1837 edition. There is no entry for it in either Hans Henning's *Faust Bibliography* or in W. Heinemann's *Goethes Faust in England und Amerika*.]

This edition was actually published by the New York firm of Radde and Paulsen as the second volume of a five-volume set issued between 1837 and 1840 entitled MUSEUM DER DEUTSCHEN KLASSIKER and its appearance as part of a set is probably the reason why it seems to have eluded the bibliographers.

In their own way, Radde and Paulsen were sowing the foreign seeds as actively as Margaret Fuller and Elizabeth Peabody. William Radde and George Henry Paulsen were agents of J. G. Wesselhoeft and importers of French and German books. At 471 Pearl Street they offered the works of Jean Paul and Wieland, Schiller and Körner, as well as all the advantages of a German intelligence office and a homeopathic apothecary shop. Indeed in this the Verlags-Handlung resembled the Peabody bookshop where homeopathic remedies were also available along with German literature. Besides the works of Hahnemann, Radde and Paulsen sold tinctures, milk sugar, and homeopathic chocolate.

In 1840, when Elizabeth Peabody published a *Catalogue* of her Foreign Library, her fourteenth entry was "Faust, Tragedie von Goethe. (See Hayward's Faust.)" One wonders if this was a copy of the edition published in New York by Radde and Paulsen. Its appearance, preceding Miss Peabody's entry for the 55-volume set of Goethe's *Sammtliche Werke*, seems to indicate that it was indeed a separate edition and if so it may well have been the Radde and Paulsen edition.

At all events, that New York firm merits the distinction of issuing the first German *Faust* with an American imprint and so of helping to stir up that tempest in the transcendental teapot that has been engaging the attention of scholars ever since.

Elizabeth Peabody's Foreign Library (1840)

IN November, 1840, Margaret Fuller wrote Emerson: "Will you send to me at Miss Peabody's the remaining volumes of Pietro della Valle which she is to have in her Foreign Library, and foreign they will surely be.—The other day I was sitting there and two young ladies coming in asked first for Bettina and then for Les Sept Chordes—I suppose next time they will ask for Pietro and Munchausen."[1]

The importance of foreign literature and philosophy to transcendental New England has long been recognized by scholars and the means by which the foreign seeds were imported to this country have been traced. Visits abroad, such as that made by Edward Everett; lessons and readings in foreign tongues at Longfellow's Bowdoin and Harvard; articles in American periodicals; the influence of Carlyle; the work of Emerson and Margaret Fuller—all played a part in awakening the American mind to the cogency of German, French, and Italian thought. So, too, did the library and bookstore opened by the Massachusetts bluestocking Elizabeth Palmer Peabody at 13 West Street, Boston. The shop became famous as the scene of Margaret Fuller's Conversations, the meeting place of New England's reformers and, between 1842 and 1843, the place of publication of *The Dial*, the organ of Transcendentalism. It was also recognized as the principal means for the dissemination of foreign literature, indeed as "the only [shop] in Boston carrying a stock of foreign books."[2] As Elizabeth Peabody herself recorded: "About 1840 I came to Boston and opened the business of importing and publishing foreign books, a thing not then attempted by any one. I had also a foreign library of new French and German books."[3]

The Foreign Circulating Library in the front parlor of the house on West Street in Boston's south end was recalled by enthusiastic visitors as "a notable centre of intellectual and reformatory interest."[4] Plans for the

Reprinted from *American Transcendental Quarterly* 20, Supplement, Part One (Fall 1973): 5–12.

community at Brook Farm were discussed there along with anti-slavery and Margaret Fuller's latest Conversations. It boasted as patrons Emerson and Alcott, Holmes and Lowell, Ripley, Bancroft, and James Freeman Clarke, as well as Miss Peabody's future brothers-in-law, Nathaniel Hawthorne and Horace Mann. Among them all the "desultory," "dreamy," but bustling proprietrix happily circulated. One side of the shop was supervised by Miss Peabody's father, Dr. Nathaniel Peabody, who sold homeopathic medicines. Artists' materials were available—thanks to the suggestion and aid of the painter Washington Allston. But the "atom of a shop" was most remarkable for the books circulated or sold. Edward Everett Hale recalled that "a counter ran across the parlor" and that "the books of the circulating library stood on shelves in brown-paper covers."[5] Only a few of them have been specifically cited by browsers, who remembered the atmosphere rather than the details of the Foreign Library. Hale himself mentioned the *Revue des Deux Mondes* and Strauss' *Leben Jesu*, whereas Thomas Wentworth Higginson enumerated Cousin and Jouffroy, Constant's *De la Religion*, Leroux' *De l'Humanité*, Schubert's *Geschichte der Seele*, and German ballads. Kraitsir's *Lectures on Language* and General Bem's *Historical Chart* were on hand.[6] Emerson grandly advised his wife Lidian: " . . . if you see anything you want there, do not fail to buy it."[7]

Now, through the discovery of a printed *Catalogue of the Foreign Library*,[8] the actual books and periodicals circulated by Miss Peabody may be more accurately identified. Of the 1,161 items listed,[9] the greatest number of foreign works—some 300—were French, including Molière and La Fontaine, Mirabeau and Voltaire, Stael, Chateaubriand, George Sand, Balzac, Béranger, Cousin, Hugo, and De Gerando, whom the proprietrix herself had translated. Next in quantity were the German books, which numbered about 250. Of these, however, a great many were represented by collected editions, including a 55-volume set of Goethe and other multiple-volume sets of Herder and Schiller, Wieland and Jean Paul, Schlegel and Lessing. Among the 70 items in Italian were the writings of Dante and Petrarch, Ariosto and Bonarelli, Guarini and Metastasio. A small selection of Spanish books completed the foreign showing except for several foreign periodicals: *Revue Française, Revue des Deux Mondes, Journal des Literarische Unterhaltung*, etc. Many of the English books were themselves of foreign interest, including some translations—notably Abraham Hayward's translation of Goethe's *Faust*, the first translation of that work to be published in this country (1840). Carlyle and Emerson, Alcott and Channing, Hawthorne (to be published by Miss Peabody) all appeared in their brown-paper covers on the shelves of the West Street bookshop, in that front parlor where the transcendental Zeitgeist was fostered.

Miss Peabody's methods of cataloguing left something to be desired. Her alphabetizing was casual, sometimes by author, sometimes by title, sometimes by both; her numbering was erratic upon occasion, and one is not always sure whether a repeated entry indicates a duplicate copy or a double listing by title and by author, as in the case of Hayward's *Faust*, for example, which is entered as No. 991: "Faust, trans. by Hayward" and again, out of numerical order, as No. 1062: "Hayward's Faust." Of far more importance is the fact that such books as these might be borrowed at the subscription price of $5 or at 12½ to 25 cents per week "according to . . . sizes" in the Boston of 1840. This "brief Catalogue . . . furnished for the subscribers' convenience" at that time may now serve as an index to the contents of Elizabeth Peabody's "atom of a bookshop," the foreign seeds of which came to flower in transcendental New England.

Notes

1. *The Letters of Ralph Waldo Emerson*, ed. Ralph L. Rusk (New York, 1939), II, 354 note 421.

2. "Elizabeth Palmer Peabody," *D A B.* For twentieth-century accounts of the shop, see Doris Louise McCart, *Elizabeth Peabody: A Biographical Study* (Typescript, Master's Thesis, University of Chicago, 1918), pp. 31–36; Leona Rostenberg, "Number Thirteen West Street," *Book Collector's Packet*, IV:1 (Sept., 1945), pp. 7–9; Madeleine B. Stern, *The Life of Margaret Fuller* (New York, 1942 & 1968), pp. 181–198; Louise Hall Tharp, *The Peabody Sisters of Salem* (Boston, 1950), pp. 133–147.

3. George Willis Cooke, *An Historical and Biographical Introduction to The Dial* (Cleveland, 1902), p. 148.

4. *Ibid.*, p. 148.

5. Edward Everett Hale, *A New England Boyhood* (Boston, 1920), p. 246.

6. James Freeman Clarke, *Autobiography, Diary and Correspondence* (Boston & New York, 1899), p. 143; Cooke, *op. cit.*, pp. 149ff; Hale, *op. cit.*, p. 246.

7. *The Letters of Ralph Waldo Emerson*, II, 359.

8. The *Catalogue* is in the Department of Rare Books and Manuscripts of the Boston Public Library and is here reproduced through the courtesy of James Lawton, Esq., Curator of Manuscripts.

9. Excluding the 27 periodicals which were given a separate enumeration at the beginning, and gaps, presumably for new arrivals. Generally, in this pre-Dewey system, the initial digits 1–2 seem to have been assigned to German books, 3 to Italian, 4 to Spanish, 5–8 to French, and 9–11 to English.

CATALOGUE

OF THE

FOREIGN LIBRARY,

NO. 13 WEST STREET.

N. B.   This Library is on the increase, but a brief Catalogue is furnished for the subscribers' convenience at present.

BOSTON:

PRINTED BY S. N. DICKINSON, 52 WASHINGTON-ST.

1840.

RULES OF THE LIBRARY.

1. Subscribers only are permitted to take out the Periodicals. These begin to circulate as soon as they arrive. A list of them is here furnished.
2. A New Periodical must not be kept out more than a week; and the subscribers are requested to return it in less time if possible.
3. Other books must be returned, or at least reported, once a month. When no other subscriber wants them they may be retained longer.
4. All books must be returned to the Library to be counted, the first week of November, on penalty of a fine amounting to the cost of the volume.
5. It is requested that the books shall not be lent.
6. The subscription price is $5.00. Subscribers will be preferred with respect to books; but when they are not wanted by subscribers, they may be hired for 12 1-2 or 25 cents per week, according to their sizes.

CATALOGUE.

PERIODICALS.

1 Annals of Natural History.
2 Annales de Chimie et de Physique.
3 Annales des Sciences Naturelles.
4 Bentley's Miscellany.
5 Blackwood's Magazine.
6 Boston Quarterly Review.
7 Christian Examiner.
8 Dial.
9 Edinburgh Review.
10 Fraser's Magazine.
11 Foreign Quarterly.
12 Gentleman's Magazine.
13 Galignini's Messenger.
14 Hallische Jährbucher.
15 Journal des Literarische Unterhaltung.
16 Jährbucher du Litteratur.   Wiener.
17 Jamieson's Philosophical Journal.
18 London Quarterly.
19 London and Edinburgh Philosophical Magazine.
20 Monthly Chronicle.
21 Metropolitan Magazine.
22 Musical Journal.
23 New York Review.
24 Revue Française.
27 Revue des Deux Mondes.
25 Westminster Review.
26 Western Messenger.
N. B.   Some of the above periodicals will not arrive till January, and some may be changed for others in the course of time.

GERMAN BOOKS.

1 Ackermann's Christliche in Plato.
2 Carlos Don, von Schiller.
3, 4, 5, 6, 7 Erzahlungen.   9 Banden in 5.
8, 9, 10 Eichhorn—Einleitung Alte Testament.   3
   Banden.
11, 12, 13 Eichhorn—Die Hebräischen Propheten.   3
   Banden.

4

14 Faust. Tragedie von Goethe. (See Hayward's Faust.)
15—70 Goethe. Sammtliche Werke. 55 Banden.
71—100 Herder's Werke. 60 Banden in 30.
101—105 Junger's Lustspiele. 5 Banden.
106—110 Körner's Werke. 4 Banden.
111—113 Krummacher's Parabeln. 3 Banden.
114 Lessing's Nathan der Weise.
115 Lessing's Emilia Gallotti.
116—130 Lessing's Sammtliche Werke. 30 Banden in 15
131 Menzel, die Deutsche Litteratur.
132 Novalis Schriften.
133 Oehenschlager's Dramatische Werke.
134—138 Pfeffer's Erzahlungen. 5 Banden.
139—168 Richter, Jean Paul's Sammtliche Werke. 60 B.
168—200 Schiller's Sammtliche Werke. 18 Band.
201—204 Schlegel's Shakspeare. 4 Band.
205—206 Schlegel Ueber drammatische Kunst &c. 3 B.
249 Schleiermacher über Religion.
207—210 Titan, von J. P. Richter. 4 Band.
211—225 Tieck's Werke. 30 Banden in 15.
226 Undine.
227—242 Wieland's Sammtliche Werke. 32 Band. in 16.
243 Weichtnacht's abend.
244 Wallenstein von Schiller.
245—248 Zschokke's Erzahlungen. 4 Ban.
249 F. Schlegel's Werke. 14 Band.

ITALIAN BOOKS.

300 Ariosto—Orlando Furioso.
301 Bacco in Tuscano—Ditirambo di Rede.
*302 Bonarelli—Filli de Sciro.
*303, 304 Constantini, Nuova Scelta di Poesie Italiana.
*305—308 Cesarotti. Poesie de Ossian. 4 tomes.
309—312 Dante. Divina Comedia. 4 tomes.
313—321 Denina della Revoluzioni d'Italia. 9 tomes.
*322 Guarini—Pastor Fido.
323 Gravina, della Ragion Poetica, &c.
324—329 Lanzi, Storia Pittorica. 6 tomes.
330 Maroncelli—Addizioni alli "Miei Prigioni."
331—344 Metastasio. 14 tomes.
345 Monti—Tragedie.
346 Monti. In Morte de Ugo Bass Ville—La Rivoluzioni
     Francese, Visone alla Dantesca, in quattro Canti.

5

347, 348 Mengs—Opere di. 2
349—351 Manzoni—Promessi Sposi. 3
352, 353 Notti Romane. 2
354 Ortis—Ultime Lettere de Jacopo.
355 Pepoli—Prose.
356 Pepoli—Verse.
357 Pignotti Poesie.
358 Petrarca, and Scelta di Poesie, &c.
322 Pastor Fido—Guarini.
359 Silvio Pellico—Miei Prigioni.
360—365 Silvio Pellico—Opere, Tragedie, Canteche, Dei
   Doveri degli Uomini.
366 Saffo—Dramma Lirico—da T. J. Mathias.
367 Soave—Novelle Morali, &c.
368, 369 Torquato Tasso—Gerusalemme Liberata e Aminta.
370 Tassoni, La Secchia Rapita.

SPANISH BOOKS.

400 Armistades Pelligrosas.
401 Bernardo del Carpio.
402 Cuentos Morales.
403 Cadalso—Cartas Marruescas.
404 Cervantes—Ejemplares Novellas.
405—408 Don Quijote. 4
409 El Epicureo.
410 Familia di Primrose.
411—415 Gil Blas—Santilliano. 5
416 Iriarte—Fabulas Litterarias, e Las Niñas de Moratin.
417—430 Metastasio. 14
432 Sales Comicas.
431 La Utopia.

FRENCH BOOKS.

501—507 D'Abrantes, Mémoires de la Restauration, &c. 7 tomes.
508 Affaires de Rome, par la Mennais.
509—512 Aimé-Martin, Lettres à Sophie. 4 tomes.
513—522 Anacharsis, Voyage du Jeune, par Barthelemy.
   9 tomes, avec Atlas.
767 André, par George Sand.
523—526 Andryane, Mémoires d'un Prisonnier d'Etat au
   Spielberg. 4 tomes.
  1*

6

527 Balzac. Les Chouans.
528, 529 " Le Père Goriot. 2 tomes.
530 " La Dernière Feé.
531, 532 " Le Livre Mystique. 2 tomes.
533, 534 " Le Medecin de Campagne. 2 tomes.
535 " La Recherche de l'Absolu.
536 Béranger—Chansons de.
537—546 Barante—Histoire des ducs de Bourgogne. 10 t.
547—549 " Mélanges Historiques et Litteraires
    3 tomes.
550 Belisaire, par Mad. de Genlis.
551 La Belgique—Esquisses Historiques de la Revolution,
    en 1830. 1 tome.
552, 553 Supplément au même—2 Livraisons.
554, 555 La Belgique—Ed Dupectiaux, de l'instruction de
805 Bombet—lettres sur Haydn et Mozart.
556, 557 Capefique, Histoire de la Restauration. 2 tomes.
667 Chants du Crepuscule, par V. Hugo.
558 Charbonnières Histoire Abrégée de la Litterature Française.
559—590 Chateaubriand. 32 tomes.
591—598 Christianisme, Histoire du, par de Potter. 8 t.
599 Cinq Mois aux Etats Unis de l'Amérique nord, par Ramon
    de la Sagra.
600 Code Civile, Manuel Complet de la Politesse, &c.
601 Code de la Conversation, Manuel Complet, &c.
602 Conjurations des Espagnoles Contre la republique de
    Vénise, par St. Real.
603 Constant, J. T. Essais sur l'instruction publique.
604—606 Corinne, ou l'Italie, par Mad. de Stael.
607—611 Corneille. 5 tomes.
612, 613 Correspondence de Victor Jaquemont sur l'Inde.
    2 tomes.
614—625 Cousin—Plato. 12 tomes.
626 Cromwell, Histoire de, par Villemain.
674 Cromwell, Drame, par V. Hugo.
627 Dumont—Souvenirs de Mirabeau.
628 Damiron, Essai sur l'histoire de la Philosophie en France
    au 19me Siècle.
629—632 De Gerando, sur la Perfectionnement Morale.
    2 tomes.
805—808 De Gerando, sur la Bienfaisance Publique. 4 tomes.
633 De Stael, vie de, par Madame Neckar de Saussure.
634, 635 Dumeril, Elemens des sciences Naturelles. 2 to.

7

636, 637 Duport P. Essais littéraires sur Shakespeare.   2
638 De la Vigne—Evènemens de Paris des 26, 27, 28,
         29 Juillet, 1830.
639 Etats Unis, Histoire des.
640 Empéreurs, Histoire des.
641 Florian—Guillaume Tell.
642   "   Fables.
643—645 "   Gonsalve de Cordova.   3 tomes.
646, 647 "   "   1 tome, 2 copies.
648—651 Foy, General de—Histoire de la Guerre d'Espagne
         et du Portugal sous Napoleon.   4 tomes.
652 Guizot, de la Peine de Mort.
653   " Histoire de la Civilization en Europe.
654—658 " Histoire de la Civilization en France.   5 tomes.
660, 661 " Essais sur l'histoire de France.   2 tomes.
662, 663 Gaucheraud—Pélérinage de Jeune Fille.   2 tomes.
642 Guillaume Telle, par Florian
644—648 Gonzalve de Cordova, par Florian.   3 copies.
664 Hugo, Victor—Cromwell, drama.
665   "   Notre Dame de Paris.   3 tomes.
666   "   Littérature et Philosophie Melées. 3 tomes.
667   "   Les Chants du Crépuscule.
           "   Lucrèce Borgia.
668, 669 Hoffman—Contes.   2 tomes.
805 Haydn et Mozart lettres sur.
670, 671 Italie, lettres de l', par M. Pierre de Broux.   2 tomes.
612, 613 Jaquemont, Victor, Correspondence sur l'Inde.
672, 673 Lettres persanes, par Montesquieu.   2 tomes.
674 La Fontaine's fables.
675—677 Las Cases—Esprit du Mémorial de St. Helène.
         3 tomes.
678, 679 La Martine.   2 tomes.
680 Llorente—Histoire de l'Inquisition.
681, 682 Langlois—Theátre Indian.   2 tomes.
683—691 Magasin Pittoresque.   (9 examples.)
692—703 Mirabeau—Mémories, biographiques, litteraire et
         politiques de, écrits par lui-même, par son père, par son
         oncle, et par son fils adoptif; précédés par une étude
         sur Mirabeau, par V. Hugo. 11 vols. in 18mo.
704 Mirabeau, souvenir de, par Dumont.
705, 706 Mignet, histoire de la Revolutione Française.   2 tomes.
707—714 Molière, histoire de la vie et des ouvragerde
           " Euvres complet.   8 tomes.

8

715, 716 la Martine. 2 tomes.
805 Mozart et Haydn lettres sur.
717 Norvins vie de Napolean.
665 Notre Dame de Paris, par V. Hugo.
718 Paroles d'un Croyant, par l'able de Mennais.
719 Paroles d'un Voyant, par Faider.
720, 721 Physiologie du Gout. 2 tomes.
722, [7]23 Persanes lettres par Montesquieu. 2 tomes.
724 Poussin, vie de.
725 Polignac's Considerations politiques sur l'epoque actuelle.
726—731 Racine. 6 tomes.
732 Roland, Mad.—Lettres Autographe.
733, 734 Robespierre, Mémoires de. 2 tomes.
735 Riquebourg, la famille de.
736—738 Saussure, Mad. Neckar de, sur Education progressive.
      3 tomes.
737   ''   vie de Mad. de Stael.
740, 742 Segur—Mémoires ou Souvenirs et anecdotes, par M. le
      Comte de. 3 vols.
743—748 Sand, Georges—Mauprat. 2 tomes.
                     La Marquise.
                     Sept Cordes de la Lyre.
                     Les Maîtres Mosaistes.
                     Simon.
                     André.
749, 750 Soirées de St. Petersbourg, par Josef de Maistre.
      2 tomes.
751—758 Sismondi—Histoire des Republiques Italiannes.
759—774   ''   ''   '' Français.
775—778 Thierry—Histoire de la Conquêtc de l'Angleterre.
779   ''   Lettres de l'histoire de France.
780—783 Thiers—Histoire de la Revolutione Française.
      4 tomes.
784—789 Toqueville de, Democratie en Amerique. 6 to.
790 Vinet, Résumé de l'histoire de la Litterature Française.
791 Vertot, Révolutions de la Suède.
792   ''   Histoire de Russie.
793 Voltaire, La Henriade.
794 Valérie.
795—797 Villemain. 3 tomes.
798—804 Voyage en Italie, par La Lande. 7 tomes.

9
ENGLISH BOOKS.

901 Aids to Reflection, on the formation of a manly character, by S. T. Coleridge.

902, 3, 4 Alfieri's life and writings, transl'd from Italian.

905 Agricultural Documents relating to the Introduction of Tropical plants into Florida.

906 Abstract of School Returns for 1837.

907 Arabian, poetry, by Carlyle.

908 Adams, Mrs. John, Letters.

909 Adams, Miss Hannah, Life.

910, 911 Allen Prescott, 2 vols.

912 Andryano's Memoirs of his arrest and imprisonment at Milan, trans. by F. Prandi.

913 Ali Pasha, life of, by R. A. Davenport.

914 Animal Magnetism.

915 Abbot's Sermons, (J. E.)

916—18 Bancroft's History of the United States,   3 v.

919—21 Bettine Brentano. 3 vols.

922 Bonnycastle's Spanish America.

923 Buckminster's Sermons.

924, 25 Bulwer's England and the English.   2 vols.

926 Byron's Corsair, Lara and Giaour.

927 Brownson's New Views.

928 Browning's History of the Hugenots.

929, 30 Buche's Ruins of Cities.

931 Bastille, History of the.

932 British Lawyers, by Roscoe.

932 Bulwer's Last days of Pompeii.

933 Carlyle's Sartor Resartus.

934, 35   "   French Revolution, 2 vols.

936—939   "   Miscellanies. 4 vols.

940   "   Life of Schiller

941   "   Chartism.

942 Cappe's Sermons.

953 Chaucer, Riches of, by C. Cowden Clarke.

944 Channing's Miscellaneous Works.

945   "   Eleven Discourses.

946   "   Sermons and Tracts.

947   "   Temperance.

948   "   Self-Culture.

949   "   Laboring Classes.

950   "   Slavery.

951   "   Letter by Jonathan Philips.

952   "   Letter to Henry Clay.

10

953—955 Characteristics of Goethe. 3 vols.
956, 57   "   of Women. 2 vols.
958—960 Coleridge's Poetical Works. 3 vols.
961 Coleridge's Church and State and Lay Sermons.
962   "   Friend.
963   "   Table Talk. (See Aid to Reflection.)
964 Companions of Columbus, Voyages of.
965, 66 Conversations on the Gospels, by A. B. Alcott. 2 vols.
967 Cousin's History of Philosophy, by Linberg.
968   "   Examination of Locke, by Henry.
969 Chapone, Gregory and Pennington.
970 Crocker's Fairy Legends.
971 Clarke's Travels in Russia, Tartary and Turkey.
972 Cervantes Life.
973, 74 Dante, translated by Cary. 2 vols.
975, 76 Dabney's Annotations on the N. Testament. 2 vs.
977 Dewey's Sermons.
978—980 Euripides, trans. by Potter. 3 vols.
981 AEschylus,   "   "
982   "   " into Prose.
983, 84 English Poets, Lives of, (Lardner's Cycl.) 2 vols.
985, 86 English Dramatists, Lives of, (Lard. Cycl.) 2 vols.
987 Early English Writers.
988 Emerson's (R. W.) Orations, &c.
989 Ellis' Journal of Embassy to China.
990 Freeman's Sermons.
991 Faust, trans. by Hayward.
992 Fisher Ames' Life and Works.
993 Faber on the Prophecies.
994, 995 French Literary Men. 2 vols.
996 Fairy Legends.
997 Grace Abounding, &c. Bunyan.
998, 1000 Goethe's Characteristics, by Mrs. Austin. 3 vols.
1001 Goethe and Schiller's Songs, trans. by Dwight.
1002—1004. Gil Blas. 3 vols. translated.
1005 Gustavus Adolphus' life, by Hollings.
1006 Gurley's Life of Ashmun.
1162 Hayward's Faust.
1006, 1007 Hall's Journal of Residence in Chili, Peru and
        Mexico.
1008 Hall's Voyage to Java, China and Loo Choo.
1008—1011 Hallam's Introduction to Literature. 4 vols.
1012 Heeren's Greece, trans. by Bancroft.
1013, 1014 Herder's Hebrew Poetry. 2 vols.

11

1015 Howard's Life, by Mrs. Farrar.
1016 Huber's Ants.
1017—1019 Hebrew Prophets, trans. by Noyes. 3 vols.
1020, 21 Heads of the People. 2 vols. illustrated.
1022 Hesiod, trans. by Elton.
1023 Hutchinson, Col. Memoirs by his wife.
1024, 25 Iliad, trans. by Cowper. 2 vols.
1026 Indian Biography.
1027 Imposture, Sketches of
1028 Idler in Italy, by Lady Blessington.
1029—1031 Italian and Spanish Literary Men. (Lardn. Cycl.)
    3 vols.
1032 Job, trans. by Noyes.
1033, 34 Jouffroy's Ethics. 2 vols.
1035 Joanna of Naples.
1036 Junius, Letters on the Authorship of.
1037, 38 Jerusalem Delivered, trans by Wiffen. 2 vols.
1039 Kock's Revolutions of Europe.
1040 Louis on Fever.
1041 La Martine's Travels in the East.
1042, 1043 Macauley's Miscellanies. 2 vols.
1044 Mason on Self-Knowledge.
1045 MacIntosh's Progress of Eth. Philosophy.
1046   "   History of England.
1047   "   English Revolution,
1048—1050 Montaigne's Essays. 3 vols.
1051—1052 Martineau's Society in America.
1053—1068   "   Illustrations of Political Economy.
    16 vols.
1069—1072 Müller's Universal History. 4 vols.
1073 Natural History of Enthusiasm.
1017—1019 Noyes' Hebrew Prophets. 3 vols.
1032   "   Job.
1074 Nature, by R. W. Emerson.
1075—1078 Our Village, by Miss Mitford. 4 vols.
1079, 80 Odyssey, trans. by Cowper. 2 vols.
1081 Oberlin's Life.
1081, 82 Phantasmion. 2 vols.
1083 Plato's Phædo.
1084 Pictures of the French.
1045 Progress of Ethical Philosophy, MacIntosh.
1085 Prize Essays on the Congress of Nations.
1086 Picciola, trans. from the French.
1087 Physiognomy, by Lavater.
1088, 89 Phrenology, by Spurzheim. 2 vols.

12

1090—1093 Parterre, (Novels and Stories.) 4 vols.
1094 Pringle's Residence in South Africa.
1095 Peter Wilkins, Life and Adventures of.
1096 Quincy Josiah, Jr., Memoirs of.
1097 Richard 1st, Life of.
1098, 99 Ruins of Cities, Buche. 2 vols.
1100—1102 Ranke's History of the Popes. 3 vols.
1103 Ripley's Letters to Mr. Norton.
1104 Riches of Chaucer.
1105—1107 Romilly's Memoirs. 3 vols.
1108 Rousseau on Man.
1109 Shakspeare, Wisdom and Genius of.
1110, 11 Spirit of Hebrew Poetry. 2 vols.
1112, 16 Spenser. 5 vols.
933 Sartor Resartus.
1117, 1118 Society in America. 2 vols.
1120 Sismondi's Decline and Fall of the Roman Empire.
1121   "   Italian Republics, abridged.
1122 Spurzheim's Physiognomy, with plates.
1088, 1089   "   Phrenology. 2 vols.
1123 Spark's Letters to Episcopalians.
1124—1134 Scott's Novels. 11 vols.
1135—1136   "   History of Scotland. 2 vols.
1137—1141 Seward's Letters. 6 vols.
1142 Schlegel's Lectures on Dramatic Art, &c.
1143 Sketcher's Manual, by F. Howard.
1144, 1145 Thucydides, trans. 2 vols.
1146 Tourist in Europe.
1147 Twice-told Tales.
1148 Tytler's Elements of History.
1149 Valentine Vox, with illustrations by Cruikshank.
1037, 1038 Wiffen's Tasso. 2 vols.
1150 William Tell, trans. by Brooks.
1151—1154 Wordsworth's Works. 4 vols.
1155—1157 Wilhelm Meister. 3 vols.
1161 Wilberforce, Life of, by his Sons.
1158 Xenophon's Memorabilia, trans.
1159 Yarrow Revisited, Wordsworth.
1160 Young Lady's Friend, by Mrs. Farrar.
1161 Wilberforce.

3

A Murder and a Meeting

A Murder for Bibliophiles

The Case of John Caldwell Colt

IF EVER an unlikely book conjured up a tale of passion, violence and bloodshed, it is an innocuous looking quarto volume with a long and prosaic title: *The Science of Double Entry Bookkeeping, Simplified, Arranged and Methodized, after the Forms of Grammar and Arithmetic; Explained by Definite Rules, and Illustrated by Entries Classed, in a Manner Entirely Different From any Work Ever Before Offered to the Public.*

The author of this popular textbook published in 1838 is described on the crowded title-page as J. C. Colt, Accountant. John Caldwell Colt was indeed an accountant, but he was more than that. He was the brother of Sam Colt of Colt's Revolver fame; he was a bookseller and publisher. John Caldwell Colt was also a murderer and the defendant in one of the most publicized trials of the nineteenth century. But he was no ordinary murderer, for on September 17, 1841, this bookseller-publisher slew his printer, Samuel Adams. [See Plate 2.] It is entirely possible that many a bookseller-publisher has entertained with some degree of relish the thought of murdering his printer, but few if any have carried the thought into action with the dispatch and decisiveness of John Caldwell Colt. That gentleman has therefore earned a place not only in the annals of crime, but in the history of the American booktrade.

Where should one begin his disastrous story? With the spring day in 1837 when he quite literally had his head examined by a phrenologist who was disturbed by the size of Colt's organs of Combativeness and Destructiveness? Or with another spring day two years later when he opened an office for the sale of his books in New York City? Or at the time of his partnership with the publisher, Nathan G. Burgess? Or in the late summer of 1841 when a fateful trade sale was scheduled? Or with the announcement in

Reprinted from *AB Bookman's Weekly Yearbook* (1968): 25–28.

PLATE 2. A publisher murders his printer—Colt's cruel crime.

the papers of the disappearance of printer Samuel Adams under the arresting heading: APPREHENDED MISFORTUNE?

There are many points at which the blood-stained thread might be taken up, but doubtless it would be best to begin at the beginning in which inevitably the end is implicit.

John Caldwell Colt began his ill-starred life in 1810 in Hartford, Connecticut, the third child and first son of Sarah Caldwell and Christopher Colt. His father, who was engaged in the West Indies trade, failed in business when John was ten and the following year his mother died. The introduction of an antagonistic stepmother into the Colt household compounded the young boy's trials and, frustrated in his choice of school and profession, he entered upon what is customarily called a "checkered" career. His studies alternated with periods of teaching in a ladies' seminary in Baltimore, with mercantile trade and with lectures on chemistry in New Orleans. His early life was punctuated by two tragic suicides—the first that of a well-loved sister who took arsenic in 1829; the second that of a young woman in Cincinnati who terminated her unrequited love for him by self-destruction.

Firmly built and slender, with curling hair, aquiline nose and hazel eyes, John Caldwell Colt had the wherewithall to inspire romance—and tragedy. By 1834 his professional interests had centered upon bookkeeping and he spent the subsequent three years teaching and lecturing on that subject in the midwest. By this time he had amassed material for a book on "the science of double entry book-keeping" which was published in Cincinnati by N. G. Burgess & Co. in 1838.

It was at this point in his career that Colt earned his place in the booktrade with which he was thenceforth "deeply connected." The opportunity arose in Cincinnati in the Burgess office. In order to stimulate the sale of his manual on book-keeping, Colt joined forces with the publisher. Nathan Burgess was then engaged in issuing a far more elaborate tome—*An Inquiry into the Origin of the Antiquities of America* by John Delafield, Jr., a book adorned with a folding facsimile, color plates and lithographs of Mexican hieroglyphics and paintings, which it was estimated "must have cost some $2000 to bring out." It was "brought out" in 1839 both in Cincinnati and in New York, the New York edition bearing two different imprints—one that of Colt, Burgess & Co., the other "published for subscribers, by J. C. Colt."

With two such books as *The Science of Double Entry Bookkeeping* and *The Antiquities of America* on their list, each "commanding readers of a different but numerous class," the partners anticipated nothing but prosperity. Unfortunately readers were less interested in American antiquities than in American arithmetic, and the Delafield book seems to have been a slow seller. Called away for a while, John Colt returned to Cincinnati to find his partner in a state of extreme indebtedness. Some adjustment was made by the transfer to Colt's account of $2500 in bills due and his partner's note for $1500—along with 700 copies of Delafield's *Antiquities of America.*

With this capital, in April 1839, Colt set up his shingle at 14 Cortlandt Street, New York City. His stock in trade consisted of his book-keeping manual and his colorplate archeological tome. His modus operandi was simple and may be described in one word—barter. By exchange with his own two books he would accumulate a stock of various other books and pack cases of them off for auction or for a fresh exchange. The trade sales were obviously of prime importance to him. Thus John Colt, living frugally in his office, doing his own packing and carting, "kept his chances moving."

For a short time he set up a business in Philadelphia at the corner of 5th and Minor Streets, but all he seems to have derived from his venture in the City of Brotherly Love was a mistress, Caroline M. Henshaw, who returned to New York with him and in due course bore him a child. Back in Gotham, Colt occupied an office in the Granite Building at the corner of Broadway and Chambers Street, renting it from Asa H. Wheeler, who ran a writing school in the adjoining apartment.

Colt was deeply engrossed in bringing out a new edition of his popular *Double Entry Bookkeeping*, for his manual had been introduced into the schools and seminaries of the country and boasted the distinction of being the only work on the subject sold "in the great valley of the Mississippi." Actually, he was publishing two editions of the book—one a Teacher and Clerk's Edition priced at $1.50 and the other, in smaller format, a School Edition priced at $1.00. This innocuous seeming work has an unprecedented claim to bibliographical interest, for its paper was provided by none other than Cyrus W. Field and its typography by none other than Samuel Adams. The future—when Samuel Adams would suffer a violent end and Cyrus Field would bear witness in court—was closing in.

Adams, partner of a recently deceased gentleman with the unlikely name of Scatchard, operated his business on Gold Street, where he employed the services of a foreman and several apprentices. Colt had hired him for previous impressions of his manual and now, with the trade sales looming up, he was especially eager to get the two editions of his book off the press as promptly as possible. The paper had been bought by Adams from Cyrus Field and Colt's note had been given for the amount. Charles Wells, also on Gold Street, was to do the binding. The sheets were sent to be folded and arrangements were made to send the bound volumes to the trade sales.

A New York trade sale was scheduled for August 30, 1841, and a Philadelphia sale for September 6. On those occasions, new works went off in large quantities to the assembled dealers who often bought from samples, paying either cash or notes as soon as the books were supplied—not more than two or three weeks later. From the proceeds of 400 volumes Colt anticipated a return of between $125 and $150. Obviously, however, his books must be ready in time. The printer did not seem to share the publisher's eagerness to expedite the job and Colt's impatience with the dilatory Samuel Adams was mounting.

On his part, the printer was harassed with anxiety and doubts of his own. Colt, he claimed, already owed him $71.15—an amount which the publisher questioned, admitting to a debt of only $55.80. Moreover, Colt's stereotype plates, worth $500, were already in Adams' hands, along with unbound books worth as much more. The printer, apparently preferring ready cash to stereotype plates and unbound sheets, was "vexed," and refused to be rushed in his work. The trade sales came and went. "While there was hurrying on the one side and procrastinating on the other," Colt's impatience increased at about the same rate as Adams' suspicion that moneys due him would be withheld. Arrayed in his gambroon pantaloons, his black coat and black stock, the printer, between three and four o'clock on Friday, September 17, 1841, paid a fatal and final visit to the publisher in his offices in the Granite Building.

The scene of that truly historic meeting was reconstructed subsequently at the trial. Colt was seated at his table, looking over a manuscript account book, when Adams entered. The gentlemen discussed the printer's bill, Colt insisting that it was wrong, Adams retorting that Colt did not understand printing. The discussion became heated as both figured parts of the account on separate papers. "Word followed word till it came to blows. The words 'you lie' were passed." The men grappled and Colt, thrust to the wall, seized a hammer that lay conveniently on the table and struck the fatal blow. Adams, bleeding profusely, breathed loudly for several minutes, threw his arms about and finally was silent. The blood spread over the floor. Colt tried to stop the flow by tying his handkerchief tight around his victim's neck. Fearing the blood would leak through the floor, he took a towel and soaked up all he could, rinsing it into a pail. After an interim devoted doubtless to probings, self-analysis, panic and remorse, it occurred to the publisher that he might pack the printer's body in a cask and ship it to a remote destination. He proceeded to strip Adams' body of clothing and he may possibly have salted it down (this was never fully established). Thereupon, using a rope, he bent his victim's knees as close as possible to his head in an attempt to give the body a compact format. It was not, however, until Colt actually stood upon Adams' projecting knees that he could get them down so the corpus delicti would fit into the box. Once the cover was nailed down, Colt marked the cask to a false address and hired a cartman to take it to the New Orleans packet "Kalamazoo" at the foot of Maiden Lane.

Between that bloody day and Colt's arrest six days later, he actually visited Adams' shop to see that his stereotype plates were put into the vault, although "from the great depression of business and unhappiness that he felt," he neglected to attend to the binding! At least Colt did have his nose to the grindstone.

Other noses were occupied with other matters, notably with the discovery of a decomposing and noisome-smelling corpse in a box aboard the "Kalamazoo." Less than a week after the crime—on September 23, 1841—John C. Colt was arrested. Between that day and the opening of his trial the following January, he occupied himself in The Tombs by writing letters, reading Oliver Goldsmith, and objecting to the press reports of "the late horrible murder" that threatened to condemn him without a hearing.

Colt had his hearing none the less. He was brought to trial in January 1842, Judge Kent presiding, Dudley Selden and Robert Emmet defending. It was a trial which, like the crime, was unparalleled in the annals of both book history and court procedure. In the course of it, Adams' bloody garments were shaken out before his widow and the printer's head, which had been severed from his trunk, was—after the ladies had retired—exhibited to the jury and discoursed upon by Dr. Valentine Mott. Sam Colt was given the opportunity to testify about his firearms and several witnesses discussed the blood spots on the wall, the borrowing of a saw by the publisher, and the carting away of the gruesome box.

But the testimony of greatest interest was that which cast light upon the booktrade, for among the witnesses was a grand array of printers, booksellers, and others connected with the manufacture of books. Seldom if ever has there been a trial of such bibliophilic interest. The roll of witnesses included many printers who testified regarding the character of Samuel Adams, among them his foreman, apprentices and colleagues. Perhaps the best known of the printers called to court was Robert Hoe, son of the founder of R. Hoe & Company, who, with his brother Richard, succeeded to the great business of printing press manufacturers. Cyrus W. Field, just building up the paper firm of Cyrus W. Field & Company from the financial wreck of its predecessor, was duly sworn and revealed the terms by which he supplied reams of paper for Colt's publication. Robert Carter, who had opened his bookstore in 1834 and was to become a well-known publisher of religious books, took the stand in the Colt trial to report on the mildness and amiability of the victim. The bookbinder, Charles Wells, made his appearance, giving his account about the bindery, and Nathan Burgess, the publisher and Colt's erstwhile partner, testified about their joint venture with the Delafield book which, "published in the name of Colt, Burgess & Co., . . . lost a thousand dollars." The trial in short was a free-for-all for the booktrade, whose members had the unprecedented opportunity of discussing at length their favorite subjects: printing and papermaking, publishing and bookselling.

Despite, or perhaps because of this preponderance of bibliognostic witnesses, the verdict rendered by the jury was that of WILFUL MURDER and John C. Colt was sentenced to be hanged on November 18.

Like every author, Colt could not resist a sequel, and while his story found its way into Philip Hone's Diary and Governor Seward's Autobiography, the sequel unfolded. On the day scheduled for his execution, John C. Colt was married to his mistress, Caroline Henshaw, the ceremony being performed in prison by the Rev. Mr. Anton at high noon. Four hours later, when the sheriff, with his deputy and a clergyman, went to the cell to escort the prisoner to his fate, they found John Colt on his bed, a dirk thrust into his heart. At that very moment, the cupola of the prison went up in flames and the cry was raised: "Colt has committed suicide and the Tombs are on fire!" The fire provided a graphic subject for Currier and Ives, and had Beadle been at work in 1842, John Colt's story would have vied with the bloodiest paperbacks.

So, amidst blood and thunder, fire and gore, ended the drama of the publisher-bookseller-author, John Caldwell Colt. Or did it end? While his onetime partner, Nathan Burgess, went on to write his *Ambrotype* and *Photograph Manuals*, while his brother Sam Colt built his immense armory, while Cyrus W. Field laid the Atlantic cable and Robert Carter and Robert Hoe prospered in their trades—was all ended for the man who had once brought them all together? No story such as his is complete without a legend, and legend has it that somehow Colt escaped, perhaps in the clothing of Caroline Henshaw, substituting the body of a dead convict for his own.

Some said that with the help of Lewis Gaylord Clark and James Fenimore Cooper he was spirited away, to live on in anonymity in California or in Europe.

Wherever he may have wandered, his gory ghost still haunts the impatient publisher and the dilatory printer, recalling the bloody deed that brought together for a brief moment in court a parade of witnesses for the booktrade.

CAVEAT TYPOGRAPHUS! ! ! ! ! !

The Fruits of Authorship

O_N September 27, 1855, the Crystal Palace, that "beautiful edifice constructed wholly of iron and glass"[1] in what was then uptown New York—Forty-second Street, between the Reservoir and Sixth Avenue—was the scene of a festival, which, because of its significance as a register of author-publisher relations, deserves to be rescued from oblivion. Indeed, the New York Book Publishers' Association itself had been reorganized for the purpose of sponsoring the "Complimentary Fruit and Flower Festival."[2] William H. Appleton was President and George P. Putnam Secretary; and the entertainment committee, by the undeniable finesse of its arrangements, made it amply clear that the nineteenth century could launch a celebration that would eclipse many a twentieth-century cocktail party given to herald a new book or expand an author's ego.

On August 14, Putnam, on behalf of the Association, wrote to the caterer, Colonel Stetson of the Astor House, requesting entertainment for six hundred guests not to exceed $2,500.[3] Invitations were dispatched; and the replies received at the Association's headquarters at 348 Broadway gave promise of a stimulating evening and an almost united front on the desirability of cementing author-publisher relations. Speeches of the evening actually arrived at rather precise conclusions regarding the kindred interests of the two groups and the intellectual obligations of publishers.

The literary fruits were important. But so, too, were the more tangible ones, largely because of the many features that distinguish the occasion from modern imitations:

1. "The beverages were altogether destitute of alcoholic stimulant."
2. "The gentlemen refrained from indulgence in cigars."
3. "The place was kept at a temperature unusually comfortable for such an occasion."
4. "Gentlemen with ladies, and gentlemen without that privilege, alike endeavored to be polite, and displayed excellent capabilities of enjoyment."[4]

Reprinted from *American Notes & Queries* VIII, no. 7 (October 1948): 99–105.

All this—a far cry from the present-day receptions, at which "100-odd guests spend an hour or so blowing smoke at one another and milling around in search of the waiter"[5]—may be studied in closer detail in the September 29, 1855, issue of the *American Publishers' Circular and Literary Gazette*. The entire number is given over to a report of the Festival, with apologies to the advertisers whose space had been consumed for that purpose. There, beneath the headlines "Authors Among Fruits" and "Genius in the Crystal Palace," the reader may unearth a close-range view of the forebear of the authors' cocktail party.

The whole of the north end of the Crystal Palace was enclosed in the form of a pavilion, with alternating strips of red, white, and blue. Six long tables were flanked by a dais upon which rested the table for the officers and speakers of the evening. Covers were laid for six hundred and fifty guests. There were place-cards for all, and small bouquets wrapped in filigree for the ladies. In front of the President's chair was a cornucopia. From the mouth of it poured "a luscious flood of the gifts of Pomona"; and from the other extremity hung a cord bearing the inscription, "May plenty crown the humblest board." Facing the President also was a figure representing Gutenberg with his printing press. On the wainscoting around the enclosure was an array of greenhouse plants and "vases of gorgeous flowers." Behind the dais, and reaching toward the great dome of the Crystal Palace, was a raised amphitheatre with seats for ladies. The whole edifice was brilliantly illuminated, "the gas working admirably." The chandelier under the dome and the lights in the picture gallery were ablaze, and from under the stained roof hung a spread of gas jets setting off this inscription: "COMPLIMENTARY FRUIT AND FLOWER FESTIVAL,/GIVEN TO AUTHORS,/BY THE/NEW YORK PUB-LISHERS' ASSOCIATION/SEPTEMBER 27, 1855."

Lines of gaslights were arranged to represent the Temple of Wisdom, in which was placed a small white statue of Clio, the Muse of History, and above her in letters of light one saw: "HONOR TO GENIUS." On the walls hung portraits of the publishers, Mathew Carey, Thomas Desilver, Daniel Appleton, and E. L. Carey.[6]

At a little after six, the guests gathered beneath the rotunda and entered, two by two, to the banquet. As the orchestra, under the direction of Messrs. Noll and Ritzell, struck up, genius prepared to be served. The President's table was graced by such distinguished personages as Washington Irving, "fresh and genial, and the object of universal remark," Dr. Valentine Mott, President Woolsey of Yale, the Hon. Charles King of Columbia, Mayor Wood, the Rev. Henry Ward Beecher, William Cullen Bryant, and Prof. S. F. B. Morse. At other tables were E. A. Duyckinck, Alice and Phoebe Cary, Charles A. Dana, T. S. Arthur, Epes Sargent, Charles G. Leland, "Fanny Fern," Park Benjamin, L. A. Godey, the Bottas, S. Austin Allibone, N. P. Willis, Benjamin J. Lossing, and H. T. Tuckerman. As one journalist put it,

"On no former occasion has there been an opportunity to enjoy the sight of so many great lions at once." Another remarked that in view of the

> brilliant and splendid array presented by the . . . guests, no doubt much of the singular beauty of the ornamental arrangements and their novelty as a public entertainment, were lost upon those who witnessed . . . them.

All in all, it was said, the whole effect was one which "perhaps no other public occasion in this country has surpassed." The "demi-toilets" of the ladies formed a pleasing ensemble; the palace of glass and iron rivaled the temple of the Pythian Apollo. The "coup d'oeil" was indeed brilliant.

The feast itself came as close to nectar and ambrosia as the caterers, Coleman and Stetson of the Astor House, could conceive. The promises inscribed on the satin bill of fare were fulfilled at the tables, where, amid devices of books in singular bindings and a profusion of fruits—"from the blushing peach to the red-lipped melon"—dinner was served. Among the cold ornamental dishes were boned turkey, "Noi of Veal, en Bellevue," "Serpents destroying Bird's Nest," and "Bastions ornamented." The creams were horticultural; the fruit romantic and historical, Vicar of Wakefield Pears and "Pommes d'Neigles." The pastry was ornamental, introducing models of Gutenberg, the Temple of History, and a Monument of Literature; or geographical, indicating maps and books of travel, from Charlotte Russe to Swiss Meringues, from Bavarian Cheese to Champagne Jelly.

After proper obeisance had been paid to so ingenious a bill of fare, Mr. Appleton arose to welcome the guests. He felt the occasion historic:

> Under the guise of a light floral banquet, it is very possible that we may be inaugurating a new era in the history of that trade which ministers to the intellectual wants of a great and powerful people. Our present social gathering of authors and publishers may lead to unanticipated results. It can hardly fail to promote a good understanding among those who exert an important influence on the education of the national mind.

He then followed this with a significant remark on the obligations of his own profession:

> It is in our power, and therefore it becomes our imperative duty, to lend the most important aid in raising the intellectual and moral tone of the literature which is daily and hourly sent forth among the people of our native land.

The second meaningful note of the evening was sounded by the Secretary of the Association. Putnam asserted that the interests of

> writers, and publishers, and sellers of books, in this great and thriving country, . . . are, or should be, mutual and identical.

William Cullen Bryant, responding to a toast of the evening, reiterated this motif, which, indeed, had been the inspiration of the Festival itself:

Authors and booksellers are each other's best allies. . . . When I hear of a rich bookseller, I know that there have been successful authors.

Putnam drew attention, also, to the increasing importance of American literature, when he offered yet another answer to the question, "Who reads an American Book?" and reported for the benefit of our English cousins that

the sheets from our book-presses alone, in a single year, would reach nearly twice round the globe; and if we add the periodicals and newspapers, the issues of our presses in about eighteen months would make a belt, two feet wide, printed on both sides, which would stretch from New York to the Moon!

A final interesting point was scored in a poem by James T. Fields,[7] who, contrasting earlier publishing methods with those of his own day, perceived that by 1855 publishers had learned at least one lesson in the art of commerce:

> How slow and sure they set their types,
>   How small editions ran!
> Then fifty thousand never sold—
>   Before the sale began.
>
> For how could they, poor plodding souls,
>   Be either swift or wise,
> Who never learned the mighty art
>   Of *how* to advertise.
>
>   . . .
>
> But yet a hint may not be lost,
>   Altho' 'tis dropped in fun,—
> Don't publish books that *from* your press
>   Whoever reads may run!

Though the toasts were downed in "crystal Croton," they were as potent as the speeches:

THE REPUBLIC OF LETTERS—Boundless as the world, it should guarantee equal rights to every section: pure genius should be its only badge of honor, and the sure passport to substantial reward.

After the hopeful air, "Behold how brightly breaks the morning," the toasts continued:

AMERICAN LITERATURE—Its youth gives brilliant promise of an honorable future: may its riper years show that it has been trained in the right schools.

THE PUBLISHERS OF BOSTON—A Fraternity that has been illustrated by the patriotism of Knox, and the practical intelligence of an Armstrong, a Lincoln and a Brown, may still be proud of the products of their cultivated Fields.

THE BOOKSELLERS OF THE UNION—So long as they are the mediums for diffusing sound intelligence and the pure products of true genius, they deserve an honorable position in the community; for, in the ordinary business of their lives, they become benefactors to their country.

Until nearly midnight the toasts were offered, responses made, and letters from absentees read. E. H. Chapin gave an address on that "revolutionist," the Printing Press, that "voice for the groaning people," whose rumble is "better than the rattle of artillery." Samuel Goodrich was called for, but his only reply was that the last time he had heard of Peter Parley, he had gone somewhere up the Connecticut River to see if he could find Rip Van Winkle. Washington Irving, in the midst of all the bustle, enjoyed an unexpected meeting with his old friend Moses Thomas, the ex-publisher from Philadelphia, whom he had not seen for a quarter of a century. The female authors were honored in a punning toast:

> The *New England Tale* is re-echoed from the *New Home* of the Far West; and from a *Cabin* on the banks of the Ohio, a touch of Nature vibrates among *The Lofty and the Lowly* through the *Wide, Wide World.*

The authors present appeared to be united in their belief that the Festival might usher in an era of harmony in author-publisher relations. Letters from those unable to attend reiterated this same hope. Nor should one short sentence be omitted from the report of so splendid an occasion. A letter from Robert Winthrop, discussing the publishers and booksellers of America, declared, "Theirs is the only *imprimatur* to which a Free People can ever submit." Indeed, there were several "fruits" of this reunion. Some of them, less tangible than the Vicar of Wakefield Pears, are virtually as sound as they were almost a century ago.

Notes

1. James G. Wilson, *The Memorial History of the City of New York* (N. Y., 1893), III, 444. *See also* Georg Carstensen and Charles Gildemeister, *New York Crystal Palace* (N. Y., 1854).

2. George Haven Putnam, *A Memoir of George Palmer Putnam* (N. Y. & London, 1903), I, 378.

3. G. P. Putnam to Colonel L. Stetson, August 14, 1855; included in the Festival Correspondence (*See Appendix, next page*).

4. This and the subsequent quotations relating to the Festival appear in "Complimentary Fruit Festival of the New York Book Publishers' Association To Authors and Booksellers, At the Crystal Palace, September 27, 1855," *American Publishers' Circular and Literary Gazette*, September 29, 1855, pp. 65–79. An interesting account of the Festival by a Chicago publisher appears in D. B. Cooke, "My Memories of the Book Trade," *Publishers' Weekly*, March 25, 1876, p. 404. *See also* J. C. Derby, *Fifty Years among Authors, Books and Publishers* (N. Y., 1884), pp. 34 ff.

5. Ralph Thompson, "In and Out of Books," *New York Times Book Review*, October 17, 1948, p. 8.

6. Two of the letters in the Festival Correspondence refer to the shipping of

portraits: those from Henry C. Carey, Philadelphia, September 22, 1855, and from Mr. & Mrs. C. C. Little, Cambridge, September 21, 1855.

7. Fields had written to Putnam from Boston, September 17, 1855, "I should like to know what guns are to speak on the 27th, so that if there is too much ammunition and my cartridge is not needed, I shall not be obliged to pull my small trigger." The letter is printed on page 380 (Vol. I) of G. H. Putnam's *A Memoir of George Palmer Putnam.*

Appendix

Replies to Festival invitations were carefully saved by G. P. Putnam and eventually found their way into the New York Public Library, where they have been mounted in two volumes labeled *New York Book Publishers Association. Fruit Festival Correspondence.* These materials are of interest not merely because they include notes from such figures as Melville, Holmes, Whittier, Bryant, and Longfellow, but because letters from some of the lesser lights constitute a short symposium on author-publisher relations. The following excerpts are cited by courtesy of Mr. Robert W. Hill, Manuscript Division, New York Public Library:

THE PROFESSION OF PUBLISHING

"I entertain a great respect for the Booksellers & Publishers of the U. States as a class; . . .

"The vocation of the printer & publisher, in its various departments, is among the most important in the community, closely connected with the promotion of its best interests."—Edward Everett, Boston, September 25, 1855. [Everett, 1794–1865, the celebrated statesman and editor of the *North American Review.*]

"They [Authors, Publishers and Booksellers] are the caterers . . . of the mental food for the immortal mind."—John Grigg, Philadelphia, September 15, 1855 [Grigg, 1792–1864, Philadelphia publisher.]

AUTHOR-PUBLISHER RELATIONS

"The occasion will be of special interest. It would be pleasant to sit at feast with so many, who, as authors, have adorned our national name. And it would be pleasant also to be the guest of those active, enlightened & generous publishers who have done so much for authors. . . .

"At your table there will be an aggregation of various genius & talent, constituting a true *Wittenagemote*, which may justly gratify an honest pride of country. But grateful as this may be, as a token of power, it will be more grateful still as a token of that concord, which is growing among men in all the relations of life. The traditional feud between authors & publishers promises to lose itself in your festival, even as the traditional feud between

England & France is all absorbed in the welcome of Victoria by Louis Napoleon. . . . And the whole scene, . . . will be an augury of that permanent co-operation & harmony which will secure to the pen its mightiest triumphs."—Charles Sumner, Boston, September 26, 1855. [Sumner, 1811–1874, the eminent statesman and opponent of slavery.]

"My own share in literature though humble, has been sufficient to make me estimate highly these efforts to promote confidence and good will between Authors and Publishers."—Sarah Josepha Hale, Philadelphia, September 21, 1855. [Sarah J. Hale, 1790–1879, editor of *Godey's Lady's Book.*]

"For myself, I needed no assurance that this Festival will be 'a pleasant and acceable reunion of those connected in the book-world, both as authors and as business-men.'

"I have long been of the opinion that the prevailing idea of the natural enmity of authors and publishers was a popular fallacy." Grace Greenwood, Coldwater, Michigan, September 17, 1855. [Sara J. C. Lippincott, 1823–1904, wrote numerous books under the pseudonym of "Grace Greenwood," and was one of the first women in the United States to become a regular newspaper correspondent.]

"To one who has watched, for half a century, the simultaneous growth of native literature and publishing enterprise in this country, this occasion suggests curious recollections and . . . hopes. The first time I had the pleasure of witnessing a social gathering of American Publishers, was at the Old City Hotel, Broadway, in 1802, at your primary organization I believe, and under the auspices of the remarkable Matthew Carey. [An outcome of Carey's book fair of 1802 was the earliest national booksellers' organization, which came to be called the American Company of Booksellers.] About thirty years after I was one of the large assembly brought together by the Brothers Harper. If you compare the annual list of new works, the authors, bookstores, processes of manufacture at the beginning of the century and now, you will realize the vast progress of our country in this the noblest department of her industry; and feel how much of interest the history of your Guild might possess for one who has followed it with sympathy and circumspection. It is to me a most grateful reminiscence that *Stereotyping*, which has so multiplied the capabilities of your pursuit, was originated by one of our eminent fellow citizens of New York.

"Having, at times, during a busy professional life, become somewhat familiar both with the composing stick and the pen, I am proud to claim fraternity with both hosts and guests; and as the latter are chiefly authors, I cannot but hope that a better mutual understanding may be one of the fruits of this re-union."—John W. Francis, New York, September 13, 1855. [Francis, 1789–1861, the well-known physician and author of *Old New York*, had been apprenticed to a printer in his youth. He commented upon the three publishers' meetings he attended in *Old New York* (N. Y., 1865, p. 354), and stated, "A comparative view of these three periods in literary progress would furnish an instructive illustration of the workings of the American mind and of the enterprise and capabilities of the American press."]

ONE DISSENTING VOICE

"I feel honored and flattered, but my dear Sir I freely confess that this scheme for setting Gog and Magog face to face has appeared to me eminently preposterous. I cannot learn that any harmonious reunion of the beasts of the earth for fruit-eating purposes has taken place since their lamentable dispersion after the fall of Adam.

"[But] . . . The venom of critics will certainly be harmless when their fangs are buried in peaches. The most heartless and avaricious publishers cannot receive plums otherwise than with complacency—and I allow that it is next to impossible to conceive of a poet, melancholy and heart-broken, over grapes.—I will come if I can."—Erastus W. Ellsworth, East Windsor Hill, Connecticut, September 14, 1855. [Ellsworth, 1822–1902, poet and inventor.]

4

Books and Their Fates

The Long and the Short of It

Whitman's Leaves of Grass

T HE FIRST TWO editions of *Leaves of Grass* are essential for any collector who would pry below the surface of Walt Whitman's life and work. They are far more than two editions; they are really two completely different books. They reflect light not only upon the nature of Whitman's poetry but upon the nature of the poet, their publisher, and the taste of the times. Together they tell a fascinating story of American authorship and publishing at the mid-century.

On May 15, 1855, Walt Whitman walked into the clerk's office of New York's Southern District Court and inquired about the correct wording for a copyright notice for his forthcoming book.[1]

He had set some of the pages of type himself at Rome's Printing Office in Brooklyn. Not long afterward, a visitor "found him revising some proof, (his) blue striped shirt, opening from a red throat . . . His beard and hair . . . greyer than is usual with a man of thirty-six. His face and eye are interesting, and his head rather narrow behind the eyes; but a thick brow looks as if it might have absorbed much . . . His eye can kindle strangely; and his words are ruddy with health. He is clearly his Book."[2]

He was also his own publisher. On July 4, 1855 "his Book"—*Leaves of Grass*—which has been called "America's second Declaration of Independence," appeared, a thin quarto volume bound in green cloth, without the name of the author-publisher, with "only his photograph as signature."[3] Some seven or eight hundred copies were printed,[4] not all of which were immediately bound. In later copies Whitman bound in eight pages of comments and reviews. Meanwhile, priced at two dollars a copy, *Leaves of Grass* was advertised in the *New York Tribune* on July 6 as "for sale by SWAYNE, No. 210 Fulton St., Brooklyn, and by FOWLERS & WELLS, No. 308 Broadway, N.Y."

Reprinted from *American Book Collector* XXVI, no. 2 (Jan./Feb. 1976): 23–24.

Besides being bookseller-publishers, Fowlers & Wells were phrenologists or head-examiners, who believed that a human being's talents and disposition, mind and character could be ascertained from the shape of his skull. They also believed that, with phrenological guidance, the various faculties of the mind were improvable. Their philosophy was an affirmative one; their confidence in man's perfectibility unshakeable.

In this they stood on common ground with Walt Whitman. As a matter of fact, six years before his book was published, on July 16, 1849, he had walked into the Fowlers & Wells office and submitted his own massive head to the test of phrenology. Lorenzo Fowler's phrenological description of W. Whitman was a penetrating sketch of a man who thought for himself, who could "see much that is unjust and inhuman in the present condition of society" and who had but "little regard for creeds or ceremonies." Whitman's Amativeness got a high rating—6 on a scale of 1 to 7. "You . . . are yourself at all times," Fowler had summed up. Walt Whitman was fortified by Lorenzo Fowler's insightful analysis. He kept his phrenological chart to the end of his life and published it on five different occasions including the first and second editions of *Leaves of Grass*.[5]

Meanwhile, before his book was published, Whitman's association with the firm of Fowlers & Wells was strengthened. In 1850 and 1851 he bought and sold some of their publications. Later on, in November 1855, he became a staff writer for a Fowler & Wells[6] periodical, *Life Illustrated*.

The phrenological publishers continued to advertise the first edition of *Leaves of Grass* in brief notices that convey their own sad story of a nonselling book.[7]

Four days after the first advertisement had appeared, the name of Swayne's Bookstore vanished from the *Tribune*. Possibly having found the book objectionable, Swayne refused to handle it, leaving the field to Fowler & Wells as sole agents for its sale. By September the price of *Leaves of Grass* was lowered from $2 to $1. Not many of the copies that had been dispersed had been sold. Some had been distributed with the compliments of Walt Whitman; others had been sent out by Fowler & Wells for review; still others had found their way to England. One of Whitman's copies was to go to Ralph Waldo Emerson; some of the review copies would be reviewed by Whitman himself; and the Fowler & Wells London agent was to play an important part in establishing Whitman's English reputation.[8]

Leaves of Grass was not well reviewed. The three best reviews, published anonymously, were written by Whitman himself.[9] But the *New York Tribune* in October 1855 ran the now famous letter from Emerson. Its printing has been called "perhaps an event of greater importance in the history of American literature than the printing of any other letter has ever been."[10] That letter, in which Emerson greeted the poet "at the beginning of a great career," had been addressed to him in care of Fowlers & Wells.

Having done their best to sell the first edition of *Leaves of Grass*, Fowler & Wells were prepared, by August 1856, to announce another edition. This new edition of *Leaves* was more than a reprinting—it was in effect an altogether different and expanded book. Fowler & Wells were its publishers in deed but not in name. Encouraged perhaps by Emerson's endorsement, as well as by their own personal knowledge of the poet, they consented to publish the second edition of *Leaves*, but, loath to tilt openly with Dame Grundy, they refused to take credit for it. Hence their imprint does not appear on the title page. Nonetheless they played a vital part in the production of the second edition of *Leaves of Grass.*

The possibility of a new edition had been broached as early as June 1856 when a firm partner—Samuel R. Wells, chief of the publishing division—wrote the following letter marked "Private" to Walt Whitman: "After 'duly considering,' we have concluded that it is best for us to insist on the omission of certain objectionable passages in Leaves of Grass, or, decline publishing it . . .

". . . it will be *better* for *you* to have the work published by clean hands, i.e. by a House, not now committed to unpopular notions . . . "[11]

By July, Wells' reluctance was to some extent overcome and the decision was made. Despite the slow sales of the first edition, Whitman had written so many additional poems that a second edition would be less a new edition than a new book. With twenty previously unpublished poems, more than half the volume would offer "entirely new material" including the frank paean to sex, "A Woman Waits for Me," which had doubtless caused Wells to hesitate. Now he compromised: Fowler & Wells would offer publication without an imprimatur, and a thousand copies of the new *Leaves of Grass* would be printed.

Copyright for the new edition was recorded on September 11, 1856. The book looked altogether different from the first edition. This was a chunky, squat volume bound in drab green cloth—so different indeed from the first *Leaves* that one wit distinguished the two editions as "The Long and the Short of it." The "Short of it" consisted of 384 pages, a volume swollen not only with the new poems but with a section of quoted comments called "Leaves-Droppings," among which were Whitman's own review of himself from the *American Phrenological Journal*, Lorenzo Fowler's phrenological notes on the poet, and Emerson's laudatory letter.

Emerson's letter—at least one sentence of it—was also emblazoned, without Emerson's authorization or knowledge, upon the backstrip of each volume. There, stamped in gold, were the words: "I Greet You at the Beginning of A Great Career   R W Emerson."

Despite this, however, the new *Leaves* did not fare well. The second edition was "even more unfavorably reviewed" than the first because of its "exploitations of the sexual theme." As for Emerson, he commented that "If he had known his letter would be published he might have qualified his praise. 'There are parts of the book where I hold my nose as I read. . . . It is all there, as if in an auctioneer's catalogue.'"[12]

Understandably, therefore, the already timid publishers took fright and "quietly asked to be excused from continuing the book any further."[13] The third edition of *Leaves of Grass* would not be published until 1860, when Thayer and Eldridge of Boston would bring it out. Yet, the Fowler & Wells edition of *Leaves of Grass*—the second edition—is really the edition that laid "the foundation of future editions."

Collectors who would study Walt Whitman must have not only the first edition of "his Book," but the second and indeed as many subsequent editions as possible. Since Whitman was clearly "his Book," to know Whitman one must know "his Book" in all its many metamorphoses and with all its accretions. All the editions of *Leaves* that appeared during the poet's lifetime are indispensable sources for a great career, from its beginning to its end.

Notes

1. Madeleine B. Stern, *Heads & Headlines: The Phrenological Fowlers* (Norman, Okla., 1971) pp. 99–123, 291–296. This treats in full the relationship between Whitman and Fowler(s) & Wells.

2. Moncure Daniel Conway, *Autobiography Memories and Experiences* (Boston and New York, 1904) I, 215 f.

3. Emory Holloway, *Whitman* (New York and London, 1926) p. 117.

4. *Walt Whitman A Catalogue Based Upon the Collections of The Library of Congress* (Washington, 1955) pp. xi–xii places the number of printed and bound copies at 795.

5. It was also published in the *Brooklyn Daily Times* of September 29, 1855 and in the third edition of *Leaves of Grass*. The fifth reprint was made by Whitman's literary executors.

6. In 1855 Fowlers & Wells became Fowler & Wells with the departure from the firm of its founder, Orson Fowler.

7. *New York Daily Tribune* (July 6, 1855–August 4, 1855, September 25, 1855–November 24, 1855, February 18, 1856–March 1, 1856) p. 1.

8. William Horsell, the Fowler agent who introduced Whitman to England, was a British counterpart of the Fowlers, being a vegetarian and water cure enthusiast as well as a publisher. Both Horsell and Fowler imprints appeared jointly on some copies of the 1855 *Leaves of Grass*. In 1868, William Michael Rossetti's edition of *Leaves* finally brought Whitman to the excited attention of the British public.

9. In *The United States Review* (September 1855), the *Brooklyn Daily Times* (September 29, 1855) and the *American Phrenological Journal* (October 1855).

10. Ralph L. Rusk, ed., *The Letters of Ralph Waldo Emerson* (New York, 1939) IV, 520.

11. S. R. Wells to Friend Whitman, New York, June 7, 1856 (courtesy Charles E. Feinberg, Detroit, Michigan).

12. Conway, *op. cit.* I, 216 f.

13. John Burroughs, *Notes on Walt Whitman, as Poet and Person* (New York, 1867) p. 19.

The First Beadle Dime Novel and Its Author

T HE WRITER of the first Beadle Dime Novel should, by rights, have been an adventurous trailer in buckskin, a scout of the Great Plains familiar with powder horn and painted Indian. It is one of the delightful paradoxes of American literary history, however, that the "Star of American Authors" who produced *Malaeska: the Indian Wife of The White Hunter* was neither trailer nor scout, nor indeed a man at all. She was a woman, fair, fat and fifty, who hailed from New England, named Mrs. Ann Sophia Stephens.

By 1860, when Beadle's first dime novel was published, Mrs. Stephens had married, borne two children, been closely associated with Edgar Allan Poe on the staff of *Graham's Magazine*, flowered as the chatelaine of New York's literary society, gained a powerful reputation as the author of serials that appeared with cosmic regularity in *Peterson's Magazine*, and had a finger in various political pies served up to an expanding nation on the eve of war.

Like its prolific author, *Malaeska*, too, had had a history before it appeared in orange-colored paper wrappers as Beadle's Dime Novel Number One. The story had first been published as a serial in William W. Snowden's New York magazine, *The Ladies' Companion*, between February and April 1839, when Mrs. Stephens was twenty-nine years old. The author had prepared for its composition by a fairly serious study of the Indian language as well as by an earlier experiment in Indian narratives, "Mary Derwent. A Tale of the Early Settlers," for which she had won a $200 prize.

Despite its gaudy pictures of Indian life, the three-part serial, "Malaeska," lay unnoticed in the pages of *The Ladies' Companion* for more than two decades in the course of which its author established so enviable a reputation that by 1860, when the firm of Beadle was searching for a novel to begin its dime series, they could do no better than turn to Mrs. Stephens' work.

Abridged from Madeleine B. Stern's *We the Women: Career Firsts of Nineteenth-Century America* (New York: Schulte Publishing Co., 1963) and reprinted from *The American Book Collector* XIV, no. 2 (Oct. 1963): 27.

It may have been through Orville Victor, who had been a contributor to *Graham's Magazine* and who was to become the Beadle editor in 1861, that overtures were made to Mrs. Stephens for the right to reprint "Malaeska." The story had been chosen "as the initial volume of the Dime Novel series," the publishers explained, "from the interest which attaches to its fine pictures of border life and Indian adventure, and from the real romance of its incidents. It is American in all its features, pure in its tone, elevating in its sentiments." The offer of $250 for the right to reprint was accepted and in the June 9, 1860 issue of the *New-York Daily Tribune*, Irwin P. Beadle & Co. announced that "Beadle's Dime Novels, No. 1" was "Ready This Morning."

First 10,000 copies, then 20,000 more were issued. In time, 300,000 copies were said to have been sold—perhaps as many as half a million copies in the various reprints. A new best seller was in the making. Everywhere, as the 1860's catapulted by, readers devoured the sad but moral story of an Indian princess wed to a white hunter—union soldiers in army camps to whom Beadle bundled off the paperbacks in carloads, young men and boys at home who would recall the year 1860 less as the year of South Carolina's secession than as the year of Beadle's first dime novel.

With just the right proportion of savagery and civilization, Victorian sweetness and wild melodrama, Mrs. Stephens had found the formula for dime novel success. *Malaeska* was swiftly reprinted, first as a Fifteen Cent Novel, then in the American Six-penny Library for London consumption.

Meanwhile, Mrs. Stephens followed the pattern she had set by unearthing more serials for transformation into Beadle Dime Novels, supplying the firm with six more tales between 1860 and 1864—stories that stirred in the dime novel cauldron a delectable broth of covered wagons and border scouts, fur-traders and savage Indians. To a nation hungry for historical romance she served up its own romantic history.

By the 1880's, although the lustre of the "Star of American Authors" showed as yet no signs of dimming, the Beadle firm entered into a decline. Despite the fact that they reprinted *Malaeska* yet again in a series of New Dime Novels, both the nature and the reputation of their product were waning. The critics who had at first found the dime novels "free from any immoral tendency," now castigated them as "distinctly evil in . . . teachings and tendencies." The Hon. Abel Goddard made his bid for immortality by introducing into the New York Assembly a bill declaring guilty of a misdemeanor "any person who shall sell, loan, or give to any minor . . . any dime novel . . . without first obtaining the written consent of the parent or guardian."

On August 20, 1886, the seventy-six-year-old Ann Stephens, who had been "among the most prolific authors of the age," died. By 1897, the House of Beadle reached its debacle, its dime novel spurned as "an atrocity."

Yet, like Mrs. Stephens' own serials, *Malaeska* was to enjoy a "sequel." In

1929, the first Beadle dime novel was reprinted and hailed with fervor by nearly every reviewer in the country. With its "roots in the American scene" it was re-interpreted as "the nearest thing . . . to . . . a true 'proletarian' literature" and as "a landmark on the road of American literature."

Malaeska had become an American document and the few extant copies of that orange-colored paperback first edition were exalted as rarities. Upon the first Beadle Dime Novel, time had once again worked its little ironies.

Behind the Mask of
Louisa May Alcott

ANY STORY that has kept the secret of its authorship for eighty years presents enticements to a literary sleuth. If that story was a gaudy, gruesome Gothic the enticements are enhanced. And if the author turns out to be none other than America's best-loved writer of children's books the enticements become irresistible.

Not one such story but nine were dashed off in secret by a young woman in her thirties whose equipment included a riotous imagination, a dramatic instinct, and an indefatigable right hand. Seated at her desk, an old green and red party wrap draped around her as a "glory cloak," Louisa May Alcott dipped her pen into gory ink and produced shockers for the 1860s—tales of jealousy and revenge, murder and insanity, feminist anger, passion and punishment, drug addiction. By the end of the decade, with the publication of Part II of *Little Women*, the author of those thrillers would be known to most of the literate world as the Children's Friend.[1] Having found a comfortable and eminently respectable literary niche, she no longer had the need to produce sensational tales. Their secret was well kept. Eventually it would be unearthed as a chapter in publishing history.

Louisa Alcott was no Children's Friend when she wrote "Pauline's Passion and Punishment"; "A Whisper in the Dark"; "A Marble Woman: or, The Mysterious Model"; "V.V.: or, Plots and Counterplots"; "The Abbot's Ghost"; "Behind a Mask: or, A Woman's Power." She was a compulsive writer, churning out narratives anonymously or pseudonymously—sensational stories that provided her with a psychological catharsis at the same time that they filled an economic need. Because she was a highly skilled professional writer even before *Little Women*, those shockers of the 1860s are still page-turners more than a century later. They are also interesting revelations of a complex mind, a multi-faceted writer experimenting with varied literary techniques.

The money her blood-and-thunders earned were sorely needed by the Alcott family. The four "little women" had grown up not only in the climate of love and transcendental idealism but in the climate of poverty. Bronson Alcott, their father, had no gift for money-making, and the cost of coal, the price of shoes, discussions of economic ways and means formed an obbligato to Louisa Alcott's early years. Later on she was often the only breadwinner in the family.

But it was not economic need alone that drew her to a gory inkstand. In her flamboyant narratives Louisa Alcott could give vent to the passions and frustrations of thirty difficult years. In so doing she achieved an emotional catharsis for herself and, in an oblique manner, foreshadowed the feminist anger of a later century. Her anger had traceable biographical sources. Life in Concord, Massachusetts, despite the proximity of such illustrissimi as Emerson, Thoreau, and Hawthorne, was far from a haven of sweetness and light. At mid-century the family poverty was extreme, and the Alcotts moved temporarily to Boston where Mrs. Alcott opened an employment agency. At the age of nineteen Louisa herself went out to service for the Richardson family of Dedham, Massachusetts. After seven weeks of drudgery as a domestic she received four dollars which her outraged family promptly returned. The experience left its mark upon an impressionable young woman. A few years later, frustrated in all her attempts to find work, she contemplated suicide. The temptation was evanescent, but, like her humiliation in Dedham, it became part of the psychological equipment of a writer of thrillers. Finally, the illness Louisa Alcott suffered after she had served six weeks as a nurse during the Civil War provided her with a backlog of sinister dreams, nightmares, and fevered delirium that could be interwoven into the fabric of her blood-and-thunders.

For the searcher after sources, there are other strains in Louisa Alcott that reappear in her sensational tales. Her lifelong devotion to the theater, the melodramas she concocted with her sister Anna for performance before the Concord neighbors, her omnivorous reading of fiction—all contributed details for her Gothics. The disguises, desertions and suicides, the magic herbs, love potions and death phials of her early plays could be introduced with subtle variations for flamboyant weeklies. Indeed much of her skill in lively dialogue, suspenseful plotting and broad-stroke character delineation may be traced to her persistent romance with greasepaint. As for her reading, there is little doubt that she dipped from time to time into the gore of the Gothic novel, whose ruined abbeys and frowning castles supplied her with background touches and whose unholy motifs introduced her to pacts with the devil and all sorts of supernatural agencies from ghouls to ghosts.

With such grist in store, Louisa Alcott at the age of thirty was well prepared for her nightmarish excursions. Even then she was a compulsive writer. She had been the mainstay of the *Saturday Evening Gazette*, author of *Flower Fables*, contributor to the *Atlantic Monthly*. Her *Hospital Sketches* were to appear in 1863. She had experimented with a variety of literary techniques from tales of sweetness and light to realistic war narratives. By 1862 she was ready for her literary Walpurgis night.

Despite the fact that the secret of her double literary life was kept for eighty years, the author scattered clues to lure the detective working in the field of publishing history. One such clue was the letter she wrote to a young friend in June 1862:

> I intend to illuminate the Ledger with a blood & thunder tale as they are easy to "compoze" & are better paid than moral & elaborate works of Shakespeare so dont be shocked if I send you a paper containing a picture of Indians, pirates, wolves, bears & distressed damsels in a grand tableau over a title like this "The Maniac Bride" or The Bath of Blood A Thrilling Tale of Passion." [2]

What was that paper with graphic illustrations of bears and distressed damsels? What was the actual title of "The Maniac Bride or The Bath of Blood"?

There were other hints that peppered her journals of the 1860s, veiled allusions to a succession of thrillers, manuscripts sent to editors identified only by enigmatic initials. For example, this, in 1862:

> Wrote two tales for L. I enjoy romancing to suit myself; and though my tales are silly, they are not bad; and my sinners always have a good spot somewhere. I hope it is good drill for fancy and language, for I can do it fast; and Mr. L. says my tales are so "dramatic, vivid, and full of plot," they are just what he wants. [3]

Who was Mr. L.?

In 1865 she wrote:

> . . . fell back on rubbishy tales, for they pay best, and I can't afford to starve on praise, when sensation stories are written in half the time and keep the family cosey. [4]

What were those sensation stories? How much did they pay?

A year later she revealed:

> Wrote two long tales for L. . . . One for E. for which he paid $75. [5]

Who was the mysterious E. who had now joined the equally mysterious L.?

Little Women itself was filled with clues for the literary sleuth and publishing historian:

> Jo . . . began to feel herself a power in the house, for by the magic of a pen, her "rubbish" turned into comforts for them all. *The Duke's Daughter* paid the butcher's bill, *A Phantom Hand* put down a new carpet, and the *Curse of the Coventrys* proved the blessing of the Marches in the way of groceries and gowns.

For the editors of the *Blarneystone Banner* or the *Weekly Volcano*, Jo March "like most young scribblers, . . . went abroad for her characters and scenery; and banditti, counts, gypsies, nuns, and duchesses appeared upon her stage."

... as thrills could not be produced except by harrowing up the souls of the readers, history and romance, land and sea, science and art, police records and lunatic asylums, had to be ransacked for the purpose. . . . Eager to find material for stories, and bent on making them original in plot, if not masterly in execution, she searched newspapers for accidents, incidents, and crimes; she excited the suspicions of public librarians by asking for works on poisons; she studied faces in the street, and characters, good, bad, and indifferent, all about her; she delved in the dust of ancient times for facts or fictions . . . and introduced herself to folly, sin, and misery.[6]

What were the titles of those tales of folly, sin, and misery, and where had they been published?

Even toward the end of her life, Louisa Alcott retained a taste for the lurid. In an interview she confessed:

I think my natural ambition is for the lurid style. I indulge in gorgeous fancies and wish that I dared inscribe them upon my pages and set them before the public. . . . How should I dare to interfere with the proper grayness of old Concord? The dear old town has never known a startling hue since the redcoats were there. Far be it from me to inject an inharmonious color into the neutral tint. And my favorite characters! Suppose they went to cavorting at their own sweet will, to the infinite horror of dear Mr. Emerson, . . . To have had Mr. Emerson for an intellectual god one's life is to be invested with a chain armor of propriety. . . . And what would my own good father think of me . . . if I set folks to doing the things that I have a longing to see my people do? No, . . . I shall always be a wretched victim to the respectable traditions of Concord.[7]

But Alcott scholars and publishing historians were convinced that Louisa May Alcott had not always been a wretched victim to the respectable traditions of Concord, that she had indeed indulged in gorgeous fancies and inscribed them upon her pages. Where were those pages? What extravagant, perhaps outrageous stories had she penned in secret behind some pseudonymous mask?

It was while I was researching the life of the author of *Little Women* for a biography entitled *Louisa May Alcott* that I met the well-known Alcott collector, the late Carroll Atwood Wilson of New York. I visited him with my lifelong friend and future partner, Dr. Leona Rostenberg, whose interest in printing history had already been manifested in several articles and monographs. Mr. Wilson proudly showed us his first editions of Alcott, and at the end of the evening turned to me, saying, "Miss Stern, you should apply for a Guggenheim Fellowship to complete your biography of Louisa May Alcott." Then to Leona Rostenberg he remarked, "Miss Rostenberg, we are all quite sure that Louisa Alcott must have had a pseudonym and must have written thrillers under that pseudonym. Why don't you find out what the pseudonym was and locate the stories?"

Mr. Wilson's provocative injunctions were promptly followed and the secret kept by Louisa Alcott for eighty years was at last disclosed. The thrillers we were trailing had been written, we were sure, before the publication of *Little Women* and some time during the Civil War. It was in the course of another war—the Second World War—that Leona Rostenberg discovered them.

One bright and auspicious spring morning we were seated side by side at a desk in Harvard's Houghton Library, delving through piles of manuscript and mountains of Alcott family letters. Suddenly the dignified atmosphere of Houghton Library was rent by a loud and triumphant warwhoop emanating from Miss Rostenberg. She had come upon five letters from a Boston publisher to Louisa Alcott—letters that disclosed her pseudonym, the titles of three of the thrillers, and the name of the periodical that had issued them. She had identified Jo March's *Blarneystone Banner* or *Weekly Volcano*; she had penetrated the secret of "The Maniac Bride or The Bath of Blood"; she had removed the mask from the Children's Friend.

All five letters had been written in 1865 and 1866 by James R. Elliott of Elliott, Thomes and Talbot, Boston—the E. of her journal—to Louisa Alcott. In them the publisher proposed printing her stories "V.V.: or, Plots and Counterplots," "A Marble Woman: or, The Mysterious Model," "Behind a Mask: or, A Woman's Power." Her pseudonym was revealed as A. M. Barnard, a name probably devised from her mother's initials (Abigail May) and the name of a family friend, the educator Henry Barnard. Publisher Elliott concluded with his terms of payment—$50 or $65 for a four-part serial. His letterhead disclosed the periodical in which the stories were to appear, *The Flag of Our Union*.

In 1943 Leona Rostenberg announced her discovery in an article entitled "Some Anonymous and Pseudonymous Thrillers of Louisa M. Alcott," published in *The Papers of the Bibliographical Society of America*.[8] The announcement made a bit of a splash among scholars. Carroll Atwood Wilson sent a charming note of appreciation. Librarians began searching for the anonymous and pseudonymous stories to add to their collections. The fact that Louisa May Alcott had indeed written thrillers under the pseudonym of A. M. Barnard was clearly established.

The stories themselves, however, were buried in the rare and crumbling periodicals that had printed them in the 1860s, and they remained buried for another thirty years. It was not until the spring of 1974 that the idea of reprinting the Alcott thrillers in book form came to mind. In 1975 four of them were published as *Behind a Mask: The Unknown Thrillers of Louisa May Alcott*; the following year the remaining five were issued as *Plots and Counterplots: More Unknown Thrillers of Louisa May Alcott*—both volumes published by William Morrow & Company of New York.[9]

And so, books have their fates, in this case a fate that was well over a century in the making. It was not only the author writing compulsively in secret who shaped that fate, but the publishers of her wild forays into the domains of madness and mind manipulation, opium addiction, and murderous revenge. Two publishing houses were involved in the original publication of Louisa Alcott's sensational tales.

Her first "sensational" publisher was the Mr. L. of her journal—the colorful magnate of New York's Publishers' Row, Frank Leslie[10]—a name that was itself a pseudonym. Born Henry Carter in Ipswich, England, in 1821, he had adopted the name of Frank Leslie because his father had not approved of his interest in woodcuts and engravings. As Frank Leslie he had worked on *The Illustrated London News* and in 1848 had migrated to America. Ruddy-faced, black-bearded, dynamic, young Leslie by 1855 had launched his *Frank Leslie's Illustrated Newspaper* which would make him a power in American journalism. With its graphic cuts of murders, assassinations, prize fights, and fires, it dominated the field of illustrated journalism for nearly three-quarters of a century. It sported just enough text to float the pictures—often huge double-page engravings that graphically depicted the *causes célèbres* of the century. This was the paper which in 1862 offered a $100 prize for a story.

Louisa Alcott wanted the prize and was ready with a story. With "Pauline's Passion and Punishment"—the first of her sensational narratives—she let down her literary hair and began the roster of her blood-and-thunders. Throughout the transactions she remained anonymous, in public at least. *Frank Leslie's Illustrated Newspaper* announced that after deliberating over two hundred manuscripts the editor had decided to award first prize to "a lady of Massachusetts" for a story of "exceeding power, brilliant description, thrilling incident and unexceptionable moral." To the author herself the Leslie editor wrote the glad tidings:

> Your tale "Pauline" this morning was awarded the $100 prize for the best short tale for Mr. Leslie's newspaper. . . . Allow me to congratulate you on your success and to recommend you to submit whatever you may hereafter have of the same sort for Mr. Leslie's acceptance.[11]

With "Pauline's Passion and Punishment"[12] the anonymous Louisa Alcott began her association with the L. of her journal. She followed "Pauline" with "A Whisper in the Dark,"[13] a story of mind control, and some years later provided another Leslie periodical, *Frank Leslie's Chimney Corner*, with the last and perhaps the most eyebrow-raising of her shockers, "Perilous Play,"[14] a brief narrative concerned entirely with hashish experimentation. In 1866, Leslie's seductive editor and future wife, Miriam Squier—herself a *femme fatale* who might have sat for an Alcott heroine—reminded Louisa May Alcott that Frank Leslie would be glad to receive a sensational story from her every month at $50 each.[15]

By that time the tireless author was receiving between $2 and $3 a column for thrillers produced for the Boston publishing firm of Elliott,

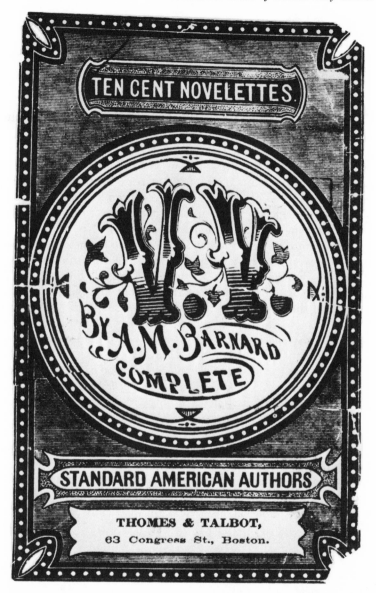

PLATE 3. *V.V.* by A. M. Barnard. Courtesy of the Rare Book Division, New York Public Library, Astor, Lenox and Tilden Foundations.

Thomes and Talbot.[16] They were a remarkable trio, those partners. One had edited tales of the wild, a second had yielded to the lure of the wild by sailing to New Granada, and the third had been the hero of a sensational novel which, if written, would have included chapters on gold digging and a jaunt to the Fiji Islands. If A. M. Barnard was ever at a loss for a plot she had merely to hearken to the lives of her Boston publishers. William Henry Thomes had sailed aboard an opium smuggler, encountered Indians and grizzlies, and succumbed to gold fever. James R. Elliott, who penned the letters that eventually disclosed the Alcott secret, had edited the type of story Thomes had lived. The two formed a publishing partnership in 1861 and, joined by Newton Talbot, they set out their shingle on Boston's Washington Street where they issued a chain of periodicals and novelettes to distract a nation at war.

The mainstay of their business was *The Flag of Our Union*, a miscellaneous weekly that specialized in violent narratives peopled with convicts and opium addicts. It was for that periodical that Louisa Alcott devised her pseudonym of A. M. Barnard and produced her bloodiest and most thunderous thrillers. "V.V.: or, Plots and Counterplots"[17] appeared as a four-part serial in 1865 and was later reprinted as No. 80 in the firm's series of Ten Cent Novelettes of Standard American Authors, a series issued in pink or blue wrappers designed to rival the Beadle dime novels. [See Plate 3.] "A Marble Woman: or, The Mysterious Model"[18] followed. In 1866 "Behind a Mask: or, A Woman's Power"[19] was emblazoned in *The Flag of Our Union*, and the next year the prolific author supplied the Boston firm with "The Abbot's Ghost: or, Maurice Treherne's Temptation."[20] In 1867 *The Skeleton in the Closet* and *The Mysterious Key* provided the publishers with material for their Ten Cent Novelettes.[21]

And so, behind the mask of the Children's Friend has been discovered a writer who delved in darkness. The author of *Little Women* knew much of the wholesome pleasures of apples and ginger cookies. The author of "A Marble Woman: or, The Mysterious Model" knew much of the macabre attractions of opium and hashish. Her sensational tales, written out of economic and psychological need, help complete the portrait of a literary experimenter, a skillful, complex, professional writer. With their reappearance the Concord Scheherazade emerges full-face from behind her mask. An extraordinary fate has attended her secret shockers—a fate determined by the author and her publishers as well as by the sleuths who trailed them both.

Notes

1. For biographical details throughout, see Madeleine B. Stern, *Louisa May Alcott* (Norman, Okla.: University of Oklahoma Press, 1950, 1971).

2. Louisa May Alcott to Alf Whitman, Concord, June 22, [1862] (Houghton Library, Harvard University).

3. Ednah D. Cheney, ed., *Louisa May Alcott: Her Life, Letters, and Journals* (Boston: Roberts, 1889), p. 131.

4. *Ibid.*, p. 165.

5. *Ibid.*, p. 184.

6. Louisa May Alcott, *Little Women* (New York & London 1975), pp. 302, 385, 386.

7. L. C. Pickett, *Across My Path: Memories of People I Have Known* (New York 1916), pp. 107–108; Madeleine B. Stern, "Louisa M. Alcott's Self-Criticism," *More Books: The Bulletin of the Boston Public Library*, XX:8 (October 1945), p. 341.

8. Leona Rostenberg, "Some Anonymous and Pseudonymous Thrillers of Louisa M. Alcott," *The Papers of the Bibliographical Society of America*, XXXVII:2 (1943).

9. Both volumes were edited with introductions by Madeleine B. Stern.

10. For Leslie, see Madeleine B. Stern, *Imprints on History: Book Publishers and American Frontiers* (Bloomington, Ind.: Indiana University Press, 1956), pp. 221–232, 448–450; John Tebbel, *A History of Book Publishing in the United States* (New York & London: Bowker, 1972), I, 357–358.

11. E. G. Squier to Louisa May Alcott, ca. December 18, 1862 (Orchard House, Concord, Mass.).

12. "Pauline's Passion and Punishment," *Frank Leslie's Illustrated Newspaper*, XV:379 and 380 (January 3 and 10, 1863).

13. "A Whisper in the Dark," *Frank Leslie's Illustrated Newspaper*, XVI:401 and 402 (June 6 and 13, 1863).

14. "Perilous Play," *Frank Leslie's Chimney Corner*, VIII:194 (February 3, 1869).

15. Miriam F. Squier to Louisa May Alcott, New Rochelle, September 17, 1866 (Houghton Library, Harvard University). For Miriam Squier, who later became Frank Leslie's wife and successor, see Madeleine B. Stern, *Purple Passage: The Life of Mrs. Frank Leslie* (Norman, Okla.: University of Oklahoma Press, 1953, 1970).

16. For Elliott, Thomes and Talbot, see Stern, *Imprints on History*, pp. 206–220, 445–448; Tebbel, *A History of Book Publishing in the United States*, I, 438–440.

17. "V.V.: or, Plots and Counterplots," *The Flag of Our Union*, XX:5, 6, 7, 8 (February 4, 11, 18, 25, 1865).

18. "A Marble Woman: or, The Mysterious Model," *The Flag of Our Union*, XX:20, 21, 22, 23 (May 20, 27, June 3, 10, 1865).

19. "Behind a Mask: or, A Woman's Power," *The Flag of Our Union*, XXI:41, 42, 43, 44 (October 13, 20, 27, November 3, 1866).

20. "The Abbot's Ghost: or, Maurice Treherne's Temptation," *The Flag of Our Union*, XXII:1, 2, 3, 4 (January 5, 12, 19, 26, 1867).

21. *The Skeleton in the Closet* was published with Perley Parker, *The Foundling*, as No. 49 in the Ten Cent Novelettes series (Boston: Elliott, Thomes and Talbot, [1867]). *The Mysterious Key, and What It Opened* was issued as No. 50 in the series (Boston: Elliott, Thomes and Talbot, [1867]).

The First Appearance of a "Little Women" Incident

THE November, 1867, issue of *Merry's Museum*, an unpretentious juvenile monthly that had just fallen into the hands of a new owner, Horace B. Fuller, carried a prospectus for 1868, announcing, among the "pleasant improvements," a new editor, described as "an experienced and competent person." This newcomer was identified a month later as "Louisa M. Alcott, the brilliant author of 'Hospital Sketches,'—who has hardly an equal, and who has no superior as a writer for youth, in the country. . . ."

Mr. Fuller's description of Miss Alcott bore traces of publishing if not poetic license, for she was at that time known to the juvenile public through only her *Flower Fables* (1855) and *Morning Glories* (1867). For the *Saturday Evening Gazette* she had, it is true, written several saccharine tales ("A New Year's Blessing," "The Sisters' Trial," etc.), and the penny dreadfuls, *The Flag of Our Union*, and *Leslie's Illustrated Newspaper* had been emblazoned with her sensational contributions.[1] Such reputation as she could honestly claim was based upon *Hospital Sketches*, not her juvenilia. The new publisher, however, should be credited with considerable foresight, since *Little Women* was under way when Mr. Fuller offered Miss Alcott five hundred dollars a year for the editorship of the *Museum*.[2]

In order to fulfill her employer's promises Miss Alcott had supplied the January, 1868, issue of the "rejuvenated" monthly with a story and two poems; had garnered in two serials and a number of tales; and had maintained the various popular departments. She herself, moreover, was responsible for filling the section known as "Merry's Monthly Chat with His Friends." The policy of publishing the letters of young readers was altered somewhat in order to include what Louisa Alcott called her "editorial." As Cousin Tribulation—carried over from the Tribulation

Reprinted from *American Notes & Queries* III, no. 7 (October 1943): 99–100.

Periwinkle letters in *Hospital Sketches*—she wrote for "Dear Merrys" various incidents, principally autobiographical, that could be twisted to offer a lesson in virtue and good works.

The episode chosen for the January, 1868, "Chat" was one that was to be reprinted, with slight changes, in *Little Women*. Since it was not until July that she finished the first part of the classic, and not until the end of August that she received the proofs, this early appearance of a section of the story gives to that issue of *Merry's Museum* a bibliographical significance it would otherwise lack. The episode selected relates the manner in which the March girls gave up their breakfast to a poor family on Christmas morning, and a comparison between the *Merry's* version and that which was to appear later in chapter 2 of *Little Women* may be fruitful.

The most interesting variation within the two forms is the fact that the *Merry's* version is the more autobiographical. The writer uses the first person, gives truer names to the sisters—Nan, Lu, Beth, and May, instead of Meg, Jo, Beth, and Amy—and her characterization of herself is, if harsher, more realistic. Lu's first thought upon hearing her mother's suggestion that the girls give their breakfast as a Christmas present to their poor neighbors is, in the *Merry's* version, "I wish we'd eaten it up." It is Nan who exclaims, "I'm so glad you come [*sic*] before we began." In the *Little Women* version it is the impetuous Jo who takes those words from her sister's mouth and thus appears more generous than hungry. The poor family is the same in both versions, with the exception that they bear the name of Hummel in *Little Women* and go nameless in *Merry's*. Louisa Alcott had already, in an anonymous story, "Living in an Omnibus," which appeared in the October 1867 issue of *Merry's Museum*, used the Hummel family as her protagonists.

She published no further *Little Women* incidents as "editorials" in *Merry's*. Perhaps Thomas Niles objected to this manner of preprinting the story. Perhaps the editor, "finding that a good deal of disappointment is felt by some of our readers at the discontinuance of the correspondence,"[3] decided to give less space to Cousin Tribulation and more to the W-e's and A.W.'s who deluged the office with stories and poetry.[4] At any rate, although Cousin Tribulation did continue "moral" episodes as part of her "Chat," she also found space to insert an account of Van Amburgh's Menagerie or the new "Potatoe [*sic*] Pantomime."

To be sure, this is only one of the many narratives which Louisa Alcott wrote originally for a periodical and afterward incorporated into a book of some kind. Her tales in the *Youth's Companion*, the *Independent*, and *St. Nicholas* saw later publication in the various volumes of children's stories issued by Roberts Brothers. She was, indeed, more than the "competent" juvenilist whom Mr. Fuller had so heartily introduced in his prospectus— she was a shrewd Yankee who liked her bread buttered on both sides.

Notes

1. Leona Rostenberg, "Some Anonymous and Pseudonymous Thrillers of Louisa M. Alcott," *The Papers of the Bibliographical Society of America*, XXXVII:2 (1943).

2. Ednah Dow Cheney, ed., *Louisa May Alcott: Her Life, Letters, and Journals* (Boston: Roberts, 1889), p. 186.

3. "Merry's Monthly Chat with His Friends," *Merry's Museum*, April, 1868, p. 164.

4. *Ibid.*, May, 1868, p. 208 and October, 1868, p. 420.

A Book from Garfield's Library

J AMES A. GARFIELD, 20th President of the United States, was shot in the waiting room of the Washington depot on July 2, 1881, and died on September 19, 1881. The sensational and tragic event made news, stopped the presses, and filled the country's stands with "extra" editions and illustrated papers. It was not until November 19, 1881, however, that the Literary Society of Washington met to offer a *Tribute of Respect* to the late President. Among the observations made in that *Tribute* was one relating to Garfield as book collector and bibliophile:

> Garfield's library motto was *"inter folia fructus"*—fruit among the leaves. His interest in libraries was great, and he made the Library at the Capitol the recipient of his large annual collection of pamphlets.[1]

That "library motto," *Inter folia fructus*, was printed in italic type above the words "Library of James A. Garfield. No. . . . ." on a small book ticket approximately 1½ by 2¼ inches in size. In one recently discovered work on political theory from Garfield's library, a number "273 c" has been inked in above the words: "Case 4 Shelf a." Number 273 c also bears a presentation inscription from the author: "To General Gardfield [sic] with the respectful Compliments of Chambrun May 23d 1875." The book containing that inscription and book ticket is an extremely fitting volume for any presidential library and singularly so for the library of a future President marked out for assassination.

Le Pouvoir exécutif aux États-Unis, Étude de droit constitutionnel, by M. Adolphe de Chambrun, covers such subjects as the election of President and Vice President, the constitution of executive power, relations between President and Congress, federal administration, the Senate as executive council, executive power under Lincoln, impeachment proceedings and acquittal of Johnson, and circumstances that could modify the Constitution of the United States. The assassination of Lincoln at a crucial moment in

Reprinted from *Quarterly Journal of the Library of Congress* XXX, no. 3 (July 1973): 205–209.

American history is considered as well as the balance of legislative and executive power. This French study in American constitutional law provided James A. Garfield, Republican Representative from Ohio in the U.S. Congress, with considerable food for cogitation and eventually prompted him to express interesting opinions on "the character and tendencies of the Government of the United States."

The book was written by Charles-Adolphe de Pineton, Marquis de Chambrun[2] (1831–91), legal adviser to the French legation in Washington and husband of the French ambassador's daughter, Marie Hélène Marthe de Corcelles. On February 10, 1873, their son, the future diplomat Charles de Pineton, Comte de Chambrun, was born in Washington. Eight days later the author wrote the foreword or *avertissement* to his work on the executive branch of the U.S. government, expressing his indebtedness to the teachings of Charles Sumner, Caleb Cushing, and Carl Schurz.

There is no doubt that, either at the Literary Society of Washington (of which both were members) or in the course of diplomatic meetings in Washington, Adolphe de Chambrun, as he signed himself, met "General Gardfield." Although the former hailed from a family illustrious in French military and diplomatic history and the latter was to be known as the last President born in a log cabin, the two gentlemen had much in common, especially their interest in American constitutional law. Chambrun's interest was reflected in *Le Pouvoir exécutif aux États-Unis*; Garfield's concern with the subject was manifested when in 1874 he provided a preface to the English translation of Chambrun's work.

The original French publication of 1873 bore a somewhat unusual imprint: "Rouse's Point, N.Y.: Imprimé Et Publié Par John Lovell." In 1873 John Lovell's printing and publishing establishment at Rouses Point on the New York-Canadian border was both in its infancy and under a cloud. Chambrun's book was either the first or among the first books to issue from that press. It is true that John Lovell, who had founded the Lovell Printing and Publishing Company at Montreal in 1835, pioneered in Canadian schoolbooks, imported the first steam press into Canada, and published the first Canadian Directory, merited a niche in Canadian publishing history.[3] Shrewd and enterprising, by 1872 he was planning a vast printing establishment on the American-Canadian border, but his project was promptly denounced by the Book Trade Association as a scheme designed "to defraud the revenue of both countries and to undersell all the traders who pay their honest dues."[4] Lovell replied to this "injurious and offensive libel" in a letter of January 17, 1873, to *Publishers' Weekly* which outlined his grandiose plans:

> My proposed Rouse's Point printing and publishing house will be an American industry, planted on American soil, and will be conducted on the same principles as every other respectable and responsible printing and publishing house in the United States.

I selected Rouse's Point because it combines the advantages of water traffic by Lake Champlain, railway connections with every State in the Union, and is the nearest available site in the United States to my long-established Montreal business.

My printing office and bindery, instead of being built straddle-wise across the boundary line, in order to baffle Custom House authorities, . . . will be situated one and a half miles inside the American boundary line, in close proximity to an important American Custom House, and under the guns of the celebrated United States fortress of Rouse's Point.

. . . The buildings I purpose erecting next summer will cost over $60,000, and the presses, types, stereotype apparatus, bindery material, etc., will cost at least $100,000. . . .[5]

Lovell's plant had obviously just begun operation in 1873, very possibly with the publication of Chambrun's *Le Pouvoir exécutif aux États-Unis.* The reasons for Chambrun's choice of this publisher must be conjectured. During the Panic year of 1873 publishers were probably loath to issue a work of such limited appeal as a French text on American government; perhaps the author had met Lovell during a journey in French Canada; perhaps Garfield, who had had publishing experience in Ohio as a founder of the Standard Publishing Company,[6] had suggested his name to Chambrun. The reason for Lovell's selection of what may well have been his initial publication at Rouses Point is more apparent. "My proposed Rouse's Point . . . house," he had insisted, "will be an American industry, planted on American soil." What better way to carry out this proposal than by publishing a book, albeit in French, on American constitutional law.

Upon its publication in 1873, the book was well received. It was reviewed enthusiastically in *The Nation* on August 28, 1873, and favorable notices appeared in the *Baltimore Gazette, Appleton's Journal,* and elsewhere.[7] The most significant review, however, appeared in the form of a preface to the English translation of the following year—a preface by a future President of the United States, James A. Garfield.

Written by a Frenchman, published by a Canadian, *Le Pouvoir exécutif aux États-Unis* was translated into English in 1874 by a woman certainly known to both Chambrun and Garfield. Madeleine Vinton Dahlgren[8] (1825–98) had been born in Garfield's native Ohio, the daughter of a Congressman from the district. Her mother was the daughter of French émigrés. Having served as her father's hostess in Washington and been twice widowed, Mrs. Dahlgren lived in her father's home in the national capital, where she wrote the *Etiquette of Social Life in Washington.* She founded the Literary Society of Washington, of which Garfield and Chambrun were members.

In a diary entry dated February 14, 1874, Garfield wrote: "The Marquis de Chambrun and Mrs. Dahlgren united in requesting me to write a preface to Chambrun's book which Mrs. Dahlgren has just translated."

Eight days later he noted, "In the afternoon read Mrs. Dahlgren's translation of the Marquis de Chambrun's book on *The Executive Power*."[9]

For that translation Garfield wrote a preface which seems to have missed the attention it deserves.[10] Reflecting as it does the political philosophy of a future President of the United States, it merits reprinting in its entirety:

> It will be generally conceded that the most profound and searching discussion of the democratic principle and of the character and tendencies of the Government of the United States, which has appeared in modern times, is that of De Tocqueville. Many of his chapters sound like prophecy when read in the light of recent events. The monograph of the Marquis De Chambrun on the Executive Power of the United States is a worthy continuation of De Tocqueville's discussion. It is the first of a series of four volumes, which the author proposes to publish, on the several departments and functions of our Government. Should the series be completed with the thoroughness and ability manifested in this volume, it will have a repertory of the most valuable political results of our republican experiments.[11]
>
> This volume offers a new and striking illustration of the fact that many of the characteristics and tendencies of a nation are better understood and appreciated by foreigners than by native citizens. The foreign student has an advantage in the stand-point from which he makes his observation. He studies the institutions from a distance, and is able to measure them by other standards with less bias, perhaps, than those whose opinions have become a part of the public thought of the country whose institutions they discuss. This truth has frequently been exemplified in the criticism of National literature.
>
> It is worthy of remark that the efforts to recover the fame of Shakespeare from the oblivion into which it had fallen at the end of the 17th century was made by men who did not speak the language of Shakespeare. It was to Voltaire, Gœthe and Schlegel, that the world was chiefly indebted for the Shakespearian revival.
>
> This volume of the Executive Power of the United States is another striking illustration of the same truth, applied to political philosophy. While the author is an ardent supporter of republican government, he has evidently escaped the error that so many writers have fallen into—that of believing that our forms can be safely adopted by all nations.
>
> Throughout the volume the author keeps two objects constantly in view, viz.: To study our institutions in relation to the traditions, spirit and tendencies of our own people; and to ascertain what features of our institutions are adapted to the tradition and spirit of European nations. This comparative study will be most interesting to the student of political philosophy.
>
> In discussing the relation of the office of the Vice-President to our system, the author notices the fact, which I think has not been elsewhere discussed, that the office of Vice-President, while it is valuable for the purposes of an election—the candidate being usually selected with a view to supplementing the opinions of the candidate for the Presidency—yet this very fact makes the Vice-President an inharmonious element for purposes of administration. The author traces to this cause the fact that whenever our Vice-President has become

President, his administration has not been satisfactory to the country. On the whole, the author doubts the value of the office of Vice-President, and says that our example in this particular should not be followed elsewhere.

After giving a masterly analysis of the constitutional power of the Executive, the author discusses the advantages and disadvantages of the frequent changes in the Presidency by popular elections, and concludes that the instability of the office is in the interest of liberty.

The fourth chapter contains a very clear and interesting sketch of the conflicts that have occurred from time to time between the Executive and the Legislative departments, and concludes with the declaration that on the whole "The prerogatives of the President are today nearly what they were in the time of Washington, though they have been rather increased than diminished."

The chapters of this work which will be of most interest to the people of the United States are those in which the author discusses the effects of the late civil war upon our system of government. It is hardly possible for those who have been actors in the Executive, Legislative, or Judicial Departments of the Government to realize the changes which recent events have produced. The author of these chapters has rendered a great service to every thoughtful American, in setting forth with remarkable clearness and force the changes which recent events have wrought.

Starting from the antagonistic views of Hamilton and Jefferson, the one insisting upon a strong central Government—the other upon the preponderance of power in the people and the States—the author traces clearly the influence of those two forces upon all our subsequent history, and predicts that the safety of our system depends upon the equilibrium of these two forces. He concludes this portion of his discussion by saying that "so long as political activity in the States remains undiminished, and the existing division of sovereignty between them and the national government continues, the equilibrium will not be deranged. The Executive authority cannot imperil the Constitution, unless the local autonomies first disappear or become sensibly weakened." [12]

The author has been peculiarly fortunate in his selection of the translator. His thought has been faithfully rendered into clear and elegant English; and the work has been done with so much grace that the reader discovers nothing in the style to indicate that it is a translation.

JAMES A. GARFIELD.

Washington, March 16, 1874. [13]

Doubtless it was in gratitude for so incisive and perceptive a judgment that Chambrun on May 23, 1875, presented to Garfield a copy of the original French edition published in 1873 by John Lovell. Taking time from his work as Chairman of the Committee on Appropriations, James A. Garfield pasted inside the front cover of *Le Pouvoir exécutif aux Etats-Unis* his small book label: "*Inter folia fructus.*" In the pages of that book there had been much to instruct a future President, to stir up thoughts on assassination and impeachment, on the future of the Republic, and on political philosophy in general. There was indeed "fruit among the leaves" of the volume numbered 273 c that reposed on Shelf a in Case 4 of James A. Garfield's library.

Notes

1. Literary Society of Washington, *A Tribute of Respect from The Literary Society of Washington to its late President James Abram Garfield* (Washington, 1882), p. 25. For Garfield's membership in the Society, see Theodore Clarke Smith, *The Life and Letters of James Abram Garfield*, 2 vols. (New Haven: Yale University Press, 1925), 2:906.

2. Harry James Brown and Frederick D. Williams, eds., *The Diary of James A. Garfield*, 2 vols. ([East Lansing, Mich.]: Michigan State University Press, 1967), 2:290, n. 37; *Dictionnaire de biographie Francaise*, s.v. "Chambrun, Charles de Pineton." Chambrun had been sent as a special envoy to the United States in 1865 by the French foreign minister.

3. Madeleine B. Stern, *Imprints on History: Book Publishers and American Frontiers* (Bloomington, Ind.: Indiana University Press, 1956), p. 261.

4. *Publishers' Weekly* 2 (December 12, 1872): 643.

5. *Publishers' Weekly* 3 (January 30, 1873): 107. Lovell's plant at Rouses Point printed the sheets of British copyright works in the United States and, through the Montreal firm, circulated them in Canada. Eventually over 800 people were employed in typesetting and platemaking, printing and binding good books at cheap prices. The five-story factory, equipped with foundry and electrotyping apparatus, boasted an auditorium and running track and became known as the largest New York printing and publishing establishment north of Albany. See Stern, p. 262.

6. Stern, p. 377.

7. See "Opinions of the Press" at the end of Adolphe de Chambrun, *The Executive Power in the United States: A Study of Constitutional Law* . . . , translated from the original French by Mrs. Madeleine Vinton Dahlgren (Lancaster, Pa.: Inquirer Printing and Publishing Company, 1874).

8. *Dictionary of American Biography*, s.v. "Dahlgren, Sarah Madeleine Vinton."

9. Brown and Williams, 2:290–293.

10. The editors of Garfield's *Diary* mention the introduction in a footnote (2:290, n. 37), but it is not included in Burke A. Hinsdale, ed., *The Works of James Abram Garfield* (Boston: J. R. Osgood and Company, 1883), 2 vols.

11. The series was apparently never completed.

12. Cf. Garfield on "The Powers of Government" in William Ralston Balch, comp., *Garfield's Words* (Boston: Houghton, Mifflin and Company, 1881), p. 142: "We are accustomed to hear it said that the great powers of government in this country are divided into two classes: national powers and state powers. That is an incomplete classification. Our fathers carefully divided all government powers into three classes: one they gave to the states, another to the nation; but the third great class, comprising the most precious of all powers, they . . . reserved to themselves. This third class of powers has been almost uniformly overlooked by men who have written and discussed the American system."

13. Chambrun, pp. iii–vi.

The First Feminist Bible

The Alderney Edition, 1876

DURING the early 1840s the excitement stirred up on the eastern seaboard by William Miller's prophecy of the Second Coming took varied forms. In anticipation of the advent or the world's end, some purportedly donned ascension robes or spoke in strange tongues while others attended camp meetings, watched for heavenly signs, or assembled in graveyards. One strong-minded individual, a slight and wiry woman in her early fifties who hailed from Glastonbury, Connecticut, turned not to the stars but to her Bible to check the veracity of the Millerite forecast. In so doing she launched for herself a program of intense intellectual activity which would eventually culminate in the first English translation of the whole Bible by a woman.

The woman who accomplished this monumental labor was the eccentric but delightful Julia Evelina Smith. Though she uncovered no satisfactory proof of the Millerite prophecy in the course of her biblical studies, she did succeed in shaping a milestone in feminist history that demands attention.[1]

The five Smith sisters of Glastonbury grew up less in the odor of sanctity than in the aura of erudition. Their very names testified to the lofty nature of their background: Hancy Zephina, Cyrinthia Lucretia, Laurilla Aleroya, Juliette Abelinda, and Abby Hadassah. The penultimate sister, Juliette Abelinda—the name was changed to Julia Evelina after a reading of Frances Burney—was born on May 27, 1792, and it was as Julia Evelina Smith that she made her claim to fame. Except for Julia, who at the eleventh hour entered into an octogenarian union, none of the sisters ever married. Apparently the "maids of Glastonbury" were content with parental relationships. Their father, Zephaniah Hollister Smith, entered the Congregational ministry after his graduation from Yale but, deeming it wrong to

Reprinted from *Quarterly Journal of the Library of Congress* XXXIV, no. 1 (January 1977): 23–31.

accept money for preaching, he abandoned the ministry and turned to the law. A follower of the Sandemanian sect who held that "faith is mere intellectual assent," Zephaniah influenced his daughter to seek salvation not in the church but in the Bible. The mother of the family, Hannah Hadassah Hickock Smith, was in her way equally remarkable. Linguist and poet, astronomer and mathematician, she drew up both her own almanac and an antislavery petition to Congress. Indeed, an imaginative journalist would one day assert that she was "such an intense student" that she studied in a specially constructed "glass cage." [2]

With such a background Julia Evelina Smith took naturally to study in general and to languages in particular. At eighteen she commenced a diary in French which she continued for thirty-two years.[3] Latin and Greek she acquired both at home and, as she would recall, at "our academy."[4] For a time Julia Evelina Smith taught French at Emma Willard's school in Troy, New York, but for the most part her life was centered in the Glastonbury farm where, with her sisters, she kept house in their "roomy old mansion built in 1739" and made butter and cheese from the milk of their Alderney cows.[5] It was said of the Glastonbury maids that their "speech and manner reflected rural New England."[6] So did their point of view, for they were indignant at wrong and forthright in their pursuit of truth.

It was in the pursuit of truth, during the early 1840s, that Julia Evelina Smith studied her Bible intensively to seek corroboration of the Millerite predictions. By 1847, when she was fifty-five, she launched into the labors of translation that would preoccupy her during the next seven or eight years and result eventually in a feminist first.[7] By the time she had finished, Julia Evelina Smith had translated the Bible five times: once from the Latin, twice from the Greek, and twice from the Hebrew. As for Hebrew, this tongue was self-taught. As the years passed the "old quarto Bible was so interlined with Miss Julia's fresh translations as to be one of the curiosities of literature,"[8] and the manuscript version of her translation occupied three boxes.[9] Word for word, the work of literal translation continued. As Julia Smith put it: "I cannot express how greatly I enjoy the work of translating, and now the real meaning of different texts would thrill through my mind, till I could hardly contain myself."[10]

The results of this word-for-word translation are best conveyed by quoting Julia Smith's rendition of the Twenty-third Psalm.[11] It is possible that this translation is more accurate than that of the King James Version but the likelihood of its thrilling through the mind is somewhat remote:

> Chanting of David. Jehovah my shepherd, and I shall not want.
> He will cause me to lie down in pastures of tender grass; he will lead me to the water of rest.
> He will turn back my soul: he will guide me into the tracks of justice for sake of his name.

Also if I shall go into the valley of the shadow of death, I shall not be afraid of evil, for thou art with me; thy rod and thy staff they will comfort me.

Thou wilt set in order a table before me in front of mine enemies: thou madest fat mine head with oil; my cup being satisfied with drink.

Surely goodness and mercy shall pursue me all the days of my life: and I dwelt in the house of Jehovah to the length of days.

It was not until 1876, by which time Julia had lost three of her four sisters and engaged in struggles more secular than scriptural, that her version of the Bible was published. The preface she wrote at that time describes in detail the labors involved, the stages passed, and the techniques employed in her translation. Since the Smith translation was indeed unique this autobiographical exposition merits quoting:

It may seem presumptuous for an ordinary woman with no particular advantages of education to translate and publish alone, the most wonderful book that has ever appeared in the world, and thought to be the most difficult to translate. It has occupied the time and attention of the wisest and most learned of all ages, believing, as the world has believed, that such only could give the correct rendering of the language in which the Bible was written.

Over twenty years ago, when I had four sisters, a friend met with us weekly, to search the Scriptures, we being desirous to learn the exact meaning of every Greek and Hebrew word, from which King James's forty-seven translators had taken their version of the Bible. We saw by the margin that the text had not been given literally, and it was the literal meaning we were seeking. I had studied Latin and Greek at school, and began by translating the Greek New Testament, and then the Septuagint. . . . We all had a strong desire to learn the signification of the proper names, and I wrote to a learned friend about it, and he advised me to study Hebrew, saying, "it was a simple language, and easily learned, there being but one book in the world, of pure Hebrew, which was the Bible." He added that, "then I could see with my own eyes, and not look through the glasses of my neighbors." I soon gave my attention to the Hebrew, and studied it thoroughly, and wrote it out word for word, giving no ideas of my own, but endeavoring to put the same English word for the same Hebrew or Greek word, everywhere, while King James's translators have wholly differed from this rule; but it appeared to us to give a much clearer understanding of the text.

It had never at that time entered my mind that I should ever publish the work, but I was so much interested and entertained to see the connection from Genesis to Revelation, that I continued my labors and wrote out the Bible five times, twice from the Greek, twice from the Hebrew, and once from the Latin—the Vulgate. . . . It may be thought by the public in general, that I have great confidence in myself, in not conferring with the learned in so great a work, but as there is but one book in the Hebrew tongue, and I have defined it word for word, I do not see how anybody can know more about it than I do. It being a dead language no improvements can be made upon it. As for the Latin and Greek, I have no doubt many have searched deeper into the standard works than I have, but I think no one has given more time and attention to the literal meaning of the Bible texts in these languages.

... It took me about seven years to accomplish the five translations, at least, I was engaged in it that length of time, not giving my whole time to it. I should probably have been much longer, had it come into my head that I should ever consent to have it published. There may be some little inaccuracies, ... but I think never has the sense of the Original Tongue been altered.[12]

When, after a shelf rest of some twenty years, Julia Smith's version of the "Original Tongue" was finally published, one or two wits referred to it as the Alderney Edition of the Holy Bible. For this there was good reason. During the late 1860s and the early 1870s, Abby Hadassah and Julia Evelina, the only surviving Glastonbury maids, boldly entered the feminist arena. In the sisters' struggle for women's rights, the Alderney cows of the Glastonbury farm played important roles.[13]

Assessed for what they considered a disproportionate share of taxes, the ballotless sisters of Glastonbury refused payment. Their determination to protest taxation without representation culminated in January 1874 with the attachment of seven of their fine Alderneys. The cows were paraded to the Glastonbury signpost where, to cover delinquent taxes amounting to $101.39, they were auctioned off. Upon at least two different occasions the bovine march and auction took place until only two Alderneys, Taxey and Votey, were left. When the town fathers turned from the Smiths' movable property and auctioned off eleven acres of their meadowland valued at $2000.00 for $78.35, the sisters initiated a lawsuit against the tax collector.

Meanwhile, as one newspaper put it, "Though Miss Julia, the older of the two sisters, is the one who raised the cows, Miss Abby is the one who raised the breeze."[14] The breeze was raised in several directions. At a town meeting, Miss Abby protested taxation without representation, and when the town meeting was closed to her she climbed an oxcart outside the building to deliver her speech. Sometimes the sisters made joint appearances at suffrage meetings, standing side by side on the platform, Abby reading a prepared lecture, Julia speaking less formally. Their message caught on. The *Springfield Republican* declared that the sisters "as truly stand for the American principle as did the citizens who ripped open the tea chests in Boston harbour or the farmers who leveled their muskets at Concord."[15] Isabella Beecher Hooker, the suffrage leader, suggested "kine couchant" for the suffrage emblem,[16] and in the office of the *Woman's Journal* a framed bill ordering the sale of the pet cows was hung. As far afield as Chicago, souvenirs appeared, made from the hair of the Glastonbury cows. When Julia Smith's Bible was published, newspaper articles formed "a remarkable blending of cows and Biblical lore, dairy products and Greek and Hebrew."[17]

Like their country, the Glastonbury sisters were stirred to remembrance during the Centennial year. As they put it in a letter to the *Woman's Journal*: "Would our revolutionary ancestors have felt better to have yielded to taxation? which they declared to be tyranny, and endured a seven years war, and yielded up their lives for it. Did not women as well as men inherit this spirit? And this Centennial year they were going to rejoice over this principle! And did Great Britain use our forefathers anything like so badly as our town had used us?"[18]

This Centennial year, Julia Smith reasoned that she could give a spur to the feminist movement by offering to the world proof of one woman's accomplishments. The proof had lain on her library shelf for years. Now she would publish it. As early as July of 1875 the sisters had written to the editor of *The People* for advice on the project, informing him that "She [Julia] had never intended publishing these translations, till our town had persecuted us so unjustly about our taxes." They went on to say:

> We thought it might help our cause to have it known that a woman could do more than any man has ever done, while we are denied all protection from any quarter, made to pay more money than any of the inhabitants of the place, without any voice in the matter. . . .
>
> We rode over to Hartford, yesterday, and called at several houses to learn the cost of publication. Shall learn definitely, tomorrow, the actual cost from one of the best houses. But it occurred to us, this morning that perhaps you would know if it could be done with less expense in Philadelphia. . . . If there is anything to be made by publishing this work, we would like it to be made by *suffragists*. We do not expect in our life-time to realize enough from the sale of the books to pay the cost of publication. We should publish one thousand copies, at first as soon as could be done.[19]

The editor in replying suggested that the sisters would better serve their cause by a direct contribution of money, at which they demurred, commenting, "It seems our State has given twenty-five thousand dollars to your Centennial, to glorify principles which neither the men who got it up, or our forefathers, ever practiced, or ever intended to practice; neither do those who vote this money: but they may be obliged to, for truth ever comes up at the last. It is never suppressed." Then they added:

> We learned, last week, there was a publishing-house in Hartford that favored our cause, and will assist us in selling our books. We have never expected the sale of the books would pay the expense of publishing, which will be about five thousand dollars. We can spare this money, and we propose, also, selling off half our land, (owning one hundred and thirty acres, from half of which we derive no profit,) that our town may not be able to take more from our property than from any of its citizens, as it has done heretofore.[20]

The house in Hartford that favored their cause was the American Publishing Company, a firm whose major claim to fame is Mark Twain's association with it as a director and as author.[21] Located at 284 Asylum Street, the American Publishing Company was a subscription house. Its books were sold not in bookstores but by agents who carried their wares across the country soliciting individual orders. Its contracts were signed "on the basis of sample dummies, the required number of copies periodically supplied by the publisher on a cash basis." 22 As Julia Smith had remarked, it was "more sensible to spend $1,000 on printing a Bible than to buy a shawl." 23 By November 1875, the sisters Smith contracted with the American Publishing Company to print Julia's Bible. From their Hartford bank stock they paid $4,000 for the printing of 1,000 copies, and the publication date was set for April 1876.

Like most subscription houses, the American Publishing Company regarded religious books as a staple of the business. Its list included a family Bible "so arranged that 'Family Portraits may be preserved within its sacred lids.'" 24 During the Centennial year, under the aegis of its president, Elisha Bliss, the company issued, besides Mark Twain's *Tom Sawyer* and works by Charles Dudley Warner and Bret Harte, a biography of the evangelist D. L. Moody and a book entitled *Bible Lands Illustrated.* Through canvassers such books found their way to thousands of readers who never entered a bookstore. The firm boasted that by means of subscription selling "they reach directly the whole reading public." 25

The American Publishing Company, advertising for agents to sell its publications, made a strong appeal to women: "The sale of our works is an honorable and praiseworthy employment, and is particularly adapted to disabled Soldiers, aged and other Clergymen having leisure hours, Teachers and Students during vacation, &c., Invalids unable to endure hard physical labor, Young Men who wish to travel. . . . *Women who can devote time to the work, often make the best of canvassers.*" 26 It is therefore entirely probable that women canvassers sold Julia Smith's feminist Bible. It is even more probable that women compositors worked on the publication. According to the *Hartford Daily Times* of December 11, 1875, "The work is now going through the press of the American Publishing Company, Hartford, and is to be brought out next April. This work seems to make a new departure in several directions. It is not only the first translation of the Bible by a woman, but it is (or will be) the first work 'set up' by a type-setting machine; and this machine is itself run by a woman—and another woman does the proof reading. Everything connected with this Bible seems to be on a new and original plan." 27

It was eminently fitting that that new and original plan was feminist in nature. Typesetters customarily entered only their first names or their surnames or their initials at take-marks in the printer's copy of books. Mark Twain's *Adventures of Tom Sawyer* was published in 1876, the same year that saw the emergence of Julia Smith's Bible. The printer's copy of *Tom Sawyer* bears the names of four compositors, of whom two are women: Lizzie and Nellie.28 May it not be assumed that either or both of those women compositors worked on the printer's copy of the Smith Bible?

It was indeed a feminist Bible that rolled from the press of the American Publishing Company. In May 1876, between the eighth and the twenty-seventh of the month, 1,000 copies of what was called "Miss Smiths Bible" emerged from the binderies, 950 bound in cloth and 50 in library bindings.[29] A royal octavo priced at three dollars—a price that prevented the translator from breaking even—*The Holy Bible:/Containing the/Old And New Testaments;/Translated Literally from the Original Tongues* was a somber-looking affair.[30] Yet, bound in black cloth with gilt-stamped lettering on the front cover, it presented in its 1,170 double-columned pages proof of what one woman could accomplish.

In its sale and distribution the translator was aided by other women. For example, Sara Andrews Spencer of the Spencerian Business College in Washington wrote to Isabella Beecher Hooker: "Miss Wooster [a student] pasted Miss Smith's autograph in all of her Bibles and, as enclosed receipt will show, I took them to Ballantynes to be sold on commission." She added that she would "advertise the Bibles . . . in the Star & Post upon the best terms I can make."[31] [See Plate 4.]

If Abby Smith had raised a breeze with her cows, Julia Smith raised something of a whirlwind with her Bible. Amos A. Lawrence, the merchant-philanthropist, wrote to the translator: "You remember that the Devil was said to be afraid of the Bible in Martin Luther's time. So now, according to your account, the selectmen of Glastonbury and the lawyers begin to dread the appearance of the new translation. May the result be the same as in Luther's time, and may Glastonbury become as renowned as Wittenburg."[32] One reader went so far as to pontificate: "My opinion of it is that it has power to reach to a substratum of thought at a depth beyond where King James's can reach."[33] Although some poked fun at the "Alderney Edition" of the Bible that had appeared out of Glastonbury, and bovine allusions punctuated scriptural commentaries, the general reaction must have gratified the translator, then in her mid-eighties. One reaction did more than gratify—it led to her marriage. Amos Andrew Parker of Fitzwilliam, New Hampshire, a retired judge, who had recorded his personal recollections of Lafayette, was attracted by a notice of the Bible. He ordered a copy and proceeded to Glastonbury to meet the translator. On April 9, 1879, almost three years after publication, the octogenarians would be married.

Meanwhile, despite the impact of the "Alderney" Bible, taxation without representation continued for the Smith sisters. In 1877, Julia compiled a pamphlet, *Abby Smith and Her Cows*, which she published through the American Publishing Company. The death of Abby Hadassah in 1878 left Julia bereft. The two sisters had shared all the humiliations and struggles, all the triumphs and achievements of a long lifetime. Now Julia, at eighty-six, was on her own. The next year, probably out of her loneliness and the desolation of the Glastonbury farm, she married Amos Parker and moved to his home in Hartford. Despite their common scriptural interests, the marriage does not appear to have been happy. Julia's closing years were

A LITERAL AND EXACT TRANSLATION

OF THE

HOLY BIBLE,

BOTH OLD AND NEW TESTAMENTS, FROM THE ORIGINAL TONGUES,

By JULIA E. SMITH.

The announcement of this translation of the Scriptures from the Hebrew and Greek tongues, by a woman, unaided and alone, so attracted the attention of many prominent scholars, that they have taken the trouble to closely examine the Bible since its publication, and have subjected it to the closest scrutiny. The result has been most complimentary to the translator, and she has received thousands of congratulatory letters from all parts of the country.

This translation will prove of great service to all who desire to read the Bible in its purity, and who wish to apply their own judgment in deciding the meaning of its original terms. Nothing has been altered, but the old text has been literally and exactly translated, and rendered word for word and sentence for sentence. It is worthy the attention of all.

As the object of publication was not profit, the price has been made very low, in order to place it within the reach of all, and is as follows:

Bound in a Handsome and Durable Manner, $3.00 per copy.

The volume will be sent by mail, postpaid, to any part of the country, upon receipt of the price. Usual discounts to the trade. Orders and remittances can be made to JULIA E. SMITH, Glastonbury, Conn., or to

AMERICAN PUBLISHING CO.,
Hartford, Conn.

PLATE 4. Advertisement of the first feminist Bible.

marked by a few noteworthy events: in 1881 she edited *Selections* from her mother's poems,[34] and in 1884 she addressed the Hartford Woman Suffrage Association. On March 6, 1886, in her ninety-fourth year, she died in Hartford but, in accordance with instructions left in her Bible, she was buried in the family plot at Glastonbury and on her tombstone her maiden name was carved.

The *Woman's Journal* pronounced her "remarkable for learning, her public spirit, and her love of justice."[35] All three attributes had played a part in the first translation of the whole Bible by a woman. With her "Alderney" Edition, Julia Evelina Smith fired a feminist shot for America's Centennial year that still echoes a century later.

Notes

1. The writer is grateful to Patricia Ballou, Barnard College Library, for bringing Julia Smith's Bible to her attention. For biographical sketches of Julia Smith and her family, see *Dictionary of American Biography*, s.v. "Smith, Abby Hadassah"; Helen K. Greenaway, "Sarah Josepha Hale and Julia Evelina Smith," *Germantowne Crier* 20, no. 2 (May 1968): 45-51; Addie Stancliffe Hale, "Those Five Amazing Smith Sisters," *Hartford Daily Courant*, May 15, 1932, p. e3; "In Memoriam [Julia E. Smith]," *Woman's Journal* 17, no. 11 (March 13, 1886): 85; *Notable American Women, 1607–1950*, 3 vols. (Cambridge, Mass.: Belknap Press of Harvard University Press, 1971), 3:302–4; "Obituary. Julia E. Smith Parker," *Hartford Times*, March 8, 1886, p. 2; "Abby Smith," *Woman's Journal* 9, no. 31 (August 3, 1878): 244; Elizabeth G. Speare, "Abby, Julia, and the Cows," *American Heritage* 8, no. 4 (June 1957): 54–57, 96.

2. Elizabeth Cady Stanton, Susan B. Anthony, and Matilda Joslyn Gage, eds., *History of Woman Suffrage*, 6 vols. (New York: Arno Press & The New York Times, 1969), 3:337.

3. Her diary is now in the Connecticut Historical Society, Hartford.

4. Julia E. Smith, *Abby Smith and Her Cows with a Report of the Law Case Decided Contrary to Law* (Hartford: American Publishing Company, 1877), p. 64.

5. *Ibid.*, p. 63.

6. *Dictionary of American Biography*.

7. According to Rev. P. Marion Simms, *The Bible in America* (New York: Wilson-Erickson, 1936), pp. 149 and 252, Julia E. Smith was "the only woman in the world's history to translate the entire Bible into any language." Simms described her translation of the New Testament as an "'immersion' version, made from the commonly received Greek text." See also Margaret T. Hills, ed., *The English Bible in America* (New York: American Bible Society and the New York Public Library, 1961), pp. 288–89; Smith, *Abby Smith and Her Cows*, especially pp. 57 and 62.

8. "Abby Smith," *Woman's Journal* 9, no. 31 (August 3, 1878): 244.

9. The manuscript is deposited in the Connecticut Historical Society. It is composed of numerous small folios, unbound, made from paper of the period, and including over ten thousand pages.

10. Smith, *Abby Smith and Her Cows*, p. 64.

11. *The Holy Bible: Containing the Old And New Testaments; Translated Literally from the Original Tongues* (Hartford: American Publishing Company, 1876), p. 636.

12. *Ibid.*, pp. [1–2].

13. For the sisters' suffrage activities see especially Stanton et al., eds., *History of Woman Suffrage*, 3: 76, 98, 328–29, 336–37 and Smith, *Abby Smith and Her Cows*. On January 29, 1878, the sisters petitioned the Connecticut State Senate, "praying we may be relieved from the stigma of birth. . . . We cannot even stand up for the principles of our forefathers . . . without having our property seized and sold at the sign-post, which we have suffered four times; and have also seen eleven acres of our meadow-land sold to an ugly neighbor for a tax of fifty dollars—land worth more than $2,000. . . . For being born women we are obliged to help support those who have earned nothing, and who, by gambling, drinking, and the like, have come to poverty, . . . And when men meet to take off the dollar poll-tax, the bill for the dinner comes in for the women to pay" (*History of Woman Suffrage*, 3: 336).

14. *Windham County Transcript*, August 19, 1875, quoted in Smith, *Abby Smith and Her Cows*, p. 58.

15. Quoted in Greenaway, "Sarah Josepha Hale and Julia Evelina Smith," p. 50.

16. *Ibid.*, p. 50.

17. Stanton et al., eds., *History of Woman Suffrage*, 3: 337.

18. Quoted in Smith, *Abby Smith and Her Cows*, p. 67.

19. *Ibid.*, p. 57.

20. *Ibid.*, p. 58.

21. For the American Publishing Company, see Frank E. Compton, "Subscription Books," *The Bowker Lectures on Book Publishing. First Series* (New York: The Typophiles, 1943); Hamlin Hill, *Mark Twain and Elisha Bliss* (Columbia, Mo.: University of Missouri Press, 1964); Marjorie Stafford, "Subscription Book Publishing in the United States, 1865–1930" (M.S. thesis, University of Illinois, 1943); John W. Tebbel, *A History of Book Publishing in the United States*, 2 vols. (New York and London: R. R. Bowker Co., 1972–75), 2: 104, 541–42.

22. Hellmut Lehmann-Haupt, *The Book in America* (New York: R. R. Bowker, 1951), p. 252.

23. Speare, "Abby, Julia, and the Cows," p. 57.

24. Hill, *Mark Twain and Elisha Bliss*, p. 15.

25. Advertisement in Smith, *Abby Smith and Her Cows*, in the New York Public Library.

26. *Ibid.*

27. *Hartford Daily Times*, December 11, 1875, quoted in Smith, *Abby Smith and Her Cows*, p. 64. The writer exaggerated about the typesetting machine. For considerably earlier typesetting machines, see John W. Moore, *Moore's Historical, Biographical, and Miscellaneous Gatherings . . . relative to Printers* (Concord, N.H.: Republican Press Association, 1886), p. 79.

28. Information from Paul Baender of the Department of English, University of Iowa, who is editing *The Adventures of Tom Sawyer*.

29. American Publishing Company, Books Received from the Binderies, December 1, 1866, to December 31, 1879 (ledger in Berg Collection, New York Public Library).

30. Lynds E. Jones, comp., *The American Catalogue . . . July 1, 1876* (New York: Peter Smith, 1941), p. 68. The Bible's collation is [2], 892; 276 pp.

31. Sara Andrews Spencer to Isabella Beecher Hooker, Washington, D.C., May 8, 1878. In the Stowe-Day Foundation, Hartford (courtesy Diana Royce, librarian, Nook Farm Research Library). The receipt of Wm. Ballantyne & Son is for twenty-four Bibles at $2.50 each.

32. Greenaway, "Sarah Josepha Hale and Julia Evelina Smith," p. 50.

33. Smith, *Abby Smith and Her Cows*, p. 74.

34. Hannah Hadassah (Hickock) Smith, *Selections from the poems of . . . by her daughter, Julia E. Smith* (Hartford: Press of the Case, Lockwood and Brainard Company, 1881). This publishing firm was also a subscription house.

35. "In Memoriam [Julia E. Smith]," *Woman's Journal* 17, no. 11 (March 13, 1886): 85.

5

The Move West

William N. Byers Had
His Head Examined!

THERE can scarcely be a Coloradan who has not heard the colorful story of William Newton Byers, the Omaha surveyor who in the Spring of 1859 arrived in the place now called Denver with a few assistants, a Washington hand press, and a "shirt tail full of type," determined to publish the first newspaper in the diggings. His race with John Merrick (whose press had been fished out of the Missouri River) to make Rocky Mountain newspaper history is common knowledge. The story of how his *Rocky Mountain News* beat Merrick's *Cherry Creek Pioneer* by twenty minutes is almost as much a part of Western history as the Gold Rush.

Since the *Rocky Mountain News* has appeared continuously since its auspicious beginning on April 20, 1859, it may interest students of Denver publishing history to read a previously unknown account of William N. Byers. The account is particularly unusual since it was based in part upon a phrenological examination. Phrenology,[1] the "science of the mind," was the nineteenth century's closest approach to psychoanalysis. A phrenological examination involved the measurement of the head and the study of the skull for various faculties of the mind—amativeness and cautiousness, conjugality and ideality, benevolence and veneration. It also involved an analysis of the temperament and physiognomy, all of which helped to make the man. A phrenological examination might be based upon an actual sitting or, as is most likely in Byers' case, upon a photographic likeness.[2]

At all events, in January 1872, the *American Phrenological Journal* carried the following sketch of the Denver printer. The *Journal* was published monthly in New York by Samuel R. Wells, publisher, author, editor and phrenologist. Following his general custom in running a feature story on a subject, he included not only a biographical sketch, but a character analysis based upon the contours of the subject's skull, his physiognomy and

Reprinted from *Occasional Notes, Norlin Library, University of Colorado*, No. 10 (April 1969): 1–3.

temperament. As will be evident from what follows, Byers' skull came out very well indeed, for the enthusiastic Eastern publisher predicted "a useful and successful career" for his Denver colleague.[3]

William N. Byers, the Rocky Mountain Printer

Here we have a Rocky Mountain pioneer, not a wild native of those regions, but a civilized, cultivated, and refined Christian gentleman. The story of his interesting life—were it told even in simple, unvarnished English—would touch the heart of every reader. Mr. Byers stands about five feet eight, weighs not far from one hundred and fifty pounds, is of fair complexion, and in temperament the Mental predominates over the Vital and Motive. His brain is well developed, of symmetrical proportions, and the mind is active, intense, and definite. He is thoroughly alive "from top to toe," and drives straight to the mark. He is strictly temperate, and is always in good working order.

Besides a fine practical intellect—perceptives and reflectives alike well developed—he has very large Benevolence, and hence is charitable. He has high moral sentiments, and is thoroughly honest and reliable. He is full of push and perseverance, being in all respects a thoroughly executive spirit. Grass will not grow under his feet. What he finds to do he does with his might.

He is very affectionate, and is popular in the social circle. As a business man, he would be enterprising and careful. If he had been educated for the law, he would have excelled in that profession. He would shine in legislation or literature, and grace any place of honor or of trust. Here is a sketch of this young Western editor, for whom we predict a useful and successful career.

WILLIAM N. BYERS was born in Madison County, Ohio, February 22, 1831. His early paternal ancestors were originally Scotch, who subsequently settled in Ireland, and were represented in the siege of Londonderry in 1688–9. His maternal ancestors were of German stock, from Brandenburg. His later progenitors were early settlers in Pennsylvania, and afterward among the first to emigrate to the valley of the Ohio. His father, being a farmer in moderate circumstances, William, at ten years of age, was first sent to the district school, where he attended about three months each winter for eight years. During the remainder of the year he had charge of certain farm work which kept him closely occupied, and rendered his winter's schooling irregular. Two "quarters" at a village academy completed his school education. As a school-boy he was proficient in spelling, but made no unusual progress in other studies. In the last term of his school he took up surveying, and learned it readily. From boyhood, however, he was a great reader of newspapers and periodicals, and attributes his education and knowledge of the world, men, and things mainly to that source. In 1850—when William was about nineteen years of age—his father sold the farm in Ohio and moved West, finally locating near Muscatine, Iowa, and he availed himself of an opportunity to spend several months in traveling in the Northwestern States, and especially along the frontier in Iowa, then about half way across the State.

In 1851 he was employed as *chainman* to accompany a party of Government surveyors to Western Iowa; but the second day in the field he was given a compass and placed in charge of a party of men, and continued in that capacity until the completion of the contract in the spring of 1852. He was at Council Bluffs the same spring, during the great rush to the Pacific coast, and determined himself to cross the Plains, which he accomplished successfully, reaching Oregon in the fall of the same year, after a journey of one hundred and forty-five days during the whole of which he saw not one house and but one person whom he had met before, and then only for an hour or so. There was great mortality on the Plains that year, almost entire loss of stock, and great destitution. He reached his destination an utter stranger, with but twenty-five cents, and a terribly ragged suit of clothes. He first engaged to chop rail timber; then to saw logs; next he was put in charge of a saw-mill, and then was employed in measuring and rafting lumber to vessels at the head of the tide water on the Columbia River. In a few weeks he was offered a situation on the Government Surveys, and again took charge of such work in Oregon and Washington for a year. The year completed, he goes to California, from thence to Central America, and *via* Havana and New York, home.

But he did not think of remaining at home. The new "march of empire," under the "Kansas Nebraska Bill," in 1854, found in young Byers a warm co-operator, who pitched his tent at Omaha when there was but one log cabin on the site. Here he engaged in surveying for town, company, and private parties. Late in the fall he returned to Eastern Iowa and married a Miss Summer[4]—granddaughter of Gov. Lucas, the first Territorial Governor of Iowa. Going back to Omaha, he was in the next week elected to the first Nebraska Legislative Assembly. In 1855 he was appointed U. S. Deputy Surveyor and ran the first township lines in Nebraska. In the next two years he surveyed nearly all those lines for 150 miles front on the Missouri River. Meantime he engaged in real estate operations, and made money rapidly. Besides his Government work, he was also county surveyor and member of the city council of Omaha. In the money crisis of 1857–8 he lost heavily, and his property, being almost entirely in real estate (mainly town lots), and unsalable, rapidly reached the "ground floor" again. In the midst of these losses, in the summer of 1858, while performing an official duty and an act of humanity, he received a terrible gun-shot wound, the weapon being a Springfield musket, double charged, first with goose-shot and then buck-shot. In a consultation of seven physicians, six pronounced the wound necessarily fatal; the seventh said there was one chance in a hundred for life.

The result proved the one chance good—attributable mainly to an elastic vitality and *determination*.[5]

As his recovery progressed, supposing incapacity for active out-of-door work would last to the end of life, he began to cast about for something which he could do. At length, as result of a banter, he agreed to take a printing press to "Pike's Peak."

March 8th, 1859, he left Omaha with press and material, while still suffering and almost helpless from his wound. A snow-storm occurred every week on the road to the Platte valley, then entirely uninhabited, except by half a dozen traders, who were stationed at the best points as far up as O'Fallon's Bluffs. However, he pressed on, and in forty-two days reached Denver. Three days after, there was issued the first newspaper ever printed at the foot of the Rocky Mountains. There Mr. Byers has maintained his business ever since, and engaged more or less in farming, mining, and in railways and other enterprises of the country. Meantime, during the winter of 1858–9, he wrote and published "Hand and Guide Book to New Mines," but unfortunately lost his entire venture in this new line by the failure of the printing firm (in Chicago) which held the copyright.

In 1860 he lost his dwelling-house and contents by fire. In 1864 he lost his printing office and farm improvements, aggregating nearly $30,000, by flood. Most of the time he has had one or more partners in the ownership and publication of the *Rocky Mountain News*, but now owns and controls it entirely alone.

Mr. Byers was appointed postmaster (the third) of Denver by Mr. Lincoln when he became President. He says that he did not ask for the position, and was surprised when notified by telegraph of the appointment. After about two years' experience in this new capacity, he resigned the position on account of the pressing nature of his other business. A man of indomitable will and persevering energy, Mr. Byers can scarcely be said to have known an idle moment. By no means a creature of circumstances, he has made opportunities and carved a future for himself, despite misfortunes and calamities. He is one of the most industrious and upright men the Far West has to show.

Notes

1. The grand sachem of phrenology was Dr. Franz Joseph Gall (c. 1758–1828), a Viennese physician who, not unlike another Viennese physician of a later century, founded a so-called science of the mind. His doctrine was imported to the United States by his disciple, Dr. Johann Gaspar Spurzheim, who in 1832 delivered a series of lectures on the subject in Boston. Although some dismissed the theory as humbug, it took hold for a time and many an illustrious head was bared for the exploring fingers and "manipulations" of the practical phrenologists.

2. The presence of the actual head, though not essential, was, of course, a decided

advantage in making a phrenological analysis. The three-quarter view of Byers' head as it appeared in the portrait did not give the examiner too much to go on. The only faculty actually marked for size was his Benevolence which probably received a 6 (the phrenological scale for sizing the different faculties ranged from 1 for very small to 7 for very large). Beyond that, the general aspect and measurement of Byers' skull revealed a well-developed brain, strong Adhesiveness and Amativeness ("he is very affectionate, and is popular in the social circle") and strong Individuality.

3. After he had been immortalized in the columns of the *American Phrenological Journal*, Byers continued a leader in his community. According to Mr. John A. Brennan (Western Historical Collections, University of Colorado Libraries), he "engaged in various speculative ventures after he sold the *Rocky Mountain News*, including lead promotions and mining. In these he usually was successful. In 1901 he published a "Biographical History of Colorado." Byers died on March 26, 1903.

4. I.e., Elizabeth Minerva Sumner of Muscatine, Iowa, whom Byers married in 1854.

5. This case of the gunshot wound leads to some interesting Sherlockian speculation, for it certainly seems as if some game had been afoot. What area or areas of W. N. Byers was/were affected? Why the goose- and buck-shot? Whence gathered the seven physicians? What "official duty and . . . act of humanity" triggered so reprehensible a reaction? There are simply not enough facts to go on. All we can conclude is that the strong Destructiveness of the would-be killer met its match in the strong Vitativeness (clinging to life) of the intended victim.

A Rocky Mountain Book Store

Savage and Ottinger of Utah

A PREVIOUSLY UNCHARTED bypath in Western Americana leads directly to a nineteenth-century Salt Lake City business partnership. The firm, which gave an impetus to the development of Western art and photography, was known as A ROCKY MOUNTAIN BOOK STORE. In its history three protagonists were involved.

Charles R. Savage,[1] destined to become one of the most outstanding photographers of the West, was born in Southampton, England, in 1832. Converted to Mormonism by a missionary, he ventured to New York during his twenties. From there, having decided to become a photographer, he journeyed west and practiced his trade supplied with a camera. a grey blanket which he used for background and a large tea chest that he converted into a darkroom. In June of 1860 he crossed the plains to Salt Lake City, where sagebrush grew high in the streets and prairie schooners carried their cargoes. He was equipped with an observant eye and a camera, a faith in Mormonism, and a background of Rocky Mountain scenery. All he needed was a partner.

This need the second protagonist filled. George M. Ottinger,[2] soon to become a pioneer artist of the West, had been born a year later than Savage, in Springfield Township, Pennsylvania, the descendant of German Quakers who had immigrated to America. His youth was varied and colorful, including some formal schooling, much daubing in water colors, and a three-year voyage before the mast when as a sailor he shipped to Panama and China, India and Africa. Tinting photographs to earn money, he subsequently made the westward journey; and, having adopted the Mormon faith, Ottinger arrived by oxteam in the valley of the Great Salt Lake just a year after Charles R. Savage.

The two men complemented each other. While Savage took photo-

Reprinted from *Brigham Young University Studies* IX, no. 2 (Winter 1969): 144–154.

graphs, Ottinger colored them. The art work that resulted could be exchanged for molasses, wheat, and provisions, and so the partnership of Savage and Ottinger prospered. Ottinger was promised the job of scene painting for the new Salt Lake Theater and was soon able to purchase a home lot from Brigham Young. By 1863, the Deseret Academy of Arts was organized. The territory developed a taste for Rocky Mountain scenery that could be photographed by one partner and tinted by the other. . . .

In 1866, when the Civil War was over, Charles Savage, who did most of the field work for the firm, went east to augment his stock of photographic materials. It was doubtlessly at that time that he met the third protagonist in the story of A ROCKY MOUNTAIN BOOK STORE, Samuel R. Wells.

Wells, proprietor of the New York City firm of phrenologist-publishers, Fowler and Wells, had an understandable interest in art and photography. Besides publishing and selling books on phrenology—the science, or pseudoscience, of the mind—and giving phrenological examinations based either upon heads or accurate photographs of heads, he operated a cabinet at 389 Broadway. In the galleries of that Golgotha of Gotham, visitors found much of interest, from skulls and mummies to busts, engravings, and paintings. The latest techniques in making plaster casts, new developments in photography, and modern styles in painting had a fascination for Wells who, in addition, was an enthusiastic traveler to the West. He was well equipped to guide Charles Savage in photographic purchases. At all events, on the return trip Savage fitted up a supply wagon from which he did photography en route; and once back in Salt Lake City he sent to Samuel R. Wells a photograph of Brigham Young which duly appeared in *The Illustrated Annual of Phrenology and Physiognomy*, "through the politeness of Mr. C. R. Savage, photographic artist of Salt Lake City."[3]

As the 1860s rushed to their completion, so, too, did the great Overland Railroad, and the firm of Savage and Ottinger found a ready market for "views of the Overland Route and of all places of interest in Utah and Montana." They supplied for *The Salt Lake City Directory* a huge folding plate of the town, advertising their "photographs taken in the best style of the art."[4] In his celebrated lecture on Mormonism, the humorist Artemus Ward used a series of painted panoramas based upon photographs by Savage. In time the Union Pacific and the Central Pacific met at Promontory Point, Utah, on May 10, 1869; the thrilling ceremony was captured by Charles R. Savage in a scene to be reproduced in most of the history textbooks of the country.

Meanwhile, however, the firm had received most desirable publicity at the hands of Samuel R. Wells, and a business arrangement had been entered into by which Savage and Ottinger sold the Wells publications while Wells sold the handiwork of Savage and Ottinger. It was through this arrangement that Savage and Ottinger were spurred on to greater artistic achievements.

The picture of A ROCKY MOUNTAIN BOOK STORE appeared in the May 1868 issue of the *American Phrenological Journal*, a long-lived periodical edited by Samuel R. Wells. Beneath the picture was the following announcement:[5]

> The above engraving represents the book store and photographic art emporium of Messrs. Savage & Ottinger, in Great Salt Lake City, Utah Territory. Besides supplying the "Saints" and the "Gentiles" with the best literature of the Old World and the New, they produce good pictures—we may safely say some of the best we have ever seen. Portraits of the "saints" and "sinners" . . . Indians, pictures of trees, mountains, water-falls . . . and some of the most sublime scenery in the world.
>
> These gentlemen are artists! They combine business with art, and supply school books, phrenological books, and every variety of *useful* books.
>
> . . . Here is a store, . . . three thousand miles west from New York, in the center of a vast Territory teeming with life, enterprise, education, and MORMONISM! A hundred thousand hardy people now have their homes in these mountains; . . . Look now on one of its first book stores.

After an apostrophe to the "grandest portion of the American continent," Wells concluded by quoting a paragraph from the Salt Lake *Daily News*:

> Books.—The attention of our readers is directed to the advertisement of Messrs. Savage & Ottinger. They are the agents for several valuable publications, including those of Mr. Samuel R. Wells, of New York, of which we can not speak too highly. Visitors from our Territory to that establishment speak very highly of the courtesies extended to them. The house certainly deserves credit for the number of progressive works it publishes. We are glad to learn that they have an extended circulation among us.

After this burst of mutual esteem, George M. Ottinger apparently sent to the head of Fowler and Wells one or more of his paintings, among them a picture of the great creek that ran through Brigham Young's premises, entitled "City Creek Falls." This Wells had no difficulty in disposing of. Its purchaser was none other than Schuyler Colfax,[6] who in 1865 had visited Salt Lake City with Samuel Bowles, editor of the *Springfield Republican*, and who by 1868 had been elected vice-president of the United States.

The following letter, written by Ottinger to Wells from Salt Lake City on November 6, 1868,[7] refers not only to "City Creek," but to Wells' part in publicizing the artist's work:

Salt Lake City, Utah
Nov 6, 1868

> Mr Wells
> Dear Sir
>   Your letter of the 22d ult recd and I assure you it is no small gratification to me to hear you are so well pleased with the picture. Not only a gratification & satisfaction to feel that so small a gift has been appreciated & accepted in return for

the many—many kindnesses you have extended to S. & O but it is also with no little satisfaction I hear that yourself & friends have discovered some merit in my work, enough indeed to place it among your other gems. Now Mr Wells the only part of the business I'm not satisfied with is your placing $50 to our credit *We will not stand that.* We have been more than doubly paid for that picture. It is a free gift fresh from the hearts of the givers as a slight token of their esteem and friendship, and as such you must accept it. We will not have it otherwise.

In a few days I shall send you another Cañon View as good as the one you have. I send it to you to sell for us and if successful I shall send you more and allow any commission you think proper.

I have been for years struggling and studying with brush & palette to gain or at least approximate to that point of fame, so coveted by all artists. The little picture I sent you has broken the ice—(in New York, the great center of American art) and its success emboldens me to venture another. Your influence judgement, and facilities for Exhibiting pictures in your rooms until my name has become known in the art world would be a kindness extended to me of more value than a thousand pictures like City Creek.

I shall send you another picture take your choice, sell one keep the other, sell it for $25—50 or $100 sell it for what it will bring and place to our credit of course deducting your commission cost of frame & stretcher & c. The CP.RR is drawing close to our doors and in a few months we shall be linked to civilization. Then Mr Savage & I shall look for you and do our best to show you the wild & Rocky beauties of Utah. And until that renewal of our friendship & better acquaintance believe me

Yours truly
G. M. Ottinger

To S. R. Wells Esq.
New York City

P.S. If you can advance my name or add to my reputation by exhibiting my pictures at the National Academy I would be very thankful Use your own good judgement about it—

A Phrenologist Describes Ottinger

A few months after he had received Ottinger's letter, Wells struck out once again in behalf of the Mormon painter. He devoted several columns of the March 1869 issue of his *American Phrenological Journal* to the phrenology, portrait, and biography of George M. Ottinger, "The Utah Artist."[8]

Here is a full-sized brain; a tough, flexible, and enduring body, made up of the motive, mental, and vital temperaments fairly blended. It is comparatively easy for such an organization to work hard, . . . The head is high and long, rather than low and broad. Benevolence is the largest of the moral organs, and Destructiveness is among the smaller of the propensities. . . . Approbativeness,

Conscientiousness, and Firmness are large; while Self-Esteem and Concentrativeness are less fully developed. He will be ambitious to excel; honorable and honest in his transactions with others. Acquisitiveness and Secretiveness are small, and his love of money is limited by his necessities. . . . The social feelings are fully indicated in the chin and lips. There is large Imitation and full Constructiveness. He can copy nature, and would be expert in the use of tools.

The intellect, as a whole, is above the average. He is both a correct observer and a clear thinker. There is enough Ideality to give taste, refinement, and love for the beautiful; but not enough to make him a wild, imaginative romancer. He will work with nature in her calm and quiet aspects, rather than in her wild and tempestuous moods. Still, there must be an ardent love for her hills, her forests, and her plains, . . . We know our subject to be an artist, and claim nothing for Phrenology in this delineation. But he is more than an artist,—he is a fully fledged man—a matured human being. . . .

Mr. Ottinger has not suffered the grand landscape about the "city of the saints" to remain unappreciated. His pencil and brush have been much employed in transferring to paper and canvas its peculiar features. . . . his productions . . . evince the free touch, originality, and freshness of a sprightly and progressive lover of nature, and point to future achievements of enviable excellence.

Some of his paintings—the most noteworthy—we may mention. "Who Will Care for Mother Now?"—an incident of the battle-field "Independence Rock;" "City Creek Falls," now in the possession of Mr. Schuyler Colfax; "Overland Pony Express," engraved and published by *Harper's Weekly*; "The Last of the Aztecs," a large picture, telling of departed greatness.

Not long after Ottinger's portrait looked out from the pages of the *American Phrenological Journal*, the phrenologist Wells paid a visit to Salt Lake City, finding it regularly laid out in blocks with wide streets and large mansions, the office of Wells Fargo not far from the Salt Lake Hotel. "Utah," he concluded, "is a great country, and Brigham Young was her prophet."[9]

Wells' enthusiasm for the city and its artists persisted and was reflected in the pages of his monthly, where in 1870 and 1871 he featured articles on the sociological problems of the Mormons, the Utah Gentiles, and the Mormon question. He was especially interested in "The Utah Reformers, as they styled themselves," who in November and December 1869 had "made a bold stroke of rebellion against the power of Brigham Young." This apparent schism in Mormon ideology inspired Wells to make the following interesting comments:

> Though we did not lecture or make any professional examinations on our recent visit to Salt Lake City, we have examined the heads of hundreds of the representative men and women of the Mormons, and made ourselves acquainted with the people.
>
> Savage and Ottinger, of the artists, are, . . . one from England, the other from Philadelphia; but Mr. Ottinger is an American artist who has settled down

and cast his destiny with the Mormons rather than an original Mormon Elder. . . .

Reformers—men of large heads, with the philosophical and idealistic development, and they design to publish an elaborate system of spiritual and moral philosophy, and also a complete system of social science from the standpoint of "Reformed Mormonism." They are . . . universalian in their mental tendencies, and therefore unfit for a theocracy of "chosen people." [10]

A feature on "Leaders in the Mormon Reform Movement," with portraits of such "new movers" as Eli B. Kelsey, the iconoclast of Utah Reformers, and Joseph Salisbury, leader of the working classes, continued to be emblazoned in the pages of the *American Phrenological Journal.*[11]

It was Wells' articles on those Utah Reformers that motivated the following letter from C. R. Savage:[12]

Salt Lake City
June 27th 1871

Friend Wells -

Yours to hand—I am much flattered at your opinion of me. I do not think however that while you represent the great living spirits of the present day that I am entitled to any prominence above my fellows—certainly I have pioneered the interior west photographically moreover I have endeavoured to infuse a love of art among the people and have maintained the only art Gallery in any of the Territories. I have also pulled the sage brush and planted the vine, so have hundreds of others here—

We the Mormons do not realize that the eyes of the world are on us so much; the love of money will make some men do almost any thing, but it was not the love of money that built up our country—it was a higher, loftier, principle and power of action. New Moveism would never have accomplished this much—it lacks the power of concentration—it lacks unity—it lacks faith— for my part my faith in the overruling power of God towards us was never greater than at present.

I notice you give prominence to some of the so called reformers of Utah— *Heaven save the mark* What the Communists were to Paris, so would the *New Movers* be to Utah They *the Reformers* would pull down and destroy what has taken 22 years to build up—What can they give in return for the faith *once delived* [sic] *to the saints—vain philosophy*—wordy *moonshine* of an impracticable character. If I could find one less drunkard a less number of thieves—or *blasphemers* through any of their *reforms* I would thank God for the movement.

I think, Bro. Wells, you ought to go slow in lending your paper too much to the interests of the so called *liberal party*—did you live here you would pronounce them unmitigated tyrants that same Salisbury was known to utter the following sentiment while denouncing his old faith said he—*damn Jesus Christ.* As the party deny the mission of Christ you can see where they land— but I must stop—I denounce them as a set of humbugs—whose efforts will destroy more than build up—and their counterpart may clearly be seen in the doings of the Communists of Paris—they have refused to celebrate the 4th of July in our Tabernacle because it is devoted to the interests of the Kingdom of

God—they have taken sides against the sovereign people here—and look forward to the speedy overthrow of the Mormon Church, & people. They will look in vain—we'll weed them out.

This is the character of the reformer But I am sorry to say the reverse is the case. Men who under the influence of the old faith left off tobacco—whisky, &c, now think they have the liberty to use the article the reformers can be seen exemplifying their liberty by falling back upon errors they once left—the same Eli B Kelsey you speak of so highly would have cut me off from the Church years ago, for the commission of any act violating the word of wisdom he now struts our streets smoking the biggest cigar he can find. I only mention this to show that their reform is a humbug—no reform will help a people if it does not make them better—What I love in my faith is that it brings to bear upon our every day life a constant controlling power to restrain men in all their actions.

I do not say there are not some good men amongst them, but they are very few. Co-operation that they please to style an oligarchy—is a great success and a godsend to the people.

You must excuse the scrawl I send you I am attending to the counter and trying to write this—the foregoing are my honest sentiments. When you call such men reformers you ought to go slow—

My regards to Mrs Wells—
and best wishes to yourself—

C. R. Savage

When next you dwell upon *Utah give the men who make the country prominence* and not upstarts under the guise of reformers—You may think me severe but I have strong reasons for it.

During the few years still allotted to him Samuel R. Wells dwelt less upon Utah Reformers than upon reforms closer to home. Both Savage and Ottinger, however, continued their work, although their partnership was dissolved. While Ottinger became the spokesman for the glories of Utah art,[13] Savage opened his own Art Bazaar as "headquarters for views of Rocky Mountain Scenery and Portraits of Utah's Celebrities."[14] At his establishment on Main Street, visitors having sat for their photographic likenesses might purchase not only Mormon publications, books and albums, but a souvenir casket of Great Salt Lake containing a vial of the water and the sand of the shore. Mrs. Frank Leslie, visiting Salt Lake City during the grand transcontinental tour organized by her husband, the newspaper magnate, Frank Leslie, naturally paid a visit to Charles R. Savage, the town's "principal photographer," who "freely admitted himself to be a Mormon, somewhat defiantly stating that he had nailed his colors to the mast."[15] By that time, his erstwhile partner, Ottinger, had painted hundreds of pictures and, when Brigham Young died on August 29, 1877, it was Ottinger who made the cast of his face and took the measurements—a technique which he had perhaps learned from the phrenologist, Samuel R. Wells.

At all events, the trio of Savage, Ottinger, and Wells had learned much from one another, and their relationship, though brief, had been fruitful. The Rocky Mountain Book Store, built up by Savage and Ottinger, specialists in Utah art and photography, had, through Wells' publicity, been made known to the East. With the country's increased awareness of the beauties of Western scenery, a powerful impetus was given to the arts that recorded it.

Notes

1. Edward H. Anderson, "Events and Comments," *The Improvement Era* XII, 406; Kate B. Carter, *Heart Throbs of the West* (Salt Lake City, 1943–1948), V, 54, IX, 107–110, 115–119; Information from Mr. Harold B. Kelly, Western Americana, University of Utah Libraries; Robert Taft, *Photography and the American Scene* (New York, 1938), p. 272.

2. Kate B. Carter, *Heart Throbs of the West* (Salt Lake City, 1943–1948), II, 3–4; H. L. A. Culmer, "Art and Artists in Utah," *Tullidge's Quarterly Magazine* (January 1881), pp. 217–220; Frank Esshom, *Pioneers and Prominent Men of Utah* (Salt Lake City, 1966), p. 1080; Alice Merrill Horne, *Devotees and Their Shrines: A Hand Book of Utah Art* (Salt Lake City, 1914), pp. 24–27, 115; Information from Mr. Harold B. Kelly, Western Americana, University of Utah Libraries; Heber G. Richards, "George M. Ottinger, Pioneer Artist of Utah," *The Western Humanities Review* III:3 (July 1949), pp. 209–218; Robert Taft, *Artists and Illustrators of the Old West 1850–1900* (New York, 1953), p. 323.

3. S. R. Wells, *The Illustrated Annuals of Phrenology and Physiognomy for the Years 1865–1873* (New York [1873]), p. 38 of *Annual* for 1866.

4. E. L. Sloan, *The Salt Lake City Directory and Business Guide. For 1869* (Salt Lake City, 1869).

5. *American Phrenological Journal* 47:5 (May 1868), p. 195.

6. See *American Phrenological Journal* 49:3 (March 1869), p. 110.

7. The original is among the Fowler Family Papers, Collection of Regional History, Cornell University Library, and is reproduced by courtesy of Mr. Herbert Finch, Curator and University Archivist.

8. *American Phrenological Journal* 49:3 (March 1869), pp. 109–110.

9. *American Phrenological Journal* 51:6 (December 1870), p. 416.

10. *American Phrenological Journal* 52:1 (January 1871), pp. 44–45. See also *Ibid.* 51:5 (November 1871), pp. 328–333.

11. *Ibid.* 53:1 (July 1871), pp. 30–40.

12. The original is among the Fowler Family Papers, Collection of Regional History, Cornell University Library, and is reproduced by courtesy of Mr. Herbert Finch, Curator and University Archivist.

13. G. M. Ottinger, "The Salt Lake City," *The Art Journal* XIV (1875), p. 268.

14. C. R. Savage, *Pictorial Reflex of Salt Lake City and Vicinity* (Salt Lake City [1893]); C. R. Savage, *Views of Utah and Tourists' Guide* (Salt Lake City [1887]).

15. Mrs. Frank Leslie, *California A Pleasure Trip from Gotham to the Golden Gate* (New York: Carleton, 1877), pp. 75–77.

Anton Roman

Argonaut of Books

A MANIFEST DESTINY seemed at work not merely upon the lips of statesmen and historians, but upon the whole great continent itself. Fast upon the heels of the peace treaty that concluded the Mexican War came the discovery of gold in the California hills. A new State was in the making, and with the opening of the Far West came the need not only for miners to work the diggings, but for farmers to work the soil, teachers to instruct the new generation of children, writers to lift the hearts and expand the minds of settlers in the far-flung reaches of the country. Settlers and farmers, teachers and tradesmen—all who thronged to the bustling, roaring, colorful communities that sprang up overnight in the wake of the mining camps— needed books almost as much as they needed tools. Books, in fact, were their tools, and in San Francisco as the 1850's rolled their swift, vivid course, the sharp need for men who could publish those books was answered. The Golden Fleece that was California had many Argonauts, not the least of whom was the Argonaut of Books who, purveying wares that would ease the path of pioneers and enlighten and enrich their lives, became himself a pioneer in the distant West whose bloodless conquest rounded out a nation and determined its borders forever.

As always, when the need arose, such an Argonaut was on hand. In December of 1851 he appeared in San Francisco, a bearded miner with thick hair and a prominent nose. His name was Anton Roman. Born in Bavaria some twenty-three years before, he had migrated to America in his youth and in 1849 had crossed the plains to California. He had joined the gold-seekers on the Trinity River at Weaverville, along the Klamath, in Siskiyou, and in the northern regions of Shasta, striking rich diggings at Scott Bar. But Roman had washed more than dust from the sand at Scott Bar. He had lived

Reprinted from Madeleine B. Stern, *Imprints on History: Book Publishers and American Frontiers* (Bloomington, Ind.: Indiana Univ. Press, 1956), pp. 136–154 and 426–432.

among traders and prospectors, had worked the rich placers, had been on hand at the Scott Bar decision between rival mining groups, had seen a claim opened, gold extracted with iron spoons, pans filled with solid gold; but he had observed, too, the bustling camps, the stores, the saloons, the hotels. He had seen Ozarkers and York Staters stake their claims and wash dust from the sand. He had heard the sound of shovel on gravel, and in the tents and huts on the banks of the creek he had listened while miners exchanged their tales of rich diggings. He had lived the uproarious days that would soon become history and literature. And, along with a fund of mining anecdotes with which he would one day regale a young man named Bret Harte, he had taken with him his awareness of the need for books among prospectors and tradesmen and lonely men.

And so, in December of 1851, the bearded miner might have been seen strolling about San Francisco. In Brenham Place on the west side of the Plaza he paused before the bookstore of Burgess, Gilbert and Still; and, though he had no clear intention of making any purchases, he entered the shop. The clerk was interested in the visitor's tales of the miners at Scott Bar. More particularly, Roman showed an extreme fondness for books; and in short order the conversation between miner and clerk culminated in a business transaction whereby over a hundred ounces of gold dust, the current earnings of Roman's share of a claim on Scott Bar, were exchanged for books. Though probably neither the miner nor the clerk was aware of it, that little transaction opened an important page in the history of bookselling and publishing on the west coast.

At the moment Roman's problem was not to consider his place in history, but simply to dispose of his books. During the winter months in the Shasta mining region, he knew, prospectors could be induced to exchange their gold for reading matter; and so Anton Roman peddled his wares from camp to camp, with such success that he soon decided to abandon mining for migratory bookselling. From Eureka he moved on to Shasta City, during the golden period when the town was almost as proud of its stores as of its diggings. In the *Shasta Courier* of March 12, 1853, Roman inserted an advertisement of his Shasta Book Store, opposite El Dorado Hotel, where new books might be purchased wholesale and retail, and where might be found at all times "a large and splendid assortment of Books and Stationery . . . at the lowest prices. Among the late works just received are the following: The Necromances [sic], Parricide . . . Fair Rosamond, Amy Lawrence, Mad Cap . . . Stanley Thorn . . . &c. Also, the works of Shakspeare, Byron, Milton, Gray, Campbell and other distinguished poets. All the latest newspapers, both home and foreign, constantly on hand." In addition, musical instruments were available at the Shasta Book Store, for the proprietor had "just received an assortment of . . . Flutes, Flagelets, Clarionets," as well as note and song books and violin and guitar strings. Anton Roman hoped, "by strict attention to his business, to merit a continuance of the patronage heretofore bestowed on him," and his hopes were realized, for by the fall of 1853 his purchases in books and stationery for the three counties of Shasta, Trinity, and Siskiyou amounted to $42,000. It was apparently simpler to extract gold dust from a miner than from a mine.

Yet Roman extracted more than money from his patrons. Before his eyes rolled the gaudy panorama of the gold mining fields. At his feet were spread the rude communities of men whose tools were picks and shovels and gold pans. His comrades were the "sourdoughs," with their shaggy beards and broad hats, their boots and rolled-up trousers. Picture after picture flashed before his observant eyes, a kaleidoscope of history in the making— colorful images of pack and pan, shovel and rifle, colonies of tents with lofty mountains in the background. Roman saw the gold-bearing earth washed down, watched the rush from camp to camp; and his ears were filled with the twang of the guitar at night and the congenial murmur of tall tales exchanged by candlelight. Among villain and outlaw, lucky and luckless, gambler and drinker, he wandered, trading his books and his pamphlets for gold dust—for more than gold dust—for a rich, inexhaustible store of adventure from the flashy and crude and notorious days of the Gold Rush.

It was not until 1857 that Roman left the northern counties and, having purchased a large stock of standard and miscellaneous books in the eastern cities, set up his stand in San Francisco. Roman's trade covered about a dozen of the interior counties besides the city, and by 1859 he had so expanded that, with a still larger stock, he opened a permanent store on the west side of Montgomery Street, north of California. The migratory bookseller had settled down, a fact to which the San Francisco *Directory* of 1860 bears evidence, for there "Anthony" Roman is listed as an "importer and wholesale bookseller" at 158 Montgomery Block and 78 and 80 Merchant. Having provided miners with books to while away their weary hours, he was ready at last to fill the larger needs of the more stable community of settlers who had followed the miners to the West in a second wave of migration.

Roman had learned, in the years that had elapsed since his eventful purchase from Burgess, Gilbert and Still, that demand governs supply and that books to be bought must be needed. The books he sold, therefore, answered the requirements of a newly expanding community on the Pacific coast. The farming settlements near the seaboard were attracting immigrants; prospective settlers would want information about their new home. If books on the subject were not available, they could be printed; and Anton Roman, importer and wholesale bookseller, responded to the needs of his time and his place by entering a new phase of his career, that of publisher.

One of the earliest books bearing the Roman imprint was *An Outline of the History of California, from the Discovery of the Country to the Year 1849*. The Argonaut of Books, who had already helped make the history of

California, was ready to record that history and publish it abroad. The little paper volume consisted of an address delivered by Edmund Randolph before the Society of California Pioneers at their celebration of the tenth anniversary of the admission of the State into the Union. Printed at the Alta California Job Office, the work was published by Roman in 1860 and marked the beginning of a long line of books that were designed to instruct gold-seekers and settlers in the history and resources of their new State. Roman was akin to John S. Hittell, who wrote in the preface to the first edition of his *Resources of California*:

> I undertake to write the resources of a state, which, though young in years, small in population, and remote from the chief centres of civilization, is yet known to the furthest corners of the earth, and, during the last twelve years, has had an influence upon the course of human life, and the prosperity and trade of nations, more powerful than that exerted during the same period by kingdoms whose subjects are numbered by millions.

The publisher had been quick to seize the opportunity of sponsoring this book, the extended title of which was *The Resources of California, comprising Agriculture, Mining, Geography, Climate, Commerce, . . . and the Past and Future Development of the State;* and his interest was justified, for it passed through several editions, a compendium by, for, and of the Californian. In the third edition of 1867 is an affidavit stating that the "book is exclusively Californian in composition and manufacture," from the paper and paste-board to the morocco, thread, and gold leaf. The publisher had grown conscious of his place in California's history. Through the years Roman published similar works, from Mowry's *Geography and Resources of Arizona and Sonora* to Ferris's *Financial Economy of the United States Illustrated, and Some of the Causes Which Retard The Progress of California Demonstrated*; from *A Youth's History of California* by "Lucia Norman" [Louise Palmer Heaven]—a volume "Californian in authorship and execution"—to Cremony's *Life Among the Apaches*. The Indian fighter, Cremony, astutely dedicated his book "To the Pioneer and Liberal Publisher, Anton Roman, The Zealous and Enterprising Friend of Literature on the Pacific Coast."

By 1868 Roman had indeed become a pioneer publisher, who watched the expansion of the State and provided books that would inform prospective settlers of the nature of the west coast. In a prefatory note to Hutchings's *Scenes of Wonder and Curiosity in California*, the publisher later explained his point of view:

> Since the completion and appointments of the great Overland Railway have made travelling to the Pacific Slope easy, pleasant, speedy, and safe, a general desire has arisen for information concerning its remarkable scenery, the cost of travelling, distances, hotel charges, etc.

This general desire Roman fulfilled, giving to the public in well-printed volumes, bound in cloth or paper, a variety of works ranging from Morse's *Treatise on the Hot Sulphur Springs, of El Paso De Robles* to Stillman's *Seeking the Golden Fleece; A Record of Pioneer Life in California.* Not Stillman's book alone, but, metaphorically at least, all these publications were dedicated to the "Argonauts of California," who, at prices ranging from 50¢ to $3, could receive by mail, post-paid, the literature that would inform them of the resources of their new home. In some of these books, such as *A Sketch of the Route to California, China And Japan, via the Isthmus of Panama*, Roman's device was printed on the title-page: surmounting his initials was the grizzly bear; below them, in a significant union, the miner's pan, pick, and shovel.

In the broader aspects of his publishing activities, Roman had not forgotten the miners.

> The rapid extension of Silver Mining enterprise, in consequence of numerous discoveries of rich and extensive silver-bearing lodes in California, . . . has excited a general desire for information of such methods of extracting Silver and Gold from the . . . ores, as are practical and adapted to our circumstances.

Although the name of Frank D. Carlton, Roman's associate, appeared on the imprint of Küstel's *Nevada and California Processes of Silver and Gold Extraction*, Roman advertised and circulated the book, and, in addition, it was he who published Gregory Yale's important and authoritative *Legal Titles to Mining Claims and Water Rights, In California*. Roman had not forgotten the Scott Bar case, nor the necessity for prospectors to learn the principles governing the laws on mining property. Another volume bearing the Roman imprint was William Barstow's *Sulphurets*, designed to help miners make their own assays. Besides entering the publishing field with such works, Roman had for sale in his Montgomery Street bookstore a remarkable collection of volumes on minerals and their processing. There miners might exchange their gold dust for manuals and reap benefit from the transaction.

As the completion of the "great Overland Railway" stimulated the need for books on Western resources in general, so the discovery of new lodes created a need for books on allied and other phases of mining. Upon the successful pioneer voyage of the Pacific Mail S.S. *Colorado* to Hong Kong in 1867, a third field had opened to publishers. China was brought closer to California than ever before; and this fact, together with the presence of a great many Chinese in the State, emphasized the need for "books to enable one to understand their character." This need the enterprising publisher was eager to fill, his imprint appearing on A. W. Loomis's edition of *Confucius and the Chinese Classics*—the first book printed from stereotype plates in California. As Roman declared, "No question is more frequently asked by curious and thinking people than this: What is the literature of the Chinese? They are a reading people; then what do they read? They are a peculiar people; what has made them so? They are an unchanging people; what is it that has fixed their habits?" It was to the advantage of Californians that such questions be answered. While Loomis's compilation was designed to supply those answers, still another work published by Roman, Lanctot's *Chinese and English Phrase Book*, was intended "to enable all classes of citizens, especially merchants, shipmasters, contractors, families, and travelers to acquire an elementary and practical knowledge of the spoken language of the Canton dialect . . . the dialect most generally understood by all classes of Chinese immigrants on the Pacific Coast." The author—and, one might add, the publisher—had been induced to undertake the work because of "a daily increasing necessity, consequent upon the extended employment of Chinese, and the now established regular line of communication with China and Japan." In the preface to his own compilation Loomis had stated that, to meet the demands for understanding the Chinese, "a Book Firm of this city has spared no pains or expense to bring together as complete a collection of works on China as was possible. Such as were not to be obtained at home have been ordered from abroad." The name of that book firm must have been apparent to all, for Roman had established in his Montgomery Street bookstore a section devoted to Orientalia. There one might have found Huc's *Travels in Tartary* or Davis's *China and the Chinese*, books on Yedo and Peking, or Upper and Lower Amoor, a dictionary of the Chinese language, or a tome on the Middle Kingdom, books to charm the alien and nostalgic Oriental, and books to help the Occidental understand him.

It was not the merchants only who wished to learn something of the Asiatic industries adapted to California. The fertility of the soil along the western seaboard was attracting farmers to the coast, and for them Roman published Kendo's *Treatise on Silk and Tea Culture*. "As there is, at this time, much attention being paid to the cultivation, in this State, of many trees, shrubs and other vegetable productions heretofore only grown extensively in Japan and the Orient," Kendo's treatise was issued to acquaint the farmers of California with the requirements of the plants named in the title, and to give advice on the growing of mulberry and persimmon trees. For their more general needs, Roman added to his bookstore a section on horticulture that offered works on garden vegetables or greenhouses, facts about peat and grape culture, farm implements or landscape gardening. There were shelves devoted to the mysteries of bee-keeping, to poultry, to horses, cattle, and sheep, simply because the soil and climate of California were attracting homesteaders, just as its placers had attracted the men with pan and shovel.

As the years passed, another need made itself felt among California settlers. They were raising not only horses and grapes and roses, but children, too; and Roman, enterprising and public-spirited as ever, was ready to enrich his own coffers by facilitating the education of youth. For their amusement he published the Inglenook and Golden Gate series; for their instruction he published textbooks. The children's stories that appeared over his imprint were adapted to, and concerned with, California. In them, Roman advertised, Californians would "recognize many familiar places and personages." "Elegantly illustrated from original designs," Roman's California juveniles rolled from the press—May Wentworth's *Fairy Tales from Gold Land*, Carrie Carlton's *Inglenook*, Clara Dolliver's *Candy Elephant*—and with them were issued such texts as Layres's *Elements of Composition*, or Carrie Carlton's *Popular Letter Writer*, "particularly adapted to the wants of California." The children's teachers were urged to call and examine the textbooks and pedagogic apparatus.

Less practical than treatises on mining or agriculture, of less immediate need than works on Oriental customs or school texts, books for relaxation began to find a place on Roman's crowded shelves. Besides selling standard literary treasures, he himself published works of fiction, such as novels by "Laura Preston" [Louise Palmer Heaven] and Mrs. Embury, as well as volumes of poetry, to encourage native talent and to manifest to the world the possibilities of Californiana. James Linen's *Poetical and Prose Writings* included accounts of the missions of Upper California; Patterson's *Onward: A Lay of the West* sketched "a hasty picture of our great and growing West, at this period of its magical progress"; and the poem, *Madrona*, was "conceived and begun during a trip made by the author through the picturesque County of Sonoma." The *Poems* of Charles Warren Stoddard appeared in an elegant edition, illustrated by William Keith and printed by Bosqui on the finest paper, with a subscription list including nearly every well-known name in the professional and social circles of California.

Another verse collection, published by Roman and now a bibliographical rarity, gave rise to as much excitement as the discovery of a new lode and paved the way for a general interest in the literary enterprises of California. The story behind its publication is of extreme interest. One Mary Tingley, having filled a large folder with clippings culled from periodicals, had offered the collection to Anton Roman, who held it for possible publication. Having become acquainted with Bret Harte, the publisher requested the young man to edit the collection and obtain additions to it. The arrangements between them were not very clear, for after its publication Harte was to write to Roman:

> From your remarks concerning the cost of the volume . . . am I to infer that you propose to recompense me from the profits of the edition? I do not think we made any agreement whatever as to the amount or manner of remuneration, but I certainly cannot consent to any that is to be *contingent* upon the success of the volume, if that is your intention.

Whatever the intention, the book appeared as a small quarto, beautifully printed on fine, tinted paper, handsomely bound in cloth, priced at one dollar, and entitled *Outcroppings: Being Selections Of California Verse.* Today it is of interest as the first book with which Bret Harte was associated. In

December, 1865, when it first appeared, it proved of interest for another reason. "Its contents," Harte's preface explained, "have been selected partly from contributions made by local poets to the California newspapers during the past ten years, and partly from material collected three years ago for a similar volume, by Miss M. V. Tingley."

That Miss Tingley objected to the work, disavowing Roman's right to use her selections, is understandable. That the poems of Ina D. Coolbrith, Emilie Lawson, B. P. Avery, J. R. Ridge, C. H. Webb, and other local littérateurs should have called down upon the head of the compiler a storm of abuse is scarcely comprehensible today. None the less, there was "Commotion on Parnassus" when *Outcroppings* made its bow. Within two hours after its arrival was bruited abroad, a mob of poets besieged Roman's bookstore, all eager to learn whether their effusions had been immortalized among the selected gems. *Outcroppings* had become "the salient literary topic of the day." Heralded as a "beautiful specimen of typography," it was also condemned both for the geological character of its title and the limited nature of its contents. According to one paper, *Outcroppings* was "a Bohemian advertising medium. . . . As a collection of California poetry, it is beneath contempt." The contempt was aired, however, and the newspapers enjoyed a field day at the expense of Roman's little gift book. "All of which," the editor astutely observed, "ought to make the volume sell." It did more than that. While Ward's Furnishing Store, with tongue in cheek, issued "Outcroppings No. 2, by A Rum-Un & Co.," Hubert Howe Bancroft was quick to publish a rival anthology, *Poetry of the Pacific*. Edited by May Wentworth, this collection was, as its title indicates, more complete and ambitious in scope than Roman's undertaking. Though many of the authors were the same as in *Outcroppings*, and though their utterances paid similar tribute to such poetic staples as autumn, love, and trees, *Poetry of the Pacific* was, quantitatively at least, superior to its predecessor. Decades later Harte recalled the excitement attending the publication of *Outcroppings*, in his *My First Book*; but long before that the anthology had spread Roman's reputation abroad and had indicated to him the interest in California that a native literary work might arouse. By 1868 even a Bancroft publication could declare that "the leading publishing houses in California are those of H. H. Bancroft & Co. and A. Roman & Co." It was time for Anton Roman, miner, bookseller, and publisher, to embark upon yet another enterprise, and to prove—if proof were needed—that California was rich not only in its natural resources, but in its literary products as well.

He himself needed no such proof. His bookselling and publishing activities had acquainted him with many of the writers of the coast. Manuscripts were constantly being submitted to him, and he was confident that abundant material, not suitable for publication in book form, would be valuable for use in a magazine. Shortly before his death, Roman explained the purposes behind his entrance into the field of magazine publishing:

I considered the geographical position of San Francisco and California, the large extent of territory surrounding it, its immense seacoast both on the American side and across the Pacific. . . . Here I saw an opportunity for a magazine that would furnish information for the development of our new State and all this great territory, to make itself of such value that it could not fail to impress the West, and the East also.

Financial support and advertising patronage were sought by means of the following circular:

A. Roman & Co. propose taking immediate steps for issuing a first-class monthly magazine, the first number to appear July 1st, 1868.

The nature and character of the magazine will embrace, to the fullest extent, the commercial and social interests of California and the Pacific Coast.

We ask your assistance in this enterprise in the shape of an advertisement of your business for the term of one year, which we think will fully repay you.

Our intentions are to have every article original; to employ only the best talent in the country; to pay for every article; and to distribute 3000 copies monthly, until its permanent circulation reaches or exceeds this number.

The rates of advertising will be $50 per page monthly, or $25 for a half page.

The circular brought in contracts for advertising which would assure the magazine an income of $900 monthly for a year. With such support, and with the confidence that he himself could procure at least half the articles for the first six months of the magazine, Roman was ready to seek an editor.

Charles Warren Stoddard, whose *Poems* Roman had published, recommended the writer who had edited *Outcroppings* and who was then serving as secretary of the U.S. branch mint—Bret Harte. Harte entertained some doubts about the project, and, to win him over, Roman indicated on a map of the two hemispheres in his office the central position of San Francisco on the Pacific coast, and its potential influence upon the entire territory. The prospective editor was convinced. Harte had visited Roman at the moment when the publisher was considering a change of die for the cover. The line-cut of the grizzly now seemed too unadorned and Roman desired some alteration. Harte took out a pencil and drew two lines beneath the bear, placing it on the tracks of the Pacific Railroad. If Roman had had any doubts about Harte's abilities, they were dispelled by this inspired touch. Both editor and publisher were ready to proceed with a magazine that needed only a title, and this too was supplied by Harte, who dubbed the periodical *The Overland Monthly*. [See Plate 5.]

The first number of *The Overland Monthly Devoted To The Development of the Country* appeared in July, 1868. Harte's editorial section, entitled "Etc.," explained the reason for its name:

Shall not the route be represented as well as the *termini*? And where our people travel, that is the highway of our thought . . . what could be more appropriate for the title of a literary magazine than to call it after this broad highway?

THE

Overland Monthly

DEVOTED TO

THE DEVELOPMENT OF THE COUNTRY.

VOLUME I.

SAN FRANCISCO:
A. ROMAN & COMPANY.
1868.

PLATE 5. Anton Roman's *Overland Monthly*, showing the grizzly
on the tracks of the Pacific Railroad.

Noah Brooks, who had agreed to serve as a joint editor with Harte and W. C. Bartlett, contributed "The Diamond Makers of Sacramento"; B. P. Avery discussed "Art Beginnings on the Pacific"; and a poem, "San Francisco," was supplied by Harte. The section on Current Literature included the review of a Roman publication, Swift's *Going to Jericho*. *The Overland Monthly*, priced at $4 a year, with appropriate reductions in the rates for clubs, had been launched.

Perhaps one of the most interesting concomitants of the enterprise was Roman's relationship with Bret Harte. Roman wished to obtain from Harte a story for at least every other number. This plan threw publisher and editor together much of the time; and, as they journeyed by train up and down

Santa Clara Valley or rode across the Santa Cruz Mountains by stagecoach, Roman shared with Harte his anecdotes and reminiscences of the gold rush, pointing out to him their literary possibilities.

The results of this association appeared in the second number of *The Overland* in the form of "The Luck of Roaring Camp." At Santa Cruz Harte had outlined the tale to Roman, and one Sunday afternoon the duplicate galley proofs arrived on the stagecoach. Roman's wife, Eliza Fletcher Roman, read the story aloud to him until she was too affected to continue. The next day, upon his return to San Francisco, Roman was greeted by his chief clerk with the announcement that the proofreader, Mrs. Sarah B. Cooper, had objected to the immorality of "The Luck." Roman decided to print the story, none the less, and it became the sensation of the day. By October, 1868, Harte could write in "Etc.":

> The prophet has been honored in his own country. Throughout the Pacific Slope, from San Diego to Portland; on the Sierras and along the Great Highway . . . wherever a printing press has been carried or a ream of printing paper packed, the Overland has been kindly welcomed.

What is more, the local talent of the west coast found in it a medium for their writings, and, through earthquake and sunshine, *The Overland* pursued its successful way, crossing the continent on the completed Pacific Railroad. By the end of its first year, however, Roman fell ill, and at the advice of his physician left San Francisco for a rest, selling out his proprietorship in the magazine to John H. Carmany for $7,500, an amount that represented a profit of $3,000.

By the terms of his contract with Carmany, Roman had agreed not to enter the magazine field again for ten years. Magazine publishing was, however, as he himself described it, "in his bones." At the same time that he had sponsored *The Overland*, his imprint appeared on the *California Medical Gazette*, a monthly devoted to medicine, surgery, and the collateral sciences. As soon as the ten years had elapsed, therefore, Roman returned to the field with another venture in periodicals, *The Californian A Western Monthly Magazine*. The first number of January, 1880, included an editorial section appropriately called "Outcroppings," in which the publisher introduced his new enterprise:

> Keenly alive to the fact that we have here on this coast the elements of a literature as strong, original, and characteristic, as the people themselves, the projectors of this periodical warmed it into life . . . to stand the exponent of our life and letters, such as they now are, and such as they may in time become. In the language of its prospectus, and indicative of its name, "The Californian will be thoroughly Western in its character, local to this coast in its flavor, representative and vigorous in its style and method of dealing with questions, and edited for a popular rather than a severely literary constituency." . . . With . . . a sincere desire of arousing a local literary pride among our people, the new magazine

clasps hands with all interested in the working out of a common and continued prosperity.

Under the editorship of Fred W. Somers and later of Charles H. Phelps, *The Californian* became a medium for the "outcroppings" of a later generation of the West, publishing the writings of Joaquin Miller and Ambrose Bierce. By May, 1880, however, Roman was again compelled—because of "lack of means to push the enterprise"—to yield his proprietorship in the magazine, this time to the California Publishing Company for the sum of $275; and, with the revival of the old *Overland Monthly*, which had been suspended, *The Californian* was merged with it. Both magazines had been the offshoots of Anton Roman's ingenuity and confidence in the literary possibilities of California, and though he himself was never to return to the field, he could rest content with the contributions he had made to periodical publishing on the west coast. He could write, "I have always felt grateful to the public and to the many good friends who readily and cheerfully . . . aided my endeavors in magazine publishing, but above all to the many contributors to the early issues, who worked for the success of the enterprise."

In the years that passed between Roman's withdrawal from *The Overland* and his connection with *The Californian*, his bookstore had expanded to such an extent that it offered works not only for miners and farmers, settlers and Orientals, children and littérateurs, but "for the million" as well. As a publisher he had undertaken such travel books as Swift's *Going to Jericho*; he had sponsored the writings of local theologians, publishing the sermons of the San Francisco minister, Charles Wadsworth, and the scriptural commentaries of the California bishop, William Kip. But, in order to attract "the million," Roman was forced to import and sell. As early as 1861 he had issued a 259-page *Catalogue raisonné*, consisting of "a classified collection of prominent standard authors—embracing a wide range . . . and of use to all seeking the best works in any branch of Literature." As the years passed, the Montgomery Street bookstore became a market for books "for the million," books standard and miscellaneous, medical and scientific, legal and theological, books appealing to every class of society and every profession. At Roman's stand might be found, therefore, the works of Eastern publishers—G. W. Carleton and T. B. Peterson, D. Appleton and Harper, Loring, and Lee and Shepard; so many of the books published in New York, Philadelphia, and Boston were sold by Anton Roman in San Francisco that he could advertise "a complete stock in every department of literature." His shelves were filled with "the finest library bound books, embracing all the standard works in the English language." On the center tables might be found "the rarest and most costly editions of the poets and favorite authors of the age, together with the choicest gift-books and other *recherche* publications of the English and American press." Globes, maps, charts, atlases, school apparatus, toy books, and juveniles completed a stock that increased yearly, and indicated, as it increased, the development of California's interest from the regional to the universal. In 1865 Roman's establishment ranked next to Bancroft's as the leading firm on the Pacific coast. The annual sales for two years past were represented as between $175,000 and $200,000, while the stock of books on hand was valued at $75,000 or $85,000. Here was a far cry from the California of only eighteen years before, when "there were not probably 300 volumes of English books within the territory." Now Roman's firm had agents in London and Paris, as well as in New York, from whom shipments were received. His relations with the Eastern publishers were generally equal, if not superior, to those of any other house on the coast, and he advertised that thus he was able to supply books in larger quantities and at cheaper rates than other importers.

With one Eastern publisher Roman's relations were more closely knit. In 1866 he established, for some six years, a residence in New York, but even before that date the firm of William J. Widdleton had served as his New York purchasing agent. Widdleton's business was substantial, and as the publisher of standard books and belles-lettres, he had earned a fairly solid reputation. Many of Roman's publications appear with a double imprint— that of the Montgomery Street establishment in San Francisco and that of Widdleton at 17 Mercer and later at 27 Howard Street, New York. It was through this New York agency that Roman offered Bret Harte's *Condensed Novels* to the publisher, G. W. Carleton, and it is on the back of Widdleton's lists in the *Publishers' Trade List Annual* that Roman's advertisements appear. In addition, Roman could observe publishing conditions in the East. With Widdleton in particular he could discuss the close affiliation of the book and stationery trades, current methods of book distribution, publicity devices, seasonal trends in books, the growth of the reprint field, changes in popular taste, the relative appeal of English novels or American travel books, juveniles or household helps, and could cull many ideas for California circulation.

As a west coast publisher and bookseller Roman needed such an association. The books he sold were carried by semi-monthly steamer between San Francisco and the East; and his relationship with Widdleton provided him with the best facilities for obtaining the latest issues of the American and English presses. In other directions, ships for Japan and China, Honolulu and Australia, Mexico and British Columbia carried heavy shipments of his goods. "We are constantly in receipt of all new publications by steamer," he advertised, "as fast as issued from the press. Books imported to order on shortest notice." Roman catered not only to the interests of the "million," but to their pocketbooks as well, building up his business on the principle of "quick sales and small profits," and advertising that his "extensive and elegant assortment" might be purchased "cheap for cash." The trade was supplied on liberal terms, special inducements were offered to libraries, and particular care was taken "in filling all wholesale and retail orders by mail and express, with promptness and at the lowest cash rates." Roman was prompt, indeed, as a letter of his sent in 1876 to the publishers of the *New-York Tribune* indicates:

> Do you propose republishing Chas. Reade's Letters on International Copyright in any form? We have tried to obtain copies of your issues containing the several letters without success, and as we have repeated inquiries for the letters, either in a collected or in the original form, we take this means of finding whether you will republish or not.

Roman's letter shows not only his expeditiousness but the status of his business as well, for it is signed "A. Roman & Co." In his early business career, Roman had associated with himself Frank D. Carlton, who had had his training as a clerk with W. T. Coleman & Co., shipping merchants. Boarding with Frederick McCrellish, publisher of the *Alta California*, he had become interested in printing and in 1862 had joined Roman's company. Later on, after Carlton listed himself as a "capitalist" instead of a publisher in the San Francisco *Directories*, his place in the firm was taken by Joseph A. Hofmann, who had served as Roman's chief clerk and afterwards as salesman in the concern.

In 1871 announcement was made that Messrs. Roman & Co. had removed from their old quarters to "new and larger premises" at 11 Montgomery Street. Equipped in lavish style befitting California's spectacular, silver seventies, the store in the Lick House Block displayed to its customers a ceiling painted in fresco, appointments of white picked out with walnut, and the whole "a magnificent temple of letters." The firm that had long before advertised itself as "the largest miscellaneous book buyers in this country," and "the only exclusive book store on the Pacific Coast," now offered its customers, for the Christmas season of that year, "a royal literary feast." The "noble hall has its long tables covered with the choicest mental food culled from all climes and served up in the most magnificent style of binding." A. Roman & Co. could proudly boast, "Here we are, geographically isolated from the great world's throng, and yet the greatest cities cannot show a more complete establishment than ours." Besides the books, the annuals, the photograph albums of earlier times, 11 Montgomery Street could provide its patrons with Russian leather *porte-monnaies*, and "a complete trousseau of stationery, from the maiden card to the family Bible." Furniture, too, was for sale in the Lick House Block: carved book shelves and brackets, book stands and pouches for the wall, card stands and ink stands of cut glass or ormolu. The window display gave an earnest of the riches within; and by that Christmas of 1871 Anton Roman had reached the zenith of his success. The miner of Scott Bar, the proprietor of the Shasta Book Store, had come a long way in twenty years.

The general panic of 1873, however, resulted in a continued business depression on the Pacific coast, which, by 1879, had affected booksellers as well as farmers and industrialists. In consequence of this economic crisis, an announcement was made in April, 1879, that A. Roman & Co. had made an assignment for the benefit of their creditors. The firm's liabilities were estimated at from $85,000 to $90,000; their nominal assets at $80,000, consisting of about $15,000 in book accounts and the balance in stock and claims in equity. At the same time, W. J. Widdleton disposed of the bulk of his publications to A. C. Armstrong and discontinued his service as Roman's New York agent.

Roman's failure did not overwhelm him. Enthusiastic and venturesome as ever, he emerged from bankruptcy as the A. Roman Publishing Company, 511 California Street, and by 1882 had opened an agency in Room 15, 120 Sutter Street. In order to give the widest possible publicity to his undertaking, the publishers of *The Californian*, which he himself had projected, announced that "Mr. Roman has again started in business as bookseller and publisher . . . and . . . is prepared to supply anything and everything in his line, from a sheet of note-paper to a complete library in bindings warranted to match the carpet. We mention this last with the special purpose of influencing the patronage of our rich men in his favor."

Such patronage, however, does not seem to have been extended to him. It was less as bookseller and publisher that he resumed business than as general agent for subscription books. Roman had earlier in his career served as agent for *The National Almanac and Annual Record*, the publications of the Sunday School Union, and *The California Mail Bag*. He had also handled subscription books, such as Palmer Cox's *Squibs of California* and Hugh Quigley's *Irish Race in California*; he had been the San Francisco agent for the first edition of Mark Twain's *Roughing It*, and his imprint appears, in conjunction with that of the American Publishing Company, on the first American edition of *The Adventures of Tom Sawyer*. Along such lines he continued his business during the 1880's, no longer in a "magnificent temple of letters," but in a single room on Sutter Street. By that decade, however, the handling of subscription books had fallen into disrepute, and this aspect of the book business, impinging as it did upon the regular trade, had not only become the object of attack but was less lucrative than it had once been. Roman's first imprint had appeared in 1860 on *The Still Hour* by Austin Phelps, a work copyrighted by Gould and Lincoln and offering "standard thoughts" on religious subjects. His last imprint appeared in 1886 on a book far more characteristic of his own interests, Walter M. Leman's *Memories of an Old Actor*, for Leman's memories embraced the Sacramento Theater and the San Francisco theatricals of the early days. Though Roman never wrote his "Memories of an Old Publisher," he might well have recorded his history now, for by 1888 he had abandoned the book field forever.

At that time, and until his death in 1903, Roman appears in the San Francisco *Directories* as real estate agent, dealer in city and country property and timber lands, and loan broker. At first with Arthur H. Breed (with whom—as Holcomb, Breed and Bancroft—Harlow P. Bancroft, nephew of H. H. Bancroft, became associated after the turn of the century), Anton Roman sold the land he had loved instead of the volumes that had been written about it.

On June 21, 1903, he accompanied his son and daughter to a funeral, traveling on the North Shore Railroad. A car was derailed near Tomales, and among the victims of the wreck whose injuries proved fatal was the seventy-five-year-old Anton Roman.

Roman had been naturalized in Shasta County during the summer of 1885. In reality he had been naturalized long before that. Although his activities were neither so elaborate nor his reputation so celebrated as Bancroft's, his choice of publications served as a kind of marker to the progress of the Pacific coast. In this way Roman's career was both a parallel and a herald to the story of westward expansion, and the narrative of his life reaffirms the sometimes forgotten American tradition which asserts that every man is a debtor not only to his profession, but to his country. Anton Roman had paid that debt in full. With tools of type and ink he had helped to settle the Far West and round out a nation. The miner from Bavaria, who had crossed the plains to seek gold, had enriched the land of his adoption. When he placed his initials between grizzly bear and pick, pan and shovel, he had taken up the task of Argonaut in a broad sense. He had given to settlers the books they needed to establish a new community, and he had published abroad the literary treasure that could be found in El Dorado. In the settling of the Far West he takes his place, along with miner and farmer and teacher and builder. He, too, was a builder of empire—his masonry the printed word.

Notes on Sources

Opening of Far West

See Allan Nevins and Henry Steele Commager, *The Pocket History of the United States* (New York, 1951), pp. 197, 314 f.

Roman's Appearance

A photograph of Anton Roman is reproduced in Noah Brooks, "Bret Harte: A Biographical and Critical Sketch," *The Overland Monthly* XL:3 (September 1902), p. 205.

Roman's Early Life & Mining Activities

For the early phases of Roman's life, see Idwal Jones, "The Man From Scott Bar," *Westways* (June 1948), pp. 8–9; Robert O'Brien, *California Called Them* (New York, London, Toronto, [1951]), pp. 162, 234; "Anton Roman," *San Francisco Chronicle* (June 22, 1903), p. 2 (courtesy Mabel R. Gillis, formerly of the California

State Library); "Anton A. Roman, Romance Of Early Days In His Life," *San Francisco Examiner* (June 22, 1903), p. 3 (courtesy Mabel R. Gillis); Charles H. Shinn, *Mining Camps A Study in American Frontier Government* (New York, 1885), pp. 219 ff.; Franklin Walker, *San Francisco's Literary Frontier* (New York, 1939), p. 259.

There is a possibility that Roman was in New Mexico in 1846. In the Huntington Library is a summons to the constable of Santa Fe commanding him to summon Marcus Quintane [Marcos Quintana?] before the justice of the peace to testify concerning an assault and battery made on the person of Maubrecie Duran by A. Roman. The summons is signed by John R. Tulles and is dated December 22, 1846 (courtesy Ernest R. May, and Haydée Noya of the Huntington Library).

Details of the rich Scott Bar gravels appear in H. H. Bancroft, *History of California* (San Francisco, 1884–90), VI, 365 ff., 494. See also *History of Siskiyou County, California* (Oakland, 1881), p. 217. An account of the arbitration effected between rival mining camps at "Scotch" Bar may be found in Shinn, *op. cit.*, pp. 220–23.

Roman's Bavarian origin is shown by his registration record in *Index to San Francisco Great Register of Voters*, 1898, 42d assembly district, 10th precinct (courtesy Mabel R. Gillis). Special acknowledgment is due to Mabel R. Gillis, Rollo G. Silver, and Neal Harlow for their aid in the preparation of this chapter.

A brief sketch of Roman's life appears in Robert E. Cowan, *Booksellers of Early San Francisco* (Los Angeles, 1953), pp. 11 ff.

The Purchase from Burgess, Gilbert & Still

"Reminiscences of Bret Harte (a symposium: 'The Genesis of the Overland Monthly,' signed by Anton Roman)," *The Overland Monthly* XL:3 (September 1902), p. 220; Henry R. Wagner, "Commercial Printers of San Francisco From 1851 To 1880," *The Papers of the Bibliographical Society of America* XXXIII (1939), p. 76.

Roman's Migratory Bookselling & Shasta Book Store

"Reminiscences of Bret Harte," p. 220; George R. Stewart, Jr., *Bret Harte Argonaut and Exile* (Boston & New York, 1931), p. 130.

Roman's advertisement is reprinted in M. H. B. Boggs, *My Playhouse Was A Concord Coach* (Oakland, 1942), p. 155.

Further details of Roman's book business in Shasta and his finances appear in Anton Roman, "The Beginnings of the Overland As Seen By The First Publisher," *Overland Monthly*, 2nd Series, XXXII:187 (July 1898), p. 72.

Roman in San Francisco

Roman, "The Beginnings of the Overland," *Overland Monthly* (July 1898), p. 72 and "Reminiscences of Bret Harte," *ibid.* (September 1902), p. 220.

Between 1862 and 1871 Roman is listed in the San Francisco *Directory* at 417 and 419 Montgomery Street, and later at 11 Montgomery. For these listings thanks go to Mabel R. Gillis, Neal Harlow of the University of California Library, William Ramirez of the San Francisco Public Library, and Dorothea E. Spear of the American Antiquarian Society.

According to "Notes On Books And Booksellers," *American Literary Gazette and Publishers' Circular* V:6 (July 15, 1865), pp. 121–22, Roman "first started in this city by selling books at auction in 1859. He leased for that purpose a portion of W.

B. Cooke & Co.'s store, on Montgomery Street. After remaining there about a year, he removed into the old stand of J. G. Gilchrist, now occupied by the Telegraph Company. . . . After staying in this store about a year and a half, his success was secured beyond peradventure, and so rapid was the increase of his business that he was obliged to look out for a larger store. In the beginning of the year 1862 he obtained the store now occupied by him on Montgomery Street, between California and Sacramento Streets, which is the largest and most elegant single room occupied for such purposes in San Francisco."

Californiana Published by Roman

See, besides the books themselves, *American Literary Gazette* IX:3 (June 1, 1867), p. 73; Ethel Blumann and Mabel W. Thomas, eds., *California Local History A Centennial Bibliography* (Stanford, 1950), *passim*; Robert E. and Robert G. Cowan, *A Bibliography of the History of California 1510–1930* (San Francisco, 1933), *passim*; Ruth Doxsee, "Book Publishing in San Francisco (1848 to 1906)," Special Study (MS in University of California, School of Librarianship), 1931, pp. 13–16 (courtesy Ruth Doxsee); list of books bearing the Roman imprint in *Overland Monthly* (July 1898), p. 72 n. 2; Roman's advertisements in many of his publications, as well as in *Publishers' Trade List Annual* 1877 and 1878, *Publishers' Weekly* III:14 (April 5, 1873), p. 359, VIII:1 (July 3, 1875), p. 56; San Francisco *Directory* 1868–69, between pp. 80 and 81; C. F. Tiffany and A. C. Macdonald, *The Pocket Exchange Guide of San Francisco* (San Francisco [1875]), p. 10; *Uniform Trade List Circular* (September 1867), p. 181.

Hittell's preface appears in John S. Hittel [sic], *The Resources of California* (San Francisco: A. Roman & Co., and New York: W. J. Widdleton, 1863), p. v. For the affidavit in the third edition of 1867, the writer is indebted to Neal Harlow, University of California. See also Robert E. Cowan, *A Bibliography of the History of California . . . 1510–1906* (San Francisco, 1914), pp. 111–12.

For Cremony's dedication, see John C. Cremony, *Life Among the Apaches* (San Francisco & New York: A. Roman & Co., 1868), Dedication.

For the publisher's note in Hutchings, see J. M. Hutchings, *Scenes of Wonder and Curiosity in California* (New York & San Francisco: A. Roman & Co., 1872), prefatory note from publisher.

Roman's Works for Miners

Guido Küstel, *Nevada and California Processes of Silver and Gold Extraction* (San Francisco: Frank D. Carlton, 1863), p. 3; "List of Valuable Works on Mining . . . For Sale by A. Roman & Co.," advertisement in William Barstow, *Sulphurets* (San Francisco & New York: A. Roman & Co., 1867), p. 118.

Roman's Orientalia & Farming Books

T. A. Kendo, *Treatise on Silk and Tea Culture and Other Asiatic Industries Adapted To The Soil And Climate Of California* (San Francisco & New York: A. Roman & Co., 1870), Preface; at the end of this work is the list of "Important Books for Farmers, for sale by A. Roman & Co." Benoni Lanctot, *Chinese and English Phrase Book* (San Francisco & New York: A. Roman & Co., 1867), Preface; at the end of Lanctot is the list in which "A. Roman & Co. invite particular attention to the following works on China and Japan." A. W. Loomis, ed., *Confucius and the Chinese Classics* (San

Francisco & New York: A. Roman & Co., 1867), pp. vii–viii. See also advertisement of Loomis's work at the end of John Franklin Swift, *Going to Jericho* (New York & San Francisco: A. Roman & Co., 1868). Loomis's work was announced as "the first book printed from Stereotype Plates in California," in *Publishers' Weekly* VIII:1 (July 3, 1875), p. 56.

Juveniles & Schoolbooks Published by Roman

Publishers' Weekly VIII:1 (July 3, 1875), p. 56, X:5 (July 29, 1876), *passim*; advertisement of Roman's "California Juvenile Books" at end of Hutchings, *op. cit.* (1871); Roman's list at end of Gregory Yale, *Legal Titles to Mining Claims* (San Francisco & New York: A. Roman & Co., 1867).

For the juveniles and texts, and school apparatus sold by Roman, see *The California Mail Bag* I:5 (December 1871), p. 112; Roman's advertisement at end of Hittell, *op. cit.* (1874); *San Francisco Business Directory and Mercantile Guide* 1864–65, p. 31.

Roman's Literary Publications

Besides the works themselves, see Edgar J. Hinkel, ed., *Bibliography of California Fiction, Poetry, Drama.* W.P.A. Project (Oakland, 1938), I, *passim*; list of Roman imprints at Huntington Library (courtesy Lyle H. Wright); *Madrona Etc. By D.T.C.* (San Francisco: A. Roman & Co., 1876), Note; A. W. Patterson, *Onward: A Lay of the West* (New York & San Francisco: A. Roman & Co., 1869), Remarks; information from Jacob Zeitlin, Los Angeles.

For discussions of Charles Warren Stoddard's *Poems*, edited by Bret Harte and published by Roman in 1867, see Francis O'Neill, "Stoddard, Psalmist of the South Seas," *The Catholic World* CV:628 (July 1917), p. 511; Charles H. Shinn, "Early Books, Magazines, and Book-Making," *The Overland Monthly*, 2nd Series, XII:70 (October 1888), p. 347; Walker, *op. cit.*, p. 230.

Outcroppings

For the preparation and journalistic reception of *Outcroppings*, edited by Bret Harte for Roman in 1865 but dated 1866, see Bret Harte to Anton Roman, San Francisco, January 8, 1866, in Geoffrey Bret Harte, ed., *The Letters of Bret Harte* (Boston & New York, 1926), pp. 3–4; Bret Harte, "My First Book," California edition of *Works* (Boston & New York, 1929), III, 427 ff.; *Outcroppings: Being Selections Of California Verse* (San Francisco & New York: A. Roman & Co.—W. J. Widdleton, 1866), p. 3; "Outcroppings of California Verse," *San Francisco Evening Bulletin* (January 6, 1866), p. 1; "Reminiscences of Bret Harte," p. 220; Stewart, *op. cit.*, pp. 129 ff.; Walker, *op. cit.*, pp. 211 ff.

Roman's Reputation

Titus F. Cronise, *The Natural Wealth of California* (San Francisco: H. H. Bancroft & Co., 1868), pp. 683–84.

The Overland Monthly; Bret Harte & Anton Roman

H. H. Bancroft, *Essays and Miscellany* (San Francisco, 1890), p. 600; Henry J. W. Dam, "A Morning with Bret Harte," *McClure's Magazine* IV:1 (December 1894), pp. 44–45; Charles S. Greene, "Magazine Publishing in California," *Publications of the Library Association of California* (San Francisco, 1898), No. 2, pp. 3 ff.;

George Wharton James, "The Founding of the Overland Monthly," *Overland Monthly* LII:1 (July 1908), pp. 5, 10; Idwal Jones, *Ark of Empire* (Garden City, N.Y., 1951), pp. 204 ff.; B. E. Lloyd, *Lights and Shades in San Francisco* (San Francisco, 1876), pp. 301 ff.; Henry Childs Merwin, *The Life of Bret Harte* (Boston & New York, 1911), pp. 44–45; Frank Luther Mott, *A History of American Magazines 1865–1885* (Cambridge, Mass., 1938), III, 56, 402 ff.; *The Overland Monthly* (July 1898, September 1902), *passim;* "Overland Reminiscences," *Overland Monthly*, 2nd Series, I:1 (January 1883), p. 1; T. Edgar Pemberton, *The Life of Bret Harte* (London, 1903), pp. 82, 87–88; "Reminiscences of Bret Harte," pp. 220 ff.; Roman, "The Beginnings of the Overland," p. 73; "A. Roman," *San Francisco Alta California* (August 4, 1879), p. 1 (courtesy Mabel R. Gillis); Stewart, *op. cit.*, pp. 162–63; Charles Warren Stoddard, "Early Recollections of Bret Harte," *The Atlantic Monthly* LXXVIII:469 (November 1896), pp. 675–76; Walker, *op. cit.*, pp. 259 ff.

See also *The Overland Monthly* I:1 (July 1868), p. 99, I:4 (October 1868), p. 385.

For details of its later history, see "'The Overland Monthly' Sold," *Publishers' Weekly* LVIII:10 (September 8, 1900), p. 484.

There is some confusion regarding the story behind "The Luck of Roaring Camp." In "Reminiscences of Bret Harte," prepared for *The Overland Monthly* of September 1902, Roman indicated that he had read the proofs before he received word of the tale's "immorality." In an interview with Roman reported in the *San Francisco Alta California* of August 4, 1879, p. 1, however, he states that he read the proofs after he had received a letter from his partner denouncing the story as "indecent." Moreover, according to James Howard Bridge, *Millionaires and Grub Street* (New York, 1931), p. 214, Roman occasionally remarked that the lady proofreader was a "fanciful creation." There was also some difference of opinion between Harte and Roman regarding Mrs. Roman's part in "The Luck." See Harte's letter to Nan, August 29, 1879, in Geoffrey Bret Harte, ed., *op. cit.*, pp. 152–53: "Do you remember the day you lay sick at San José and I read you the story of 'The Luck,' and took heart and comfort from your tears over it, and courage to go on and *demand* that it should be put into the magazine. And think—think of fat Mrs. Roman claiming to be its sponsor!!!" This explosion was doubtless a result of the *Alta California's* report of the interview with Roman (August 4, 1879), in which Roman stated, "I told my wife that she was truly the sponsor of Bret Harte."

Other Magazine Projects of Roman

Information from Dr. Archibald Malloch, New York Academy of Medicine. Roman also reprinted articles from the *California Medical Gazette* (San Francisco), such as Arthur B. Stout's "Hygiene, as regards the Sewerage of San Francisco," in 1868 and 1869.

For details about *The Californian*, see *The Californian* I:1 (January 1880), p. 90, II:7 (July 1880), p. 100, VI:33 (September 1882), p. 291; Greene, *op. cit.*, p. 7; Mott, *op. cit.*, III, 56, 406; "Reminiscences of Bret Harte," p. 222; Roman, "The Beginnings of the Overland," p. 75. *The Californian* (1880–82) superseded *The Overland*, which was suspended 1876–82 and the second series of which, begun in 1883, in turn superseded *The Californian*.

Roman's Books of the Million

Roman's books "for the million" are advertised in *The California Mail Bag* I:5

(December 1871), p. 112. His *Catalogue raisonné: a general and classified list of the most important works in nearly every department of literature and science, published in the United States and England, with a bibliographical introduction* (San Francisco, 1861) is owned by the California State Library.

See also "Notes On Books And Booksellers," *American Literary Gazette* V:6 (July 15, 1865), pp. 121–22, where the stock is summarized as follows: "Standard and miscellaneous books, 50,000 volumes; medical works, 3,000 volumes; theological works, 8,000 volumes; scientific books, 5,000 volumes; military books, 500 volumes."

For the wide variety of his stock, see also *San Francisco Business Directory and Mercantile Guide* 1864–65, pp. 30–31.

The eastern publications sold by Roman are listed in "Books of the Month," *The Overland Monthly* V:1 and 2 (July and August 1870), pp. 104, 200; in *The California Mail Bag* II:3 (June–July 1872), pp;. 11, 41; and at the end of *The Californian* II:9 (January 28, 1865). According to William McDevitt of San Francisco, Roman had his name appended to the title-pages of some of the books of which he procured quantities. His agents are mentioned in J. Price and C. S. Haley, *The Buyers' Manual and Business Guide; being a description of the Leading Business Houses . . . Of The Pacific Coast* (San Francsico, 1872), p. 48.

Roman & Widdleton

For Roman's connections with W. J. Widdleton, see *The American Bookseller*, N.S. I:10 (May 15, 1882), p. 226; Bret Harte to James R. Osgood & Co., May 30, 1870, in *Concerning "Condensed Novels" By Bret Harte Introduction And . . . Notes By Nathan Van Patten* (Stanford University, 1929), pp. xix–xx; "Obituary. W. J. Widdleton," *New-York Tribune* (May 3, 1882), p. 5; "Obituary. William J. Widdleton," *Publishers' Weekly* XXI:18 (May 6, 1882), p. 478; "Sketches of the Publishers. William J. Widdleton," *The Round Table* IV:54 (September 15, 1866), pp. 107–8.

Roman's Business Methods & Associates

See Roman's advertisements on the covers of the San Francisco *Directory* 1861 and 1862 (courtesy Neal Harlow and Dorothea E. Spear); his advertisements at the end of Barstow, *op. cit.*, Hittell, *op. cit.* (1874), *A Sketch of the Route to California, China And Japan, via the Isthmus of Panama* (San Francisco & New York, 1867); Price and Haley, *op. cit.*, p. 48; *San Francisco Business Directory and Mercantile Guide* 1864–65, p. 30. San Francisco *Directory* 1859–1865, listings for Frank D. Carlton, and 1863–1872, listings for Joseph A. Hofmann (courtesy Dorothea E. Spear, American Antiquarian Society, and Oscar Wegelin, New York Historical Society).

For Roman's letter about Charles Reade, see A. Roman & Co. to the publishers of the *New-York Tribune*, February 8, 1876, MS Division, New York Public Library (courtesy Robert W. Hill).

The Lick House Block Store

American Booksellers' Guide III:12 (December 1, 1871), p. 446; *American Literary Gazette* (December 1, 1871), p. 23; *The California Mail Bag* I:5 (December 1871), p. 112; Price and Haley, *op. cit.*, p. 48.

Roman's Failure & New Start

"The Affairs of A. Roman & Co.," *American Bookseller* VII:8 (April 15, 1879), p. 309; *The Californian* IV:22 (October 1881), p. 358.

Roman's Later Years & Death

In 1894 he was an unsuccessful non-partisan candidate for recorder. See *San Francisco Chronicle* (June 22, 1903), p. 2 (courtesy Mabel R. Gillis).

For Roman's death, see also "Death of Anton Roman," *The Argonaut* LII:1372 (June 29, 1903), p. 427; *Sacramento Union* (June 23, 1903), p. 1 (courtesy Mabel R. Gillis); *San Francisco Examiner* (June 23, 1903), p. 6 (courtesy William Ramirez, San Francisco Public Library).

Henry Frank

Pioneer American Hebrew Publisher

THE SUDDEN DEATH of the pioneer American Hebrew publisher, Henry Frank, at Saratoga Springs, N. Y., on July 31, 1868, went unnoticed by the non-Jewish press of New York. Indeed, it was apparently only in the *Hebrew Leader* that his productive life was summarized, the editor remarking that, "during his long career in this country, which brought him in contact with persons of all creeds and nationalities, he quickly convinced them of his many noble qualities both as a man and a scholar." Then—nearly a year after Frank's death—his biography and his portrait were blazoned forth in one of New York's most unlikely media, the *American Phrenological Journal*. There, under the hyperbolic caption HENRY FRANK, THE FIRST HEBREW PUBLISHER IN THE UNITED STATES, three columns were devoted to his life and work, and a large portrait was accompanied by a phrenological analysis of his faculties and temperament.[1]

The publisher of the *American Phrenological Journal*, Samuel R. Wells, was, of course, a student of phrenology or the science of the mind, the nineteenth century's equivalent of psychoanalysis. As such, he was deeply interested in so-called "national types," among whom the Jew, standing "at the head of the Semitic sub-races," always found a place in his ethnological analyses. As an example of a race characterized by a "lofty coronal arch, . . . breadth above the ears, and . . . broad, arched, and prominent nasal bone," Henry Frank may have engaged the attention of the phrenologist-editor Wells. At all events, the *American Phrenological Journal* was apparently the only periodical that carried Frank's portrait and gave his career the space it deserved. As a German-Jewish-American publisher, Henry Frank had indeed supplied the needs of a growing, changing country, and though he was not, as Wells believed, "the first Hebrew

Reprinted from *American Jewish Archives* XX, no. 2 (November 1968): 163–168.

PLATE 6. Henry Frank, publisher of American Hebrew books.

publisher in the United States," he was a pioneer who merits a niche in American publishing history.[2] [See Plate 6.]

Born at Walsdorf, Bavaria, in 1804, young Frank became an apprentice printer at the age of thirteen in the neighboring city of Bamberg. Having, as the *American Phrenological Journal* was to put it, "gained a reputation highly flattering and deserving for one so young, which soon won him . . . fame as a practical printer," the twenty-year-old Frank was invited to superintend the Hebrew publishing firm of Arnstein & Sons in Sulzbach. There he continued for fifteen years until the concern retired from business. Only then, when he was in his thirties, did Frank strike out for himself. As Wells commented, ambitious to establish himself, he succeeded in obtaining a license from the Bavarian Government, which, at that time, was a very difficult thing for an Israelite to obtain. His first publication was the Pentateuch, or five books of Moses, in Hebrew and German, of which we have a copy before us. This book was, through his energetic endeavors, introduced in all the theological schools and colleges of the kingdom, and thus laid the foundation of his fame. He carried on the publication of Hebrew books with great success until the year 1848, when the revolution, which spread all over Germany, gave a rather gloomy aspect to business. Expecting a brighter state of affairs in America, he emigrated to this country in that year with his family, and founded the pioneer Hebrew publishing house of America in the city of New York.

Obviously, with the migration of the "48'ers," a large market for German-Jewish books and Hebrew prayer books was created, and the need in New York City especially for a German-Jewish printer was apparent. Where there had been 5,000 Jews in this country in 1820, by 1848 there were 20,000. Henry Frank was one of them, who brought with him not only his hopes and his ambitions, but also a more tangible stake in the future—his ability as a practical printer, his experience as a publisher, a stock of Hebrew books, and his fonts of type.[3]

Establishing his press at 205 Houston Street, he appeared in the New York City directories for 1849/50 as a "printer." By 1850 he had published at least five books which set the pattern for his future list.[4] Of these perhaps the most important was a Passover Haggadah, which he entitled *Service for the First Two Nights of the Passover*, "printed and published by H. Frank" in Hebrew and English and in Hebrew and German under the title *Die Pessach-Hagada*. The Haggadah would remain a staple publication of the House of Frank through the years. In addition, his imprint appeared upon the *Gebete und Gesänge zur Seelenfeier*, published in German and Hebrew for New York's Temple Emanu-El, as well as upon Salomon Herxheimer's *Catechism of the Faith* and Maurice Mayer's *Volksbuch über Moral und Sittenlehre*.

Frank's principal publications, the *Daily Prayers* and *Festival Prayers*, would, in their various editions, continue to fill the needs of Jews who swelled the westward migration after 1848. Despite the competition offered by Isaac Leeser, of Philadelphia, or "N. Ottinger," of New York, Frank prospered, supplying the demands of the increasing number of German Jews who had settled in America and required books for the festivals in Hebrew, German, and English.[5] As the *American Phrenological Journal* explained,

> In the outset he labored under many difficulties to procure journeymen printers, but finally succeeded . . . after five years' steady and unflinching labor he finished the publication of the "Prayers for the Festivals," or *Machsor*, in five volumes, in Hebrew, with an English translation. This work proved his greatest success. After the foregoing, he published numerous minor books, calculated for the Jewish faith, but which found sale among many learned and intelligent Christians. . . . A good proof of his industry may be drawn from the

fact that there is scarcely a Jewish family on this continent who is not in possession of some Hebrew book published by Mr. Frank.

Among those books were scholarly or devotional works by the learned Rabbis Samuel Adler and Moses Mielziner, along with Wolf Schlessinger's *Religioese Betrachtungen & Gebete* and Fanny Schmiedl Neuda's *Stunden der Andacht.* This last was published also in an English translation as *Hours of Devotion.* Besides issuing the liturgy in the German and Polish rite, the firm saw through the press several works in English including Pyke's *Scripture History* and Bernhard Felsenthal's *Practical Grammar of the Hebrew Language.*[6]

Frank's patrons included the members of New York's Congregations Emanu-El, B'nai Jeshurun (for whom he published the Pyke's *Scripture History*), and subsequently Anshe Chesed (for whom his firm would issue the *Ordnung der Gebete beim Gottesdienst*). They numbered not only his fellow "48'ers," but also those who followed, bringing the Jewish population in America to some 250,000 by 1870. For them, "Frank's Hebrew Book Store" not only published books, but also imported Hebrew books published elsewhere. Moving about as the years passed, from Houston Street to Broome, from Cedar to Pearl and Division Streets, operating sometimes from his home, Frank supplied his patrons not only with books, but also with synagogue and society stationery, *etrogim,* and silk and woolen prayer shawls "selected by our agents in Europe." In addition, he annually distributed a Hebrew Calendar throughout the United States.[7]

The calendar marked for Henry Frank the passage of years kindly and prolific. The publisher was rich not only in his imprints, but also in his sons. One of them, Leopold H. Frank, had studied under his father's tutelage until he was able to superintend the firm on his own. Two other sons, inheriting perhaps their father's pioneer blood, struck out for the West Coast and by 1864 had established a branch of the business in San Francisco. There, Frank & Co., wholesale stationers on Sacramento Street, was managed by Jacob J. and Joseph H. Frank.[8] Doubtless through their West Coast connections, the New York firm was able to publish *A Class Book for Jewish Youth of Both Sexes* by Henry Abraham Henry, rabbi preacher of San Francisco's Congregation Sherith Israel, in an edition which, it was hoped, would "be found useful not only to Israelites but also to all enlightened Gentiles who may desire to inform themselves of those subjects." The growing Jewish, and possibly "enlightened Gentile" population in the golden West created the market that Frank's sons were swift to supply.

Sacramento Street was a far cry from Walsdorf, Bavaria, and by the mid-1860's, Henry Frank, having, as the *American Phrenological Journal* mused, "achieved his aim, . . . to establish a well-organized Hebrew publishing house on this continent," retired from business and left the firm in charge of his son Leopold. The firm name Henry Frank was altered to L. H. Frank & Co., although the firm's original purposes remained unchanged. In 1868, during a visit to Saratoga Springs, Henry Frank was stricken with apoplexy and, "after lingering in a state of unconsciousness for four days, he died, at the age of sixty-four years, surrounded by his children."

The business he had founded continued to prosper. L. H. Frank & Co. expanded the list begun by Henry Frank with a new illustrated edition of the Haggadah and by 1872 reached the thirteenth edition of the *Prayers of Israel* with English translation. For the Hebrew Free Schools of New York, the publishers issued *Daily Prayers, with English instructions*, while additions to the list included Bible Selections, Samuel Cahen's *Catechism . . . for children of the Hebrew Faith* translated from the French, and Hymen Polano's *Hebrew Speller . . . according to the German and Portuguese Mode of Pronunciation*. One of the most interesting of the later Frank publications, reflecting the changes in Judaism, was *The American-Jewish Ritual*, the Reform liturgy issued in 1870 for Temple Israel in Brooklyn. It was followed two years later by the Reform liturgy for New York's Congregation Ahavath Chesed.

Shortly after Henry Frank's death, in September, 1868, when Isaac Leeser's executives held a final sale of the Philadelphia leader's publications at Bangs, Merwin & Co. in New York, the "Messrs. Frank" had been "among the larger purchasers." Advertising themselves as "Publishers and Importers of Hebrew Books," L. H. Frank & Co. persisted in the sale and publication of works for German- and English-speaking Jews.[9] Their books were "also for sale" at the San Francisco branch of Frank & Co. Both in the East and in the West the business weathered the Panic of 1873, surviving in the San Francisco and New York City directories until 1878/1879. For thirty years the Frank family of publishers had supplied the intellectual and religious needs of German Jews who had migrated to this country, adding to the rich store of what has come to be called Jewish Americana. Yet, when the founder of that family died, his achievements were celebrated principally by the *American Phrenological Journal*. That *Journal's* analysis of Henry Frank's character has an abiding interest:

> . . . The brain was large and the body well formed. The face indicates the character he was. There was length, breadth, and fullness in nearly every part. Observe how large the perceptive faculties! How broad the forehead between the eyes! No little mechanical talent is indicated by that amplitude. There was also much energy here. See how broad the head is between the ears! The top-head is also high, and the whole contour speaks the language of respect, kindness, affability, and executiveness. Such qualities, with integrity, ingenuity, and perseverance, would work their way up, as this man did. There is care as well as *work* in this countenance, but it is not the face of groundless fear or discontent. Nothing of timidity or irresolution is evinced. He evidently was at once self-relying and self-helpful. . . .

Surely this was as thoughtful and as laudatory an obituary as Henry Frank might have desired. He needed no other, for he is best remembered in the many books that bear his imprint and the imprint of his son Leopold. By these he takes his place as a pioneer in the long stream of American Hebrew publishing, and by these he gains his immortality.

Notes

1. *Hebrew Leader*, August 7, 1868, p. [5]; *American Phrenological Journal*, XLIX, No. 4 (April, 1869), 161. A simple death notice was carried by the *Jewish Messenger*, August 7, 1868, p. [6].

2. Samuel R. Wells, *New Physiognomy, or, Signs of Character, as manifested through Temperament and External Forms* (New York, 1875), pp. 444–45.

3. Eric E. Hirshler, ed., *Jews from Germany in the United States* (New York [1955]), pp. 120, 153; Hyman B. Grinstein, *The Rise of The Jewish Community of New York 1654–1860* (Phila., 1945), p. 219; Guido Kisch, "*Israels Herold:* The First Jewish Weekly in New York," *Historia Judaica*, II, No. 2 (October, 1940), 83.

4. A. S. W. Rosenbach, "An American Jewish Bibliography . . . until 1850," *Publications of the American Jewish Historical Society*, XXX (1926), Nos. 665, 672, 687; Jacob R. Marcus, ed., *Jewish Americana . . . A Supplement to . . . An American Jewish Bibliography* (Cincinnati, 1954), Nos. 224, 226.

5. "N. Ottinger" may be one with the *sofer* Nathan Oettinger.

6. Allan E. Levine, *An American Jewish Bibliography . . . 1851 to 1875* (Cincinnati, 1959), lists seventy Frank imprints. The Jewish Division of the New York Public Library owns various Frank publications which the writer has examined.

7. See the advertisement in the *Jewish Messenger*, August 17, 1860, and the listings in New York City directories 1849/50–1878/79.

8. See the listings in San Francisco directories 1864–1878/79.

9. *Jewish Messenger*, September 16, 1868, p. [4]; August 28, 1868, p. [3]; *Hebrew Leader*, February 26, 1869, p. [6].

6

Panacea Publishers

Mind and Body

The Fowler Family

F OR EVERY ILL suffered by 19th-century America, a panacea was put forth. Since there were many ills, a host of panaceas was offered. For slavery and the exploitation of labor, for improper soil cultivation and the oppression of women, for alcoholism and national dyspepsia, a variety of remedies enlisted crusaders. Abolition and the rights of labor, land reform and women's emancipation, temperance and hydropathy—all gathered supporters. Indeed it was said that "every possible form of intellectual and physical dyspepsia brought forth its gospel. Bran had its prophets. Everybody had a mission." [1]

One such mission, imported from abroad, seemed to some capable of curing most of the current ills of mind and body. Moreover it appealed to the love of scientific classification that prevailed during the century. Phrenology, or the science of the mind, stipulated that the skull was an index to the function of the brain. An examination of the skull would therefore provide a key to what went on within the skull. As for the brain itself, that was a kind of three-story house with a skylight. In the base of the brain the instincts had their being; above them the animal propensities; in the top story sat reason, and in the skylight spirituality was enthroned. There was a place for everything, 'and everything was in its place. Not only could those mental activities—those organs or faculties—be analyzed by an examination of the skull, but they could be improved, strengthened or diminished according to need. Sufferers from a diminutive organ of philoprogenitiveness or parental love, for example, could be taught to enlarge that faculty. There need be only a universal examining of heads to arrive at universal omniscience and hence universal reform.

This was the panacea for the ills of mind and body grasped by a family from upstate New York—the Fowlers, who became the strongest and most enduring popularizers of the new science of mind. [2] They did not rest with examining thousands of contemporary skulls. They served up the glories of phrenology and related reforms by means of books, for besides being practicing phrenologists they were publishers.

241

The possibilities of phrenology captured Orson Squire Fowler's imagination while he was a student at Amherst College, and he in turn fired the imagination of his brother Lorenzo Niles Fowler. With his strong nose and high forehead, his piercing blue eyes and electric personality, Orson beguiled many an audience as he lectured, gauged temperaments, measured heads with a tape, explored the distance between organs of the brain, and marked phrenological charts. Both brothers became itinerant examiners, peddlers of a new science, wandering from Providence to Salem, from Washington to Hannibal, analyzing the skulls of sculptors and poets, Indians and senators, criminals, reformers, even the Siamese Twins.

In 1838, Orson, not yet thirty years old, set up a stand in Philadelphia. There his examination room and museum of plaster casts and phrenological busts were in short order expanded with a publishing office. Among Fowler's earliest publishing ventures was the *American Phrenological Journal* which he issued in October 1838 with Nathan Allen as editor. Subsequently, publisher Fowler himself assumed the editorial chair. That periodical, filled with analyses of the nation's heads as well as with reprinted or original articles, persisted until 1911—a remarkable record for a monthly devoted to a cause that became more and more dubious as the century progressed. The country's longest-lived phrenological magazine, it recorded character analyses made from life or from likenesses, and it reflected the dogged perseverance of its editors along with the gullibility of its subscribers.

Shortly before he took over its editorship, Orson Fowler closed his Philadelphia office and moved the Cabinet to New York's Clinton Hall where his stand became a metropolitan landmark. [See Plate 7.] Subscribers to the *Journal* and visitors to the Phrenological Cabinet were surrounded by busts and casts, specimens and mummies, paintings and drawings of animal and human, savage and civilized, criminal and virtuous. Since admission was free, visitors often came in droves, escorted around by Orson, brother Lorenzo, and sister Charlotte. As the firm announced:

> For many years arrangements were kept open with the friends of peculiar people, to let us know when they died, so that a cast of their heads could be obtained, and many a dark, rainy night have the proprietors traveled miles to make a cast of some deceased person.
> They have visited prisons and attended executions for the purpose of taking the casts of heads, . . . Travelers, captains of ships, soldiers on the frontier, have brought home specimens of the skulls of the different nations of the world, and contributed them to this collection.[3]

The head of John Quincy Adams vied in time with a bust of Horace Greeley, while an African appeared side by side with a Choctaw chief. After their sightseeing, visitors might attend lectures on phrenology, have their heads examined, or pick up a book designed to reform the ills of the world.

The *American Phrenological Journal* was issued, according to the Fowlers,

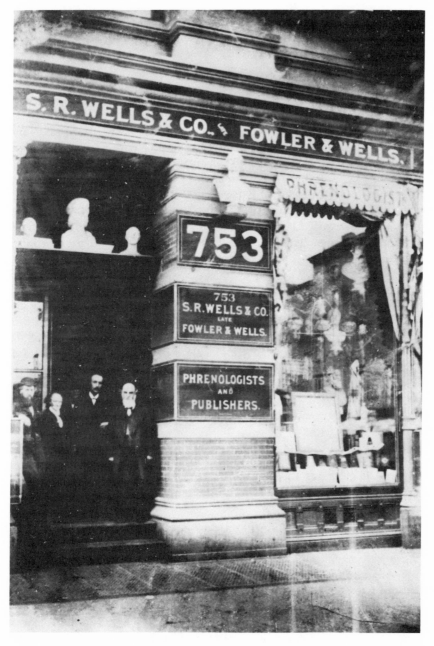

PLATE 7. The Fowler office from 1880 to 1887. Fowler Family Papers, Collection of Regional History, Cornell University.

"to Phrenologize Our Nation, for thereby it will Reform The World."[4] Several related reforms were ardently espoused by the family who took to their inkstands with as much alacrity as they took to their measuring tapes. Their subjects included child guidance and vocational guidance, prison reform and improved treatment of the insane, marriage counseling and sex education, eugenics and mnemonics, dress reform and water cure, vegetarianism and a strong crusade against the twin evils of tobacco and alcohol. In their *Journal* and in book after book written by one or both of the brothers and published by their firm, they regaled their readers with advice that would restore the health of mind and body. During the 1840s their books rolled from the press: *Matrimony: or Phrenology and Physiology applied to the selection of Suitable Companions for Life; Fowler on Memory; Temperance, Founded on Phrenology and Physiology; The Principles of Phrenology and Physiology applied to Man's Social Relations; Love and Parentage, applied to the Improvement of Offspring.* Even Lorenzo's wife Lydia, who became the first American woman professor of medicine, joined the scribblers with a trilogy of books for the young.

The family might have begun their reform writing with their interest in the child, the fountainhead of life, but they did not stop there. From the rights of children and the teaching of speed reading they went on to manuals opposed to three abominations: the noxious weed tobacco, the noxious liquid alcohol, and the detestable practice of tight lacing against which they proposed the slogan: "Natural Waists, or No Wives." Temperance men, anti-tobacco men and anti-lacing women, vegetarians and water cure advocates basked in the congenial climate of Clinton Hall, and in time the Fowlers perceived the advantage of expanding their publishing program for such a clientele.

Orson Fowler expounded his publishing credo in the preface to the American edition of Andrew Combe's *Principles of Physiology*, which he edited: "I shall publish no work which I do not think eminently *calculated* to *do good*." Moreover, "so that all, especially the *labouring* classes," might learn from them "the comforts and happiness of a virtuous and healthy life," his books were practical and low-priced. That credo was carried out by Samuel Roberts Wells, a vigorous businessman with genial temperament and winning manners who joined the brothers in 1843, married Charlotte Fowler the next year, and shortly thereafter became a member of the reorganized firm of Fowlers and Wells.

By 1845, the division of labor practiced by Fowlers and Wells promised to become a guarantee of good business. While Orson produced page after page for the *Journal* and text after text on his favorite reforms; while Lorenzo read head after head in a succession of private or group examinations, Samuel Roberts Wells served as publishing arm and business manager. Under Wells' aegis the firm became large-scale publishers, a central distribution point for reading matter on almost universal reform. As the Fowlers supplied books for those in search of health of mind and body, they found that the salubrity of mankind went hand in hand with increased business at Clinton Hall. Wells astutely saw in the reforms championed by his partners the means not only of enlightening the public but of creating and developing a sizable publishing business.

The presses hummed during the 1840s and 1850s. From them flowed such books as Justus Liebig's treatise on *Chemistry* and Cornaro's *Discourses . . . on a Sober and Temperate Life*, prize essays on tobacco by the hygienists Trall, Shew and Alcott, a series of almanacs, manuals for the masses, small, cheap, useful "Hand-Books for Home Improvement" that taught readers *How to Write* and *How to Talk*, *How to Behave* and *How to Do Business*. During an era of over-eating and national dyspepsia, popular interest in health was keen, and practical answers to practical questions were sought by practical Americans. For a public eager to learn, in a few easy home lessons, how best to live and how to make the most out of life, Fowlers and Wells supplied answers. On the cover of the *Phrenological Almanac* was inscribed the motto: "Nature's Printing Press is Man, her types are Signs, her books are Actions." It almost seemed as if "Nature's Printing Press" was the press of Clinton Hall. The firm boasted that each year the sales of its books doubled. Indeed those who came for a phrenological analysis—Horace Greeley or John Brown, Lucretia Mott or the dancer Fanny Elssler—could, if they wished, leave with a "Library."

One of the firm's Libraries—the Library of Mesmerism and Psychology—reflected the Fowler interest in yet another aspect of the newness, animal magnetism. It also reflected their fascination with that "gifted son of genius and misfortune" and author of "Mesmeric Revelation," Edgar Allan Poe. In almost every one of the Fowlers and Wells phrenological handbooks there appears as the embodiment of the so-called nervous or mental temperament the portrait of Poe with a brief biography and analysis.[5] As for the Library of Mesmerism and Psychology, that included Joseph Haddock's *Psychology*, John B. Newman's *Fascination*, and John Bovee Dods' *Philosophy of Electrical Psychology*.

On any reform of vital interest a single publication never sufficed. An entire Water-Cure Library was published, and in 1848 the *Water-Cure Journal* was taken over by the firm. Similarly, to popularize shorthand or phonography as a shortcut to the teaching of reading, Fowlers and Wells published not only a periodical, *Universal Phonographer*, but books that eventually filled *A Complete Catalogue of Works for Shorthand Writers*. Phonographic envelopes, mottoes, pencils, and gold pens were sold, and the Declaration of Independence and the Constitution of the United States were available in phonographic type.

There is no doubt that by the mid-century Fowlers and Wells were manipulators not only of heads but of big business. Their publishing department under Samuel Wells claimed to have the largest mail-order list in the city.

Their market extended "from Nova Scotia to New Mexico, including the Canadas, and all the Territories on the American continent." Orson Fowler's books alone sold by the thousands, and in New Haven "at one time his popularity . . . was so great that a bookstore in which his books only were sold was established." Without the help of the general book trade the firm's phrenological charts were circulated in "immense numbers," and "almost half a million of his [Orson's] various productions were now in the hands of the American public."[6]

One of Orson's books in particular was designed to improve domestic life in America, and its popularity was such that it went through a series of printings. *A Home for All: or a New, Cheap, Convenient, and Superior Mode of Building* was first published by Fowlers and Wells in 1848. Its purposes were "to cheapen and improve human homes," to provide comfort for the housewife, to popularize the most advanced innovations from dumbwaiters to indoor water closets, and to advance the octagonal shape in domestic architecture. Its success was so great that, while the author practiced what he preached, actually building his octagonal house in Fishkill, New York, his manual went through a succession of printings to supply orders that arrived from France, England, China, and the Sandwich Islands. Indeed, in Kansas during the 1850s, an Octagon Settlement was projected where participants were expected to work for free soil, restrict themselves to a vegetarian diet, and live in eight-sided dwellings. Sensing popular interest in the subject, the publishers promptly initiated an architectural department, selling not only Orson's *Home for All* but "Works on Architecture" by Downing, Ranlett and Gould, and inserting a feature on "The Builder" in one of their periodicals.

Fowlers and Wells was closely associated with another, far more epochal book. Long before the publication of *Leaves of Grass*, Walt Whitman, age thirty, entered the Fowler establishment for a phrenological analysis. He would write in "Good-Bye My Fancy": "One of the choice places of New York to me then was the 'Phrenological Cabinet' of Fowler & Wells, Nassau Street near Beekman. Here were all the busts, examples, curios and books of that study obtainable. I went there often."[7] Subsequently he became a staff writer for yet another Fowler periodical, *Life Illustrated*, for which he wrote "New York Dissected." Meanwhile, phrenology was giving to Whitman a new language, reflected in poem after poem that would appear in *Leaves of Grass*. The first edition of *Leaves* was advertised and sold by Fowlers and Wells. The second edition of 1856 was actually published by the firm though their imprint did not appear on the title-page. Wells felt his house was already sufficiently committed to what he described as "unpopular notions" and so was reluctant to associate his name openly with *Leaves of Grass*. None the less, the firm did publish the considerably enlarged and controversial second edition of that book and, if for no other reason, merits a claim to remembrance.[8]

Among the "unpopular notions" which Wells had in mind was sex. In the course of the firm's association with Whitman, Orson Fowler withdrew in order to devote himself almost exclusively to writing and lecturing on sex education. As believers in nature's laws, Fowler (no longer Fowlers) and Wells published a variety of manuals on the subject including George S. Weaver's *Hopes and Helps for the Young of both Sexes*, a tome entitled *Passional Zoology*, and M. Edgeworth Lazarus' turgid and ambitious treatise *The Human Trinity; or Three Aspects of Life: The Passional, The Intellectual, The Practical Sphere.*

Wells' publishing list, concerned as it was with harmoniously developed man, was devoted to those "Three Aspects of Life." His how-to manuals covered the practical; his tomes on sex the passional; and a wide range of unusual books on the psyche the so-called intellectual sphere. All three aspects of life touched closely upon the mental and physical health championed from the beginning by the Fowlers and endorsed by Wells.

Wells was keenly aware both of the demands of the public and of the requirements of a successful publisher. In his *How to Do Business* he listed those requirements, doubtless basing his ideal portrait upon the publisher he knew best—himself.

> To be a successful book-publisher one requires a rare combination of qualifications. A spirit of enterprise, tact, discrimination, a knowledge of human nature, a careful and continual study of the public tastes and wants, and a general knowledge of modern literature, are indispensable. A mistaken judgment in reference to a single work may lead to serious loss, and even to pecuniary ruin. . . . The publisher, who is generally also a seller of books, should have *a thorough knowledge of the wares in which he deals.*[9]

Besides knowing his wares and gauging public taste, Wells, like the Fowlers, aimed at reforming that taste. His firm postulated that only through the "Physical Regeneration of the Race [could] the Intellectual and Moral Elevation of our fellow men [be promoted.] Health of Body and Health of Mind and Heart are . . . intimately connected."[10]

In their efforts to instruct the nation in the laws of hygiene Fowler and Wells became a potent force in the health reform movement. Their publishing division seemed indeed devoted to the complete development of the whole man. From their presses rolled books against swill milk as well as tobacco; Edward Youmans' *Alcohol and the Constitution of Man; Delia's Doctors*, a novel in which Hannah Gardner Creamer exposed her heroine to all the medical sects of the day from allopathy to homeopathy, from mesmerism to hydropathy. As for mental health, the house responded to "the increasing demand for works on Psychology . . . and other kindred subjects" with an array of volumes on mental alchemy and spiritualism, clairvoyance and electrical psychology. William Fishbough's *The Macrocosm and Microcosm* appeared under their imprint, along with Alfred Smee's *Electro-Biology, or The Voltaic Mechanism of Man.* Andrew Jackson Davis, the slim black-haired clairvoyant, was the author of *Philosophy of Spiritual Intercourse* published by the firm. In the hope of exploring the empire of the mind and improving the mental health of the country, the *Phrenological Journal* introduced a regular department devoted to "Psychology."

The coupling of universal mental health with universal physical health must surely result in social health and harmony, a subject that also had a place on the Fowler and Wells list. On it appeared *The Science of Society*, the most lucid work of that far from lucid eccentric philosopher Stephen Pearl Andrews, a book that aimed to elucidate the so-called Cost Principle expounded by the first American anarchist Josiah Warren. Warren himself was among the Fowler authors, the firm publishing his *Practical Details in Equitable Commerce*. Their "Social Harmony" division included also Albert Brisbane's *Social Destiny* and Parke Godwin's *Popular View of the Theory of Charles Fourier*, Robert Dale Owen's *Labor* and Adin Ballou's *Practical Christian Socialism*. Social reform occupied an important position in a list that offered Horace Greeley's *Hints toward Reforms*, Kossuth's lecture on *The Future of Nations*, and Hurlbut's *Essays on Human Rights and Their Political Guarantees*. For a short time, too, the Fowler imprint appeared upon *The Spirit of the Age*, successor to *The Harbinger*, organ of the communal society of Brook Farm.

That the destiny of woman played a part in social reform was recognized by Fowler and Wells. There was a strong rapport between the firm and women in general, who looked to them for advice on marriage, sex education, maternity, child guidance, and health. Publishers who had themselves written on marriage and maternity were the obvious choice for an omnibus volume on *Sexual Diseases* which included Trall's *Home-Treatment for Sexual Abuses* and Newman's *Philosophy of Generation*. Advocates of hydropathy for women, they were the logical publishers for Dr. James C. Jackson's *Hints on the Reproductive Organs: Their Diseases, Causes, and Cure on Hydropathic Principles*.

Partly through the influence of Lorenzo's wife Lydia, pioneer woman physician who practiced and taught medicine, and partly through the influence of that early feminist Charlotte Fowler Wells, the phrenological publishers agreed that "Women's Sphere of Industry should . . . be enlarged till it equals that of men. . . . What but 'female suffrage' can save our republic? Women's wages should equal men's for the same work."[11] Putting their theories into practice, they issued Mrs. Hugo Reid's *Woman, Her Education and Influence*, along with a variety of books designed to free the oppressed "Isabellas" of the country, from *Woman and Her Wishes* by Thomas Wentworth Higginson to *Woman and Her Needs* by Elizabeth Oakes Smith. In addition the firm published the *Proceedings* of the Second National Woman's Rights Convention at Worcester.

Of all the feminist books issued by the phrenologists perhaps the most interesting were those written by that New England bluestocking and citizen of the world, Margaret Fuller, who had once sat for a phrenological reading by Orson Fowler. By 1850, at the time of her tragic death by shipwreck, she seemed to many to personify the right to intellectual, personal, and political freedom which she had exercised during her life. Between 1852 and 1856 the firm reprinted her *Papers on Literature and Art*, issued a new edition of her revolutionary tract for the times, *Woman in the Nineteenth Century*, and published her *At Home and Abroad; or, Things and Thoughts in America and Europe*. Even in their manual *How to Write* they inserted among the specimen letters several penned by Margaret Fuller.

Such books as these, along with timely and useful handbooks for emigrants to Iowa or Illinois, Minnesota or Kansas, were distributed by mail from the Phrenological Depot, which moved in 1854 to 308 Broadway where it would remain until the mid-sixties. By that time the firm had undergone a significant change in personnel. In 1863 Lorenzo Fowler established himself in London, substituting Fleet Street for Broadway. There his sensitive fingers continued to examine a variety of skulls including that of Mark Twain. Meanwhile brother Orson set up an independent shingle in Boston from which base he persisted in his efforts to teach "Right Sexuality." In a tome of 1,052 pages entitled *Creative and Sexual Science* he distilled his views on the subject, and in the 1860s and 1870s on Boston's Tremont Street, when Sigmund Freud was barely in his teens, Orson Fowler used one lever only to move the world—the lever of sex.

With Lorenzo's departure, Samuel Wells became sole proprietor of the New York establishment. Aided by his wife Charlotte and the indefatigable phrenologist Nelson Sizer, he headed the firm for more than a decade. Through war and panic, fire and flood, the Phrenological Depot endured. It was a Broadway showplace that attracted to its examining room a variety of visitors who bared their heads for analysis, from Lola Montez to Horace Greeley. It was also a reforming agency and a thriving publishing emporium.

By the close of the Civil War, Wells sought to inject a get-ahead spirit, an *élan*, a newness into his business. New enticements were offered to agents, new advertisements appeared in the annuals and journals, and grander premiums lured subscribers, from Steinway pianos and Mason organs to Wheeler and Wilson sewing and washing machines. Since there were "no sexes in heaven," new lady canvassers were employed to make up clubs for trial subscriptions to the periodicals.

As a publisher Samuel Wells tried to reach "the masses of the people" and to train them to "think for themselves." Occasionally he accepted for publication a book with limited audience appeal or one "in advance of public sentiment" that had been declined by other, wealthier publishers. But on the whole, when offered a manuscript, he asked two questions only: "Will it be useful?" and "Can I afford it?" To continue the cure of a nation of dyspeptics he kept on his list the hydropathic effusions of Drs. Trall and Gully along with books on the Swedish Movement Cure, affections of the nerves, and his own pamphlet, *Father Mathew, The Temperance Apostle*. The line of how-to manuals was expanded with *The Invalid's Library* which enabled every man to be his own doctor; and *Notes on Beauty, Vigor, and Development; or, How to Acquire Plumpness of Form, Strength of Limb, and Beauty of Complexion*. For the medical profession Wells provided *A Special List of the Best Private Medical Works* designed for "private, professional and confidential use." For the general pill-swallowing public he supplied a *New Illustrated Health Almanac*, over 50,000 copies of which were distributed to subscribers and circulated by agents to counteract the trade in "powders, pills, plasters, bitters, and other poisonous preparations or slops."

Having offered sustenance for the body, the publisher proceeded to offer food for the mind. He kept abreast of the times with a pamphlet on capital punishment and a soldier's edition of his *Annual of Phrenology*. In his appeal to women he was, like the Fowlers, in advance of his times. His own book on *Wedlock; or, The Right Relations of the Sexes* applied science to "conjugal selection." More boldly than his predecessors in the firm, Wells struck out in the literary field, applying phrenology to the great writings of the past. In his edition of Pope's *Essay on Man* in 1867 he added original designs and notes that interpreted the poem phrenologically. The same procedure was carried out in other editions of such "gems of literature" as Aesop's *Fables*, Goldsmith's *The Traveller* and *The Deserted Village*, Coleridge's *Rime of the Ancient Mariner*, and Milton's *Comus*. These cheap illustrated editions, known as People's Editions, had a wide sale, supplying the masses with "reading matter of a high class" phrenologically interpreted, at low cost. To insure endorsement Wells continued the practice of sending gift copies to readers in high places who might express suitable and sometimes printable acknowledgment. Between his books on health reform and his books on literature, it was probably only a mild exaggeration to boast, as the *Phrenological Journal* did, that "every hamlet and many a cabin receives light for the mind and guidance for the body" from the publications of his house.

Indeed, despite the panic of 1873, Wells could sum up that year's accomplishments:

> Besides the Phrenological Journal and the *Science of Health* . . . we have published and republished during the present year more than 75 different books . . . relating directly or indirectly to the Science of Man. . . . We have given more than a hundred lectures . . . have delineated the characters of several hundred persons. . . .
>
> We are now sending our publications to . . . China, Japan, Africa, New Zealand, Australia. . . .[12]

For all of Wells' confidence, however, the panic of 1873 cast a long shadow. The Depot which had moved in 1865 to 389 Broadway was forced to move again ten years later, following the upward trend along Broadway

the *coup de grace* to phrenology. With the work of Sigmund Freud, phreno-analysis would be displaced by psychoanalysis. For Jessie Fowler's firm portents of the end were everywhere. In January 1911, the final number of the *Phrenological Journal*, which had endured almost seventy-three years, was issued. Five years later, the firm was split, Fowler and Wells moving to 27 East 22nd Street in the charge of Jessie's brother-in-law Michael H. Piercy, and she herself remaining associated with the American Institute of Phrenology. The split, doubtless arranged in an attempt to survive through division of labor, was not effective. The Fowler brand of phrenology and the reforms associated with it could not survive either the economic crises of the 20th century or the newer philosophy of mind introduced by Freud.

Yet the publications of the Fowler firm had answered the purposes and reflected the tendencies of the 19th century. In its books designed to improve the physical and mental health of the nation, it had supplied a very real need. And so, thoroughly to understand that century, a knowledge of the work of the phrenologist-publishers becomes remarkably useful. Both the reform movements of their time and the ills those movements were intended to cure are embodied in the publications of the Fowler family. Hence those publications disclose to the 20th century the spirit of the age that went before.

Notes

1. Arthur M. Schlesinger, *New Viewpoints in American History* (New York, [1961]), p. 215, citing James Russell Lowell in his essay on Thoreau (1865).

2. For further details about the Fowlers and phrenology, see Madeleine B. Stern, *Heads & Headlines: The Phrenological Fowlers* (Norman: University of Oklahoma Press, 1971), upon which this chapter is based.

3. *Catalogue of Portraits, Busts, and Casts, in the Cabinet of The American Institute of Phrenology* (New York, 1879), prelim. page.

4. *Phrenological Journal*, Vol. XI (1849), "The American Phrenological Journal for 1849," p. 12.

5. Madeleine B. Stern, "Poe: 'The Mental Temperament' for Phrenologists," *American Literature*, Vol. XL, No. 2 (May 1968), pp. 155–163.

6. Stern, *Heads & Headlines*, p. 84. For details of the Fowlers' success, see John D. Davies, *Phrenology Fad and Science: A 19th-Century American Crusade* (New Haven, 1955), pp. 55 f; Orson S. Fowler, *Hereditary Descent* (published at end of *Phrenological Journal*, Vol. V, 1843), p. 567; *New-York Times* (August 20, 1887), p. 5; *Phrenological Journal*, Vol. VIII, No. 1 (January 1846), p. 30, Vol. XI (1849), p. 385, Vol. XVIII, No. 1 (July 1853), p. 19; *Water-Cure Journal*, Vol. IX, No. 4 (April 1850), p. 128.

7. Walt Whitman, *The Complete Writings* (New York and London, [1902]), VII, 54 ("Good-Bye My Fancy").

8. S. R. Wells to Friend Whitman, New York, June 7, 1856 (courtesy Mr. Charles E. Feinberg, Detroit, Michigan). For further details concerning Whitman's *Leaves of Grass* and the Fowler firm, see pages 157–161.

9. [Samuel Roberts Wells], *Hand-Book for Home Improvement, How to Do Business* (New York, 1875), p. 87.

10. *Water-Cure Journal*, Vol. XII, No. 6 (December 1851), p. 136, Vol. XIX (1855), p. ii.

11. Orson S. Fowler, *Creative and Sexual Science* (N.p., n.d.), p. 167.

12. *Phrenological Journal*, Vol. 57, No. 6 (December 1873), pp. 383 f.

13. *Phrenological Journal*, Vol. 60, No. 6 (June 1875), p. 406.

14. Emily Faithfull, *Three Visits to America* (New York, [1884]), pp. iii–vi.

15. For the firm's publishing of the *History of Woman Suffrage*, see Katharine Anthony, *Susan B. Anthony* (New York, 1954), pp. 341 f, 344, 370 ff; *Phrenological Journal*, Vol. 75, No. 3 (September 1882), p. 172, Vol. 109, No. 4 (April 1900), p. 116.

16. *The American Kindergarten and Primary Teacher*, N.S. Vol. I, No. 7 (March 1887), advertisement.

17. J. A. Fowler, *Phrenology. Its Use in Business Life* (New York and London, 1898), p. 25.

18. Jessie Allen Fowler, *Brain Roofs and Porticos* (New York and London, [1908]), p. 97.

Laughter in America

G. W. Carleton

T HE PANGS of failure could be softened, the pomposities of success could be pricked, indeed all the outrages of fortune could be tolerated, with a touch of humor. Like a man, a nation must learn to laugh at itself and its own self-consciousness, and that was the bridge that led to the nation's maturity.

The need for humor in America was never so sharp as in the nineteenth century when Civil War threatened to divide the country South from North, when migrations into distant geographical frontiers threatened to divide it East from West. Humor was the clay that could cement the union once the nation learned to laugh at itself.

There was much to laugh at—but this the so-called humorists alone could point out. For they alone, whether they came from Massachusetts or from Ireland, from New York State or from Maine, whether their wanderings had carried them to the West or the South, could gently but pointedly expose the weaknesses of the country. How many Achilles' heels were ready for their darts: from the war to political office-seekers, from Yankee notions to frontier conditions, from Fourth of July orations to the Negro question, from free love to woman's rights, from scheming Yankees to bragging Kentuckians, from circuit lawyers to politicians in caucus, from manifest destiny to every gaudy feather in the spreading wings of the American eagle. Humbug, quackery, absurdity, and insincerity, the sentimental and the highfalutin—all awaited the pin that would prick the empty balloons that floated over the continent.

And it was a pin rather than a barbed arrow that performed the national operation. It was a genial humor, a mild satire, a combination of parody and burlesque, tall tales and distorted spellings. It was good humor—compounded partly of the conventions of backwoods wit and partly of a characteristic form of fantastic exaggeration; it was the good humor that Mark

Reprinted from Madeleine B. Stern, *Imprints on History: Book Publishers and American Frontiers* (Bloomington, Ind.: Indiana Univ. Press, 1956), pp. 191–205 and 441–445.

257

Twain eventually inherited, and it was this good humor that led a nation to chuckle at its own foibles. Like most humor, it was topical, contemporary; and though it has therefore suffered the fate of becoming outdated, it has for that very reason become invested with a historical, a documentary importance. The humor may be less funny today; but it is an open window upon the mores of yesterday.

Sometimes the humorist paraded under the disguise of an itinerant showman, and Lincoln enjoyed his extravagances so much that he read them to his Cabinet members before submitting to them the final draft of the Emancipation Proclamation. Sometimes the humorist assumed the character of an Irish private in the Union Army; sometimes he donned an all-revealing pseudonym—"Orpheus C. Kerr" (office seeker); sometimes he began to look, with his sharp features and rustic demeanor, like the country farmer he was impersonating. Whether his name was "Artemus Ward" or "Private Miles O'Reilly," whether it was "Orpheus C. Kerr" or "Josh Billings," he frequently practiced his "trade" or tested the effect of his broad burlesque at one of two rendezvous. One was Pfaff's restaurant in a basement on Broadway near Bleecker Street, where the so-called "Bohemians" gathered to air their witticisms while they downed their beer. Another was perhaps a more significant rallying place, for it was the bookstore of their publisher, George W. Carleton. Like the men whose works he published, Carleton was a humorist of sorts, and by placing their extravagant phrases, their vivid caricatures and atrocious spellings before the public, he helped a stumbling and self-conscious nation to enjoy a laugh at its own expense. Setting his own unmistakable mark upon the humor that he published, he helped America become not only mature, but characteristically American.

During the winter of 1864–65 George Washington Carleton, a young New Yorker with a genial, intelligent face, a long, pointed nose, and a pair of conspicuous lorgnettes, might have been seen tearing through the narrow streets of Havana. On vacation from his publishing office at 413 Broadway, he was employing his time fruitfully, for he was exercising not only his legs but his sense of humor. Besides assisting with domino and false nose at the masquerades in the Tacon Theatre and lounging over ices at the Café Dominica, Carleton sketched many a delicious caricature in pen-and-ink, setting down in humorous fashion the sights of Cuba, from the Havana Flea to the Cuban Tooth-Pick, and his own aspect as he regarded them. The young man had had no little experience with humor—and with its publication.

In his early thirties, Carleton could already look back with satisfaction upon his brief but promising career. Born in New York in 1832, he had studied at St. Thomas Hall in Flushing and served as clerk to Burnham, Plumb and Company, an importing and commission house. During his leisure moments he had varied his occupation of deciphering foreign invoices by designing illustrations for such humorous papers and periodicals as *The Lantern* and *The Picayune*. Some of his work attracted the attention of George Merriam, who asked him to design for his firm an appropriate illustration to head an advertisement of Webster's Dictionary. Carleton's sketch of two chubby little cherubs weighted down with Webster's Unabridged had earned for the artist a copy of the Dictionary bound in full calf. In light of the fact that the sketch was to be used for nearly half a century, the reward was perhaps less weighty than it seemed at first sight. But doubtless it tickled Carleton's sense of humor.

That sense of humor had yielded more substantial results when Carleton had applied it to his more recent interest in publishing. In 1857, with the retirement of Edward Livermore of Livermore and Rudd, he had joined the firm, which was promptly transformed into Rudd and Carleton. Though young Carleton, at the age of twenty-five, could offer to his partner, who had served several years with Barnes and Burr, neither any specialized training nor any considerable capital, Rudd and Carleton had, during its short life on Broadway near Duane, proved successful. Besides publishing B. D. Emerson's *National Spelling Book* and the Rev. W. I. Kip's *Christmas Tree*, the firm had struck a bonanza in *Nothing to Wear*, the poem on fashionable city life in which the lawyer, William Allen Butler, had immortalized Miss Flora M'Flimsey of Madison Square. With illustrations by Augustus Hoppin, the 18mo priced at fifty cents had had a huge sale even during the panic year of 1857. Readers enjoyed the smooth verses and mild satire about the young lady who had shopped

> For bonnets, mantillas, capes, collars, and
> shawls;
> Dresses for breakfasts, and dinners, and
> balls;

but still had "nothing to wear." The somber note on "Spoiled children of Fashion" with which the poem ended detracted not at all from the good-humored travesty, but merely sharpened the point of the moral. The success of *Nothing to Wear* was followed by the claim of one Miss Peck, daughter of an Episcopal clergyman of Greenwich, Connecticut, to the effect that she had lost the manuscript of the poem in a Madison Avenue stage, where it was found by Butler, who had elaborated upon her idea. Although the controversy that followed did not profit Miss Peck, it did profit Rudd and Carleton, the latter of whom demonstrated his quick-wittedness by offering Mortimer Thomson, the immortal "Doesticks," one dollar a line for a burlesque on the subject entitled *Nothing to Say*. This "Slight Slap at Mobocratic Society," which had "Nothing do Do" with "Nothing to Wear," was issued in the same format and binding as Butler's poem and sported a genial but inverted snobbery on behalf of the villainous rich. Q. K. Philander Doesticks, whose *Plu-Ri-Bus-Tah* "burlesqued *Hiawatha* in meter and the American eagle in attitude," and who had already been "discovered" by Edward Livermore, helped center Carleton's interests upon humor and helped increase the profits of the Rudd and Carleton treasury.

Another poem published by the firm had yielded not only financial profit to Carleton but the trademark by which he was destined to be known throughout the next generation. Exploring Lane's *Arabian Nights* for inscriptions with which to embellish Thomas Bailey Aldrich's Persian poem, *The Course of True Love Never Did Run Smooth*, Carleton and Aldrich had come upon a curious symbol, the Arabic word for "books." Viewed upside down, the symbol seemed to spell the initials, "G. W. C." Besides selling 2,200 copies of Aldrich's versified love story, Carleton had found the trademark that would adorn his advertisements and title-pages for the next three decades. The year 1858 could be marked in red upon his publishing calendar, for that trademark, coupled often with Carleton's personal cipher, a pert little bird drawn with two or three pen strokes, was to symbolize for the reading public not only books but Carleton's books, and most particularly Carleton's books of genial satire and good humor. [See Plate 8.]

PLATE 8. G. W. Carleton's devices.

The name of Edmund Clarence Stedman had been added to the firm's publishing list, and *The Prince's Ball*, illustrated and printed on tinted paper, sold in the thousands under the imprint of Rudd and Carleton. A similar sale attended another, more enterprising undertaking of the firm—a work that was, moreover, to be accorded a niche in history. *The "Wigwam Edition." The Life, Speeches, and Public Services of Abram Lincoln*, published by Rudd and Carleton in 1860 and issued in paper wrappers for twenty-five cents, was the first campaign biography of Lincoln, the most popular *Life* of the campaign; and today it has become the keystone of any Lincolniana collection.

Then in 1861 Edward P. Rudd had died, and his father, George R. Rudd, retired, leaving Carleton to carry on alone. The genial publisher had gained from his association with Rudd some specialized training in addition to some capital, and, equipped with the fame of his two or three successes and a trademark, he was ready to make the name of G. W. Carleton a synonym for a nation's good humor.

In this enterprise Carleton was assisted by some interesting figures. Thomas Bailey Aldrich served him as clerk and literary adviser for a short period. Carleton's brother Charles was for a time connected with the publishing house, and during the sixties Henry S. Allen left Appleton to share his knowledge of the book business with G. W. C. before joining John K. Allen in the juvenile trade. Finally, George W. Dillingham, who had for some years been associated with Crosby, Nichols of Boston and had worked for A. K. Loring, became a moving spirit in the house of Carleton, first as head clerk and later as partner.

By the time Dillingham had entered Carleton's employ, the publisher had decided upon the types of books that would be associated with his name. The Arabic symbol would appear most significantly beneath humorous titles. The comic fellows who gathered at Pfaff's brought the results of their laughter to G. W. Carleton, aware that he knew wit when he saw it since he possessed such a fund of it himself. Indeed, Carleton's Broadway office could vie with Pfaff's as the rendezvous for American comic writers—for "Corry O' Lanus" or Robert H. Newell, known to his followers as "Orpheus C. Kerr," for all the clever young men who were bent on tickling America's ribs until the country could laugh at its own expense. They rallied at Carleton's establishment to swap stories or cap anecdotes, and they transformed a publisher's office into a headquarters for the humor that would set a slow and knowing smile upon the face of a nation.

The most famous of Carleton's humorists were "Artemus Ward" and "Josh Billings." The publisher had met Charles F. Browne, otherwise known as "Artemus Ward," soon after the author came to New York from *The Cleveland Plain Dealer*. Together they projected a humorous book entitled *Artemus Ward His Book*, the result of which was a sale of over 40,000 copies in six months. *His Book* had been bundled into a green baize bag, in which the publisher had found a blotted, almost illegible manuscript stuck with mucilage and plastered with newspaper clippings. Finally, both A. Ward and A. Ward's book had been straightened out, the latter edited and published; and G. W. Carleton had the pleasure of giving in exchange for the green baize bag $6,000 as the author's share of the profits.

To the artist, Carleton, Artemus had appeared like a caricature of Uncle Sam. To Artemus, the publisher became "Dear Carl," and to his "Dear Carl" the humorist announced, "You and I will get out a book next spring, which will knock spots out of all comic books in ancient or modern history. And the fact that you are going to take hold of it convinces me that you have one of the most *massive* intellects of this or any other epock. Yours, my pretty gazelle, A. Ward." When the "pretty gazelle" made too many alterations in A. Ward's manuscripts, however, the author, with tongue—where it usually was—in cheek, declared, "The next book I write I'm going to get *you* to write."

In the guise of an itinerant showman, "Artemus Ward" tilted at the windmills of sentimentality and insincerity, exposing, by means of graphic caricatures, execrable spelling, colossal exaggerations, and tall tales, the absurdities of American life. He was part and parcel of the Yankee tradition, from his own long, impassive face to the terse humor he purveyed. With calm mendacity he spun his brief stories about "New England Rum, and its Effects," "The Shakers," or a "Celebration at Baldinsville in Honor of the Atlantic Cable." The Negro question was simply solved—the "Afrikan" "wooden't be sich a infernal noosanse if white people would let him alone." As for politics, Artemus had "no politics. Nary a one. I'm not in the bisiness. . . . I'm in a far more respectful bisniss nor what pollertics is." At all events, whether he laughed at Brigham Young or Ossawatomie Brown, Oberlin College or the "Sences taker," he was "Yours for the Pepetration of the Union, and the bringin of the Goddess of Liberty out of her present bad fix."

At the height of his popularity Artemus was often to be seen lying on a sofa in Carleton's office at Broadway and Lispenard, puffing a cigar and framing witticisms. Carleton enjoyed the witticisms almost as much as the profits. As *Artemus Ward; His Travels* and *Artemus Ward In London* and *Artemus Ward's Panorama* rolled from the press, the anecdotes rolled also, until the publisher had collected a fund of Wardiana. By 1898, long after G. W. Dillingham had succeeded Carleton, *The Complete Works of Artemus Ward* was still a valuable item on the publisher's list. More than 100,000 copies had been printed, and the plates had become "so worn as to render it unreadable, yet the sale kept on."

"Artemus Ward" did more for Carleton than provide him with profits and witticisms. Having read a manuscript by Henry Wheeler Shaw, he recommended it to the publisher, who issued *Josh Billings, Hiz Sayings* and struck another bonanza in the comic treasury. In place of the itinerant showman, "Josh" impersonated the itinerant lecturer. In place of "Artemus Ward's" stories, "Josh Billings" depended upon brief essays. His prose was peppered with the same exaggerated misspellings that Ward had popularized, and with ludicrous sententiousness he gravely addressed "The Billingsville Sowing Sosiety" or "A Wimmin's League Meetin." At "Female Eddikashun" or Saratoga Springs, "War and Army Phrazes" or Long Branch, he tossed his gentle darts. "Yankee Noshuns" were "a kind ov noshuns that reside in Nu England, but travel awl over the world." Manifest destiny was simply "the science ov going tew the devil, or enny other place before yu git thare." Sparse of build, sharp of features, with rustic, unpolished demeanor, Henry Wheeler Shaw was himself transformed into the comic lecturer, "Josh Billings."

Josh Billings' Proverbs and *Josh Billings on Ice* cleared the way in time for *Josh Billings' Farmer's Allminax.* Carleton had suggested a burlesque of the popular old farmer's almanac, and Billings' manuscript, written on newspaper wrappings, was transformed into a book which eventually sold more than half a million copies. Although it started off slowly, taking nearly a year to exhaust the first edition of 2,000, it suddenly struck fire and turned the year with 150,000 copies to its credit. The twenty-five-cent paper volume was succeeded by an annual comic *Allminax*, the author writing five or six little paragraphs, stuffing them into his hat, and reading the sayings aloud to his friend and publisher. Finally, the wit and wisdom of all the *Allminaxes* from 1870 to 1879 were gathered together as "Josh Billings'" *Old Probability*, bound in one volume and priced at $1.50. The laughter of Carleton and Billings must surely have been as hearty as the public's. Josh Billings' arrows were not dipped in gall. His wit was rather a "Feejee club that makes those who feel it grin while they wince." His victims might be slaughtered, but they expired with a smile upon their faces, for his shafts against humbug and pretension were genial, and though the highfalutin received a mortal wound from his darts, it died laughing at itself.

If "Artemus Ward" and "Josh Billings" anticipated to some degree the humor of Will Rogers, another "comic fellow" whom Carleton added to his list foreshadowed the Private Hargrove of a later generation. "Private Miles O'Reilly" (Charles G. Halpine) of the 47th Regiment of New York Volunteers was feted at Delmonico's and pardoned by the President for his breach of decorum in publishing songs relative to the joint naval and military operations against Charleston. *The Life and Adventures . . . of Private Miles O'Reilly* was advertised as one of the funniest and most satirical collections of military and political humor the war had produced. Certainly, in the guise of an Irish private in the Union Army, the author was able to spin his gentle satire about a visit to the White House or the Miles O'Reilly caucus, city politics or the war itself. This "Irish Pickwick" followed his success with *Baked Meats of the Funeral*, and Carleton found that he had once more tickled the funny bone of the public.

Carleton was able to produce the same effect not only as publisher but as artist and author in his own right. Urged by Morris Phillips to issue his sketches of Havana in book form, Carleton had offered to the public *Our Artist in Cuba*, consisting of fifty drawings on wood depicting G. W. C., after a nautical departure entitled "Sick Transit," struck dumb with admiration at the sights he had witnessed. "Our Artist" enjoyed an equally fruitful sojourn in Peru, where he trapped with his comical pen the streets and the fleas of Lima, the boiled monkeys and pretty women of South America; and *Our Artist in Peru* was followed in 1877 by a composite volume of sketches from Cuba, Peru, Spain, and Algiers, which brought the author-publisher a clear profit of $10,000 and the public a humorous run for its money.

To Charles H. Webb, "author of books too humorous to mention," Carleton suggested a burlesque of one of his most successful ventures, a novel by Augusta Evans Wilson entitled *St. Elmo*. The burlesque, *St. Twel'mo* (published by Webb), sold fast, at the same time increasing the sale of the novel. In the course of *St. Twel'mo; or, the Cuneiform Cyclopedist of Chattanooga*, Webb took occasion to describe what happened when Etna, the heroine, produced a bestseller:

> This thing must be kept up, thought Etna, and she next published a book. This made a hit—striking the publisher favorably, as he announced in a series of fantastic advertisements. Type of the most wonderful characters had to be cast expressly for the production of this work, and the services of the Learned Blacksmith were engaged as chief proof-reader—he should be kept well up in tongs, said Etna. Fifteen cylinder presses were kept running night and day to supply the demand, and the publisher was so broken down in health by the labor of writing advertisements, answering questions, . . . that he took in a partner and sailed himself for an uninhabited island to recuperate his shattered constitution.

Carleton indeed had had experience with best-sellers. The humor he published appealed to the American public, and readers plunged their hands into their pockets to pay for the privilege of laughing at themselves or their current enthusiasms. Carleton had taught the American eagle to pluck out a feather and tickle itself.

The publisher's Arabic symbol was a portent of good fortune not only upon the title-pages of humorous books but upon many a "sensational" novel and "meteoric" volume with which his trademark also came to be associated. When Carleton was described as the "largest publisher of sensational books by native American authors," the intention was to link his name not with blood-and-thunder works, but rather with novels that were sensationally successful. Priced at $1.50 or $1.75, the effusions of such best-selling authors as Mary J. Holmes, "Marion Harland" (Mrs. M. Virginia Terhune), Miriam Coles Harris, and Julie P. Smith were successfully launched by the publisher, along with "brilliant love stories" by "Ouida" (Marie Louise de la Ramée), Epes Sargent's *Peculiar*, and May Agnes Fleming's *Terrible Secret*, *Wonderful Woman*, and *Mad Marriage*. Most of Carleton's bonanzas in this line were society novels, "depicting the flirtations and follies of the married and single," spicy books that titillated nineteenth-century taste for hammock literature.

With an eye toward his pocketbook, Carleton collected and published in uniform style the popular but "moral" novels of A. S. Roe, launched "Brick" Pomeroy's *Sense and Nonsense* "of which thousands and thousands will be sold," and struck a goldmine in the works of Augusta Evans Wilson, whose contemporary reputation for brilliant genius, magnificent word-painting, powerful plot, and intensity of interest established her as the "mother of *St. Elmo*." In addition, Carleton published under a joint imprint with Street and Smith the "cream of the contributions" to *The New York Weekly: Thrown on the World* by "Bertha M. Clay," *Peerless Cathleen* by Cora Agnew, *Faithful Margaret* by Annie Ashmore, and Mrs. George Sheldon's *Forsaken Bride*. The *Weekly* was said to have paid Mary Jane Holmes between four and six thousand dollars for a story, and with the royalties paid by Carleton for the book version she collected "a larger sum than that received by any other American authoress, with the possible exception of the author of Uncle Tom's Cabin." May Agnes Fleming's stories in turn yielded $100 an installment from the *Weekly*, and a fifteen per cent royalty from Carleton. Though they differed in content from *The New York Weekly* Series, the novels of Mayne Reid were equally "meteoric," and Carleton purchased the entire list of his romances in 1868. His *Scalp Hunters* and *Rifle Rangers* appealed to a different section of the public, but appealed none the less sensationally, while his magazine, *Onward*, brought to the youth of America the romance of the Rocky Mountains and Texan hunters, and to its publisher, Carleton, his share of the profits from yearly subscriptions at $3.50.

Another magazine published by Carleton reflected his third publishing interest. The *Record of the Year,* edited by Frank Moore, was a reference scrapbook, a compendium of important events selected from the most noteworthy articles in current newspapers and journals. This digest of information was similar in many ways to other treasuries of knowledge sponsored by Carleton, his *Tales from the Operas, Pulpit Pungencies, 100 Legal Don'ts, Popular Readings, Handbook of Popular Quotations,* and *Condensed Classical Dictionary.* Like his *Household Encyclopaedia and Handbook of General Information,* these works were reference books that gave to a public eager for a shortcut to knowledge "infinite riches and much learning in a little space."

Only a step removed from his digests of information were Carleton's courtesy books, advertised as "Handbooks of Society," and offering for those who wished to be agreeable talkers or listeners *The Art of Conversation*, for those interested in self-improvement *The Arts of Writing, Reading, and Speaking,* for those desirous of learning the nice points of taste and good manners *The Habits of Good Society.* For those who wished all three accomplishments a new diamond edition was available consisting of three volumes in one box at $3. *The Art of Amusing* gave party-minded readers hints on home amusements, while *The Ladies and Gentlemen's Etiquette Book* instructed the curious in the habits of the best fashionable society. For the ladies exclusively *Female Beauty and the Art of Pleasing* was translated from the French for American circulation.

Carleton added to his varied list many translations from the French, some of which were as "sensational" as his humorous books and "meteoric" novels. The works of Michelet and Hugo, Renan and Houssaye, for example, found a ready market. The publisher's handling of these translations indicates his methods of "streamlining" the trade, for Carleton seems to have established a nineteenth-century record in speed of publishing and liberality of advertising. Michelet's *La Femme* was translated in three days, while the 450-page volume was set, cast, printed, bound, and 20,000 copies were sold in less than thirty days. The publisher had engaged Dr. John W. Palmer to do the translation, offering him $1,000 if the work were completed in seventy-two hours, and demanding a forfeit of $10 an hour for every hour's delay. Fortified by coffee and a wet towel round his forehead, Palmer dictated the translation to his wife and delivered the manuscript according to contract. Though he trailed behind such a twentieth-century speed record as was set by the *Roosevelt Memorial* pocket book, Carleton vigorously applied assembly-line methods to the nineteenth-century trade. His advertising was also decidedly modern both in tone and in expenditure. Ten thousand dollars was spent to advertise *Les Misérables*, and results were achieved, for one dealer bought 25,000 copies at the trade sale of George A. Leavitt and Company. Edmund Kirke's *Down in Tennessee* was advertised in the following modern terms: "Enormous advance orders. Thousands of copies swept off on publication day. Subsequent orders will be executed as soon as printers and binders can turn out the books."

Carleton not only was in advance of his times in his business methods, but demonstrated in his dealings with authors tact, courage, generosity, and integrity. When he purchased the stereotype plates of Augusta Evans Wilson's earlier books, he informed the author that he had been obliged to pay so much for the plates of *Macaria* that he could allow only a moderate percentage on future sales. Subsequently, after the successful publication of *St. Elmo* and *Vashti*, Carleton on his own initiative suggested an increase in the writer's percentage on *Macaria* and earned for himself Mrs. Wilson's encomium as "a Prince of Publishers." Alice Cary also declared him "very generous . . . wide-awake and liberal." To Edmund Clarence Stedman he allowed ten per cent royalties on *The Prince's Ball* and to "Artemus Ward" fifteen cents on each copy of his work sold. When "Josh Billings" offered to sell his *Farmer's Allminax* outright for $250 and to supply one for each of ten succeeding years at the same price, Carleton "with disinterestedness rare among publishers" advised the humorist to accept instead a royalty of three cents on each copy. Outright payment would have netted the author $2,500 in ten years. The royalty arrangement brought him $30,000 in the same time. Carleton's views on copyright also indicated his generous attitude toward authors, for he upheld a "universal, absolute right and control throughout the world to eternity of the author's brainwork to the author, his heirs, executors and assigns."

Like every publisher, Carleton made mistakes. The translation of Balzac was as total a failure as that of Hugo was a success. He erred in refusing to handle "Marion Harland's" *Common Sense in the Household*, which became a Scribner bonanza, and in declining B. L. Farjeon's *Grif*, which over the Harper imprint was a great success. He added error to error by jumping at the next Farjeon book, *Solomon Isaacs*, which proved a failure. Carleton was brought to law by one Fannie Bean, who claimed that publication of her novel, *Dr. Mortimer's Patient*, had been delayed and was neither advertised nor placed on sale, except in the publisher's offices, after she had paid $900 which was to be returned after the first 2,000 copies had been sold. The breach of contract was decided in favor of the plaintiff. Perhaps the gravest mistake ever made by Carleton is revealed in a terse note written by Mark Twain about his "Jumping Frog" story: "Wrote this story for Artemus [Ward]—his idiot publisher Carleton, gave it to Clapp's Saturday Press."

Carleton upon several occasions had himself faced the difficulties of delay and postponement. *The Suppressed Book about Slavery!*, for which the stereotype plates were made in 1857, could not be published until 1864, when it at last disclosed "the hideous skeleton of the institution." The correspondence of Alexander von Humboldt had been prepared for production when it was learned that Appleton and Harper were ready to go to press with the same work, and the competing firms had to be compensated before publication could proceed. *The Love-Life of Dr. Kane*, the explorer who had brought fortune to G. W. Childs, was in press in 1862, but its publication was "stopped by a compromise with the brothers and executor of Dr. Kane," and the history of the explorer's "secret marriage" to Margaret Fox, of "Rochester Rappings" fame, did not see the light of day until four years later.

Despite such disasppointments and failures, Carleton's career was both honorable and lucrative. In 1869 he was able to open a new Fifth Avenue Bookstore for which he had leased the Worth House, and the magnificence of his quarters almost defied description. In the first story salesroom frescoes reproduced the decorations of the Pompeian Library, while pillars and griffins, bronze statues and gilded moldings vied with books to attract the public. In the ceiling of his own inner sanctum appeared his trademark, the Arabic symbol denoting books, and a French stationery department was added to make of the old Worth House "one of the finest bookstores in the world." Meanwhile, the upper section of the building was kept, under Carleton's control, as a hotel, or, in the terms of contemporary wits, as a "home for indigent authors." While still in business, half as publisher and half as hotel-keeper, in 1871, he took into partnership his head clerk, George Dillingham, and converted his house into G. W. Carleton and Company. In consequence of the increasing magnitude of its publishing business, the firm was compelled, a year later, to open a still larger establishment under the Fifth Avenue Hotel, and there, at 192 Fifth Avenue, G. W. Carleton remained for more than a decade. In 1883, when the landlord raised the rent by $4,000, the firm decided to abandon its retail trade and limit itself to its own publications. At West 23rd Street, over Dutton and Company, in quarters equipped with steam heat and freight and passenger elevators, Carleton terminated his association with the company he had founded. In 1886 he retired from business, taking with him a name that for more than a quarter of a century had been identified with American books and authors, and especially with humorous American books. G. W. Dillingham succeeded Carleton, continuing to offer to the public the "meteoric" volumes and the humor that had been launched by his predecessor.

Meanwhile, Carleton spent "half his life in exploring far-off lands and the other half in telling about them." From Egypt he sent letters to his friends about the Sphinx and the Pyramids, the seraglios and "the forty centuries of book-publishers looking down upon him" from the "hieroglyphical banks" of the Nile. The trade did not begrudge him the pleasures of his retirement. "During his long business career," *Publishers' Weekly* warmly affirmed, "Carleton had the happy knack of making friends of all the authors whose books he published, and they will rejoice to know that he is enjoying the fortune which he won through their talents. There is at least one publisher whom even Lord Byron would not desire to kill, and his name is Carleton." Fifteen years after his retirement, on October 11, 1901, the publisher died, marking the end to a full and successful career.

Most of the authors and humorists who had rallied at Carleton's office had long since scattered and died, but the seed they had planted in American soil was still fruitful. The wit and wisdom of "Artemus Ward" and "Josh Billings" had given way to the grander wit and profounder wisdom of "Mark Twain," but it was they who had helped clear the ground for the humor that was to become one of the nation's most characteristic and most flourishing products. Without their publisher, however, they would have been voices laughing in the wilderness.

The little Arabic symbol that conceals the monogram of George W. Carleton should not be forgotten, for it impressed "hys Marke" upon books that filled an urgent need in nineteenth-century America. During and after the Civil War, when the nation was rent by disunion, hatred, and embitterment, that Arabic sign became a symbol not merely for books in general, but for books of good humor touched with a mild and genial satire. America learned to look at itself and its absurdities through a mirror that reflected clearly while it distorted. The effect was comic, but somehow sound. America, beholding itself, laughed at what it saw. And so, through the humorous books that bore upon their title-pages a little Arabic symbol that concealed the initials of a publisher, a nation smiled and came of age.

Notes on Sources

Early Nineteenth-Century American Humor

Walter Blair, *Native American Humor* (New York, Cincinnati, Chicago, etc., [1937]), pp. 9 f., 124; *The Cambridge History of American Literature* (New York, 1927), II, 155 ff.; David Donald, ed., *Inside Lincoln's Cabinet The Civil War Diaries of Salmon P. Chase* (New York, 1954), pp. 149, 162; Vernon Louis Parrington, *Main Currents in American Thought* (New York, [1930]), III, 92; Constance Rourke, *American Humor* (New York, [1931]), pp. 221 ff.

Carleton's Visit to Cuba & His Appearance

George W. Carleton, *Our Artist in Cuba* (New York: Carleton, 1865), *passim;* "G. W. Carleton," *The American Bookseller* XXIV:8 (October 15, 1888), picture opp. p. 263; J. C. Derby, *Fifty Years among Authors, Books and Publishers* (New York: Carleton, 1884), p. 48.

Carleton's Early Life

"G. W. Carleton & Co.," *New-York Evening Post* (April 28, 1875), photostat courtesy Mr. Frederic Melcher; "George W. Carleton Retires," *Publishers' Weekly* XXIX:21 (May 22, 1886), p. 651; Derby, *op. cit.*, pp. 235–44; "Jubilee of G. W. Dillingham Co.," *Publishers' Weekly* LXXII:6 (August 10, 1907), p. 345; "Obituary. George W. Carleton," *ibid.* LX:16 (October 19, 1901), p. 857.

Rudd & Carleton: Their Activities; Carleton's Trademark

American Catalogue 1855–1858, *passim;* [William Allen Butler], *Nothing to Wear: An Episode of City Life* (New York: Rudd & Carleton, 1857), pp. 9, 67; *The Cambridge History of American Literature* II, 156; "G. W. Carleton," *The American Bookseller* (October 15, 1888), p. 263; "G. W. Carleton & Co.," *New-York Evening Post* (April 28, 1875); "G. W. Carleton, Retiring from Business, Tells Some of His Experiences," *Adolf Growoll Collection. American Book Trade History* IV, 10–12 (courtesy *Publishers' Weekly*); Derby, *op. cit.*, pp. 233, 235–44; Q. K. Philander Doesticks [Mortimer Thomson], *Nothing to Say* (New York: Rudd & Carleton, 1857), *passim;* Ferris Greenslet, *The Life of Thomas Bailey Aldrich* (Boston & New York, 1908), pp. 36, 52; George C. Holt, *Memorial of William Allen Butler Read before the Association of the Bar of the City of New York, March 10, 1903, passim;* "Jubilee of G. W. Dillingham Co.," *Publishers' Weekly* (August 10, 1907), p. 345; "Literary Intelligence," *American Publishers' Circular and Literary Gazette* III:9 (February 28, 1857), p. 131, and VII:32 (December 5, 1861), p. 285; "Obituary. George W. Carleton," *Publishers' Weekly* (October 19, 1901), p. 857; Morris Phillips, "The Late George W. Carleton," (October 19, 1901), *Growoll Collection. American Book Trade History* IV, 10–12; Frederic F. Sherman, *A Check List of First Editions of the Works of Thomas Bailey Aldrich* (New York, 1921), p. 5; Laura Stedman and George M. Gould, *Life and Letters of Edmund Clarence Stedman* (New York, 1910), I, 218; Ernest James Wessen, "Campaign Lives of Abraham Lincoln 1860," *Papers In Illinois History . . . For . . . 1937* (Springfield, Ill., 1938), No. 1. According to Wright Howes, *U.S.-Iana* (1700–1950) (New York, 1954), No. 6159, *The "Wigwam Edition"* was "the first life of Lincoln in book form."

Fletcher Harper had refused to publish Butler's poem in book form after he had sold 80,000 copies of *Harper's Weekly*, where the poem had run, since he believed there would be no further demand. Rudd and Carleton, who asked for and received permission to publish it in book form, later claimed to have sold 20,000 copies, although the author stated he received no benefit. For details about *Nothing to Wear*, see Blanck, *Bibliography of American Literature* I, 449 f.; William Allen Butler, *A Retrospect of Forty Years* (New York, 1911), pp. 278 ff.; John A. Kouwenhoven, "Some Ado About Nothing," *The Colophon* N.S. II:1 (Autumn 1936), pp. 101–13.

Carleton's Office Personnel

American Literary Gazette VIII:6 (January 15, 1867), p. 191, XI:6 (July 15, 1868), p. 152, XI:7 (August 1, 1868), p. 169, XI:8 (August 15, 1868), p. 177; "G. W. Carleton & Co.," *New-York Evening Post* (April 28, 1875); "G. W. Carleton, Retiring from Business, Tells Some of His Experiences," *Growoll Collection. American Book Trade History* IV, 10–12; "George W. Dillingham," *The American Bookseller* XXIV:9 (November 1, 1888), pp. 298 f.; Greenslet, *op. cit.*, p. 61; "Obituary. George Wellington Dillingham," *Publishers' Weekly* XLIX:1 (January 4, 1896), pp. 10 f.; *Publishers' Weekly* LI:15 (April 10, 1897), p. 664; *Town Topics* XVIII:11 (September 15, 1887), p. 7.

Carleton's Humorous Publications

American Literary Gazette II:5 (January 1, 1864), p. 196, II:10 (March 15, 1864), p. 354, V:3 (June 1, 1865), p. 62, V:5 (July 1, 1865), p. 110, V:9 (September 1, 1865), p. 200, V:10 (September 15, 1865), p. 223, VII:2 (May 15, 1866), p. 43; [Charles F. Browne], *Artemus Ward His Book* (New York: Carleton, 1862), pp. 79 f., 176, 179, 205, and *passim;* [Charles F. Browne], *The Complete Works of Artemus Ward* (New York, [1898]), pp. 11, 26, and *passim;* G. W. Carleton, *Our Artist in Cuba, Peru, Spain and Algiers* (New York: Carleton, 1877), *passim;* G. W. Carleton, *Our Artist in Peru* (New York: Carleton, 1866), *passim;* "G. W. Carleton," *The American Bookseller* (October 15, 1888), p. 263; "G. W. Carleton & Co.," *New-York Evening Post* (April 28, 1875); "G. W. Carleton, Retiring from Business, Tells Some of His Experiences," *Growoll Collection. American Book Trade History* IV, 10–12; Carleton's Catalogue at end of Mary E. Tucker, *Life of Mark M. Pomeroy* (New York: Carleton, 1868); Cyril Clemens, *Josh Billings, Yankee Humorist* (Webster Groves, Mo., 1932), pp. 51 ff., 115, 128, 156; Derby, *op. cit.*, pp. 235–44; [Charles G. Halpine], *The Life and Adventures, Songs, Services, and Speeches of Private Miles O'Reilly* (New York: Carleton, 1864), *passim;* "Jubilee of G. W. Dillingham Co.," *Publishers' Weekly* (August 10, 1907), p. 346; "Obituary. George W. Carleton," *ibid.* (October 19, 1901), pp. 857 f.; Morris Phillips, "The Late George W. Carleton" (October 19, 1901), *Growoll Collection. American Book Trade History* IV, 10–12; *Publishers' Trade-List Annual* 1873, 1874, 1879; "Return of Private Miles O'Reilly," *New York Herald* (October 20, 1863), clipping at New York Public Library; Don C. Seitz, *Artemus Ward* (New York & London, [1919]), pp. 117 ff.; [Henry W. Shaw], *Josh Billings, Hiz Sayings* (New York: Carleton, 1866), pp. 47, 58, and *passim;* [Henry W. Shaw], *Josh Billings: His Works, Complete* (New York: Carleton & Co., 1880), pp. xxiv, xxviii ff., and *passim;* C. H. Webb, *St. Twel'mo* (New York, 1867), p. 55.

Carleton's "Sensational" Books & Novels

American Catalogue 1876–1884, p. xxvi; *American Literary Gazette* II:3 (December 1, 1863), p. 108, VIII:3 (December 1, 1866), p. 117, VIII:11 (April 1, 1867), p. 335, IX:2 (May 15, 1867), p. 52, X:5 (January 1, 1868), p. 168, X:8 (February 15, 1868), p. 217, XI:4 (June 15, 1868), p. 106, XII:2 (November 16, 1868), p. 44, XII:4 (December 15, 1868), p. 127; "G. W. Carleton," *The American Bookseller* (October 15, 1888), p. 263; "G. W. Carleton & Co.," *New-York Evening Post* (April 28, 1875); Carleton's list at end of *Carleton's Classical Dictionary* (New York: Carleton, 1882); Derby, *op. cit.*, p. 239; Mary Noel, *Villains Galore* (New York, 1954), pp. 114, 192; La Salle C. Pickett, *Literary Hearthstones of Dixie* (Philadelphia & London, 1912), p. 293; *Publishers' Trade-List Annual* 1875; *Mayne Reid's Magazine Onward. For the Youth of America* (New York: Carleton, January 1869—February 1870); Elizabeth Reid, *Mayne Reid* (London, 1890), p. 239.

Carleton purchased the copyrights of "Marion Harland's" novels from Sheldon & Co. See *American Literary Gazette* XIV:2 (November 15, 1869), p. 57.

Carleton's Treasuries of Information & Society Handbooks

American Literary Gazette VII:3 (June 1, 1866), p. 70; *Carleton's Household Encyclopaedia and Handbook of General Information* (New York: Carleton, 1879); "George W. Dillingham," *The American Bookseller* (November 1, 1888), pp. 298 f.; *Publishers'*

Trade-List Annual 1875, 1878, 1879, 1880, 1881; *Record of the Year. A Reference Scrap Book* (New York: Carleton, 1876, 1877).

Carleton's Translations from the French

"G. W. Carleton," *The American Bookseller* (October 15, 1888), p. 263; "G. W. Carleton & Co.," *New-York Evening Post* (April 28, 1875); "G. W. Carleton, Retiring from Business, Tells Some of His Experiences," *Growoll Collection. American Book Trade History* IV, 10–12; Derby, *op. cit.*, pp. 235–244; "George W. Dillingham," *The American Bookseller* (November 1, 1888), pp. 298 f.

Carleton's Advertising, Dealings with Authors, & Views on Copyright

American Literary Gazette III:9 (September 1, 1864), p. 263; "G. W. Carleton," *The American Bookseller* (October 15, 1888), p. 263; "G. W. Carleton & Co.," *New-York Evening Post* (April 28, 1875); Clemens, *op. cit.*, p. 115; Derby, *op. cit.*, pp. 251 f., 397; *Publishers' Weekly* XV:7 (February 15, 1879), p. 197; Seitz, *op. cit.*, p. 120; Stedman and Gould *op. cit.*, I, 218.

Carleton's Mistakes & Disappointments

Derby, *op. cit.*, pp. 235–244, 566 f.; "Literary Intelligence," *American Publishers' Circular and Literary Gazette* VI:19 (May 12, 1860), p. 246; *The Love-Life of Dr. Kane* (New York: Carleton, 1866), p. viii; "The Mistakes of a Publisher," *Growoll Collection. American Book Trade History* IV, 10–12; *Publishers' Weekly* XXXVII:25 (June 21, 1890), p. 825; Donald Sheehan, *This Was Publishing* (Bloomington, Indiana, 1952), p. 63; *The Suppressed Book about Slavery!* (New York: Carleton, 1864), p. 6; *Mark Twain's Notebook* (New York & London, 1935), pp. 7, 55.

Carleton's Store, Control of Hotel, Dillingham's Partnership, & Later Firm Locations & Activities

American Literary Gazette XIII:8 (August 16, 1869), p. 219, XIV:1 (November 1, 1869), pp. 5 f., XVI:8 (February 15, 1871), p. 150; "G. W. Carleton & Co.," *New-York Evening Post* (April 28, 1875); "G. W. Carleton, Retiring from Business, Tells Some of His Experiences," *Growoll Collection. American Book Trade History* IV, 10–12; "Obituary. George W. Carleton," *Publishers' Weekly* (October 19, 1901), pp. 857 f.; "Obituary. George Wellington Dillingham," *ibid.* XLIX:1 (January 4, 1896), pp. 10 f.; *Publishers' Weekly* I:12 (April 4, 1872), p. 302, XXIII:23 (June 9, 1883), p. 689, XXVIII:4 (July 25, 1885), p. 141, XXXIII:6 (February 11, 1888), p. 333; *Trow's New York City Directory* 1869/70–1886/87.

Carleton's Retirement & Death

The American Bookseller XIX:10 (May 15, 1886), p. 255; Clipping File, Biographical Section, begun by Talcott Williams, Journalism Library, Columbia University, courtesy Wade A. Doares, Librarian; "Literary and Trade Notes," *Publishers' Weekly* XXXIII:26 (June 30, 1888), p. 989; "Obituary. George W. Carleton," *ibid.* (October 19, 1901), p. 857.

A copy of the notice of "Dissolution of Co-Partnership," dated May 8, 1886, is deposited in the Ford Collection, New York Public Library.

G. W. Dillingham Company

Announcement of the incorporation of the G. W. Dillingham Company, after Dillingham's death, appears in *Publishers' Weekly* XLIX:23 (June 6, 1896), p. 957. This company was incorporated with John H. Cook as president and John W. Hesse as secretary and treasurer, both men having worked for Carleton. The G. W. Dillingham Co. in 1906 had a capital stock of $115,000. In 1907, when it celebrated its fiftieth jubilee, *Publishers' Weekly* announced that the firm "bids fair to outlast another fifty years." In 1916 the firm was bankrupt, with liabilities of $50,000 and assets slightly more than $5,000. For details, see "G. W. Dillingham Co. Bankrupt," *Publishers' Weekly* XC:10 (September 2, 1916), p. 677; *Adolf Growoll Collection. American Book Trade History* IV, 112; "Jubilee of G. W. Dillingham Co.," *Publishers' Weekly* (August 10, 1907), pp. 345 ff.

Domesticity and Nostalgia

Dick and Fitzgerald

To THE NOSTALGIC, reminiscing twentieth-century mind, the nineteenth century has become above all the time when the family was the supreme unit of the nation and the home was the hub of America. For all of its great accomplishments, struggles, and adventures, the nineteenth century has come to mean the century of hearth and home, when people were born at home, and lived at home, and died at home.

Especially they lived at home. In its kitchen they prepared the foods now lost to an impatient age, and in its parlor they assembled to seek their joys and entertainments. In memory they assemble there again—dancing their quadrilles, the lancers and the polonaise, playing their games, patience and cribbage and whist. From the kitchen they carry their home-made rum shrub, their taffy and their caramels, those "delicious cream confections," before they settle down to watch a home-made shadow pantomime or a parlor tableau entitled "Popping the Question." Around a nineteenth-century piano they gather for songs from *Tony Pastor's Bowery Songster* or the *Bones and Banjo Melodist*. Before a nineteenth-century curtain they join to applaud a parlor theatrical entitled *Ten Nights in a Barroom* or *A Dental Engagement*. And after the performance a wealth of entertainment still awaits them, from amateur magic and fortune-telling to round and forfeit games, from puzzles to recitations, from dialogues to riddles and conundrums.

From the viewpoint of its own comparative homelessness, the twentieth century so envisions the nineteenth, romanticizing the past, over-simplifying it perhaps, but drawing an authentic picture nonetheless. To the twentieth century that has "let others sing, dance and perform" for it and has grown "more empty" in the process, the nineteenth century in America

Reprinted from Madeleine B. Stern, *Imprints on History: Book Publishers and American Frontiers* (Bloomington, Ind.: Indiana Univ. Press, 1956), pp. 290–302 and 461–464.

has become this picture of a nation at home, framed in the gold of a golden age.

There is proof that the picture is authentic, and the proof lies in those well-thumbed books of parlor tableaux and theatricals, social pastimes and songsters that the nineteenth century needed for its winter evenings' entertainments. The books, indeed, are all that is left of this vanished age, and for a later time they re-create the picture, evoke the nostalgia, restore the yesterday.

For all its varied purposes and accomplishments, the nineteenth century needed and found its publishers, those dealers in the printed word who so often shaped history while they recorded it. Two of them, joining forces on New York's Ann Street, were known as Dick and Fitzgerald, publishers extraordinary to the nineteenth-century American fireside. Across the years their books still reflect the warmth and glow of a hearthfire that has turned to ash.

William Brisbane Dick was a fortunate man whose life was marked by many auspicious days. Born in Philadelphia in 1826, the son of John and Arabella Dick, he was fortunate in claiming a close relationship with Wesley Burgess, for Burgess was to become head of the firm of Burgess, Stringer & Company, publishers and booksellers in New York. Dick was fortunate, too, in his friendship with Lawrence R. Fitzgerald, born like him in Philadelphia in 1826, a young man who had received a thorough training in the mercantile business and had served as salesman with the firm of Burgess and Zieber.

On one of Dick's auspicious days in the 1840's, he ventured to New York with his friend, embarking upon what was to become a long and prosperous career. The two young men accompanied Wesley Burgess to New York when Burgess, Stringer was being organized, and they served a useful apprenticeship with a company that dealt in periodicals, music, and books of a general nature. After Stringer retired to form the firm of Stringer and Townsend, Ransom Garrett took his place as co-partner, and the two promising young men from Philadelphia were as fortunate in their connection with Garrett as they had been with Burgess. Burgess and Garrett became, after the withdrawal of Burgess, Garrett & Company, publishers of popular fiction and games at 18 Ann Street, until the "& Company" were starred in title roles and the firm became Garrett, Dick & Fitzgerald. Garrett had only to retire for the names of Dick and Fitzgerald to stand alone in publishing history—an event signalized by the articles of co-partnership which were executed on June 30, 1858.

The New York City *Directories* of 1858/59 record the change in the firm name, listing simply Dick and Fitzgerald, books, 18 Ann Street. That narrow thoroughfare, only three blocks long and divided by Theatre Alley, was a mecca not only for gentlemen of the book trade but for sharpers, gamblers, and fireladdies. If Messrs. Dick and Fitzgerald wished diversion from their literary pursuits, they could visit Barnum's American Museum a few doors away with its famous "egress" on Ann Street, or enjoy a hearty meal with neighboring printers and booksellers at Windust's eating-house. In the Paternoster Row of America, Dick and Fitzgerald were at home. A good location and a thorough training augured well for their success in publishing.

Instead of issuing the miscellaneous books that had appeared in Burgess's lists, the two young publishers of Ann Street decided to specialize along the lines previously laid down by Ransom Garrett. They would cater almost exclusively to the mid-century's desires for entertainment and self-improvement, and since in mid-nineteenth-century America the hub of social enjoyment was the home, it was for entertainment in all the homes of America that their books were published.

Even before the execution of their articles of co-partnership, Dick and Fitzgerald had issued a monthly journal whose title alone is indicative of their purposes. *The Home Circle*, priced at three cents a copy, was "Devoted to Literature, News, Fun, Poetry, & c."; but it was devoted above all to readers who gathered at a nineteenth-century fireside, and it contained, therefore, nuggets for every member of the family. For the daughter there were poems—"The Old Clay Pipe" or "My Flora"; for the son there were tales of adventure and animals—"The Ghost Raiser," "The Western Stage Driver," or an "Adventure with Sharks." For the father there were informative articles on "Alcohol in Wine," the "Origin of Paper Money," or "Ancient Glass Manufactures." And the mother of the family would doubtless enjoy the story entitled "George Durand; or, The Profligate," a revealing account of "Quack Medicines," or the useful receipts in the "Housekeeper's Department." For them all there was a section devoted to "Family Pastime," where riddles and charades, rebuses and parlor pastimes might be found, and for them all, too, there were advertisements of other Dick and Fitzgerald publications, from the firm's Shilling Library to a series of books on the "Exploits of Highwaymen," from *The Magician's Own Book* to *The Ladies' Guide to Beauty*.

Certainly it was the "home circle," and more specifically the parlor of the home that provided the background for nineteenth-century recreation, and at least half the books appearing under the imprint of Dick and Fitzgerald may be classed as "parlor entertainments." In one of his illuminating prefaces William Brisbane Dick wrote, "There is nothing more delightful than . . . to devote the whole or part of an evening to social amusement." He had in mind, as did his readers, social amusement at home. So it was that he published several general books of parlor entertainment, *What Shall We Do To-Night? or Social Amusements for Evening Parties* by "Leger D. Mayne" (William B. Dick himself), *The Sociable; or, One Thousand and One Home Amusements, Fireside Games; for Winter Evening Amusement*, and *Uncle Josh's Trunk-Full of Fun*—books that taught the willing host the secrets of round and forfeit games, ingenious puzzles, innocent sells, musical pastimes, startling illusions, gallantry shows, and mirth-provoking exhibitions. In their pages both hosts and guests would find explained such family games as "Selling Statues" or "The Magic Handkerchief," a "Musical-Merry-go-Round" or "The Needle and Thread Trick." From "Hocus Pocus" to "Living Flowers," from "Tableaux Vivants" to "Mrs. Jarley's Wax-Works," from "Bout Rhymes" to "Hunt The Hare," there were pastimes for young and old, witty and agile, for those who loved games of action and for those who preferred games requiring memory. For all the games the setting was the home—at "merry Christmas-time, or on a wet day in the country or in the city too, . . . or on a winter's evening, when the fire is burning cheerily, pussy purring on the hearth, and the lamps lighted." The apparatus required was simple, for these parlor pastimes demanded only a family endowed with "good temper, good spirits, and gentleness, so that at any moment amusement for an evening can be obtained by anybody who wills it." And if the Dick and Fitzgerald books for the home circle were purchased, the entire winter season, including a social gathering every week, could be passed harmoniously and pleasantly by customers throughout the country.

Having once decided to limit their publications to books that would raise the spirit and improve the mind, Dick and Fitzgerald introduced a variety of works within their specialty. One of the most popular entertainments of the nineteenth century arose, in all probability, from the combination of the average person's desire to shine in society and the general ubiquity of elocution teachers. Recitation, dialogue, and joke books would meet the requirements of both, and the publishers proceeded to flood the market with collections, many of them arranged by William B. Dick himself, offering "new and bright little pieces" for "small children" or "young Thespians," and ready-made speeches for the gallant slashers of the day. When Dick's ingenuity failed him, the firm could always resort to Frost's *Dialogues for Young Folks*, Barber's *Ready-Made Speeches*, or McBride's *All Kinds of Dialogues*. While Dick and Fitzgerald flourished no program would be wanting for Washington's Birthday, no master of dialect would be unable to con the lines of "Der Drummer" or "Vat You Please," and no sharp young card would lack a joke to quote from *Yale College Scrapes; or, How the Boys Go It at New Haven*. With *Chips from Uncle Sam's Jack Knife*, "a broad grin" was guaranteed "for the domestic hearth, or boarding-house parlor, for the whole winter." From 18 Ann Street flowed recitations suited to every occasion and every elocutionist, from "The Palmetto and the Pine" to "Curfew Must not Ring To-night," from "The Blue and the Gray" to "The Drunkard's Dream," from "Aunt Patience's Doughnuts" to "The Baby's Kiss." Besides writing many of the firm's reciters, William B. Dick offered, without increasing the charge of thirty cents for a book in paper and fifty for the same in boards, some excellent advice on elocution: "Each child must so perfectly memorise its part that the text will be recited without hesitation. When this is accomplished, it is time to attend to gesture and emphasis. Let both of these be merely improvements . . . of their own natural efforts. . . . When one person is speaking, it adds greatly to the effect if the listeners seem to appreciate what is said by appropriate gestures . . . in a perfectly natural manner." As an authority on the subject, Dick was able to issue in the 1870's a series entitled *Dick's Recitations and Readings,* in which he had the remarkably good sense to render some poetical effusions in prose form to help readers avoid a sing-song inflection. While he catered to the demands of an elocuting world, William Brisbane Dick did his best to raise the standards of the art.

Almost as popular among parlor entertainments were card games, and Dick profitably explained to a world devoid of radios, television, and motion pictures the varieties of patience, cribbage, and whist. The result of two years of consultations with the best players in the country, *The American Hoyle,* appearing under the pseudonym of "Trumps," was given to an eager public. When Dick wearied of his role as "Trumps," he could publish Professor Proctor's meditations on draw-poker or an exposition of games and tricks with cards by the reformed gambler, J. H. Green. In addition to elucidating the mysteries of bezique and euchre, commercial pitch and whisky poker, the firm produced new card games—cards for courtship and fortune-telling, for popping the question or for Leap Year, the last of which were "intended more to make fun among young people than for any practical utility."

There were other games that nineteenth-century America enjoyed. Gathered in the parlor, the young folks could put on a lively exhibition of legerdemain if they had studied *The Fireside Magician* or *The Great Wizard of the North's Handbook of Natural Magic.* They could indulge in a thrilling session of mesmerism if they were equipped with De Laurence's *Hypnotism,* or amaze one another with vocal feats if they had bought *Ventriloquism Self-Taught* by Professor Ganthony. With *The Magician's Own Book* they could find "amusement sufficient to occupy the evenings of a family for three or four years, and give a new source of enjoyment each evening." While the book "*amuses,* it also *instructs,*" and with it "a man could amuse the great and small members of his family, or make himself the lion of a party, for an indefinite period." Best of all, the family could read one another's palms if they possessed a copy of *Dick's Mysteries of the Hand; or, Palmistry Made Easy.*

Reading palms was only one way of fortune-telling. Dick and Fitzgerald knew all the ways, and for nineteenth-century America's fireside evenings they published their fortune-tellers and dream-books, from *Mother Shipton's Oriental Dream Book* to *Madame Le Normand's Unerring Fortune-Teller* (with a Chart of Fate), from *The Golden Wheel Dream Book* by Felix Fontaine, Professor of Astrology, to *Le Marchand's Fortune-Teller and*

Dreamer's Dictionary by the celebrated Parisian seer. Fortunes could be told, as Dick and Fitzgerald advised an avid public, from the white of an egg or from apple-parings, from moles, fingernails, and dreams. The firm's dream books have the distinction of having introduced for the first time the lucky number device, an innovation devoutly cherished by guileless addicts.

To shine in the parlor was a worthy feat, but to shine in the ballroom was every nineteenth-century gentleman's desire. Who could master the devious steps of the polonaise, the lancers, or the caledonians without having studied *Dick's Quadrille Call-Book, and Ball-Room Prompter*? Who could bow gallantly or step gracefully through the redowa or schottische without the aid of Professor De Walden's *Ball-Room Companion* or General Ferrero's *Art of Dancing* as executed at the author's private academies? From 18 Ann Street flowed complete directions for calling figures or executing round dances, as well as for learning the intricacies of the Parisian Varieties or the Prince Imperial Set. From jigs to contra dances, from the german to the galop, instructions were available in a form at once concise, lucid, and reasonable. And for those who wished to strum a banjo while their friends enjoyed the dancing, Frank Converse's *Complete Banjo Instructor* (without a master) might be ordered for fifty cents the copy.

For only ten cents, the firm sent through the mails their song books, *Tony Pastor's Bowery Songster*, *Christy's Bones and Banjo Melodist*, *The Shamrock*, the *Camp-Fire*, *The Arkansas Traveller's*, the *Plantation*. From tent and forecastle to hearth and home there were songs for every occasion, even to *William Lingard's On the Beach at Long Branch Song Book*. There were love songs and sentimental songs, Ethiopian and comic songs, patriotic and convivial songs, and as the quartet gathered round the upright piano—a copy of *Tony Pastor's "444" Combination Songster* propped on the ledge—the strains of "Life on the Bloomingdale Road" or "The Angel Dressed in White" floated sweetly to nineteenth-century ears. With the help of the Ann Street publishers, the tunes of "She Smiled When I Had Done It" or "I Always Take It Cool," "Hunkydory" or "Humbug Now is All the Go" were familiar melodies in the parlors of yesterday.

Perhaps, in that leisurely yesterday when the home held more charms than the street, the most popular social pastime was the parlor theatrical. With wigs, a dab of grease paint, and some histrionic inclination, a group of young Thespians could convert the parlor into a magic fairyland or a dark forest, a French boulevard or an American saloon. Like Louisa May Alcott's Little Men and Little Women, they could tread the boards of a home-made stage and win the applause of their audience—provided, of course, that they owned the texts of their plays. The firm of Dick and Fitzgerald willingly supplied those scripts, sending across the country, at fifteen or twenty-five cents a copy, the farces and comediettas, dramas and vaudeville sketches that would set a stage-struck America to conning its lines. Their stock of New Plays and Entertainments was varied, ranging from *Ten Nights in a Barroom* to *Freezing a Mother-in-Law*, from *A Dental Engagement* to *Josiah's Courtship*. There were Ethiopian acts and monologues, mock trials and initiations, tableaux and shadow pantomimes, acting charades and plays—plays Irish and rural, western and temperance and military—plays to fulfill every desire of a century bent on barnstorming. For those who preferred western drama, there was *Crawford's Claim*, a play in three acts requiring nine male and three female performers and two and a quarter hours acting time. For those who inclined to farce, there was the *Darkey Wood Dealer* in one act, requiring only three male actors and twenty minutes playing time. For comedy, *Standing Room Only* might be selected— one act, three males and one female, thirty-five minutes. From colonial drama to vaudeville, from playlet to farce, Dick and Fitzgerald could recommend a variety of intriguing titles. For those who wished a ready reference theatre book, there was T. Allston Brown's *History of the American Stage*, while for those less ingenious than Miss Alcott's characters the firm facilitated matters by providing wigs and beards, Weldon's *Fancy Costumes*, colored fires, and tableau-lights, as well as a make-up box for five dollars, which contained hare's foot and nose putty, spirit gum and moustache-cosmetique, together with an assortment of crimped hair and other theatrical sundries. The parlor stage need never languish for winter evenings' entertainments while Dick and Fitzgerald flourished on Ann Street.

If half the publications of the firm centered round the parlor of the home, the other half might be said to center round the kitchen. If the upper middle classes profited most from the varied entertainments concocted by Dick and Fitzgerald, it was the so-called lower classes, the domestics, nursery-maids, and butlers, who must have proved the best customers for the firm's books on self-improvement. With these nineteenth-century courtesy books on hand, the denizens of the kitchen could rise to parlor status, in their mastery of the social amenities, by learning what William B. Dick eagerly taught: "to say or do the proper thing at the proper time and in a proper manner." For them Dick's etiquette books were bound in paper and sold at ten, twenty-five, or thirty cents, from *How to Behave in Society* to *The Art of Dressing Well*, from *Blunders in Behavior Corrected* to *Dinner Napkins, and How to Fold Them*. Doubtless for them, too, as well as for the ladies and gentlemen of the parlor, the firm published its aids to beauty and love, revealing the secrets of pomades and cosmetics in *The Ladies' Guide to Beauty* by the private physician to Queen Victoria, whose work had been revised by an American colleague, or offering "amusing" and "sarcastically instructive" hints on the art of fascinating in Madame Lola Montez's *Arts of Beauty*. For a nominal fee the willing pursuer could learn *How to Win and How to Woo*, or encompass the entire *Art and Etiquette of Making Love*, from curing bashfulness to commencing a courtship, from popping the question to acting suitably after an engagement. For those already wooed and won, of course, *Bridal Etiquette* was available at only ten cents the copy. Dick and Fitzgerald did not neglect the feminine arts. For the fair sex, the "most discriminating and exacting portion of an intelligent public," they offered works on crochet and fancy work or painting on china, and Franz Thimm's *French, German, Spanish,* and *Italian Self-Taught* to those still in need of "finishing." To meet the more urgent needs of ladies in "society, household duties, and business," a series of *Letter-Writers* was projected, the *Society*, the *Commercial*, and the *Sensible*, so that one might with perfect propriety introduce a Sunday School scholar to a clergyman in another city or thank a friend for the loan of an umbrella. The type of publication that centered most about the kitchen was naturally the cookbook, and of these the Ann Street firm offered a wide assortment, ranging from *The American Housewife and Kitchen Directory* to *How to Cook and How to Carve*, from *Dick's Home Made Candies* to *How to Cook Potatoes, Apples, Eggs, and Fish Four Hundred Different Ways*. With such indispensable reference books on hand, the mysteries of terrapin and puddings, pickles and catsups need remain mysterious no longer.

In addition to their kitchen receipts and their parlor entertainments, Dick and Fitzgerald published their Reason Why Series and their Shilling Library of reference books, "intended . . . for the use of persons whose means are limited, but who desire to . . . form their habits and character, so as to fit them for mingling in the best society." With manuals on ready reckoning and phonography, taxidermy and horse training, masonic ritual and printing, punctuation and health, the family aquarium and household pets, the firm aided both home and business. They catered to outdoor amusements with their books on sports—bowling and wrestling, calisthenics and yachting. They appealed to a more solitary type of indoor amusement with their series of cheap novels, their "Hand and Pocket Library," narratives of border adventure, detective stories, exploits of celebrated highwaymen, and, at twenty-five cents each, such Prize Novels as *The Midnight Queen* or *The Matricide's Daughter, The Rescued Nun* or *Belle of the Bowery*, tales that doubtless whetted the appetite of parlor and kitchen alike.

At the Centennial Exhibition in Philadelphia the well-known handbooks of Dick and Fitzgerald were on display, with "sample lines of their publications, which go all over the country." Though not always advertised in those terms, the firm actually was, by and large, a mail-order house. It was forced to that status by the very nature of its books, most of which were priced cheaply at thirty cents in paper or fifty cents in boards, and all of which were designed to appeal to families in Kansas or Maine, Illinois or Virginia. One needed only a parlor and a kitchen to subscribe with pleasure to the works issued from Ann Street; it did not matter where the parlor and kitchen were located. It was for that reason that Dick and Fitzgerald took such pains to recommend clarity in mail orders. "We have done a large book trade through the mails. . . . We receive so many letters every day that it is impossible for us to remember the Post-Office, County, and State where any particular person receives books. . . . Put on a plain direction." It was for that reason also that the firm reminded its patrons that "it is easier and cheaper to get books from New York than people generally imagine. You have only to write a few words . . . and the book comes free of postage, and arrives by return mail."

Because it was a mail-order house, Dick and Fitzgerald adopted a rather stringent policy in regard to payments. There was a time when books could be sent C.O.D. from Ann Street, provided five or ten dollars were sent in advance to cover freight charges. For the most part, however, no orders were filled unless sufficient money accompanied them. Remittances were to be made by express or post-office money order, a draft on a New York bank, or cash in a registered letter. Postage stamps would be accepted only if they were clean and covered sums less than one dollar. In addition to their strict policy on payments, the Ann Street firm upheld stringent rules on exchanges. No books could be exchanged, and under no circumstances could they be sent subject to approval. In spite, or perhaps because of these restrictions, the mail-order house flourished, and at their P. O. Box 2975 orders flowed in, while books, free catalogues ("no charge for catalogues or information") and stationery, playing-cards and music were supplied to booksellers and peddlers at lowest wholesale prices, and flowed out "to any part of the United States or Canada." Customers were urged to see how promptly a cash order would be executed by "the great publishing house of Dick and Fitzgerald." The catalogues themselves served as incentives to purchasers, for they were often made as attractive as possible by the inclusion of charming illustrations, delightful cuts depicting card games, banjo playing, puzzles, parlor tricks, etiquette, and even the gentle art of courtship.

Selling books was perhaps simpler for Dick and Fitzgerald than buying them, or the rights to them. When William B. Dick did not himself write the firm's handbooks or collections, he produced them after consultations with experts in the field, or ordered original selections written expressly for the works. The house was always "glad to read manuscripts (which were to be accompanied by a statement of the price demanded) . . . by any author, known or unknown, with a view toward publication." Music, needed in the ten-cent songsters, was published by W. A. Pond or William Hall of New York. Occasionally plates were purchased from such companies as Street and Smith, and occasionally, in spite of the firm's favorable attitude toward international copyright, books were pirated. Interrupted by only one lawsuit brought by an English pugilist, Dick and Fitzgerald went their smooth and merry way of supplying entertainment and self-improvement to the parlors and kitchens of American homes.

Their progress was reflected in the lives of the partners, both of whom were substantial men of affairs. While Lawrence Fitzgerald boasted membership in the Neptune Club along with a close friendship with President Arthur, William B. Dick proceeded to amass a fine dramatic library adorned with extra-illustrated books, and to join such clubs as the Lotos, The Grolier, The Church, and, since he had served as a captain in the Gettysburg Campaign, the Lafayette Post of the G.A.R. A member of St. Bartholomew's parish and a resident of the Park Avenue Hotel, the tall, fair, blue-eyed William B. Dick lent tone to his mail-order house on Ann Street.

Meanwhile, the firm was altered by changes not in its publications but in its personnel. Fitzgerald's death in 1881 was followed by a dissolution of the co-partnership, although William B. Dick continued the business under the same style until his retirement in 1898. It was then that Dick's son, Harris, who was to become one of the anomalies of nature, a "millionaire publisher," took over the affairs of 18 Ann Street, carrying on the traditions established by his father both in his business and his personal life.

Born in 1855, Harris Brisbane Dick had been trained in the ways of Dick and Fitzgerald, and now, as head of the firm, the tall, presentable, mustachioed gentleman continued to compile or edit the later series of card games and reciters first launched by his father. "Trumps" had been altered to "Trumps, Jr." and cribbage to Russian bank, but little else was changed by the stately bachelor who found time for The Union League, The Players, and his fine collection of prints, as well as for the parlor theatricals and letter-writers of Dick and Fitzgerald, and who met with equal ease the demands of the Social Register and of 18 Ann Street.

So, catering to the American hearth and home, the firm continued, aided by such faithful and steadfast employees as Rudolph Behrens and William Train, until Harris Dick died suddenly in the Boston subway in 1916. When the will of the "millionaire publisher" was probated, it was learned not only that he had bequeathed over one million dollars, much of which had stemmed from private sources, to The Metropolitan Museum of Art, but that he had directed his executor to "convert into money . . . the good-will and assets (but not the firm name) of the book publishing business now carried on . . . under the firm name of 'Dick & Fitzgerald.'"

Though the letter of the will was abided by, its spirit was not. The firm of Dick and Fitzgerald was reorganized in 1917 as the Fitzgerald Publishing Corporation, Successor to Dick and Fitzgerald, and as such it continued to do business until 1940, sending forth from Vesey Street and later from East 38th Street, reciters and dream books and amateur theatricals. But the parlor had given way to the playhouse, and, to advance with the times, the new firm issued a series of "Playhouse Plays." For many years, under the guidance of Harris Dick's friends, Arthur Howard Abendroth and Rudolph Behrens, and his cousin, Thomas Leggett, the Fitzgerald Publishing Corporation persisted. It continued for a short time under the aegis of the Walter H. Baker Company, Theodore and Carl G. A. Johnson, President and

Treasurer respectively of that firm, and William M. Sloane, playwright, later of William Sloane Associates, taking over its dramatic publications, and Rudolph Behrens of Danbury, Connecticut, its handbooks. A notation in the *New York Copartnership and Corporation Directory*, however, shows the way the wind was blowing. The firm's capital, which in 1931 had been only $18,000, had risen, under the Johnson brothers, to $50,000 by 1933. By 1934 the firm's capital had fallen to $18,000. In 1940 the Fitzgerald Publishing Corporation was dissolved.

For over eighty years the publications of Dick and Fitzgerald and its successor had brought entertainment to the American home. Doubtless it was because the center of entertainment shifted gradually away from the home that the business declined. The parlor itself has become obsolete, and with it has vanished the need for Fireside Magicians and Parlor Theatricals. 18 Ann Street has vanished, too, engulfed by a branch building of a bank. Still, the stray paper copies priced at thirty cents and bearing the old Dick and Fitzgerald imprint arouse nostalgia for the days of upright pianos and forfeit games, of gallantry shows and innocent sells, of euchre, bezique, quadrilles, and polonaises. When those paper copies can still be found, they help to brush the dust from yesterday's bandbox, revealing a way of life and a state of mind that have become historic. It was for that way of life that the firm of Dick and Fitzgerald existed, and from that way of life that it flourished. Although both have gone, the twentieth century can still recall them, for, in the paper-bound handbooks bearing the Dick and Fitzgerald imprint, yesterday is reenacted. The cast of characters is the family; the time—the latter half of the nineteenth century; the place—the parlor with warmly glowing fireside. And the curtain rises on a nation at home.

Notes on Sources

The Nineteenth-Century American Home

Details are based upon the Dick & Fitzgerald publications themselves. For the quoted remark about the twentieth-century attitude toward entertainment, see Ben Hecht, *A Child of the Century* (New York, 1954), p. 626: "The more we let others sing, dance and perform for us, the more empty we become."

William B. Dick, Lawrence R. Fitzgerald, & Their Early Connections with Burgess & Garrett

American Publishers' Circular and Literary Gazette II:49 (December 6, 1856), p. 749; information from John J. Fitzgerald, City Clerk of Pittsfield, Mass.; "Lawrence R. Fitzgerald," *The American Bookseller* XII:8 (October 15, 1881), p. 237 (courtesy Rollo G. Silver); *New York City Directories* 1853–1858; "Obituary. Lawrence R. Fitzgerald," *The New-York Times* (October 12, 1881), p. 5; "Obituary. Lawrence R. Fitzgerald," *Publishers' Weekly* XX:17 (October 22, 1881), pp. 520 f.; "Obituary. William B. Dick," *New-York Tribune* (September 6, 1901), p. 14; "Obituary.

William Brisbane Dick," *Publishers' Weekly* LX:11 (September 14, 1901), p. 434.

The will of Lawrence R. Fitzgerald, at the Surrogate's Court of the County of New York, gives the date of the co-partnership.

Ann Street

Before the move to No. 18, Ransom Garrett, William B. Dick, and Lawrence R. Fitzgerald are listed in the *New York City Directories* at No. 22 Ann Street. Wesley F. Burgess is listed at the latter address from 1849 to 1854.

For details of Ann Street at the time, see Aaron Mendoza, "Some Associations of Old Ann Street, 1720–1920," *Valentine's Manual of Old New York*, New Series, 1920–1921.

The Home Circle

See *The Home Circle* V:3 (March 1858), *passim* (courtesy Mrs. Dorothea E. Spear, American Antiquarian Society). The periodical is listed under the heading of Newspapers in Trow's *New York City Directory* 1859–1863, with Dick & Fitzgerald as publishers.

The Firm's Publications for the Homes of America

Besides the books themselves, see advertisements in *American Literary Gazette* II:10 (March 15, 1864), p. 366, III:1 (May 2, 1864), p. 33, III:9 (September 1, 1864), p. 269, IV:1 (November 1, 1864), p. 23, IV:4 (December 15, 1864), p. 130, V:4 (June 15, 1865), p. 86, VI:1 (November 1, 1865), p. 28, VII:11 (October 1, 1866), p. 267, VIII:12 (April 15, 1867), p. 367, IX:5 (July 1, 1867), p. 151, XVII:3 (June 1, 1871), p. 82, XVII:9 (September 1, 1871), pp. 272 f.; *American Publishers' Circular and Literary Gazette* VIII:7 (July 1862), p. 74; Charles Bragin, *Dime Novels Bibliography 1860–1928* (Brooklyn, 1938), p. 28; *Dick & Fitzgerald Catalogue* (New York, n.d.); *Dick & Fitzgerald's Descriptive Book Catalogue* (New York, n.d.); *Dick's Descriptive Catalogue of Dramas, Comedies, Farces* (New York, n.d.); *The Home Circle* V:3 (March 1858), *passim*; information from Albert Johannsen; Warren Elbridge Price, *Price's Catalogue of Paper Covered Books* (New York, 1905), p. 58; *Publishers' Trade List Annual* for 1875, 1876, 1886, 1888; *Publishers' Weekly* VI:24 (December 12, 1874), p. 661, Christmas Number, 1875, p. 853, IX:5 (January 29, 1876), p. 146, XII:13 (September 29, 1877), p. 382, XXXV:8 (February 23, 1889), p. 347, XLIII:4 (January 28, 1893), p. 247, XLV:4 (January 27, 1894), p. 73; R. H. Shove, *Cheap Book Production in the United States, 1870 To 1891* (Urbana, Ill., 1937), p. 140; *Uniform Trade List Circular* I:6 (April 1867), pp. 280–87; Harry B. Weiss, *Oneirocritica Americana* (New York, 1944), p.15.

Quoted passages appear in *Dick's Little Dialogues for Little People* (New York: Dick & Fitzgerald, [1890]), pp. 3 f.; *Dick's Original Album Verses and Acrostics* (New York: Dick & Fitzgerald, [1879]), Preface, p. 4; *Dick's Society Letter-Writer for Ladies* (New York: Dick & Fitzgerald, [1884]), p. 19; *Fireside Games; for Winter Evening Amusement* (New York: Dick & Fitzgerald, [1859]), p. 3; *The Home Circle* V:3 (March 1858), pp. 2, 3; Leger D. Mayne [William B. Dick], *What Shall We Do To-Night?* (New York: Dick & Fitzgerald, [1873]), Preface, p. 5.

The Centennial Exhibition

Publishers' Weekly X:1 (July 1, 1876), p. 19.

Firm Policy & Mail-Order Techniques

Dick & Fitzgerald Catalogue (New York, n.d.); *Dick's Descriptive Catalogue of Dramas* (New York, n.d.); *Publishers' Trade-List Annual* for 1875; *Uncle Josh's Trunk-Full of Fun* (New York: Dick & Fitzgerald, [1869]), verso of title-page, pp. 2, 7, 12, 19, 58.

Firm Catalogues

The undated list of Dick & Fitzgerald publications deposited in the Library of the University of Missouri, for example, is charmingly illustrated.

Firm's Methods of Obtaining Material

The *American Hoyle*, for example, was a result of the consultation method [see *American Literary Gazette* IV:4 (December 15, 1864), p. 130], while *Dick's Diverting Dialogues* (New York: Dick & Fitzgerald, [1888]) contained material "written expressly" for the work. Other methods of obtaining plates, etc., are revealed in *Dick's Descriptive Catalogue of Dramas;* A. G. Doughty, "Haliburton," *Transactions of the Royal Society of Canada*, 3rd Series, Vol. III, Sec. II (1909), p. 62; "Judge Gildersleeve Decides in Favor of Dick and Fitzgerald," *Publishers' Weekly* XLV:20 (May 19, 1894), p. 739; *Publishers' Weekly* XXV:13 (March 29, 1884), p. 381.

Personal Details regarding Dick & Fitzgerald

For such information the author is indebted to Margaret B. Harris, Charlotte Haynes of The Church Club, George L. McKay of The Grolier Club, and Andrew H. A. Thompson of the Lafayette Camp No.140.

See also The American Art Association, *The Libraries of the Late Harris B. Dick and William B. Dick* (New York, January 24 and 25, 1918); announcement of Neptune Club regarding Fitzgerald's funeral in *The New-York Times* (October 12, 1881), p. 5; *The War of the Rebellion: . . . Official Records* (Washington, 1889), Series I, Vol. XXVII, Part 2, p. 215; J. G. Wilson, *The Memorial History of the City of New-York* (New York, 1893), IV, 130.

Dissolution of Co-Partnership & Dick's Retirement

Publishers' Weekly XX:23 (December 3, 1881), p. 799, LIII:17 (February 12, 1898), p. 349.

Harris B. Dick: His Personal & Business Life

For this information the author is indebted to Rudolph Behrens, Percy L. Hance, W. M. Ivins, Jr., John Knight of The Players, Aaron and the late Mark Mendoza, Harry C. Vail, Superintendent of the Green-Wood Cemetery, Brooklyn, and F. B. Whitlock of The Union League Club.

See also *Last Will and Testament of Harris Brisbane Dick, Deceased*, p. 3 (courtesy Stewart & Shearer); Metropolitan Museum of Art, *Forty-eighth Annual Report of the Trustees* (New York, 1918), pp. 12, 24 f.; newspaper clippings on Dick Bequest (courtesy Metropolitan Museum of Art); "Obituary Notes. Harris B. Dick," *The New-York Times* (September 22, 1916), p. 7; "Obituary Notes. Harris Brisbane Dick," *Publishers' Weekly* XC:14 (September 30, 1916), pp. 1112 f.; *Publishers'*

Weekly XC:15 (October 7, 1916), p. 1161; *Social Register, New York* XII:1 (November 1897), p. 108.

At his death, Harris B. Dick bequeathed to The Metropolitan Museum of Art $1,069,298.98.

Fitzgerald Publishing Corporation

For details regarding this firm the author is indebted to Percy L. Hance, Theodore Johnson, the late Mark Mendoza, and William Sloane.

See also *Fitzgerald Publishing Corporation's Descriptive Catalogue of Plays, Entertainments and Books* (New York, n.d.); *New York City Directory* 1920/1921; *New York Copartnership and Corporation Directory* 1933 and 1934; "Obituary Notes. Arthur Howard Abendroth," *Publishers' Weekly* CI:6 (February 11, 1922), p. 358. The Minutes of the Fitzgerald Publishing Corporation are deposited with the Walter H. Baker Company, Boston. Mr. Theodore Johnson, formerly of the Walter H. Baker Company, writes: ". . . in 1931 the firm's capital was $18,000. By 1933 it had risen to $50,000. . . . One primary reason why we closed the New York office is that we found, through experience over several years, that we were merely competing with ourselves in publishing a play list both from New York and Boston."

Rudolph Behrens continued the Dick & Fitzgerald handbook line at Danbury, Connecticut, under the firm name of Behrens Publishing Company, Publisher of Dick & Fitzgerald Hand Books, and his son continued the Behrens Publishing Company.

7

"Organs" of the Book Trade

Phrenology and the Book Arts

I NSTEAD OF consulting Freudian psychiatrists or vocational guidance coun-
selors, the nineteenth-century job applicant had an opportunity denied us
today. He could knock at a phrenologist's door, remove his hat, slick back his
hair—and have his head examined. His faculties could be measured—his
Amativeness and Mirthfulness, his Adhesiveness and Conjugality. His promise
as poet or painter, doctor or engineer, printer or bookseller could be
"scientifically" extrapolated.

In the course of researching my recent book, *Heads & Headlines: The
Phrenological Fowlers* (Norman, Oklahoma, 1971), which explores the activities of America's most popular firm of phrenologist-publishers, I came upon a
fascinating volume by the Fowlers' chief examiner. Nelson Sizer, who applied
phrenology to every phase of life, applied it also to the book trade and in the
course of writing his *What To Do, And Why; and How to Educate Each Man for
His Proper Work: describing Seventy-five Trades and Professions, and the Talents
and Temperaments Required for Each* (New York, 1874), he devoted several
delightful passages to the talents essential for gentlemen (and ladies) of the
printing press. Here they are, and any bookseller-printer-papermaker-engraver-
editor who does not measure up to these yardsticks had better have his head
examined!

Book-Selling

This business requires a man of decided Mental temperament, with a
good degree of the Vital. He need not have much of the Motive temperament, for it is not hard, heavy work, but he should have a clear, sharp mind,
a taste for books and literature. The more intelligence he has, the better he
would be capable of comprehending the contents and quality of a book, and
of teaching or impressing these facts upon customers. If he is competent to

Reprinted from *AB Bookman's Weekly* (April 1, 1974): 1315–1323.

write, it is well. If he were a poet or an orator, he would succeed all the better, because he has to come in contact with that kind of people who make books and enjoy books. If he could have all the talents which any of them can be supposed to possess, he could meet each person on his own plane. A man who stands behind a bookseller's counter, and regards books as so much more merchandise, as if he were selling mustard done up in bottles, is not fitted for his position. A Bookseller should be able to run through the contents of a book, and read here and there a page, and thus come *en rapport* with the book.

To be a successful bookseller, one should love books for what they contain, and know how to talk them up, thereby creating an interest in the minds of buyers. The most eminent publishing houses have members of their firms who are writers, good critics of book-making, and are thus able to scan matter offered for publication, and to meet authors and readers intelligently.

A man should understand literature and science in order to be successful in the book business, especially as a publisher, on the same principle as one should know any other article of merchandise. The cloth manufacturer is the best cloth seller. The tanner becomes the best shoe-dealer, and one who has served his time at carpentry is just the man to keep a lumber yard, for he understands carpenters and the materials they work with. The time will come, we fancy, when clerks will be received into book houses in pursuance of the acquisition of a good rank in scholarship. They ought also to possess enough of mechanical and artistic talent to understand the quality of the work constituting the make-up of a book including the paper, printing, engraving, and binding, and also clear, far-seeing mercantile capability,—in short, good business talent and managing ability. A publisher and bookseller should be a first-class man.

Paper-Making

A man to be a thorough paper-maker needs to be a chemist, that he may learn how to clean the stock properly, for the processes are quite numerous and complicated. He needs to understand machinery, and have a nice sense of criticism, both with eye and hand. When the paper is running off from the machine, an experienced paper-maker by letting the sheet pass between his fingers will judge of the thickness of the paper so nicely that he can detect a variation of four ounces in a ream of sixty pounds weight, whether it be too thick or too thin, increasing the flow of pulp, or decreasing it accordingly.

Paper-making is a great trade, and, of course, is useful; but, like the machinist's business, it circumscribes a man's liberty, and makes it necessary for him to work for others by the week, and his wages day by day is the measure of his prosperity; whereas, if one is a tinsmith, or blacksmith, or cooper, or carpenter, he can set up the business for himself, because it does not take a great deal of capital, and can be conducted in a small way profitably; while the woolen factory, machine ship, iron foundry, or paper-mill requires a large amount of capital, must have a superintendent of each room, and the rest of the men must necessarily be subordinates.

Book-Binding

Common, straightforward book-work is a trade requiring practical talent, fair mechanical judgment, rapidity of action, and tidiness. In the binding of fine books the trade becomes more an art. But for all kinds of work in this line, whether it be what is called job, fancy, or staple work, one requires patience, attention, quick perception, order, activity, and a kind of energy which keeps the faculties at work to the best of their ability. The book-binder can work by rule when he has established his pattern or style, and has his guages [*sic*] set. When he has to make a thousand, or ten thousand, books exactly alike in appearance, the work becomes monotonous and almost automatic. The book-binder needs quickness of mind, rapidity of motion, artistic taste, and energy to secure success. In some styles of work it is difficult to have fresh, cool air, and though most of the work is not heavy or laborious, it can hardly be called a very healthful trade.

Printing

The setting of type should be done mainly by men who are not able to knock about in the rough work of life or by women. It is light work, and that which is plain requires simply a quick eye, a quick hand, and a good English education, especially in orthography. The secret of successful type-setting is this: that when one type is being adjusted, the eye of the compositor shall look to the box containing the next letter, and fix the eye on a particular letter, so as to see which end up, and which side first it lies, and having got hold of it he need have no further thought, his hand will do the rest, while his eye selects a letter in the next box, and thus he will throw in the types as fast as he can pick them up. But if he give his entire attention to the type which is being adjusted, before he looks up the next, he learns to "duck and bob," makes many false motions, and does not work nearly so fast as one who lets his eye precede his hand. It requires large individuality, to set type rapidly, and large Size, to give the idea of proportion and distance, not only in reaching for the type, but in spacing and "justifying" the lines.

To follow the printing business, a person needs large Continuity, to give a quiet, persistent, plodding patience, without which he will become nervous, restless, and either quit the Confining business in disgust, or accomplish little if he remain. As this pursuit requires an abundance of light, printing offices are usually at the top of the building, which must be full of windows, giving to the printer an abundance of air and light, which promote health. Printers are generally intelligent, and a steady man who is adapted to the business may retain his health and earn good wages. Working nights on morning newspapers soon breaks down all but those who are very tough. The Mental-Motive temperament is best for this trade.

Stereotyping requires a quick eye, sharp criticism, carefulness, rapidity of motion, and in some departments of it considerable physical strength, especially in shaving the plates.

The printer ought to be of a calm, patient, and unruffled disposition; for the whims of authors, bad manuscript, bad grammar, and sometimes worse sense, with unreasonable alterations of proof-sheets, overrunning of matter, and then being scolded for extra charges, are calculated to call into exercise all the Christian graces if they are possessed; or, if these are absent, something quite of the other sort. Writers for the press ought to spend three months at least at the case to learn the feasibility or possibility of required changes and sources of vexation caused by slashing alterations after columns or pages are in type. An experienced type-setter will alter matter, changing phraseology in such a way as to cause little trouble to the compositor. Another would add a word or two, causing the overrunning of a whole page. Every editor or habitual writer should, for his own sake, as well as that of the compositor, first learn to be a compositor himself.

Printing can be done by women as well as by men. Certainly they can do the type-setting with quite as much taste and skill. We think at least one-half of all the type-setting should be done by women, if not eight-tenths of it. We have known among them some very active and successful type-setters, and we see no reason why the nimble fingers and delicate touch of women should not be thus employed.

Engraving

The steel engraver, like the die-sinker, requires accuracy of eye and fineness of execution. In the main, his work is quite artistic. He needs quiet nerves, a strong, clear eye, and a very steady hand. A blue-eyed, sandy-haired, round-cheeked, ruddy-faced boy, who would prefer to drive a horse, or play a game at ball, rather than to sit either at books or business, should never undertake to be an engraver, for he would run away from himself, if he did not from his master. He would almost "die daily," and feel like an eagle chained to a rock. An engraver should be a man who likes sedentary habits.

Die-Sinking, like engraving, is an art, yet it is called a trade. No man should touch this work who has not large Imitation, Form, Size, Order, and Ideality. He needs first-rate eyesight, and large Continuity, to give him patience, for he must sometimes work for days on a field not larger than a silver dollar. A man of dark complexion, with the Mental rather than the Vital temperament, should follow this business.

Job Printing

Thus far we have considered the printer as a mere straightforward type-setter on plain book or newspaper work. The job printer must be an artist as well as a mechanic to produce a handsome job. Constructiveness, Imitation, and Ideality are required to fit a man for such work. In cards, circulars, title-pages, and show-bills nice taste and critical judgment are required to harmonize different styles of letter and give a fine effect to the whole. The process of printing or doing the press-work is really another trade, and those who use the hand press on plate printing or other fine work require decided mechanical skill and correct artistic taste. Machine press-work requires a good knowledge of machinery, with great watchfulness and prudence.

Wood Engraving

Wood engraving is different from that of steel or copper; the material is softer; the work is done more rapidly, and there is not so much danger of spoiling the job as in steel and copper work. The wood engraver must work by the eye and judgment rather than by rule. We have been informed, by an eminent wood engraver, that he has found out, by experience, that if a boy is fond of mathematics, and therefore feels the necessity to demonstrate everything in connection with his work, he will never succeed in wood engraving. So firm is he in this idea, that when a boy applies to him to become an apprentice, he inquires if he is good in figures and mathematics. If the boy blushingly confesses to a deficiency in this respect, the engraver considers it a favorable indication, and is willing to try him. To illustrate the point: a father brought his son to me for an examination. They looked sad, as if the world went ill with them. The father wanted to know what the boy could do best. The reply was, "Almost anything that can be done by rule. But a trade like wood engraving he would not succeed in, because that can not be done by rules and scales and gauges, but by taste and judgment." They exchanged smiles, and at the close of the examination informed me that the boy had been six months in an engraver's office, and had that day been dismissed because he would not, or could not, work by the eye; but in making tints or shading, he wanted a fixed guage [*sic*] or scale, so that it could be done, as it were, by machinery, or by demonstration and measurement. He was recommended to become a carpenter, where he could make his lines and work by them; and at once showed skill and judgment, and rapidly became successful.

Wood-engraving is practiced by woman successfully. The work can be taken home from the office and done at one's residence, for it has all to be done by the eye and hand of the engraver. Supervision, while the work is in progress, is not required. The proof determines what has been done, and how. Woman is endowed with great fondness for pictures, and naturally adopts something of an artistic character. Whatever is ornamental attracts her, and calls out her taste and skill.

Editorship

The question is frequently asked, "What abilities should be possessed, and what books should be studied, to enable one to become a first-class composer and correspondent for a daily or weekly journal?"

To be a first-class editor or correspondent, one ought to know as much of the subject-matter on which he writes as can be known; certainly he ought to know more respecting it than those who read his articles.

We may therefore say that an editor ought to have a comprehensive intellect, which signifies, first, a large development of the perceptive organs, which give prominence to the brow and lower part of the forehead. These faculties enable their possessor to gather knowledge rapidly and accurately; to see all that is going on, and to appreciate whatever is related. They give also the basis of scientific information or power to acquire the necessary knowledge for scientific subjects, that he may be intelligent in that direction. These faculties also enable one to acquire knowledge from books and retain it.

The editor should have, secondly, the reasoning or philosophical faculties well developed, that he may comprehend the logic of subjects and the law of things. The majority of American editors will be found with the lower half of the forehead more amply developed than the upper half. They are fact-gatherers rather than thinkers, and the result of their labor is very apt to contain much crude matter. Many editors are much more like the farm-rake, which gathers up wheat and tares, hay, thistles, and thorns together, than like the winnowing mill, which separates the chaff from the wheat. As evidence that the generality of editors are mere observers and not deep thinkers, it may be remarked that if one of the editorial fraternity happens to possess large reasoning organs, and ventures to reach forward in the realm of ideas much in advance of his age, he is laughed at through many of the newspapers as being a "philosopher," a "dreamer," a "speculative theorist." If all editors and newspaper writers had large Causality and Comparison, they would not jeer and laugh at a man who was inclined to originality of mind, and boldly struck out into the untrodden realms of thought.

In one aspect of the subject, the editor is required to be merely an arranger of the matter produced by others—a digester, a critic, a compiler. One who edits a great Review is not expected, for he has not the time, and probably not the varied learning and information necessary, to write well upon all subjects which go to make up the contents of the Review. One man has spent his life in the field of chemistry, another in mining, another in metaphysics, another in mechanics, another in medicine, another in agriculture, another in political economy; and these several subjects can be presented by those who have made them a specialty, respectively, more clearly and forcibly than any one man can be expected to do. But an editor of such a Review ought to have a first-class head and generous culture, so that he may estimate the labors of these special coadjutors; otherwise, if he were acting as a mere bricklayer, putting in place the productions of others, he would be likely to give to the world a good deal of crude matter.

A political editor needs an excellent memory to hold the general knowledge which is requisite to the editorial profession, that he may remember the history of politicians and legislators, the history of nations, of science, of literature and law, and also that he may remember what he himself has said and done years before. An editor should be able to carry in his memory all that he has ever written and published, so that he shall be consistent, and that one year's experience shall give him light for the next year's labor. But we would not make a man a slave to the past through a retentive memory. We would have him open to progress, to improvement, to new truths, and to reforms; but we would have his memory sufficiently tenacious not to forget the pit from which he had been digged—the old errors and ignorances in which he had at some time floundered. We have known reformers who forgot the ignorance and weakness from which they had emerged, and who seemed to delight in charging with wickedness and folly those who occupied the same position which, but a few years before, they had left. This is as ridiculous as it is for a man who, by accident or energy, has made himself rich, and then turns around and abuses and denounces "poor people" because they are poor. It is both ridiculous and pitiable to read the editorials of some newspapers, to see how to-day subjects and persons will be petted and praised who, five years ago, were vilified and denounced. A better memory of the past should serve to correct such folly in the present. Besides, an editor needs conscience in strong measure. He wields a wondrous power, and can be a tyrant if he is so disposed. An editor who lacks conscience, and has excessive selfishness and severity, can slaughter reputation, can plant thorns in the pillow of innocence without incurring legal penalty, and without the power of undoing his own mischief. An editor, therefore should be truthful, just, upright; he should have large Benevolence, so as to be tender of other people's feelings and interests.

Moral Courage Required

An editor should also have courage—no position needs greater; having a selfish world to deal with, he should be willing to utter the truth when justice demands that an unpleasant truth be spoken, and then to back it up. A want of courage in an editor is as bad as a lack of courage in a soldier; for while cowardice or treason in a soldier may cause the loss of a battle, a lack of courage or conscience in an editor may poison the public morals, and, perhaps, contribute to the loss of a battle as well. An editor should have large Language, that he may write with ease and facility; he should have good taste, that his style may be smooth and elegant, and that his writings shall not offend the tastes of his readers. We would not give him excessive Benevolence and Ideality; while lack of Combativeness, Firmness, and Self-Esteem renders the editor pusillanimous, and leads him to soften the truth until its very back-bone is withdrawn; but there is such a thing as manly courage, unyielding determination, serene dignity, and unflinching justice, combined with kindness, affection, and proper consideration for the rights, prejudices, and even the ignorance of others.

Men of power should carry that power gently; one does not lose his vantage ground, who really possesses it, by trying a gentle method of accomplishing results. He who has a hundred cannon at his back can afford to be polite to an opponent, and request the favor of a compliance with his wishes. A general who is capable of backing up his demands, need not insult a foe when he requests his surrender. An editor who has the best of a controversy loses nothing by being modest; he who has a clincher for an argument can afford to suggest it, instead of rudely cramming it down his opponent's throat.

An editor also needs large Cautiousness and Secretiveness, so that he shall not rashly adopt any course, or imprudently lead others into wrong by the expression of undigested opinions. There is quite as much wisdom in the silence which large Secretiveness imposes as there is in dashing courage which large Combativeness inspires; but with large Benevolence and Strong social affection, the editor will be inspired by general good-will to the weak and the wicked, as well as to the good and the noble. This good-will will give him a tendency to put the best face on everything; to remember that the accused may have a good defense; that there is generally another side to every bad story. A rash, unkindly man, as editor, will hunt the accused before he has time to enter his plea of "not guilty," or to "put himself upon his country" for defense.

As to the works which should be studied to aid one to become a first-class writer, we may say what we have often said to persons who were receiving private phrenological examinations at our hands, viz., that an editor, a lawyer, or a minister should know everything that can be known, in order to completely fulfill the duties of their respective offices. All literature, all science, all history will aid the editor, and the more he can have of general culture the better.

In the first place, he should be a good English scholar or a master of his mother tongue, whatever that may be; if he can have classical learning, all the better. He should be well read in the history of nations, and especially in the history of individuals; for if such history be properly written, it will open the character, and motive, and purpose, and effort of historical persons, as well as reveal the result.

The editor should understand human nature physiologically, phrenologically, and theologically. It is not enough that he should study external things; he should study men, mind, the inner life of humanity, that he may know to whom he is talking, as well as what he is talking about.

Moreover, and finally, an editor should be imbued with a religious spirit, that he may ever remember that the noise and bustle, the excitements and strifes of today are of less consequence than those subjects which, while they have their roots in time, have the life to come for their complete development. An irreligious witticism may raise a laugh and give its author a momentary popularity, but that witticism may sting the heart of innocence; may blunt the moral susceptibility of some weak brother who would otherwise lead a virtuous life. For if the editor be endowed with sufficient wisdom to do his intellectual labor well, and a sufficient amount of moral and religious feeling to desire the greatest good of the greatest number for time and for eternity, he will feel that his publication is like a voice that reaches to the ends of the earth, and not only speaks to the human race of today, but that it shall continue to speak when the hand that penned it is still, and it becomes a record for all time. A clergyman may chance to speak to five hundred people, a lecturer to a similar number, but an editor may speak to millions; and his thoughts may be copied for the reading of other millions, besides remaining in print for coming generations to peruse.

The Mystery of the Leon Brothers

E<small>VER SINCE</small> the appearance, on June 13, 1886, of an article in the New York *Tribune* entitled "Romance of the Leon Brothers," that firm of New York booksellers has been endowed with a quality of mystery which has continued to tantalize bibliophiles. Like a great many mysteries, that of the Leons may now be proved somewhat overrated. If some are born to mystery, and others achieve mystery, the Leon brothers, quite undeservedly, had mystery thrust upon them.

The *Tribune* article, reprinted in *Publishers' Weekly*, stated: "Bibliophiles will learn with some surprise of the sale of the valuable library of rare books . . . collected by the Leon brothers in their store under the Fifth Avenue Hotel. . . . The three brothers belong to a Polish family. During the Revolution of 1863, in Poland, the political prejudices of the family brought them into disrepute with the Emperor of Russia, and one of the brothers was an exile in Siberia for twelve years, and the others were imprisoned. The youngest brother upon his release came to this city and opened a small cigar-store in East Washington Square. He was a great student, and then formed the nucleus of the large collection of books which was afterward placed in charge of the brother next in age, who came to this country after his return from exile in 1875. A few months later the eldest brother leased the estates of the family for a dozen years and also came here. It was then that the Twenty-third Street book store was opened. The leases in Poland are now about to expire and the eldest brother will return to Poland to take charge of the estates. The brothers acknowledge that 'Leon' is an assumed name, but they refuse to divulge their real name. Leon is the Christian name of one of the brothers, and it was adopted as the surname in this country for convenience." [1]

A cursory examination into the careers of the Leon brothers served

Reprinted from *Publishers' Weekly* (November 17, 1945): 2228–2232.

only to heighten the sense of mystery attached to them. The most important fact connected with the firm was its issuance of a remarkable *Catalogue of First Editions of American Authors* in 1885.[2] How, then, could one account for the interest of "three" Polish exiles in the specialized field of American bibliography? Further, how could one explain the apparently sudden appearance of a firm of Washington Square cigar dealers in the guise of a rare book establishment in the Fifth Avenue Hotel? Was one catalogue only associated with the Leons? Finally, what was the meaning of the almost immediate collapse of the brothers, so that after two years on the Avenue they returned to Washington Square and then vanished altogether from New York directories and New York history?

Since the brief residence of the Leons in the Fifth Avenue Hotel coincided with the appearance of their *Catalogue of First Editions of American Authors*, the answer seemed to be that the brothers were merely handling the library of some unknown collector who wished to dispose of his stock secretly. Who was this unknown collector? The few extant letters in the New York Public Library written by the Leons to Gordon L. Ford[3] hinted at a possible connection with that noted bibliophile. The mystery had become more tantalizing than ever.

Where speculation served only to increase the mystery, fact brought about its disappearance. The facts, then, must be examined. In 1878, Adam G. Leon, a refugee from Poland, set up as a "segar" dealer on Washington Square East.[4] A few years later he was joined by his brother, Francis G. Leon, who began business as a bookseller at the same address. The brothers remained at Washington Square for a decade, the one superintending the cigar trade, the other specializing in books. The mystery of the "Leon Brothers" collapses when one realizes that first of all only one Leon, Francis, was actually identified with the book business.

Francis G. Leon was a Polish nobleman, a cultivated scholar with a fine mind and a deep admiration for America. Tall, thin, black-bearded,[5] he plied his trade in Washington Square quite unaware of the mystery that was to develop about him. Nor did he wait for the advent of an unknown collector before he issued his famous 1885 catalogue. In May, 1882, Leon published his first catalogue of *American and Foreign Books, Old and New*.[6] Unlike the celebrated catalogue of American first editions, this first list was highly generalized, including works in agriculture and architecture, bibliography and fine arts, medicine and science, industry and theology. Not forgetting his Polish background, Leon included several books on Russia, Poland, and the Slavonian races. The catalogue, arranged alphabetically by subject and author, was not particularly remarkable. It offered, among more than a thousand items, a few incunabula such as the *Interpretatio in Syllium Italicum* of Petrus Marsus (Venice, 1483) at $8, and the *Opera* of Alexander de Imola (Venice, 1491–3) at $20. The first edition of Raleigh's *History of the World* was very reasonable at $7.50, but at the same price a signed letter of Mrs.

Surratt, "who was hang [sic] after the murder of . . . Lincoln," indicated that Leon was not too optimistic about his Americana. Most of the latter consisted of second-rate nineteenth century works neither unusual nor particularly reasonable. Ten per cent discount, to be used in the selection of other books, was offered to buyers who made a purchase of more than $20. Correspondence was announced in English, French, Polish, Spanish, Russian, Italian, and German. Books might be bound (for the Leons at this period had also entered business as stationers) in cloth or morocco at prices ranging from fifty cents to four dollars. Finally, all information about new or rare books would be cheerfully furnished by the polyglot Pole with a scholarly taste for literature. In September, 1882, Leon reissued his catalogue, and by the fall of 1883 had produced three supplements which brought the items to a total of nearly two thousand.[7] Another apparent mystery collapses when one realizes that Leon had had experience in compiling catalogues long before his famous work on American first editions.

Doubtless having enjoyed some success with his preliminary catalogues, and having decided to specialize in American works, Francis Leon left his brother Adam to continue the cigar business and on January 1, 1884, moved to 3 West 23rd Street, at the same time retaining "the old stand" on Washington Square.[8] In the vault on the 23rd Street side of the Fifth Avenue Hotel several shops had been constructed, and there, at Place Number 3, Leon set up his bookstore. As he ascended the wide steps leading from the cellar shop, the literary Pole found himself in good company, for he shared the street with E. P. Dutton, Henry Holt, Putnam's, and other noted booksellers and publishers.

Two Other Catalogues Issued by Leon during 1884

During his brief Fifth Avenue period Leon flourished with a new store, a new letterhead, and a new and significant interest in American first editions. Though he issued at least two catalogues in 1884, one of books relating to history, philosophy, social sciences, etc., and one of books relating to America,[9] the dealer's preoccupation with American firsts had begun to crystallize. In *Publishers' Weekly* he proceeded to list his desiderata,[10] all Americana, notably the works of Franklin, in whom Leon was particularly interested, as well as volumes by Hamilton, Hawthorne, Longfellow, Lowell, and Whittier. In all cases he wished first editions quoted. To the American Antiquarian Society, and doubtless to other libraries, he sent requests for duplicates, especially firsts of Longfellow, Poe, Hawthorne, Bryant, Barlow, Irving, Lowell, and Whittier.[11] By November of 1884 the catalogue to which Leon owes his fame today was in preparation. "With the exception of Harris's privately printed index," it would be "the first attempt of its kind in American literature."[12] Persons wishing to dispose of first editions of American authors from Aldrich to Wolcott, from Barlow to Willis, would find the dealer a ready customer at fair prices.

American First Editions Catalogue Appeared in 1885

On July 4, 1885, the *Catalogue of First Editions of American Authors* was announced as "just out." [13] It was the first catalogue to be devoted in its entirety to what were then considered American first editions as distinguished from Americana, and thus in a sense it was the first bibliography of American first editions. Its publication was an event, and the work still marks a milestone in the history of American bookselling and bibliography. [14]

Two editions were offered to the public, a deluxe large paper edition on Whatman paper, interleaved and bound in half morocco at $2, and an unbound edition in an etched cover at $1. The catalogue contained the names of over three hundred authors with as complete a list of their works as could be assembled, regardless of whether the items were then in stock. Over 1,500 items were listed, aggregating nearly $6,000 with prices ranging from $1 for Cable's *Old Creole Days* to $75 for Bancroft's *History of the United States*. The greatest number of works by any single author was 71 by W. G. Simms, Longfellow being given second place with 55, and Whittier making a close third with 53. Among others represented in quantity were Mrs. Sigourney (51), Bayard Taylor and Cooper (45 each), Holmes (38), Emerson (37), and Hawthorne (34). Among the 32 Merle Johnson "High Spots" included in the catalogue were *Huckleberry Finn* (offered at $2.75), *The Last of the Mohicans* ($3), *The Scarlet Letter* ($12.50), *Evangeline* ($25), *The Biglow Papers* ($9), *Uncle Tom's Cabin* ($5), *Walden* ($4.25), *Leaves of Grass* ($15), and *Snow-Bound* ($1.25). In addition, the list offered such notable items as *The Spy* ($5), Lowell's *Class Poem* ($15), and Poe's *Tamerlane* (unpriced). The entries were so far from complete that it is impossible today to ascertain accurately whether all the works offered as first editions were actually firsts. Some errors are obvious, such as the New York imprint for *Tom Sawyer*, and the incorrect dating of Curtis' *Prue and I* (cited as 1857). It was, though Leon did not so state, the first American and not the first edition of Jefferson's *Notes on the State of Virginia* that he offered at $3.50. Though there were considerable gaps in the list, for example, the omission of *Moby-Dick*, and though only about forty per cent of the items would today be considered literary first editions, the Leon catalogue served as an incentive to the collection of American firsts. The compiler supplied a gap in American book collecting and turned the minds of collectors from Caxton and Shakespeare, Hugo and Montaigne, to Franklin and Irving, Poe and Longfellow.

The 1885 Catalogue Won a Noteworthy Reception

The press responded to the efforts of Francis Leon. The catalogue, according to *The Literary World*, would be "consulted . . . by all students of American literary commodities." Its publication was "a sign of the times." *Bookmart* found it the "most satisfactory and complete list" that had yet been published, while the New York *World* announced it as "an indispensably valuable manual." From *The Critic* to *The Evening Post*, from *The Nation* to the *London Publishers' Circular* the reception was noteworthy.[15] Francis G. Leon had made his name in America.

He had also made connections with the most respected collectors of the day in New York. Everyone bought from him, and he in turn bought from everyone who would sell. His brief correspondence with Gordon L. Ford, preserved at the New York Public Library, indicates that he offered that noted bibliophile $30 for firsts of Whitman, Whittier, Holmes, and Longfellow. Ford apparently sold his first edition of *Leaves of Grass* to Leon for $15, at which price the item had previously been offered in the *Catalogue of First Editions*. Leon was fair, but had an eye to business, for in the same letter he requested permission to visit Ford on Sunday to look over his books.[16]

By 1891 Leon & Brother Was Listed as Out of Business

It was probably not long after the famous catalogue had been issued that Leon was informed that his estates in Poland would be restored to him. The final activities of his New York life are those of a man who is preparing to settle his business and leave his adopted country. The store under the Fifth Avenue Hotel was given up, and Francis Leon returned to Washington Square, where Adam kept house along with his retail tobacco trade. Though books were still offered for sale at Washington Square from 1886 to 1888, Francis Leon was disposing of most of his stock by auction, notably in the sale conducted by Bangs in June of 1886.[17] By 1891, when *The American Catalogue* was issued, the firm of Leon & Brother was listed as out of business.[18]

All the mysteries, then, but one, have evaporated. Not three Polish exiles, but one was associated with the book trade. His appearance as a Fifth Avenue dealer was not the sudden advent of an unknown, but an accomplishment to which he had gradually risen after some years of bookselling on Washington Square. Not one catalogue, but several were issued by him. His interest in Americana was that of a scholarly gentleman who deeply admired the country where he had sought refuge. His business did not collapse; he merely abandoned it when he learned of the opportunity to return to his native home. One mystery only still clings to

Francis G. Leon, that of his name. Speculation, sobered by so many facts, need not run riot at the possibilities suggested by an assumed name. Leon's own name was probably unpronounceable by our standards. The surmise that his last name began with "G.," the middle initial of Adam and Francis, may be entertained without leading to deeper and darker mysteries. If indeed there was a third brother, he supplied nothing to the book business beyond his first name. If the romance of the Leon Brothers is less romantic, and their mystery less mysterious than the eager bibliophile had expected, the place of Francis G. Leon in the history of American bibliography is firm and sound. The searcher after bibliographical mysteries would do well to follow in Mr. Leon's own footsteps, and be "indefatigable in his inquiries after an answer to the only question that at all concerns him; viz.—'Which is the Princeps Editio, and which is not?'"[19]

Notes

1. *Publishers' Weekly* XXIX:751 (June 19, 1886), pp. 779–780.

2. Leon & Brother, *Catalogue of First Editions of American Authors*, New York, 1885.

3. Leon & Brother to Gordon L. Ford, January 25, 1886, February 2, 1886, February 5, and February 15, 1886. The letters dated January 25, 1886 and February 5 are inserted in Gordon L. Ford's copy of the Leon Catalogue of 1885 now owned by the New York Public Library. The other letters are in the Manuscript Room of the New York Public Library, and were examined through the courtesy of Robert W. Hill.

4. For this and subsequent information regarding the address of the Leons, see Trow's *New York City Directory, 1878–1886*, and Phillips' *Business Directory of New York City, 1879–1888*.

5. For this, as well as other points of information about Leon, the writer is indebted to Lathrop C. Harper.

6. Leon & Brother, Catalogue I, *American and Foreign Books, Old and New*, May, 1882.

7. Leon & Brother, *American and Foreign Books*, September, 1882; First Supplement, September 1882; Second Supplement, January 20, 1883; Third Supplement, Fall 1883.

8. *Publishers' Weekly* XXV:623 (January 5, 1884), p. 13.

9. Leon & Brother, *Catalogue of Books Relating to History, Memoirs, Philosophy, Religion, Social, Economical and Political Sciences*, 1884, and *Catalogue of Books Relating to America*, 1884 (Courtesy Clarence S. Brigham, American Antiquarian Society).

10. *Publishers' Weekly* XXVI:667 (November 8, 1884), XXVII:698 (June 13, 1885), XXVIII:701 (July 4, 1885).

11. Leon & Brother to E. M. Barton, American Antiquarian Society, April 23, 1884, January 15, 19, 23, April 2, May 10, July 15, 20, 24, 30, August 6, and December 21, 1885 (Courtesy Clarence S. Brigham, American Antiquarian Society).

12. *Publishers' Weekly* XXVI:668 (November 15, 1884), p. 671; "Index To American Poetry And Plays . . ." By C. Fiske Harris, Providence, 1874.

13. *Ibid.*, XXVIII:701 (July 4, 1885).

14. Jacob Blanck, "Problems in the Bibliographical Description of Nineteenth-Century American Books," *The Papers of the Bibliographical Society of America* XXXVI:2 (1942), p. 131.

15. Press notices of the Leon catalogue of 1885 appear on the back of Bangs & Company's auction catalogue of June 7, 8, 9, 1886.

16. Leon & Brother to Gordon L. Ford, January 25, 1886.

17. Information from Clarence S. Brigham; *Catalogue of the Library of Wilberforce Eames*, Anderson Auction Company, December 13, 1906, Part IV, p. 527; George L. McKay, *American Book Auction Catalogues*, New York, New York Public Library, 1937, p. 189.

18. *The American Catalogue . . . 1884–1890*, New York, 1891, p. xxi.

19. Leon & Brother, *Catalogue of First Editions of American Authors*, p. 7.

Publishers' Weekly

Its First Half-Century

T HE NATURE of *Publishers' Weekly* makes it unique in trade journalism.
Books are the distilled essence of the human mind at its best and at its worst.
As they affect events, so they are influenced by events, and there is nothing in
the world, from drought to depression, from the building of a subway to an
epidemic of cholera that is not in some way reflected in the black art. Books
demand of those who would deal in them a high and farsighted view through
the windows of the world. Publishers and booksellers, those indirect
moulders and tracers of public opinion, demand in turn a trade journal that
represents their spirit and guides their fortunes, that educates while it leads,
and records the history in whose making it shares.

Publishers' Weekly supplies those demands, serving the book trade along
bibliographical, literary, practical, and historical lines, representing the book
trade as it developed from the old days of subscription "sets" and
"drummers" to the later days of reprints and traveling representatives, and
guiding the book trade in its good fight for international copyright, trade
organization, net price maintenance, and bookstore development. *Publishers'
Weekly*, therefore, occupies in trade journalism the enviable position of
historian of a history it has helped to make, of leader among those who are
themselves leaders of public opinion.

Some such thoughts as these may have been at work in the mind of
Frederick Leypoldt when, in a German restaurant near his office at 712
Broadway opposite Dutton in the center of New York's publishing trade, he
gathered his little "business family" around him to discuss the first issue of
his *Weekly Trade Circular* on Thursday, January 18, 1872. His aims and
policy were clearly defined. He would provide an accurate record, an
intelligent journal, a comprehensive bibliographical tool. The news, book,

Reprinted from *Publishers' Weekly* (January 18, 1947): 286–306.

and list columns of his *Circular* would know no party distinction, but would inform the trade fully and fairly regarding all that might interest them as dealers in books. Yet he would give publicity to every opinion which fearlessly attacked unsound business principles that crippled the book trade. His editorial columns would freely express his best judgment as to the interests of the trade at large; they would never be influenced by advertising patronage or the lack of it; they would raise his journal from a mere chronicle of events to the position of standard bearer to the trade. His correspondence columns would express views on all sides, and while his reports of news would never depend upon his opinions, neither would his opinions be determined otherwise than by the general interests of the trade.

With such a policy in mind, Leypoldt nailed to his masthead Bacon's wise saying, "Every man is a debtor to his profession." With such purposes in view, he announced his aims frankly in his first editorial: "A prompt and full business record will always form the main feature of the *Weekly*; but it is the aim of the editor at the same time to make the *Trade Circular* a representative organ of the spirit of the trade, by admitting any exchange of views, or discussion on trade matters, that may lead to a reform of abuses, to a better understanding between publishers and dealers, and to a more congenial spirit among the trade in general. The editor also aims [at] trade education."

This policy, which was to dominate the *Weekly* throughout its first half-century, had been formulated at a significant period of American history. The end of the Civil War had given birth to a revival in literature, and the development of the Far West had brought about a genesis of fresh thought. On the other hand, the Chicago fire had caused the trade to suffer serious losses and the Franco-Prussian War had restricted importations. The public was still reading *The Last of the Mohicans*, advertised on the first page of the *Weekly's* first issue, while the sensation of the year had been Joaquin Miller's *Songs of the Sierras*.

Against such a background, on January 18, 1872, was issued *The Publishers' and Stationers' Weekly Trade Circular*. [See Plate 9.]

The official organ of the Publishers' Board of Trade, the journal appeared in octavo double column, the most convenient and time-saving format for ready reference. The subscription price was $2.50 a year, and the advertising rates were tabulated upon the basis of $20 a page.

On the first page Leypoldt indicated that the issue was the first of a new series, referring by his designation to the ancestry of his *Weekly*. Leypoldt and Holt's circular of the late '60's had developed into the *Literary Bulletin*, the imprint edition of which was called the *Trade Circular and Literary Bulletin*, with the title altered in September, 1870, to *Trade Circular and Publishers' Bulletin*. It was from this journal that the *Weekly Trade Circular* was developed. On January 25, 1872, Leypoldt announced the purchase of George W. Childs' *American Literary Gazette and Publishers' Circular*, which,

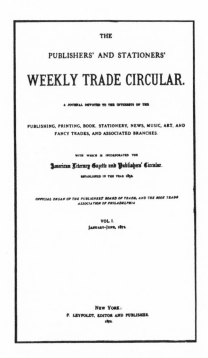

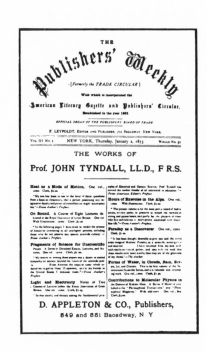

PLATE 9. Front cover of the first volume of the *Weekly Trade Circular,* as *PW* was originally known.

PLATE 10. With the first issue in 1873 (first page shown above), the magazine established by Leypoldt and Holt adopted its present name.

as it was merged with the *Trade Circular,* gave that *Weekly* an even more remote ancestry extending as far back as 1851 to *Norton's Literary Advertiser,* which the following year became *Norton's Literary Gazette.* In 1855 the *Gazette* was renamed *American Publishers' Circular and Literary Gazette,* with which *The Criterion* was merged the next year. It was this paper which in 1863 had become the *American Literary Gazette and Publishers' Circular.* Even at its inception the *Trade Circular* could therefore boast a long and proud history in trade journalism, and, changing its name on January 2, 1873, to *The Publishers' Weekly,* which clearly and briefly indicated the scope of the paper, it embarked upon what was to be an even longer and prouder future. [See Plate 10.]

The bibliographical system of *Publishers' Weekly* was its foundation stone, forming at once the bookseller's alphabet and the protoplasm of American trade bibliography. Its purpose was at all times an accurate, prompt, and complete record of American publications to guide dealers in ordering new books and to establish an authoritative national bibliography. Improved and extended continuously throughout the years with new methods of cumulation, it depended for its source material upon books provided by publishers or notations on blanks supplied to them, upon copyright cards and the accessions of the Congressional Library. Despite the difficulty involved in developing a bibliographical record whose cost exceeded its returns, the *Publishers' Weekly* system became the best in any book-producing country, challenging comparison in regard to quantity, quality, and promptness of issue with any other, and incidentally forming a monument to the life of its founder, Frederick Leypoldt.

At the basis of American book trade bibliography was, and continues to be, the "Weekly Record" of *Publishers' Weekly*, the original record entry at the foundation of American trade bibliography, and the best current trade bibliography. The basis of the "American Catalogue," was the "Weekly Record." This department is the only bibliographical tool provided by the *Publishers' Weekly* which was to be maintained throughout its entire existence. The difficulties involved in providing a complete record were enormous at first, and upon one occasion in August, 1873, the alphabetical list of books just published, when dependent only upon the publishers' supply of material, consisted of exactly three entries printed upon an otherwise blank page. The trade was educated, however, and brought to the realization of the importance of a complete record, and in 1878 the entries were augmented by annotations so that they contained notices of author, title, place, publisher, date, number of pages, size, binding, price, and a brief description of the contents supplied by Marian M. Monachesi. Later on, the record appeared in uniform type, and in 1919 the less important books and pamphlets were run in a parallel alphabet at the foot of the page.

Publishers' Weekly did not rest content with its "Weekly Record," but provided other cumulations as well. The "Monthly List," containing entries by author, title, subject and series in distinctive typography, was continued until 1919 when, with increased printing costs, it was abandoned. With the development of linotype, "Quarterly and Semi-Annual Cumulations" were provided for a decade until the rapid increase in book production necessitated their withdrawal. Finally, an "Annual Cumulation," indexed by author, title, and subject, was offered in the *Annual Summary Number* to fill the gaps left by the inattention of publishers and to serve as a sort of intercalary "Trade List Annual," summarizing for the trade the books of the past year. This finding list was discontinued only when H. W. Wilson's *Cumulative Book Index* served the same purpose. With these bibliographical tools, dealers in books could at a glance answer almost any question relating to the literature of the day or the year, from the latest in law or medicine to works on eye diseases, from the title of a book by a specific author to the author of a given book.

Still, from time to time, the *Weekly* provided other finding lists to help the trade, from the weekly order list to advance announcements of forthcoming publications, from lists of books published in England, France, and Germany to a record of cheap series, from government publications to the publications of societies, from a stationery price current to lists of new music. Nor do these comprehensive bibliographies include the special lists developed by *Publishers' Weekly* for such occasions as election campaigns or the copyright struggle, or for its own supplementary numbers. They are a substantial indication, however, of the service of *Publishers' Weekly* in supplying throughout its first half-century finding lists for the trade, and they amply fulfill the founder's primary aim to make his paper a practical tool for all who are debtors to their profession.

While its bibliographies were invaluable tools, the *Weekly* aimed also at the education of the trade along literary, practical, and historical lines. Though not primarily literary in purpose, since books were its raw material it afforded from the start many literary attractions to its subscribers.

Publishers' Weekly became, therefore, a medium for the exchange of literary news, news of periodicals or of books received or forthcoming, and its "Literary and Trade Notes," later developed into the department, "Tips From the Publishers," became actually a literary melting pot, where Frohman's purchase of the dramatic rights to *Richard Carvel* was mixed with the passing of the 400,000th mark by *David Harum*, where announcements of *Tono-Bungay*, said to be a full-blooded English novel of the old-fashioned school, but at the same time brimful of modernity, were stirred with reports from a later generation concerning works about vitamins or relativity.

The best-seller lists of *Publishers' Weekly*, garnered at first from the *Bookman* and later Herbert S. Browne Co.'s compilation and the *Weekly's* own consensus, together with its earlier prize questions on the most saleable books, became a barometer of the literary winds of the day. They recorded faithfully the change in literary taste from the turn of the century, when the public delighted in *When Knighthood Was in Flower* or *Janice Meredith*, through the early years of the twentieth century, when readers heeded *The Call of the Wild* or *The Heart of Rome* or wandered happily through *The Garden of Allah*. At the same time, they revealed the lack of social consciousness in the American mind, whose most popular novel in 1914 was *Pollyanna*, and in 1917 Tarkington's *Seventeen*. They indicated the advance in the years after the first World War, when the entire country was turning to *Main Street* or *Moon-Calf*, or, too late, to the *Outline of History*.

Since the *Weekly* dealt in books and authors, it became a medium for the literary gossip of the day. From its columns of "Personal Notes," "Authors at Work," "Notes on Authors," "Writers and Bookmen," or "Author Gossip," readers might learn, as the years passed, of the Stowe garden party or Thomas Hardy's completion of a poetical drama in six acts, of Dr. Doyle's exhuming of Sherlock Holmes or the poor breeding of *Mrs. Wiggs of the Cabbage Patch*, who had thrown a pitcher at an intruding visitor. When A. E. Housman refused payment for his verses or Oscar Wilde died an undischarged bankrupt, when no truth was found in the silly story that Sir

Edwin Arnold was about to marry a Japanese maiden, and when Frank Norris was working on *The Octopus*, the gossip was reported in *Publishers' Weekly*. A foresighted subscriber might have found the germ of tragedy in the announcement that Joyce Kilmer had enlisted in the 7th Regiment, N. G. N. Y., or a note of alarm in the report that George Sylvester Vierick had, in 1918, been expelled from the Authors' League for disseminating propagandist literature. From the days of Beaconsfield and George Ade to those of Christopher Morley and Sherwood Anderson, *Publishers' Weekly*, throughout its first half-century, painted a picture of literature in the making in these notes on men of books.

Also of a literary nature was its "Foreign Correspondence" provided by special correspondents in London, Paris, and Stuttgart, who reported the news of Carlyle's *Memoirs* or the latest in the English periodical press, Zola's royalties or notes on the German book trade. Supplemented by articles on literature in Japan or announcements from Bergen, Kiev, and Australia, the foreign correspondence of *Publishers' Weekly*, supplied by James Milne in London, H. Purper in Stuttgart, and "K. Voltaire" in Paris, presented the literary scene abroad.

The rare book departments of the *Weekly* also offered literary attractions. Its columns of "Old Book Notes" or "Old Book Chat" by "Bibliophilus," its "Notes for Dealers in Old Books" or "The Book Collector," its columns, "The Collector" and the later page of "Rare Books, Autographs, and Prints" by Frederick M. Hopkins were repositories for literary information about books of the past. Together with its series of reminiscences by members of the rare book trade and its Rare Book Numbers introduced in 1919, these columns supplied the trade with details regarding the scarcity of Dickens firsts or Quaritch's purchase of a Gutenberg Bible for £4,000, with news of J. P. Morgan's acquisition of the Irwin Library, or the discovery of the Waldseemüller maps, with accounts of Thomas J. Wise's purchase of Tennyson's *Lover's Tales* for $3,000 or the publication of Bigmore and Wyman's *Bibliography of Printing*. The great sales at Sotheby's or the Anderson Galleries were reported, the Ives Auction, the Brinley Sale, the Hoe and the Huth, marking their separate epochs in the history of rare books. Information was fully given regarding First Folios and Aitken Bibles, Grolier Club exhibitions, or Lichtenstein's "find" of Poe's *Tamerlane*, and the careers of great rare book dealers were followed from the days of George D. Smith to the later period of Rosenbach. These notes on auctions, on dealers' catalogs, on bibliographies and checklists, these reports of "finds" provided by "Anobium," the *Publishers' Weekly* bookworm, afforded a colorful pageant of the rare book trade from the time of Lenox, Brinley, and John Carter Brown to the generation of Hoe, J. P. Morgan, and Huntington. The department [was continued until 1947] with a regular weekly column by [the late] Jacob Blanck [followed by Sol M. Malkin] and articles by distinguished rare book specialists here and abroad. It supplied, in addition, an index to the literature of the past, as the best-seller lists supplied one for the present.

Primarily literary in tone was the *Publishers' Weekly Monthly Book Review*, included as an illustrated supplement in 1912, when it numbered among its contributing editors Algernon Tassin, Richard Le Gallienne, and H. L. Mencken, and later placed in the charge of Rebecca D. Moore. It was discontinued in 1932. With its book chat of the month, its classified lists of new books, its notes of books being talked about, the *Review* resembled a dignified literary magazine. Though, as a trade journal, *Publishers' Weekly* did not entertain as its primary objective that of a literary periodical, none the less, it succeeded throughout its first half-century not only in reflecting the trends of American literature, but in providing a literary education to its subscribers.

If the *Weekly* served more or less unconsciously as a literary instructor to the trade, it was definitely aware of the role it must take in the practical and technical education of its constituents. Believing in the need of an American renascence in careful book workmanship, the *Weekly* as early as 1883 presented a series of articles either specially written or reprinted, concerning the production and life of the book. In addition, it invited the discussion of current books from the manufacturing point of view, a development that naturally led in the twentieth century to the monthly column on bookmaking which contained comments on the most interesting examples of good bookmaking that came to the *Publishers' Weekly* office.

In its attempt to educate the trade, the journal covered more technical matters also. The subject of paper was thoroughly investigated, its manufacture, the introduction of the feather-weight variety, its use in bookmaking, and, especially in 1880 after the "boom" and again after the first World War, its cost. No less vital than the romance and history of paper was the matter of bindings, and the *Weekly*, in crusading for simplicity, opposed the Japanese, bric-a-brac, and gaudy fads in book covers. The use of pig skin, the duro-flexible binding, Zaehnsdorf's dictates on modern bindings, the varieties of cloth and board were all analyzed as part of the technical education of men of books. From page form to the lettering of titles, from book sizes to the correct method of interleaving, from title-pages to painting on edges, the *Weekly* provided a complete technical and artistic equipment for its subscribers. Besides encouraging technical improvements, the journal taught book illustration in all its phases, from the woodcut and engraving to the photo- and Rollergravure, and gave instruction in the methods of book repair, in washing and restoring, splitting paper, and even renewing faded inks.

In its efforts to serve as a thoroughly practical trade journal the *Weekly* developed many departments. Those in search of business opportunities could find in its pages notices of situations or help wanted. Dealers watching for new or secondhand books were facilitated in their search by lists of catalogs. Subscribers could be informed of removals, openings, or receiverships in the *Weekly*'s Business Notes. Prospective buyers scanned the advance announcements of auction sales from the days of Bangs and Libbie to those of Anderson. While dealers of a later generation watched for advertisements of specialties in the Monthly Book Trade Directory, the most effective practical departments were those headed Books for Sale and Books Wanted.

A development of the early Accommodation Department, which had served as a clearing house for books, the Books Wanted section was designed to increase the sale of books out of print and of works not readily to be had through regular channels. It was the quickest way of picking up old and rare books, and the cheapest way of disposing of them, for, from 1882 until 1919 it offered subscribers insertions of five lines free of charge. The department was often abused by misguided dealers, some of whom looked upon it as a means of keeping a standing advertisement in *Publishers' Weekly*, while others ran titles in it merely to draw out the market value of books. Some could not resist the temptation of boosting prices in answering wants, while others sent such illegible copy that upon one occasion Gonse's *Chapter on Painting* became Souse's *On Printing*. In spite of these abuses, however, the section succeeded in increasing trade by improving trade facilities. The Books for Sale department, originally used as a clearing house for "plugs," was soon developed into a correlated service with Books Wanted, until finally both sections were incorporated into the Weekly Book Exchange.

Besides offering these practical trade helps, the *Weekly* aimed also at the instruction of booksellers along equally practical lines. Believing that the bookseller was one of the most potent factors in the education of the people, it also believed that a thoroughly informed book trade was one of the greatest blessings vouchsafed to America. As early as 1890 *Publishers' Weekly* advocated the establishment of a school for booksellers, and shortly thereafter proceeded to found its own school by carrying in its pages Growoll's series of articles on the "Profession of Bookselling." The series ran for many years in the *Weekly*, giving a fund of practical information to recruits in the book trade, from preparatory training to learning stock, from the delivery, shipping and correspondence departments to pricing old books and cataloging incunabula. From that series the student-bookseller could learn to order and buy stock, to arrange it and display it, to know his customers and sell from samples. It covered completely the field of bookselling in the late nineteenth and early twentieth centuries, and incidentally helped to give that trade a professional standing.

In later years, when America was marching in preparedness parades, *Publishers' Weekly* launched its own drive for another kind of preparedness. Convinced that inadequate book distribution was the crux of the trade's problems, the journal determined to help expand the book-buying clientele, promote the increase of bookstores, and foster better bookselling through its work of information and education. As the earlier bookselling series had been inspired by Growoll this later development was largely the result of Frederic Melcher's determined efforts, and, aided this time by the slogans and posters of Year-Round Book Campaigns and the innovation of Book Caravans, *Publishers' Weekly* again became a school for booksellers.

"The Home School for Booksellers," carried by the *Weekly* under the editorship of Bessie Graham, provided a series of questions based on the "Weekly Record," along with questions and information on such specialized fields as illustrated juveniles or books on South America, anthologies of verse or translations of the classics, reference books and Bibles, cook books and Russian literature, histories, and English fiction from *Trilby* to the Trilogists. This series by Bessie Graham was the ancestor of her book *The Bookman's Manual*, first published by the Bowker Company in 1921. . . .

From the Earliest Days PW *Featured Bookseller Training*

In addition, Paul G. Ivey's "Lessons in Salesmanship" covered not only the knowledge of goods, but such essentials as store system and method, promptness and cheerfulness. These lessons may be regarded as an outcome of the *Weekly*'s "Hints to Salesmen" begun in 1891 and later extended to women booksellers. The ladies of the trade, at first considered poor business material, creatures whose chief interest was matrimony, came to be looked upon as candidates for the tearoom-book-alcove variety of store, but finally, after such enterprises as the Sunwise Turn in New York and the Gardenside Bookshop in Boston had proved their abilities, the ladies came into their own as booksellers to whom the trade owed an important debt and the *Weekly* a monthly department.

Ivey's "Lessons in Salesmanship" were supplemented with Gardner's "Selling Helps," the "Selling Talks Manual" on books of the season, and the page, "In the Field of the Retailer," with its practical suggestions on everyday problems of retail bookselling. To complete the practical education of its clientele, the *Weekly* also sent questionnaires to dealers on buying and selling, gathered consensuses, and published prize articles on the subject of bookselling.

Publishers' Weekly also supplied advice to its subscribers on the bookstore itself, giving suggestions that ranged from proper room temperature to house cleaning and furnishings, umbrella stands, retiring rooms, and general store comforts. These rather cursory hints culminated at length in a series of articles on "Successful Bookselling," containing accounts of individual stores, such as Hartman's or W. K. Stewart's, stores whose methods might stimulate and provide a model for other dealers. Narrowing the field of bookstore advice, the *Weekly* gave additional suggestions on window dressing, from the method of preventing frosted windows to the background and lighting of displays. The news element, the *Weekly* taught, might be capitalized in current events displays, and its pages were soon filled with reproductions of the shop windows of enterprising booksellers.

Other publicity devices were not neglected, from the Betty Wales dresses linked in 1915 with the *Betty Wales* books, to Knopf's device in 1921 of hiring literary sandwich men to march placarded with advertisements of *Zell* or *Moon-Calf*. Much of the *Weekly*'s attention was given to instruction in more conservative advertising, and the journal taught its subscribers the value of continuous advertising, the use of "white space," the distinction between trade and retail copy, and the problem of individualizing book advertisements and endowing them with personality. Phraseology, pictorial construction, and typography were all considered, and here again the *Weekly* offered prizes for comments on publishers' display advertisements.

As a result of these many devices, *Publishers' Weekly* not only helped in the drive for increased markets and better book distribution, but became itself the most effective practical training ground for booksellers.

PW *Always the Conscious Historian of the Trade*

The bookseller, however, must be more than a practical tradesman. His importance in the community was such that he must be endowed with a rich background and a historical perspective. Believing in the value of sketches of book trade history, *Publishers' Weekly*, therefore, became the conscious historian of the trade, running reprints or special articles from as early as 1873 on such subjects as the "Booksellers of New York Fifty Years Ago" or the "History of Chicago's Book Trade." The field of the past was thoroughly mined in papers on the "Book Trade of Ancient Rome" or "Fifteenth Century Book Advertisements," and the *Weekly* supplied an informative chronicle of the trade from the days of the mongers of Strasbourg and the bouquinistes of France to the careers of John Peter Zenger or Hezekiah Usher of Boston.

To augment such articles, the journal provided a series of reminiscences by prominent members of the book trade, printing the recollections of Peter Carter and John Keese, Henry Stevens and Henry Holt, and supplying a medium for the reminiscences of any nonogenarian bookseller or book scout in the business. Growoll's *Book-Trade Bibliography in the United States* was also carried by the *Weekly* in the form of a series of articles on Roorbach and Norton, Rode and Sabin, and Carl P. Rollins' *History of Printing* appeared in its pages.

Just as consciously as it chronicled the record of the past, *Publishers' Weekly* provided the material for the future historian of the book trade. No survey of publishing in America could ever be attempted without the source material supplied in its histories of great houses, Lippincott and Appleton, the Old Corner and Harper. Every anniversary was seized upon by the *Weekly* as a springboard for historical sketches, from Lea Brothers' century to Lee and Shepard's twenty-fifth year, from Scribner's half-century to Quaritch's semi-centennial. Removals also gave the journal an opportunity for recording the complete firm backgrounds of Dutton or Lothrop, and its obituaries were nothing but the condensed histories of Fletcher Harper or George Swett Appleton, James T. Fields or August Brentano, George A. Leavitt, Henry O. Houghton, Alexander Macmillan, on to Anson D. F. Randolph, the last of the old booksellers.

It was for the double purpose of affording a practical help to the trade and of developing an organ of trade education that the *Weekly* issued its Special Supplements. In 1875 an editorial contemplating the New Year's Outlook contained the illuminating sentence: "Once we put on our wishing cap, the *Weekly* broadens out so that we fear to follow our hopes for it." The trade itself was "broadened out" in the days before specialization, and, to aid one class of its constituents in their daily work, *Publishers' Weekly* supplied a valuable tool to the bookseller, who was also a stationer, in its Stationery Number.

The book and stationery trades were so thoroughly identified on the retail side in 1873, when this special number was introduced, that the best medium of communication for the one seemed also the best for the other. Designed to help the bookseller-stationer get customers for his books from those who came to buy writing materials, and customers for writing materials from those who came for books, the Stationery Number offered a current price and order list of staple articles in the stationery and fancy goods lines, a descriptive account of novelties, and an editorial monthly market report. The Stationery Notes of the *Weekly* regularly carried accounts of new goods with small cuts illustrating novelties, and reported business changes and personal notes among stationers, while the advertisements called attention to such non-literary items as Andrews' Dustless Erasers and Eastman Company's new Kodak Cameras. Later, when the bookseller was no longer so thoroughly identified with the stationer, *Publishers' Weekly* still retained its interest in this adjunct of the trade, describing Prang's new departures in Christmas cards, the Napoleonic craze in letter papers, Dutton's valentines, Hallowe'en novelties, the picture postcard development, the advertising stamp fad, and reporting the meetings of stationers' conventions.

From 1872 PW *Stressed Service to Libraries*

Leypoldt from the start in 1872 had recognized the library as an important means of book distribution. His Library Number therefore was devoted to lists of reference works for librarians as well as articles on the public libraries of Boston, New York, and Cincinnati. In addition, the *Weekly* found a place for a "Library Corner" which offered practical suggestions on library economy, summaries of library reports, items on personnel, and notes and queries. This section, coupled with the department of "Library and Bibliographical Notes," led the way to the foundation of the separate *Library Journal* in 1876. Even then, when there was no longer a need for a special "Library Supplement" in the *Weekly*, the journal continued to report library conferences and the books recommended by the American Library Association, and found space among its advertisements for such library aids as the Rudolph Continuous Indexer. The completeness with which *Publishers' Weekly* covered the library book-buying field astonished even itself, for in 1910 the library subscriptions to the journal represented over seventy-five per cent of the total library book-buying of the country, while at the New York State Library School the study of the *Weekly* was a recognized part of the curriculum. Throughout its first half-century *Publishers' Weekly* was the best link between publishers and librarians.

To acquaint dealers and schools with the range of school books, to serve the retail trade in handling texts, and, through imprint editions, to enable the bookseller to obtain and retain the school trade, the *Weekly* offered an appeal to the schools and colleges of the United States in its Educational Number, published in July. Containing an alphabetical price list of educational books with a supplementary subject index, this number combined a finding list for the trade with a class catalogue for schools, and became the most comprehensive list of textbooks published in the United States. In 1906 its scope was extended to include supplementary reading, augmented later on by works on vocational guidance, pedagogics, and teachers' aids. The advertisements it carried became a clearing house for educational apparatus, school series, and dictionaries, and the Supplement continued to progress through the *Weekly's* first fifty years with the constantly spreading ramifications of textbook publishing in America. In 1927 it began to be published separately as *The American Educational Catalog* by the Bowker Co., each year in May.

Early Forerunners of the Big Announcement Numbers

The special seasonal numbers of the *Weekly* came to be recognized as invaluable guides to the bookseller for the most important publishing seasons. The Fall Announcement Number, issued in September, offered in its classified list of fall publications a descriptive summary surveying the entire field. It presented not only a summary but a prophecy for the most important months of the publishing year, while its advertisements gave a comprehensive outline of publishers' plans for that period. Increasing in size through the years, the Fall Number became a milestone in the year of the book business. The Spring Announcement Number, appearing in March, provided a correlated summary and prophecy for that season. The Summer Number, issued in May, emphasized the books that found their special sale during the traveling and vacation season, the series of novels and railroad literature, the sketches of nature and books for the pocket, and, in addition, listed an index to summer books as well as guide books for summer travel. This number was developed in 1888 into the Summer Reading issue, bound in a special cover, illustrated, printed on fine paper, and prepared for imprint circulation by the booksellers. It came to resemble a magazine with its special articles and its extracts of light reading, while its practical purposes were served by the classified and selective lists of vacation books. Sunny and cheerful, avoiding gruesome books with harrowing problems, the Summer Reading Number became an appropriate literary companion for the season. It was discontinued in 1924. The Christmas Number in November was a correlated issue for the winter season which was expanded into the charmingly illustrated *Christmas Bookshelf*, called later the *Book Parade*. Through the years it became a delightful compendium of holiday gift books, birthday books and calendars, and its Christmas greeting heralded pleasant feature articles or accounts of dainty books and standard works from the Abbey Shakespeare to Victorian Songs. The publishers' display advertisements in the *Christmas Bookshelf* were little shop windows to the main body of the catalog, and despite the difficulties involved in printing cuts that varied from light to dark, close to open, woodcuts and process blocks, the number, on special light-weight paper printed in clear modern type faces, became a handsome seasonal publication. In January came the Annual Summary Number which provided the book trade statistics of the previous year gathered for permanent record, as well as a directory of publishers and statistics of foreign book production. Its editorials on the Books of the Year, as well as its advertisements, traced the Russian revival of 1887, the rise of the "new woman" or "anti-marriage" novel, the popularity of historical romances, the progress of the psychological study and social problem novel, the building of Eliot's Five-Foot Shelf, the development of whodunits, the growth of technical literature, and all the literary trends of a nation's half-century.

With the metamorphosis of the self-assertive and boisterously convivial "drummer" of the '80's into the modern traveler, *Publishers' Weekly*, recognizing not only the elevated status of this force in personnel but his importance as an advance outpost in reaching out after new markets, introduced in 1908 a supplement for the men of the road. The Travelers' Number, issued in February, was prepared so that travelers could address themselves more directly to their constituents in the retail book trade and so that competitive lines might be more effectively exploited in the mutual interest of buyer and publisher. It catered to the traveler's need for economic study, psychological analysis, and statistical tabulations, and supplied him with announcements of the houses represented by men of the road, notes of the special lines handled by them, biographies of well-known travelers, many of them members of the Brotherhood of Commercial Travelers, changes in the retail trade, and department store buyers. Later this number was curtailed as the Spring Announcement Number was expanded and the directories of travelers' representatives with biographical sketches and photographs became part of the Spring Announcement Number.

In the interest of greater trade solidarity, *Publishers' Weekly* also issued its Convention Numbers, carrying the papers read at the meetings of the American Booksellers' Association, the resolutions adopted, the banquets, plans, and even cartoons of the members.

Through the years of its first half-century, significant events were recognized by *Publishers' Weekly* as worthy of special single supplements. The Centennial Number of July 1, 1876, provided a complete account of the exhibition of the American Book Trade Association in Philadelphia, not neglecting *Publishers' Weekly*'s own exhibit in the little case designed by Dessoir, the key to which might be obtained from William E. Hibberd of the Bible Society Exhibit. The struggle for international copyright merited a special Copyright Number in 1888, presenting a compendium of the status of the international copyright movement, the history of the Copyright League, Solberg's bibliography of copyright literature, and lists of books by American authors, chiefly those living, contributed by the publishers. Later on, in 1915, in connection with the campaign for a juvenile book week, the journal began its supplement of Books Boys Like Best which later developed into the Children's Book Week Number. In the significant year 1917 the Patriotic Number of the *Weekly* supplied the trade with a guide to books for patriotic Americans. Issued in a red, white and blue cover with eagle and stars, it surveyed current books on wartime activities from drilling a rookie to hoeing a potato patch, and this was followed by a Books for Soldiers Number intended to help exploit the opportunities for private bookselling to men in uniform.

In addition to providing such devices as these, which were designed to improve facilities and educate dealers in books, *Publishers' Weekly* served as the unconscious historian of the trade, for in its attempt to become a representative organ it reflected in its communications, editorials, and news columns the developments in the publishing field throughout a half-century. In this sense, the history of *Publishers' Weekly* may be regarded as the history of publishing itself.

The change in trade neighborhoods is one of the most obvious portions of that history. In the pages of the *Weekly* may be traced the shift from a publishing center at Astor Place to a Paternoster Row on Fifth Avenue below Twenty-third Street. The uptown movement continued to influence the trade until it clustered near the "splendid home" of the New York Public Library, while Booksellers' Row on lower Fourth Avenue took a new lease on life as late as 1917.

The reports of trade sales in *Publishers' Weekly* reflected like a thermometer the developments in publishing, from the days when they were conducted by Joseph Foster, redoubtable in jokes, and when the organ could be heard from the old haunt at Clinton Hall.

The dominance of seasonal trends was mirrored in the *Weekly*, the golden fall, the Christmas rush, the January stock taking, the spring renascence, the summer dullness. These were the shibboleths that swayed the trade until the drive for Year-Round Bookselling, with the *Weekly* suggesting appropriate literary souvenirs for Washington's Birthday, St. Patrick's Day, and Leap Year, attempted to make one continuous season of the whole year.

The Book Week mania was recorded in its columns, from the Children's to the Out-of-Door, from the Religious to Book Showers for the Bride, and Baby Week.

Publishers' Weekly stands witness to the growing specialization in the trade, when the antiquarian dealer, the seller of current literature, and the handler of cheap reprints went their separate ways, and the opening of new fields in the literature of engineering or forestry or business called for newly trained specialized experts.

The drug store was noted as an outlet for books as early as 1880 and its possibilities were followed until it became a considerable market for reprints. From the automatic selling boxes of 1889 that offered "cheap johns" so that he who ran might read, to the extension of the chain store system to the literary field with the Womrath enterprise, the *Weekly* reflected every device for selling books that cropped up in a half-century.

The price increases in 1916 resulted in a column devoted to changes in price, while the *Weekly* stood aghast in 1919 at the approach of fiction to the $2 mark.

The field of reprints, entitled to a history in itself, was followed closely by the journal, from the days of the "cheap and nasty" pirates' 12mos to the authorized reprints of a later year, from the days of the *Franklin Squares*, *Seasides*, and *Unit Books* to the return of the paper-covered novel in 1921. The "Series" and "Library" fads were recorded in the *Weekly* also, the *Leisure Hour*, the *Bric-a-Brac*, the *Sans Souci*, the *No Name* of Roberts Brothers, the *Little Classics* and the *Vest Pocket Poetry*, until standard reprints came into their own with the Harper Histories and the Globe Dickens, the Riverside Aldine editions and the *Everyman Library*.

Perhaps even more significant than these publishing trends culled from the pages of the *Weekly* was the history of the world itself that was mirrored in its columns. *Publishers' Weekly* played a larger role than that of handmaid to the trade by indicating the interrelations between that trade and contemporary events. Books have always reflected the important questions of the day, and since the book trade may be regarded as a faithful barometer to world temperature, the *Weekly* likewise takes its place as the historian of global events in their relation to publishing.

Publishers' Weekly, therefore, opens a new window upon the world and provides a fresh vantage point from which to look at history. From that window one sees the Boston Fire of 1872 as an event that impoverished potential book customers or the San Francisco Earthquake of 1906 as a serious blow to the book trade of the Golden Gate. Drought or heavy rains menace the paper supply, while a plentiful harvest spells prosperity in the trade. Cholera in Italy causes the prohibition of rag importation, while the development of the apartment house curtails the space allotted for books and threatens the decay of the family library in a nomadic age.

From the vantage point of *Publishers' Weekly*, the great expositions of fifty years, the World's Fair, the Paris, the Louisiana Purchase, become the springboards for new opportunities to sell books. The death of Queen Victoria, the spread of labor and tariff problems, Christian Science, the Woman's Rights Movement, the science of eugenics, all the trends and events of a half-century become motivating forces in the production of a new literature.

The bicycle, according to the *Weekly*, injured a trade which depended upon sedentary rather than perambulatory habits, and the wheelman, though running, could not read. The automobile, on the other hand, produced not only a new literature, but an opportunity for experimental motors that carried the bookstore to the buyer.

The discovery of the North Pole was a world-shaking event that incidentally resulted in a copyright controversy regarding the protection rights of Cook and Peary, while the victrola made possible a new literary development in "Books That Sing." The subway became more than a means of transportation; it was the best place for the literary to pursue their serious reading. The telephone was not just a boon for the social-minded, but a new method of ordering books, provided, in 1908, one could get the proper connection.

The Presidential Election, long regarded as a bugbear disorganizing the trade, came at length to be considered as an opportunity for marketing campaign literature. Depressions naturally affected the trade, from the panics of 1873 and 1893 to that of 1907. But the book trade, as the *Weekly* persistently pointed out, stood to gain by those necessitated economies which forced people to purchase, especially for gifts, commodities that were midway between luxuries and essentials. Strikes were reflected in the book business, from the railroad strike of 1877, which postponed publication dates and stopped the sale of railroad literature, to the printers' strike of 1919, which suspended publication of the *Weekly* itself. In 1921, the journal found it difficult to conceive that "any group of organized workmen should . . . send to the employers a demand for a five dollar a week increase."

The movies, or, as *Publishers' Weekly* put it, the "phenomenal growth of the nickelodeon" and the "most amazingly rapid quasi-educational movement the world has ever known," resulted in a new market for books, raised up a new class of readers, effected, as early as 1908 in the *Ben Hur* case, an important development in copyright, and gave new publicity to dramatized novels, as was proved in the case of "Tarzan." In step with the times, the *Weekly* introduced a new column on motion pictures based upon published works, where Theda Bara in *The Clemenceau Case*, Marion Davies in *The Burden of Proof*, and Tom Mix in *Fame and Fortune* were duly recorded.

More noticeably than any other event, the wars of fifty years affected the book trade. The Spanish American War provided the opportunity for the sale of works on Spain and Cuba, and the Russo-Japanese War aroused interest in books on the Orient and the two opposing nations.

Musing on the first World War in 1914, *Publishers' Weekly* astutely observed, "It seems incredible that the assassination of a Hapsburg prince in an obscure town in Bosnia should affect the collections of a small bookseller in northern Ohio; but so closely interwoven is the fabric of international interdependence that some such nexus between causation and effect has been . . . shown to exist." Yet this observation was followed the next year by the complacent remark that "the happy faculty of *laissez-faire* which allows our country to loll comfortably unarmed in the face of a world war has also aided the general recovery of business by relegating the war to the somewhat objective and impersonal position of a spectacle."

The war did not remain a spectacle for long. As early as 1913 Houghton Mifflin had advertised on the same page in the *Weekly*, *Pan-Germanism* and *Justice and the Modern Law*. A new literature was in the ascendancy, and though war fiction gave way before the popularity of Conrad's *Victory*, Chesterton's *Father Brown*, and Tarkington's *Turmoil*, nonfiction assumed new proportions with serious works on Germany, accounts of eye witnesses, and books on military science and peace. At the same time, the blockade on imports gravely affected the paper market until "Notes on the Paper Situation" became a regular feature of the *Weekly*. The scarcity of material increased prices with America's entry into the war, and the scarcity of labor brought women into the field of bookselling.

Along with its lists of war books came notices in *Publishers' Weekly* on "Soldier Authors," "Rolls of Honor among Publishers and Booksellers," Liberty Bond subscriptions, War Savings Stamps, and campaigns for books for soldiers and books for camp hospitals. "Making Good in Wartime" headed a special page devoted to practical suggestions on retail methods, for the *Weekly* had perceived that there is "no such thing as private business or private interest; all business is public and all interests are vitally concerned with the public interest."

With the return of peace, this page was renamed "Making Good in the New Era," and in place of war book lists came lists of literature on the League of Nations and the New Society. New literary opportunities were once more provided by the Washington Conference, the problems of the Pacific, the development of navies, and the subject of disarmament, and *Publishers' Weekly* made the courageous though futile effort to bring to realization the prayer it had hopefully voiced in 1918: "May all . . . who believe in the power of the printed word work together for the spread of those ideas that shall ensure a just and lasting peace."

The *Weekly* had, through its first fifty years, worked staunchly for the spread of other ideas, ideas that would ensure peace and prosperity to the book trade. Perhaps more important than any of its efforts to serve, educate, or represent its constituents were its reform activities that centered round the four great milestones of international copyright, net price maintenance, trade organization, and bookstore development. In its endeavor to represent the whole trade honestly and without fear or favor, *Publishers' Weekly* fought the battle of books and tilted against the wrongs of publishers, booksellers, and all who were connected with the book trade. Its communications department became a sort of complaint box into which the grievances of the trade were dropped; its editorials became fiery channels for its crusades; and the *Weekly* itself became a leader in intellectual progress and a standard bearer for the trade.

The journal's efforts on behalf of international copyright, which culminated in the Copyright Act of 1891, were based on the broad philosophical belief that, though literature is distinctively a national product, a book is an international fact. As early as 1872 the *Weekly* stated the problem: "How shall the interests of authors, of publishers, and of the reading public, be so subserved that, first, the best productive mind of each country may receive the requisite stimulus in the way of dollars and cents, and pounds, shillings, and pence; second, that the author's indispensable deputy, the publisher, be sufficiently indemnified for the large investment which it generally falls upon him to make, in bringing a valuable book before the public; and, third, that the reading public be put in possession of the best works produced in both countries, at the smallest possible expense." From the start, *Publishers' Weekly* assumed the absoluteness of literary property, viewing the moral question of copyright as the inherent right of the author to the products of his own creation and industry, and seeing the practical question of copyright as one that would give this right to the author without putting the trade under bondage to his English publisher. The *Weekly* believed the final triumph of international copyright as sure as the triumph of truth over sophistry, and with considerable foresight regarded it as a means of bringing about the increased importance of American literature in the literature of the world.

In the fight based upon such convictions, *Publishers' Weekly* became a sounding board for authors' protests, from 1872 when Mark Twain objected to the activities of his London publisher and Henry M. Stanley demurred at unauthorized editions of works on the Livingstone Expedition. In addition, the *Weekly* printed the minutes and documents of publishers' meetings on copyright, lawyers' observations on the right of property in books, and George Haven Putnam's series of articles on international copyright. The journal sent a circular letter to leading publishers and authors on the copyright reform, and published the results in its pages. Reports of copyright suits, the Harper Treaty, bills introduced in Congress, Solberg's bibliography on literary property, the statistics of the work of the Copyright Office—all appeared in its columns. Even its advertisements became the medium for homilies on international copyright, and the *Weekly* could truthfully declare that it had given more space to the discussion of the subject than all the foreign trade journals combined, and far more than any literary journal at home or abroad.

After the passage of the Copyright Act of 1891, *Publishers' Weekly* continued to trace its effects, seeing, with the cessation of piracy of English novels, the renascence of American fiction. It continued also to work for an improvement in domestic copyright, which culminated in the Revised Code of 1909. Copyright matters became a regular feature of the *Weekly* and the Act of 1909 was heralded as a great advance, especially in the extension of the copyright term, though it retained the manufacturing clause, the chief stumbling block in America's copyright relations with the outer world. Still the *Weekly* retained its interest in the problem, printing advance portions of Bowker's *Copyright—Its History and Law*, and, after the formation of the Authors' League, aiding in a standardization of the author contract.

Against the pernicious system of inflated retail prices coupled with abnormal discounts, which made the bookstore of the '80's a shop where books were "handed down" like boots in a Chatham Street "cheap john," *Publishers' Weekly* also crusaded. It viewed abnormal discounts as a cause of demoralized prices and the deteriorated value of stock, and inflated prices as a means of inveigling weak-minded persons with imaginary deductions and bargains.

At first, the *Weekly* championed the adoption of the "twenty per cent rule," which limited the discount outside the trade to twenty per cent, and crusaded for bona fide discounts only, so that every minister, school teacher, librarian, lawyer, physician, student, friend, and friends of friends would not expect a discount on books. At the same time, the journal fought for a reduction in the retail price that would bring about a healthy condition in the trade, by making the price of a book one with its value and by substituting a real for a nominal price.

Later on, *Publishers' Weekly* supported the abolition of the "twenty per cent rule" altogether and the lowering of the retail price so that there would be no extra margin to give the public in some cases and withhold in others.

The false system of fictitious prices had to be replaced by the sounder net system based on the actual selling price of the book. Finally, the journal advocated a normal trade discount and a uniform, equitable net price honestly maintained, a price sufficiently close to the cost of the book to attract the public, and a discount large enough to enable the bookseller to make a profit, but small enough to prevent price cutting. The problem of fixing on a fair price was difficult in the book trade, for books were free of price tradition, unlike the one-cent newspaper and the ten-cent ice cream soda of 1914. After the establishment of the net price, the *Weekly* faced the problem of maintaining that price, an issue that was the basis of the trade's prosperity and the sheet anchor of its success. In answer to its own question, "Who will be the Moses to lead the children of the book trade out of bondage?" the *Weekly* might readily have answered, itself.

It was this false price system, against which *Publishers' Weekly* waged so prolonged a war, that placed a premium on underselling, led to monopolies, and promoted department store abuses. Against these enemies of the book trade, therefore, the *Weekly* unsheathed its sword. As early as 1872, the journal found underselling at the core of trade difficulties, whether practiced by state agents, book butchers, jobbers, publishers, dealers, lottery swindlers, bazaar slaves, or auctioneers. It condemned the trade sale as the auction slaughter of the newborn and an important element in the underselling problem. It saw the bazaar, as the department store was known at first, as a parasite of the city, a handmaid of monopoly, a commercial bonanza thriving at the expense of human greed and folly. Against the department store the *Weekly* launched its attack, as a slaughter house and "cheap john" business that drew trade from regular bookstore channels and sold books like groceries. The underselling by Macy was especially condemned as unfair competition that sought to create a monopoly. The Macy litigation hung over the American book trade like an ominous cloud during the first decade of the twentieth century, and though the publishers lost the fight, the suit brought to them the realization that in net prices alone, maintained by individual choice if not coercion, lay the economic salvation of the trade. It was not until the twentieth century also that the department store came to be regarded as a legitimate outlet for distribution and, provided that it conformed with book trade methods, an integral part of the bookselling trade.

Publishers' Weekly from its inception attributed the flourishing of many of these evils to the lack of unity in the trade itself. Without the goodwill and co-operation of publishers, booksellers could accomplish nothing. An *esprit de corps*, a trade solidarity was needed, for the interests of publisher and retailer were identical. The *Weekly* consistently upheld the basic principle that publishing and bookselling constituted one trade, identical in interest though diverse and complementary in field. The hope of the trade lay, therefore, in better understanding between the publisher and his natural ally, the bookseller.

No trade could be complete without both a representative press and a representative association. The first issue of *Publishers' Weekly* began its crusade for an organization somewhat on the order of the German Börsenverein, a national book trade association that would meet the problems of the trade. With uncompromising determination, the journal reported and endorsed the four rousing meetings that characterized early attempts at book trade solidarity. The meeting of the Booksellers' Protective Union at the Burnet House in Cincinnati, where the American Book Trade Union was formed in February, 1874, was proclaimed as one of the most important events in the history of the American book trade. The convention of the American Book Trade Union in July, 1874, at Put-in-Bay, which organized the American Book Trade Association, was also publicized and eagerly reported, as well as the Niagara convention of 1875, where the American Book Trade Association discussed vital legislation in regard to underselling and retail prices. The *Weekly* continued its crusade on behalf of trade organization with the fourth convention at Philadelphia in 1876, until the American Book Trade Association was wrecked on the shoals of the discount problem, failing because it was an attempt at restriction without being judged a public benefit.

Ever in sympathy with any move for higher standards in the trade, the *Weekly* watched and put on record every straw that blew in the direction of trade organization, devoting its department of Trade Associations to the activities of various local organizations and the banquets and ladies' nights of the Booksellers' League, welcoming the time when it would be necessary to print not an occasional column, but several pages every week of such notes. With the formation of the American Publishers' Association in 1900, that time came. A generation after the failure of the American Book Trade Association, the *Weekly* again reported conventions and followed the history of a consultative organization that made recommendations on price fixing. The history of the American Publishers' Association ran parallel with that of the Macy litigation, until it, too, was disbanded by suits under the Sherman Anti-Trust Law. The *Weekly* took up the cudgel on behalf of the American Booksellers' Association also, encouraging its efforts to stimulate retail bookselling. At last the National Association of Book Publishers was heralded with joy as an instrument for promoting book distribution and serving as a clearing house for publishing and bookselling information. It was through organizations such as these that the system of trade arbitration and improved working conditions championed by the journal might also be realized. *Publishers' Weekly*, surveying its accomplishments during half a century, could declare with truth that it had done more than any other single instrument to keep alive the sense of trade interest and trade solidarity.

Since the *Weekly* believed in the bookstore, the small bookstore, it fought another fight for more and better bookstores and the widest possible distribution of books. To this end it not only became a school for booksellers, but denounced whatever encroached upon regular book trade channels. Subscription book abuses were the objects of its attack, not only because they tended in 1872 to impinge upon the regular trade, but because they deteriorated that trade by extracting five-dollar bills from lean purses for worthless, padded trash in gaudy bindings on *Life Among the Mormons* or the *Royal Path to Happiness*. At the same time, however, the *Weekly* bade the retailer take a leaf of suggestion from the subscription bookseller by adopting his successful methods with "sets," his use of the installment plan, and his vigorous enterprise, so that the book business could be gradually worked back into its proper channel.

The journal also denounced as "economic grafters" those worthless author books that were presented in manuscript by a veiled lady and published at her expense to the detriment of the trade. Though, as in subscription books, there were exceptional cases that might be encouraged, the publishing house which made a specialty of author books that masqueraded as legitimate ventures gave the trade the unfortunate reputation of "plug-pusher."

Because they worked unfairly to the regular distributors, the *Weekly* condemned the club system and its successor, the pernicious premium system, which killed the goose that laid the golden eggs. For the same reason it crossed swords with the obnoxious agency system that ate the life out of the school book publishing trade, along with the delusive circular and coupon system that took the place of agents of the Ancient Mariner type, who held their victims with glittering eye and glibber tongue. Against the so-called "library associations" that were in reality nothing but commission agencies, the *Weekly* crusaded, and against the school book abuses that threw overboard the legitimate services of the book trade, from the introduction plan to state school book publications.

Publishers' Weekly tilted against any bill that was destructive of the book trade. It championed a fair tariff that did not place a "tax on ideas," and a postal system based on civil service, contesting methods "pound foolish and not altogether penny wise."

Particularly interesting was the *Weekly*'s stand on censorship. The journal believed that the publisher should take pride in presenting books that elevated rather than inflamed their readers, and roundly denounced the indiscriminate dissemination of immoral literature, productions of the "fleshly" school, obscene postcards, and even the comic supplement of the yellow journal. On the other hand, it steadfastly opposed those self-appointed, irresponsible guardians of public morals who directed their warfare against morally innocuous works. While Anthony Comstock was on the rampage, and the Watch and Ward Society nosed into the evils of Boccaccio and Rabelais, the *Weekly* declared its conviction that the Society for the Prevention of Vice might go beyond reason in undertaking prosecutions that might become persecutions. It saw a certain ludicrousness in the over-zealous suppression of borderland literature, and denounced the expurgation of textbooks and postwar censorship as subversions of the constitutional safeguards of a free speech and a free press. Those freedoms, the *Weekly* believed, were essential for the health of the trade, and nothing should interfere with any free expression of a serious and high intent.

During its first half-century, *Publishers' Weekly* fought the good fight, keeping ever in mind the millennium of the book trade, when the author could choose his own publisher, when the publisher would protect the bookseller, when the price of a book was one with its value, when a national organization would represent every branch of the trade. Fighting against abuses, struggling for their reform, the *Weekly* took its place in the vanguard of the trade.

The history of *Publishers' Weekly* has been, very properly, the history of publishing itself. Nothing has been mentioned so far of the *Weekly*'s personal history. Though its changes in address or personnel may not be as significant as its reflections of the annals of publishing, none the less they form part of the chronicle and should be recorded.

To complete the record, therefore, it may be stated that in 1873 *Publishers' Weekly*, official organ of the Publishers' Board of Trade and later of the American Book Trade Union, subsequently the American Book Trade Journal and since its founding the leading organ of the American book trade, changed its day of publication from Thursday to Saturday for the purpose of prompter delivery.

Eleven times the *Weekly* changed its address, moving in 1873 to the World Building at 37 Park Row in the newspaper center, just around the corner from the *Evening Mail*, where Bowker worked as a journalist, and where it could be in closer communication with the printing office and the mails. Six years later the office was moved to 13–15 Park Row, where it occupied Rooms 39–43, and in 1883 to 31–32 Park Row, with its P.O. Box 943. In 1887 the *Weekly* changed its location to 330 Pearl Street, near Franklin Square, and opposite the Harper Building, a district easily accessible by the Second and Third Avenue El and the Second Avenue line of horse cars. Five years later its address became 28 Elm, near Duane, close to the City Hall Station of the El and the Broadway and Fourth Avenue horse cars. Because of fire, the *Weekly* was forced to vacate these premises in 1894 for 54 Duane, two flights up, and the next year moved to 59 Duane adjoining the Edison Building and within easy reach of the Broadway cable and the Bleecker Street horse cars. In 1900 it moved again, this time to 298 Broadway, between Reade and Duane, where it occupied the sixth floor of premises accessible by the cars of the Metropolitan Street Railway System. Not till 1913 did the *Weekly* follow the uptown movement, changing its address to 141 East 25th Street in the Lexington Building, and the following year to 241 West 37th, in the printer-publishers' building, the lower portion of which was occupied by the Dutton warehouse. This move was made in connection with the new printing concern, the Rider Press, and *Publishers' Weekly* could also be nearer the new Pennsylvania Station and the new General Post Office. Here, too, it boasted a telephone, Greeley 787. [In 1919 it moved to] 62 West 45th Street.

In line with the increase of the general cost of manufacture, the price of paper and composition rates, the *Weekly* raised its subscription price to $3 in 1873, to $4 in 1907, to $5 in 1916, and to $6 in 1920. (In 1923 the price was lowered to $5 in postal zones 1, 2, 3, 4, and 5 and to $5.50 in zones 6, 7 and 8. In 1925 the price became $5 for all zones remaining so until October 1, 1946, when it was changed to $6.) Its advertising rate was reduced to $18 a page in 1877, but was advanced again to $20 in 1889 and to $25 in 1908. Between 1919 and 1920 the rate was rapidly increased from $40 for a page in the front section and $30 in the back to $60 in the front and $50 in the back.

Its path was not always smooth. The *Weekly* countered the opposition of those who would rule out from a trade journal the broader treatment of trade problems, and struggled occasionally in the conflict between editorial frankness and the honest representation of its constituents. There were difficulties at first in obtaining advertisements, so that on one occasion the *Weekly* playfully considered opening a cheap bookstore in Alaska to increase its advertising patronage. There were delays in issues, since publishers' copy did not arrive in time, and there were "accidents" in dispatch.

Nonetheless, despite such problems, the milestones were marked along its way. In 1874 the *Weekly* was recognized by the American Book Trade convention as the official organ of the entire trade, and in 1910 a resolution of the American Booksellers' Association expressed appreciation of the journal's editorial attitude in regard to net fiction and urged all booksellers to extend its influence. *Publishers' Weekly* was awarded a bronze medal at the Paris Exposition in 1889 and a silver medal in 1900. Its expansion was so great that, from 1906 on, the New York Public Library bound only three months' issues in one volume.

The American book trade must ever be one of the most important factors in American life. As the oldest living organ of that trade, *Publishers' Weekly* represented in 1922, as it does today, the highest standard of trade journalism in the country. As long as the great future of the book trade is assured, the life of *Publishers' Weekly* is assured, and it may look forward with the same hopefulness it voiced upon the completion of its fiftieth year to the milestones and achievements of the years to come.

Index